P9-DTI-940

# Moral
# Issues and Christian Response

# Moral
# Issues
# and Christian
# Response
## Third Edition

*Edited by*

## Paul T. Jersild
Wartburg Theological Seminary

## Dale A. Johnson
Vanderbilt University

HOLT, RINEHART AND WINSTON
New York   Chicago   San Francisco   Philadelphia
Montreal   Toronto   London   Sydney   Tokyo
Mexico City   Rio de Janeiro   Madrid

**Photo credits:**
   Beryl Goldberg:   53, 126, and 211
   Alan Carey:   6 and 346
   George W. Gardner:   262

**Library of Congress Cataloging in Publication Data**
Main entry under title:

Moral issues and Christian response.

   Includes bibliographies and index.
   1. Church and social problems—United States—
Addresses, essays, lectures.   2. Christian ethics—
Addresses, essays, lectures.   I. Jersild, Paul T.,
1931–     .   II. Johnson, Dale A., 1936–     .
HN39.U6M67   1982        261.8        82-15679

ISBN 0-03-062464-9

Copyright © 1983 by CBS College Publishing
Address correspondence to:
383 Madison Avenue
New York, N.Y. 10017
All rights reserved
Printed in the United States of America
Published simultaneously in Canada
3  4  5  6      090      9  8  7  6  5  4  3  2  1

CBS COLLEGE PUBLISHING
Holt, Rinehart and Winston
The Dryden Press
Saunders College Publishing

# Contents

v

# Preface to the Third Edition

This third edition of *Moral Issues and Christian Response* constitutes a substantial revision of the previous editions. Many new articles have replaced earlier selections, some chapter topics have been dropped and others added, and the five parts of the book have been expanded to six. These changes reflect in part the volatile nature of "moral issues," with some receding from the public consciousness as others gain attention.

The structure of the book remains the same. The first part acts as an introduction to the others by raising the question of the nature of our moral crisis and how Christians, both individually and corporately, should respond to this crisis and to social issues in general. The following five parts take up sexual ethics, moral issues associated with liberation movements, issues related to the economic order, issues of violence and justice, and issues in the field of bioethics. Because there is great diversity of position and perspective on the major moral issues of the day, we have sought whenever possible to include opposing points of view in the readings, not only to give balance but also to convey the issues better and to stimulate reflection. The authors, therefore, represent a variety of religious and societal perspectives—Protestant, Catholic, black, white, female, male—as well as a variety of ethical viewpoints.

Of course, many topics worthy of consideration had to be omitted because of lack of space. Those addressed deserve further research and study, and to this end we include a suggested reading list for each chapter. While the selections cannot cover all aspects of a given issue, they provide some insights into a human and Christian evaluation of the nature of the problem.

We have been gratified by the appreciative reception of the first two editions of this volume. We hope that this third edition will also make its contribution in enabling readers to develop a responsible approach to some of the major moral issues of our time.

*P. T. J.*

*D. A. J.*

# Introduction

What is the good life? What is the purpose of our life? To whom or what do our ultimate loyalties belong? Which attitudes and values are most important in determining our relationships with others? These questions have received a wide variety of answers in the history of ethical theory. But a far greater variety of answers is implicit in the kinds of lives that people live. The style of a person's life is one's own answer to the question of the meaning and purpose of life. For this reason the study of ethics does considerably more than raise questions about one's action in particular situations. It raises the question of who we are and, in doing so, challenges us to live our answers to that question.

This is both the threat and promise of ethics, and it accounts for the fascination that ethical questions hold for every thoughtful person—particularly reflective young adults. Their approach to life has been shaped from childhood, but they now seek to articulate for themselves just who they are and what their identity means in light of the new choices and broadened responsibility available to them. In this process of finding themselves, there may be a great deal of rejection —rejection of parental ideals, traditional religious values and norms, and many of society's most cherished values. But at the root of this reevaluation there is usually a fundamental moral concern to discover and develop life purposes and standards that are satisfying, both for the individual and for the society. Patterns of morality are shaped when decisions cease to be routine, when crisis situations arise in the consciousness of one or more persons, when a new problem emerges or when an older response is questioned—in short, when a particular morality becomes an "issue."

As an example, until recent years homosexuality was rarely discussed as a moral issue. Christians regarded it as sin and most people dismissed it without question as a perversion and moral evil. As our knowledge of homosexual persons has advanced, and as the burden of their rejected lives has been dramatized, new questions have been raised that challenge our traditional assessments. Our immediate reaction is to ignore or reject these new perspectives, for we find them threatening. But where ethical questions are not asked, where consciences are not pricked, moral sensitivity for the self, for the condition of others, and for the nature of the human community is not felt. We hope that current moral

1

concerns will be the catalyst for wider ethical reflection in our society; for when people do not immediately follow the factual question What is? with the ethical question What ought to be? they miss an opportunity to deal sensitively with issues facing them.

The priorities of issues, of course, will vary among individuals and will change as developments and new conditions emerge. Some issues are resolved, others are ignored, still others acquire new features as resolutions are attempted. Consideration of certain issues quickly moves beyond the immediate situation to more complex and global reflection on human life, national purpose, or existence in a multinational world. These complexities can foster different responses —from frustration and indifference to greater moral passion to contribute where one can. If it is true in our day that nothing is so permanent as change, critical ethical reflection is both more difficult and more necessary than before. In addition, the realities of pluralism and its attendant polarities between individuals and groups make simple solutions virtually impossible.

Experiences of confusion, perceptions of urgency, and awareness of emerging critical personal and social issues may all be reflected in the number of persons enrolled in academic courses in ethics. While students taking a course in ethics may be willing to investigate the nature and scope of ethics and to analyze a number of ethical systems from an intellectual point of view, more often than not they have registered because they feel that an ethics course will be more relevant to them than others they could take. When asked at the beginning of a recent semester "Why did you take this course?" one student wrote, "I find myself on the fence on various moral issues, and the position is uncomfortable. I hope this course will give me some new insights into these questions. With additional knowledge I hope to be better able to resolve the questions that face me." This personalized approach is characteristic of many students today; somewhat disenchanted by a detached, objective educational method that deals with content without adequately relating it to student needs, they may expect at least to talk about "relevant issues" in a class on ethics.

Reflecting student interest in immediate personal and social problems, many courses in Christian ethics are oriented more toward specific moral issues than toward the philosophical and theological foundations of ethics. Yet to be more than an inadequate substitute for a course in social problems, an ethics class must also consider these issues in relation to the various ethical stances they elicit. This volume should provide students with the opportunity to reflect on the different assumptions that are applied to ethical issues, as well as presenting a variety of judgments on them. Most of the material on specific issues reveals some difference of perspective and judgment and often diametrically opposed viewpoints. And so we have a twofold purpose in mind: to aid the reader in understanding the issues as they are defined by writers familiar with them, and to provide insight into the assumptions of authors who have made different judgments on the issues. The issues certainly merit considerable attention; but, beyond this, reflection on these issues should generate discussion of the ways in which moral decisions are made and of the kinds of foundational assumptions and principles that shape these decisions.

Sensitive decision making in any moral issue involves empirical, normative, and "religious" components, with the latter referring to the broadest commitments one makes concerning the nature and purpose of the individual and the society. These components indicate something of the complexity of the ethical task and point to the variety of conclusions that can be reached by equally concerned individuals. While there are other ways to proceed, much ethical reflection starts from confrontation of a specific issue. The movement might then follow with an analysis of its character, consideration of the various options for decision, reflection on the reasons or foundations for these options, and study of the theological implications or correctives that may assist in the decision making. The readings in this volume have been selected in the hope that they will provoke several aspects of this investigation.

It may seem a truism to say that careful attention must be paid to the facts before meaningful ethical judgments can be reached; yet because this seemingly obvious point is so often ignored, there are grounds for reaffirming it. For example, to talk about a "sexual revolution" does no good unless one is able to point to significant changes in sexual practice that have occurred between this generation and a previous one and to support these statements with appropriate data. Use of the term "revolution" in this context has often suggested that a major shift needs to take place in our moral and ethical reflection so that the new situation is taken into account. Of course, the term "revolution" is not a precise objective category when related to the interpretation of empirical data; it is more of a scare word. Recent sociological and psychological research might suggest that it is more appropriate to speak of "change," rather than revolution, in patterns of sexual behavior. Just what impact this change should have on sexual ethics is one area of vigorous debate.

On another issue, no one can deal with racial ethics until he or she has carefully sought the meanings of the term "Black Power" or investigated the subtle but very significant examples of racism in our society; and it would be more than curiosity to ponder why the term "Black Power" has generally been dropped in considerations of this question. In the controversy over the war in Vietnam, the moral judgments presented by either side sometimes had an air of abstractness because they were not grounded in an understanding of the history and politics of Southeast Asia. It is particularly important in a period of rapid social change that serious ethical attention be given to the hard and often confusing realities of our world, to the insights of the social sciences, and to the foreseeable consequences of particular courses of action.

The normative component involves the "ought" questions: What ought to be done? Why should it be done? One long-standing question that relates the normative to the empirical involves the ethical relationship of motivation to consequences. Another question is whether there is an objective and discernible moral order. Among the many ethical norms operating today are notions of absolute imperatives, natural law, the will of God, the greatest happiness of the greatest number, the all-encompassing significance of the state, the priority of the individual person, and, of course, love. But societal changes have affected the discussion of normative questions in several ways. Christian ethicists, particularly, have been drawn in recent years to questions of ethical method; proponents of "situation ethics," who point to the relativity of all norms except the command of love, have argued with defenders of a principle-oriented ethic; both parties have been joined by those who see merit in each side. While occasionally generating more heat than light, the debate has helped to show the frames of reference that are integral to ethical decision making. How we decide what we should do can be as important in illumining our ethical lives as what is done. A second direction has grown out of the awareness of pluralism and its impact on societal patterns. The law, which often has codified a general moral consensus, has been under increasing attack for dealing with moral issues in ways that do not reflect an agreed public morality. Law has often prohibited that which religious persons considered to be sinful; in a pluralistic society, there is considerably less support for continuing this practice. Further, there is new interest in the relationships that exist or ought to exist between the individual's liberty and conscience and particular social institutions or the society's role as a whole in moral issues. A third direction involves the search for a norm that can be used most effectively to evaluate specific issues; and this regularly leads into discussion of the final component, the religious dimension.

At the same time that traditional ethical norms have been questioned (Are there moral absolutes? Is there a natural law? Can one really know God's will?), two powers of the twentieth century, totalitarianism and technology, have called into question the basic dignity of the individual in ways never before imagined. It is no coincidence that recent ethical thinking, both religious and secular, has regularly used the norm of the authentic human person as its basic standard of reflection on moral issues. It is a recognition of our pluralism that the ethical norm is now often seen by Christian writers in "human" categories rather than in simply "Christian" ones. The overlapping moral concern of those who are Christian and those who are not is indicated by the use of phrases like those frequently occurring in the documents of Vatican II, which stress building for all persons a more truly human world and condition of life.

One also notes today a considerable disenchantment with traditional labels ("liberal," "conservative," or "Christian," for example) when applied to viewpoints on moral issues. These terms can easily confuse or mislead because a single descriptive label cannot reflect the many factors that go into the shaping of moral judgments. Because moral reflection is a task for everyone in a society, "Christian response" needs to take seriously both its own resources and the substantive reflection of those who are not Christian. We have considered this factor in selecting material for this volume. The aim is to indicate ways of discerning various dimensions of selected contemporary moral issues. Irrespective of labels, people differ in their ability to discern both moral issues and the implications of norms and religious commitments. Such differences may be due to psychological, cultural, educational, or religious factors as much as to differing ethical priorities. We might hope, however, that sensitivity would increase as one's awareness of the specific problem and the range of options increases. It is possible that confusion or frustration rather than clarity could result from the study of a variety of viewpoints on a particular moral issue. Yet the risk seems worth taking in view of the fact that the complexity of moral issues today makes it unlikely that any one position will be able to convey all of an issue's dimensions.

The religious, or theological, component provides the ultimate ground for ethical discourse. In its broadest sense this component has to deal with the question Why should I be concerned to be moral? and with the other basic questions about human life noted at the beginning of this introduction. It has to explain the contents of such a norm as "more truly human" with insights into what it may mean to be "human" in an ethical sense. If you define humanity first in terms of a relationship to God or see the ethical imperative as that of responding to God's love in Jesus, you have provided some clues toward understanding your ethical reflection and, possibly, your moral judgments. If you define humanity without these relationships, similar clues are provided. Such foundations may not be readily apparent when one starts with a specific issue, but faced with a persistent Why? or Who cares? a person will finally reach the point where he or she can only affirm "That is who I am" or "I am committed to that."

# Part One
# Taking a Stand

# I

# The Current Moral Crisis

Americans are generally likely to agree that over the last couple of decades we have witnessed a significant erosion of traditional moral values in our society. Some are disturbed over this, while many others have become rather cynical about the subject of morality. This cynicism is reflected in such comments as "Everybody's doing it" or "What business is it of yours?" or "You've got to look out for yourself—no one else will." Some would label as the immediate culprit the individual-centered thinking of the 1970s ("me-ism"), in which the individual's needs and wants were exalted at the expense of one's obligations to others or to the community.

A casual consideration of plays, novels, and films reveals the prevailing cynicism in regard to persons who are striving to be morally serious. More often than not, such people are portrayed as legalistic and offensively pious, if not self-serving. They are seen as projecting their own "hang-ups" on to the rest of us. The admired persons are free spirits, intent on doing their own thing in spite of the qualms others may have about their behavior. The ultimate norm appears to be that one be true to oneself, without much attention to whether this self is morally exemplary!

An important dimension of the current confusion over morality is the lack of consensus in our society on matters of moral judgment. This lack of consensus encourages us to suppose that moral judgments are purely a matter of one's own personal taste. Thus, when I tell you what you ought to do, it must mean that I am *imposing* my tastes on you and this is unjustified. Many people believe that in regard to morality, all judgments are relative. Of course, our society is quite heterogeneous in its ethnic, cultural, and religious mix; consequently, it is difficult to maintain a significant measure of agreement on moral issues. Another important factor is the weakening impact of the Christian tradition on the moral practice and expectations of our people. Religious conviction provides a powerful support for moral standards, and with the erosion of the religious soil that nurtures morality, we appear to be living in a "cut-flower" culture with moral

7

standards that appear simply arbitrary or at least vulnerable to challenge.

Even within a Christian context, there is a running argument over what is appropriate to Christian behavior. This is not something new, but the extent and intensity of the disagreement is noteworthy. The emergence among Christian ethicists of situation ethics (more popularly called "the new morality") has been a cause of concern for it has appeared to repudiate the tried and true standards of the past. As someone has said, "The new morality is the old immorality condoned." And yet the focus on the situation reflects a serious concern to make responsible moral judgments, acknowledging the fact that the context of moral decision has a substantial bearing on what is regarded as morally appropriate action. This is a point, however, that ethicists are more likely to appreciate than most of our citizens—especially when they sense that our society is in danger of losing its moral compass.

In addition to this confusion over what is moral and what is not, there are other indications of a weakening moral fabric in our society. The ever present opinion polls provide some interesting material on this subject. Campus surveys reveal that forty-five percent of our college students do not think it necessary to lead a moral life in order to be happy or successful. There has been a dramatic increase in blue- and white- collar crime with employees regarding their employers as fair game for outright theft, and management not hesitating, among other things, to engage in dishonest advertising and the concealment of profits. Not surprisingly, those elected to public office are no different from the rest of us; our newspapers have been full of accounts that document bribe taking and other flagrant abuses of the public trust.

In the first article of this chapter, Howard G. Garner finds a symptom of our problem in the attitudes and language of our youth. He uses the popular expression "It's a rip-off" as a window through which one can perceive both moral confusion and a displacement of traditional values. We are experiencing an emerging "society on the take,"whose guiding principle is to "maximize one's share of society's riches as quickly as possible." Perhaps one could say that this aim has always been a part of the American tradition, but it has been tempered by values of service and honesty, which now seem to be losing their hold. Or is Garner unduly pessimistic?

We move from a concern over values to a prior question about the "support system" of our values in the article by Eugene B. Borowitz. He agrees that we are in the midst of a moral crisis, but sees it as a crisis over what we believe. The real question is whether a secularized culture can provide sufficient grounds for being moral at all. Is an ethic without a transcendent dimension impoverished, finally, because it cannot provide a ground for itself outside self-interest? Borowitz's call to those who affirm biblical faith is twofold: first, to proclaim the transcendent source of life and to evaluate human affairs prophetically from this perspective; second, to demonstrate in our own lives that people can hear and celebrate the transcendent, serving others as well as themselves. The issue is awesome, requiring nothing less than a thorough assessment of such basic questions as the nature of our religious institutions and our national moral purpose, together with a consideration of the responsibility of the former for the latter.

The concluding essay, by Jim Wallis, enlarges the consideration of our social crisis well beyond the discussion of Garner and addresses the issue Borowitz raises concerning a religious foundation for our moral vision. Wallis and the Sojourner Community, to which he belongs, represent an evangelical Christian perspective that would apply biblical truths directly and radically to the social situation in a way reminiscent of the sixteenth-century Anabaptists. While many Christians might disagree with this stance, they would have to take seriously the dramatic challenge Wallis issues to embark on a way of life that provides a more noble vision of our national purpose: "Even a small group of people trying to live a new way can be a significant sign of hope."

A paramount need whenever thinking people confront a subject of this magnitude is to establish just what the real issues are in order that they may be addressed. This involves becoming a student of social and political issues, seeking responsible sources of information. Then there is the need for serious reflection that moves from the convictions of one's faith to the world of human relationships and social policy. This is not done by quoting Scripture passages in an effort to give direct and simple answers to complex questions. It involves, rather, the strenuous effort of thinking through the nature of the biblical message and the moral implications it has for human relationships. The danger concerned Christians face is to follow one of two opposite paths. The first is to exalt their institutions and become legalistic as they attempt to legislate what they perceive to be specific Christian answers to various social issues. As people become threatened, they are inclined to react in this way. Yet the pluralism of our society makes questionable, if not counterproductive, any attempt to legislate morality on the part of a particular group, Christian or otherwise.

The opposite danger is that Christians will fail to recognize the seriousness of the situation and assume that the course of our public life continues to be informed and shaped by a Christian perspective. Here the challenge is to become vigorously involved in the political process, supporting with reasoned arguments policies and programs that one believes will strengthen the social fabric of our nation. Beyond this responsibility is the challenge issued by Wallis to express in one's own life-style a moral vision that challenges the prevailing mores of a consumer society. But even here, one must be aware of the danger of legalism, which would place the expectation of a particular life-style on all who call themselves Christian. In exalting both justice and compassion within the social fabric of the nation, Christians will find themselves united with all persons who are sensitive to these ideals in the quest for a healthier social environment.

# Children of the "Society on the Take"

## Howard G. Garner

In the decade of the '60s, arrests for serious crimes in the United States jumped 71 per cent, with juvenile arrests in those categories increasing by 90 per cent. The adult rate rose by 57 per cent. Adults are more frequently guilty of crimes of personal violence, while the crimes juveniles commit are primarily those against property. Juveniles are stealing, breaking and entering, shoplifting, extorting students' lunch money at school, and vandalizing property.

Why are more and more young people breaking the law? Is it because the American family is rapidly deteriorating as an effective means of socialization? Are the schools to blame for not providing relevant academic, behavioral, and ethical training? Are the courts failing to administer consistent consequences for illegal acts? Are we reaping the results of permissive child-rearing and of child neglect as parents lead their own desperate lives to the exclusion of their children? Is the increasing frequency of crimes against property a form of rebellion against authority? Has peer pressure within the youth culture produced a personal disregard for the adult value system?

It is clear from these questions that there are almost as many theories of juvenile delinquency as there are young offenders. Yet a significant number of individual cases appear to be related to one or more of these suggested causes, and each of them accurately describes the causal factors underlying the behavior of *some* delinquents. However, none of the theories by itself is able to account for the radical upsurge of theft now occurring in this country. In this area there seems to be a more powerful and pervasive phenomenon at work than these theories describe.

## I

If, in search of that phenomenon, one were to ask a juvenile delinquent why he or she steals, the answer probably would not include the word "stealing." For the youth culture has adopted its own term for taking property without compensating the owner. It's called a "rip-off." Although originally used in a more limited sense—as a substitute for stealing or to

Copyright 1978 Christian Century Foundation. Reprinted by permission from the November 1, 1978 issue of *The Christian Century*. Howard G. Garner is Associate Professor of Special Education at Virginia Commonwealth University, Richmond, Virginia.

describe the sale of diluted drugs with a low potency—rip-off now has broad applications in the vocabulary of adolescents. It can refer to anything from high prices in the supermarket to a student's being given the grade of B when an A was expected. The expression "That's a real rip-off," now in the jargon of many adults, really belongs to the youth culture. That culture is marked by a distinctive vocabulary, style of dress and grooming, music, means of transportation, and use of intoxicants. The term "rip-off" comes out of a value system which is as complex and powerful as that of middle-class America.

There was a time when adolescents were notorious for their moralistic idealism and their keen sensitivity to injustices, whether suffered by themselves or by minority groups. Somehow in the past 15 years the sharp adolescent vision of how the world ought to be has become blurred. The young people's use of a single expression, "rip-off," to describe both a bank robbery and "being grounded" for violation of parental rules is symptomatic of their confusion. Stealing is a serious offense against society, with expected consequences, while a rip-off connotes a casual event; it sounds like tearing a sheet of paper from a pad. Stealing is a moral and legal term supported by religious and judicial codes; rip-off is a slang expression applied to any form of personal inconvenience, inequity, or larceny.

It is indeed significant that the teenage vocabulary has become so insensitive to the distinctions between degrees of human suffering, and that the adolescent peer group supports the ripping-off of personal property by so many of its members. We need to find out what is underlying these changes in our young people's values and behaviors.

## II

I am convinced that these changes are a reflection of a powerful and pervasive phenomenon now occuring in our total society: the displacement of our traditional ethics by a new collective behavior, that of the "society on the take." The guiding principle of the society on the take is that one should maximize one's share of society's riches as quickly as possible. The end justifies whatever means are necessary to attain that goal. The society on the take prefers socially acceptable get-rich-quick schemes, such as state lotteries and various rags-to-riches giveaways on TV game shows. But such means are too capricious, serving only to stimulate the desires of large numbers of people who are unwilling to leave their "take" to chance.

Hence the second principle of the society on the take: its members believe that somehow they deserve the quick wealth they pursue. As individuals look back on their past and see all the noble and honest efforts they have made to attain economic affluence, and then balance out all the barriers that the environment has placed in their way, it becomes easy to reach the conclusion that any "take" is only fair payment.

The third principle adopted by this new society which we are becoming is the widespread belief that everyone else is following the "take" ethic. Cynicism abounds regarding anyone who appears to be engaging in altruistic activities, for it is commonly believed that somewhere underneath the façade is a selfish plan to turn the act of helping others into cheap publicity and eventual personal economic gain.

Numerous and varied examples of how these principles operate are easy to find.

**The Business Community.**   When sugar prices soared to levels completely unjustified by market conditions, every product containing sugar was suddenly more expensive. For example, soft-drink prices jumped dramatically. Yet so did the cost of club soda, which contains no sugar at all. Apparently the inflationary spiral provided an opportunity for price increases which were prompted by no factor other than the business community's creed of maximizing profits to the fullest extent the market will allow. Auto prices continued to rise even though demand had fallen drastically, completely contradicting the laws of supply and demand that we learned in basic economics courses. We used to believe that the free market punished the merchant whose profit was too large. In the society on the take, that rule suddenly becomes the exception.

**Public Servants.**   The business community, which has always been blamed for promoting blatant self-interest, does not have a monopoly on that particular trait. A wide range of public servants, among them teachers, garbage collectors, police, firefighters, and nurses, has pushed up its demands for higher wages to levels that the local governments are unwilling to consider. Pressure on the community for a "fair share" of the public wealth for public workers may result in denying children their education, polluting entire cities with uncollected garbage, risking uncontrolled crime and fire, and reducing medical care for the sick.

**Sports Figures.**   Young people's sports idols are negotiating for salaries completely "out of sight." Professional boxers have been paid $5 million for 15 rounds in the ring. Players from the National Football League have secured multimillion-dollar contracts to jump to the World Football League. A hockey star asked for $6.5 million over several years. On almost any weekend, TV viewers see a tennis or golf professional receive anywhere from $10,000 to $50,000 for winning a single tournament. It becomes quickly obvious to teen-agers that people like their parents, who earn from $5,000 to $20,000 a year, will have to work a lifetime to equal these sports "takes." And despite wild fantasies of someday becoming a superstar, most teen-agers suspect that their livelihood will have to come from more mundane jobs than "making it" in the sports arena.

**Welfare Recipients.**   Since news reports have documented abuses in the welfare system, we must conclude that many young people who grow up in families of lower socioeconomic status witness their parents taking from that system. People who earn as much as $20,000 a year have remained illegally on the welfare rolls. The food-stamp program is being victimized by families who qualify under its liberal criteria but who don't really need that aid. Some third- and fourth-generation welfare recipients have come to view the system as a way of life. But to many a ghetto dweller, the small welfare checks are a pittance compared with the take of the drug pushers, bookies, and pimps. Big cars and fancy clothes are the highly visible status symbols of those who have made it the easy way, so wouldn't one be a fool not to take a little when others are taking so much?

## III

Idolization of the blatant violator of society's laws is not restricted to the poor. The success of the two *Godfather* movies is ample evidence of our fascination with people who take what they want without scruples or regard for the rights of others. Of the millions who saw these films, most came around sooner or later to pulling for the bad guys and empathizing with the shrewdest of the "family" manipulators.

Gangsters are expected to be ruthless takers, but our community leaders are not. Three high-status vocations have now been publicly labeled, whether fairly or not, as being on the take: medicine, law, and politics. It is widely believed that physicians' incomes exceed $100,000 a year. Patients pay $15 or more for a five-minute prescription-writing session. Yesterday's hard-laboring general practitioner, who was willing to accept produce from the family vegetable garden as payment, is now a joke. In his or her place, according to newspaper reports, are physicians who cheat the Medicare and Medicaid programs in a number of ways; they can get away with setting fees at ridiculous levels and charging for services never delivered when the public is paying the bill. All too frequently, unnecessary surgery is recommended and performed—when covered by medical insurance. It used to be shocking even to think that the family doctor might have faults; now it is part of the social pattern for the medical profession to share in the general corruption.

Accusations against lawyers turn largely on "ambulance-chasing." In some states physicians have actually refused to deliver medical services because of the risk posed by lawyers lurking outside the hospital door. If they are able to discover an error in medical practice which can be turned into a multimillion-dollar lawsuit, these attorneys might succeed in persuading a jury to award such unrealistic sums—and then collect half of the patient's take. The practice is to accept such cases without a set fee, in the hope of winning an enormous victory. To give another example, a recent

Supreme Court decision ruled against fee-setting by bar associations; it seems that lawyers had been engaging in price-fixing in order to maximize their take.

And, of course, the grandest example of the society on the take occurred during Richard M. Nixon's administration. The abuse of power and wealth by the Nixon White House was the logical result of a society and a political system that tolerate the "take" ethic. It's not enough that Nixon has escaped paying the price for his criminal behavior; the taxpayers now have to foot the bill for his retirement—$60,000 a year to him, plus over half a million dollars for a staff of servants and office personnel.

The post-Watergate era has been filled with revelations of corruption at all levels of government. With convictions only sporadic and jail sentences usually suspended, public cynicism grows and grows. The message is clear: those who not only take but take big may be embarrassed, but they won't be punished. They continue to be tolerated, their action considered an unfortunate occurrence which we hope will not come to the surface again. The assumption is that the taking will continue—but presumably less dramatically and certainly not overtly.

## IV

One frightening aspect of this move away from traditional values is the snowball effect that has been generated. The rising prices in the inflationary economy have quickly eaten away the security of those who worked hard and saved for the future. Investors have taken heavy losses on the stock market. Higher wages become necessary simply to maintain last year's standard of living. In the midst of this pinch, some well-publicized and prominent individuals and groups have been taking big pieces of society's economic pie. And it has become clear that these individuals and groups are not some far-removed demonic clique. They are our neighbors. Suddenly the taking seems to have changed from a game of one-upmanship into a matter of survival. The snowball rolls faster and faster down the hill; people take as much as possible as quickly as they can, before the taking stops.

Our young people are increasingly aware of this rapidly spreading "take" ethic. Recent research has documented their cynicism toward the traditional values of hard work and saving for the future. Although sometimes lacking an intellectual understanding of the dimensions of the society on the take, at a "gut level" they view the system as corrupt. Some make an attempt to justify ripping-off from this corrupt system their small piece of the crust.

Other young people, however, are not taking but destroying. Vandalism is occurring at the highest rates in history. Such total disregard for property has never been comprehensible to the adult community. Stealing is understandable, because it fits in with the "take" ethic. But malicious destruction of homes, cars, parks, and schools seems crazy. Psychologists who have attempted to explain the internal motivation of the vandal usually focus on individual and group rebellion against authority, the adult world, and the symbols of society's control and affluence. However, let's consider the possibility that the increases in vandalism are signs of rebellion against the society on the take.

Such thinking leads toward the agonizing conclusion that juvenile delinquency in the 1970s is a natural and logical result of society's present code of ethics. It suggests that the rate of delinquency will continue to rise unless the dominant values of this society change from taking and hustling for personal gain to a greater concern for our corporate well-being; from unbridled competition to interpersonal cooperation; from hoarding of resources to a democratic economy; from cynicism to caring.

Not everyone, of course, is on the take. There are groups of individuals attempting to combat the take ethic: consumer protection groups, independent political organizations, and local civic betterment movements of various kinds. It is not clear, however, whether such organizations can halt the snowball effect, or whether the majority of the American public will be engulfed by mob panic and begin "to take in self-defense." One thing seems certain: the future development of our society's code of ethics will be reflected in the behavior of our adolescent citizens.

The children of today's society on the take are our juvenile delinquents. We, the adults of that society, are the models who prescribe the behaviors they imitate. We say that we want the illegal taking and destroying of property to cease. Perhaps, when the time comes that our words and our actions match, the young people of our society will rediscover, along with us, the values we have discarded.

# Religion and America's Moral Crisis

## Eugene B. Borowitz

There is a crisis in public morality. Apparently the decline in our standard of behavior is so obvious that, despite our political and class and religious differences, we can agree upon the disorder if not the therapy. I therefore

Reprinted, with deletions, by permission of *Worldview* magazine, November, 1974. Eugene B. Borowitz is Professor of Education and Jewish Thought at the New York School of Hebrew Union College. His most recent book is *Contemporary Christologies: A Jewish Response* (1980).

propose not to document our ills any further, but I do wish first to diagnose them and only then to suggest a line of significant treatment.

I see our problem less as one of ethics than of metaethics. Our difficulty is not rules or values. There are so many of them around that our difficulty is in choosing among them. Worse, it is in caring at all about being moral. I suggest that our ethics have become so anemic because they have lost their support system. More, I shall argue that our characterological breakdown is the result of misplaced faith.

Let me begin my analysis of our condition by applying to it Paul Tillich's understanding of what it means to be religious. For him, and for me in this stage of the investigation, one's religion is best thought of in existentialist terms: What is, in fact, one's ultimate concern? This is an untraditional and uninstitutional way of thinking about having faith. For all its novelty, it is highly appropriate to our task, for we are concerned with the moral crisis of our civilization and thus require a tool which enables us to understand how believers and unbelievers alike have caught the plague.

I will begin by applying the Tillichian concept of religion to morality. I suppose my Jewish sense of the centrality of duty, of action, of good deeds manifests itself here. Yet in this enterprise I know I do not betray Tillich's sense of Christianity nor that of many other Christian thinkers, like the great nineteenth-century thinker Albrecht Ritschl, who taught that religion is primarily the realm of human value judgments. I shall, however, turn Ritschl on his head and argue with Tillich that, rather than our values being our religion, we have lost our values because we have lost what was, existentially, our religion; and that we have lost our religion, not because we never had any, but rather because we have now discovered that we have had an inappropriate one.

What has been the operative faith of most Americans for the past generation or so? Note that the question is not, What would people say to a pollster?, nor even, In what religious buildings might they, with some frequency, be found? When we inquire about ultimate concern we reach far beneath the level of conventional behavior or locations. We ask, rather: When people were faced by significant, demanding choices, to what did they give the major free energies of their lives? What did they really care about more than anything else? In phrasing the question in this existentialist fashion we are debarred from the precision of an empirical answer. Hence my response is admittedly subjective and impressionistic—but not therefore eccentric or unsupportable.

What most Americans have believed in, I submit, was not God or Church or Torah but the burgeoning American society. In simple terms, we put our trust in ever greater affluence: Once deprived, we gained sufficiency, once degraded by unceasing want, we came to the self-respect of a steady, decent income. For us Exodus or Resurrection was the libera-

tion from a slum flat to a decent neighborhood, a garden apartment perhaps, or on to a home in the suburbs, even a second home. This process,
repeated on many levels, promised not only satisfaction but, in its own
way, salvation.

I do not mean to describe us as merely economic animals. We were,
amidst our upward social striving, also concerned about the quality of our
existence. In our aspirations for our families we can most easily see the
close relationship between greater good and greater goods. And a similar
broad sense of the promise of growth was felt in other areas of our civilization. We looked to schooling not only as preparation for a good job but also
for a richer life. So as adults we turn to books and records and magazines
and concerts and hobbies to deepen our minds and increase our sensitivity. The arts would give us character; recreation would restore our
soul. Psychiatry would solve our personal problems, science our technical
ones, politics and community work our social ones.

By calling this a misplaced faith I do not mean to denigrate these activities. They were, and are, legitimate concerns, productive of much that is
morally worthwhile. The question is: Is this complex of interests and values
worthy of our ultimate trust? Does it create and sustain the morals it
contains, or must they be drawn from another, deeper source? Can the
American way of life bear the full weight of our ethical existence, or must
it derive its sense of quality and direction from something that lies beyond
it, a "more ultimate" concern?

The key issue here is the power of secularity. We had put our trust in
man and his capacities. That is, our ultimate hope was in ourselves, singly
and jointly. Either we abandoned the God of the Bible or made God
marginal to more significant concerns. In either case we based our lives
and our values on our secularity, and it is this, our old, fundamental,
existential faith, that has now been thrown into question. For it is no
longer clear that secularity mandates morality. To the contrary, it seems
abundantly clear that secularity is compatible with amorality and can even
accommodate and encourage immorality, by the standards of the Bible.
I do not think this feeling was created in the hearts of most Americans by
any of our contemporary scandals. I think they only made the issue of the
past decade or so all but inescapable.

For most of us the new realism about secularity began with a changing
sense of perspective. Instead of taking certain rules or institutions for
granted as exemplars of ethical practice, we began asking what, in truth,
they did to people. Segregation was the classic case. It had claimed the
sanction of law, tradition, established practice, and the apparent will of the
majority of voters in a wide region. But when we got down to thinking
about what it was doing to people, we knew it to be wrong. We knew that
when one cannot think of a certain group of people as persons, entitled

to the rights of all persons, then one is immoral. And that from the perspective of being a person, the great good is freedom, the great goal is being true to oneself. We also came to see the great problem in human relations as power and its abuse: If you use your power over me to constrain my freedom you render me less a person. There was recognition that when our society or members of a group coerce another group they effectively reduce their own humanity. Of course, it might be necessary for the common good for each of us to sacrifice something of our individual freedom. But too often we were not asked to participate in the process of determining what limits shall be set upon us.

With persons as the criterion of the good, with power seen as a common force for the bad, a new moral realism began to dawn on us. The institutions whose goodness we had taken for granted now showed themselves to be run by relatively insensitive power, and thus to be injurious to persons. We became aware of tyrannies we had never before noted, at home, at school, in business, in sports, in our social relationships and our politics. Noble terms were being used to cover power drives and ego trips. And it also seemed clear that we should be able to find better ways to structure our lives with others.

So we set to work. A hundred causes claimed our allegiance: civil rights, better housing, decent education, care for the aged and the sick, peace abroad and peace at home. We had some successes. They only made clear how much yet remained to be done. Increasingly we learned the hard lessons: Most of us are not very willing to change. We are comfortable with our evil and at ease with our sin. We do not propose to live up to the values supposedly inherent in our culture.

More disturbing, it began to dawn on us that the morality we thought was demanded by our secular culture was only another option to it. What was there in a secular view of things that could mandate concern for all other persons as well as self-interest? Why should we indeed care for the weak and the powerless, the ungainly and unattractive, the failures and the bores, as long as we get what we want? Our science is value-free, our economics interested in profit, our politics concerned with power, our arts dominated by questions of technique, our lifestyle devoted to strategies of escape and indulgence.

Perhaps we might have come to terms with that, for people have often lived poorly in the name of great ideals. But secularity also took away our sense of guilt. Ethics became reduced to conditioning, to convention, to education, to psychic mechanism—anything but a commandment, a duty, a summons.

A great part of our crisis, then, is that many people today are effectively amoral. In Freud's day neurosis was most commonly traceable to an oppressive sense of duty and guilt. Today it is more commonly associated with having no firm set of values and by having no sense of limits or direction, thus having no true sense of self at all.

Another part of our crisis is that those of us who still retain a strong sense of biblical morality suddenly feel alien and ill at ease. The moral America we took for granted is not the America we see around us. We are depressed and sickened by its strange hospitality to evil acts and evil people. Our civilization has become our problem—how then can it continue to deserve our existential faith? We now stand in judgment over the secularity which once comprised our ultimate concern. How can we any longer put our most basic trust in it? We are deeply disturbed because we have lost our faith. We believed in a god who was no god. The idol of secularity has fallen, and we are shaken to our core.

A number of Americans do not participate in the sense of moral crisis I am describing. For one group the old secular style still remains the only true way. Their problem is largely that they do not understand why everyone else has lost their moral nerve. They are disturbed only because they are increasingly isolated and marginal in our society. Where once they seemed to be moving with what was the major mood of the times, now they seem somehow old-fashioned and out of touch.

Unsecularized religionists are similarly untainted by our society's ethical malaise. If anything, they are somewhat elated by it. They always knew secularization was wrong. Now that the pseudo-faith created by it has come to grief, they have been justified by history. Relying now as before on revelation, they remain unperturbed. They still know what they must do. But because they have never been through the refiner's fire of secularization, I find their ethical horizons narrow and their sense of responsibility limited essentially to themselves and their kind.

One need not agree on secularity as revelation. But that does not mean there was nothing to learn from it. The notion of humanity, of one global humankind, was surely implicit in biblical faith. It took the rationalist rigor of secularity to make it clear and unavoidable. That is a precious gain I am not willing to sacrifice. I repeat: Many of the concerns of secularity are legitimate and remain morally compelling. My major quarrel with it derives from its being made a god.

No, America is not all bad, but at the very least it has lost heart. It still does many good things, but it isn't sure they still count. It no longer knows what to care about. It isn't even certain that caring itself still makes much sense.


Yet, paradoxically enough, this moment of doubt creates a new openness to a more adequate religious faith. Insofar as we are deeply disturbed we evidence deep moral concern. We show that somehow we know our ethical values are right, for it is in the name of those values that we deny the old idolatry. We have here the dawning recognition that our ethical commitments transcend us and our society, though we had, for a while, lost sight of that. We are now willing to search for a faith adequate to this new sense of personal depth. . . .

What Judaism and Christianity can uniquely bring to the American culture at this juncture (in other areas of the world we should, of course, have to add Islam) is their root religious intuition that a transcendent God stands over against us and our society, summoning us to moral conduct. These biblical religions proclaim, against almost all of Asian religious teaching, that God's ultimate character, insofar as humans may speak of such exalted matters, is not neutral. The Lord we serve is not finally beyond the categories of good and evil. Our God is not to be approached through a realm that ultimately lies beyond morality. God's holiness is intimately linked with God's ethical command. There is a direct movement from "You shall be holy for I the Lord, your God, am holy" to "You shall not hate your brother in your heart but you shall love your neighbor as yourself." True, the God of the Bible stands in covenant with us, but this intimacy never negates the distance between creature and creator, never destroys God's right to command. Our God in personal presence comes to us as compelling love and purposing forgiveness. We are summoned and sent and judged and held accountable—and in just such moral suasion we also see the signs of God's close caring.

We Jews and Christians will argue between us and among ourselves whether the new or old law is in effect and in what mode it is to be followed. We shall differ as to the form and nature of the commandments. But I think we will both insist that those who know God should devote themselves to doing good and those who love God ought to love people and dedicate their lives to creating a humane and holy social order.

Not so long ago this Judeo-Christian sense of reality linked to responsibility was taken to be the basis of the American ethos. It gave the American way of life a strong, metaphysical impetus to sustained moral striving. It was, of course, not the only and perhaps not the most important factor in creating that unparalleled mixture of idealism and opportunism we recognize as American. Yet despite the frontier and our lavish natural resources, despite immigrant vigor and extraordinary industrialization, it was the accepted sense of a transcendent ethical demand laid upon us which gave us Americans our special brand of national idealism. The hand of the Puritans still rests upon us.

In secularizing our culture in the past generation or so we have carried out an experiment, so to speak, to see what might happen to our way of life if we abandoned the Judeo-Christian view of human obligation. We did not do too badly for a while. Our commitments to our biblical past run so deep that despite our putative secularity we remain quite faithful to biblical values; much of the remaining moral content of our culture is there, I would argue, not because it is intrinsic to secularity, but as an inheritance from an earlier, more religious age. Only now is it clear what cutting ourselves off from our transcendent source of values does to us and our society.

I am not saying that if all Americans were instantly to take up Jewish and Christian religious duties or, better, were to share Jewish or Christian faith and the ethical responsibilities they entail, all the moral problems of America would be solved. The question of the ground of our values is only one of the many difficulites facing this nation. But it is our root problem. I do not see how, until we reestablish our ultimate sense of why we ought to do the good and in what direction that good lies, the rest of our moral efforts can hope to succeed.

The temptation is for religion to seek to reestablish itself in our society by denouncing secularity as it criticizes every moral evil that has been created in its name. Surely there is ample biblical precedent for us to assert our roles as the critics of society. The prophets were continually involved in political and social judgments, for they could evaluate human affairs from a transcendent perspective. Since we claim something of their vantage, ought we not be the people most sensitive to every wrong and the most courageous in pointing it out? And since our civilization is relatively understanding of the evil men do, knowing "they are only human" and "that's the way things have always been," is it not our special responsibility to remind our fellows that to be human is to bear the divine image, that the way things are must give way to how things ought to be?

I do not see how, without the greatest peril to our soul, we can shirk the prophetic role of denunciation and witness and proclamation and dissent. Better to run the risk of looking foolish by being overly sensitive to sin than to retain our respectability at the price of learning to live in peace with it.

But in a time when so much has gone wrong it is too easy to fatten one's sense of righteousness by concentrating on the sins of others. I do not think prophetic criticism is what people most need from us today. Indeed, I am far from certain that they will take our prophetic role seriously until we establish our credibility on a more substantial basis.

The truth is that institutional religion shares in the crisis of our time. The skepticism that runs so deep through our society is no less directed toward religion. Consider, for a moment, the frequent distinction made between religiosity and institutional religion. We may find some grounds for optimism in the fact that presently the sense of religious concern is widespread in our society. Yet at the same time we must acknowledge that interest in churches and synagogues seems to have passed its peak. . . .

If anything, sensitive people will set higher standards for religious bodies than for any other institution in our society. I think they are right. If we are the unique agencies of a transcendent morality, then we should exemplify it. But can we say we have done this? Have we transcended our society in moral stature? There is, at the very least, serious doubt about our moral performance. I suggest, therefore, that as people now turn to religion to help them in their search for a firm moral ground, they will want to know what religious organizations have done and are doing to merit their ethical confidence. They will care little for what we say. But they will care much about how we conduct ourselves. They will apply to us the same searching test they have used on all our social institutions: How do we use our power? They will ask: What do we do to persons in their freedom as we operate our hierarchies, our agencies, our commissions, our seminaries, our churches and synagogues, our ministries? So if we are to be able to carry out our mission as transmitters and celebrators of transcendence in a decadent age, we shall have to pass at least three key tests.

*First,* how do we, as we go about preserving what is good in our heritage, encourage the creation of the new and the better? Surely there is something timeless about God and what we ought to do for God. Yet people are not timeless. We do not, cannot, should not be expected to live as our grandparents did, perhaps not even as our parents lived. And we know that our religious traditions have changed in previous ages, sometimes radically. If we now change too much, we run the risk of losing what was good in the past, those truths and practices which carried the generations forward and linked them to each other in a history-transforming continuity. Yet if we do not change, we run the risk of losing the present generation and thus our necessary link with the future. The question then is: How will we place the burden of the past on the shoulders of the present?

The *second* challenge puts the same question in more individual terms: How do we propose to maintain the purity of our faith while fostering individual expression? We cannot be all things to all people; the recent decades have surely established that. We do see clearly that God is the source of our individuality and personal dignity. But if God can make no claim upon us and must be satisfied with whatever we choose to be, then God has no dignity; we who are created in God's image, for all our vaunted freedom, will have only the hollow worth of our freedom to choose it matters not what. Yes, we have a right to be persons and to be true to ourselves, but God has a right to be God and thus to make demands upon us. The proper question is: How will we lay God's command to humanity upon the individual?

But mainly, I think, people will judge us by seeing to what extent we serve ourselves and to what extent we serve others. To be sure, if Judaism and Christianity are to be strong enough to influence America, they must be organized and institutionalized. That means a structured constituency which shares a common dream and supports its members as they seek to achieve it in a hostile environment. And it means a social apparatus that transcends any group of persons and thus can survive to keep the old hope alive from generation to generation.

Yet, in this process, what happens to people? How do we now relate to other human beings who are not of our group, whether of another faith or of no faith at all? What happens to our need for human community with other believers in our faith as church and synagogue rightfully seek to maintain their institutions? This *third* issue, I am convinced, is the most sensitive we face. For surely religion ought to bring us together as people, to show us how to share our true humanity with one another in the presence of the one God who is the source of our unity. Yet so often, in religion's name, we feel we are attending the clergy or the lay leadership rather than God; or we are too busy carrying out the heavy formalities of religious etiquette to be able to feel for one another. If we are to be God's people, then surely we should be encouraged to feel like people, sensitive, individual, concerned, open to one another, as we gather in God's name. We should be more a community of human sharing as we gather in God's assembly than anywhere else. And at the moment that is rarely true.

What makes these demands on us so difficult is that they cannot be met by following a rule. They are true dilemmas, mutually contradictory demands, and we must learn to live with these dilemmas. For even as we affirm the continuity and tradition and institution, so we affirm the precious significance of each individual soul. In the face of such demands we have no security and can only act out of our most basic faith and intuition. That is what many people know, and that is why they will examine this focus of our power and their need to make their judgment as to who and what we truly are. And we shall restore our credibility with them only insofar as we have met this searching test.

I do not see that we can approach this challenge with any special confidence. We have been tried in the past and found wanting. We must acknowledge that it is quite possible that this beloved country of ours, and we with it, have passed by the moment of our highest moral potential and entered into a period of moral stagnation, if not decline. The crisis is real, our loss may be quite serious indeed. But for all their realism, Judaism and Christianity are religions of hope. We not only believe in the coming of God's kingdom, we believe that, with God's help, we can live in it here and now. It is our difficult task in this difficult hour to live in the reality of God's rule despite all pessimism, and by our words and deeds to summon people from their sinfulness to God's steady service.

# "Without a Vision the People Perish"

## Jim Wallis

Everything is coming apart. Nothing works anymore. We move from one crisis to another so fast that the word has become a description of our whole way of life.

We are in a period of major social disintegration. The economy is rapidly being destroyed by the twin devils of unemployment and inflation. Despite the proliferation of government regulations, our water becomes dirtier, our air is harder to breathe, and our land poisoned—all from the massive wastes of a consumer society. Even our bodies show the consequences of a polluted environment as one out of every four of us now is afflicted with cancer, the plague of our technological age. Meanwhile, the number and sufferings of the poor mount daily throughout the nation and the world, as a privileged few grow ever richer.

The resources of our finite world are reaching their limits as we who were charged to be stewards have instead been exploiters. Yet despite our dwindling resources, we now spend more than half of our public monies to increase our military arsenals. Constructing the most sophisticated and lethal weapons of war the world has ever known has required precious human and material resources, undermined the economy, and escalated the prospects of war. And now, war will be total.

It is a period of political withdrawal and instability. Politicans are suspect. The country hasn't had a president serve two terms in 30 years. Only half of those eligible in the last presidential election even bothered to vote. The standard reason: "It doesn't make any difference." The major institutions of government, business, and labor generate no confidence. Corruption is assumed on every level by a cynical public. Self-interest and apathy are the two poles of public life.

Fewer and fewer people are enthusiastic about the system, the way things are, or the world around them. All this is creating a deep insecurity that is evident everywhere. People feel like sheep without a shepherd. Unfortunately, there are many wolves who would devour the flock, or turn it to their own purposes.

It is a time of spiritual decay. Material wealth and military superiority have become idols. Our low value for human life is evident both in escalat-

From *Sojourners*, June, 1980. Reprinted by permission of *Sojourners* Magazine, 1309 L Street N.W., Washington, D.C. 20005. Jim Wallis is editor of *Sojourners* and author of *Agenda for Biblical People* (1976).

ing military expenditures and rising abortion rates. Only our hardness of heart allows us to accept a global economic system that starves children and consigns one billion people to grinding poverty. Crime runs out of control in the streets and in corporate boardrooms and corridors of power. Sexual values reflect the selfishness of a consumer society whose watchwords are always "more" and "better." Personal gratification replaces commitment and undermines the integrity of marriage, family, and the whole notion of relationships based on covenants.

It's an open question whether we will have hindsight for our time. But if there is hindsight, it will show this period to be a time of transition, a time of change from one era to another. We are either at the end of all the epochs or we're in a time between epochs, which means that old assumptions, values, and the structures they gave rise to are no longer adequate; they are unraveling. However, new assumptions, values, and structures have yet to take concrete shape. During times of transition, people are nervous about their lives, their world, and their future. Young couples agonize over whether to bring children into the world. Tomorrow looks to be only a time when today's problems get worse. People become defensive and begin to react more than to act.

In such a time the great need is for a new social vision. When confusion and uncertainty abound, the future belongs to those who can see it and begin to live it. By a new social vision I mean a new understanding of how people can relate to one another and live together. It must encompass our social, economic, political, sexual, and family relations. It must have the capacity to both change personal lives and generate new social and institutional patterns.

That new social vision will most likely arise from religious roots. The changes now necessary have to do with our most basic values and assumptions, with questions of ultimate reality and authority in people's lives. They have to do with our spiritual or religious foundations.

Visions rooted merely in secular ideology will not be enough. In American history, major social transformation has most often grown out of religious revival and spiritual awakening. The renewal of faith more than the spread of ideology has been the catalyst for change.

In an era of transition many solutions will be offered. Some people will seek desperately to hang on to the status quo. Those who profit most from the existing order will fight with all their might against any change that would deprive them of their wealth and power. Always there are those whose social vision is simply an affirmation of what already is, or a hearkening back to an earlier version of it. The language of returning to a mythical time of blessing, tranquility, and righteousness offers a sense of security.

Some religious leaders seek to justify the present system in spiritual terms. They call us to an earlier day when the nation was supposedly more pure and righteous. They refer to America as a nation like Israel, specially chosen by God, set aside for divine purpose. They argue that God has a special stake in America, as if we as a nation are indispensable to his purposes in the world. The nation has been compromised, they say, and we must return to the principles upon which it was founded. But that claim is illusive as those "principles" are defined according to the ideology of those who would preserve the old order.

Many seek to return to an era like the '50s, when the United States had clear nuclear superiority, the poor were quiet, and women stayed at home. It was the golden era of the American empire to which they long to return —a time when the United States could do what it wanted in the world without fear of challenge.

Such a vision is, in fact, reactionary. Masquerading as Christian, it runs contrary to basic biblical demands for justice and peace. Ultimately it is a vision designed not to defend the faith but to preserve narrow economic and national interests. What is needed is not a return to the past, but something that leads us to a new future.

There are now two primary questions on which the world hangs. They are also two issues on which the gospel is at stake. The first is economics. The second is military violence. It is interesting that among Right and Left, most now agree that these are the crucial questions.

Some argue a gospel of wealth. They proclaim material prosperity as a sign of God's blessing and, by implication, poverty as a consequence of sin.

Similarly, some define our nation as better and more blessed than others, and proclaim our military purposes to be righteous and just. Our national self-interest becomes elevated to the level of God's own purpose. Our enemies are the perpetrators of evil while we are the defenders of freedom. Our pursuit of military supremacy becomes, by this twisted logic, the key to peace in the world. The prospect of war, and now even nuclear war, generates no horror but takes on the character of a moral crusade.

A look at what the Bible says about these questions would serve us well here. Biblical economics begins with the affirmation that the earth is the Lord's. Its care is given to humankind in sacred trust. Its sustenance is to be shared by all God's children. The biblical doctrine of stewardship renders a clear judgment against any economic system based on ever-expanding growth, profit, and exploitation of the earth.

The early Hebrew law codes built in provisions for periodic redistribution of wealth to counter the sinful human tendency toward accumulation and to insure equity and justice. The Jubilee tradition required, at regular intervals, the remission of all debts, redistribution of land, and freeing of slaves.

The Old Testament sees poverty as neither accidental nor natural but rooted in injustice—in the way the society is organized. The prophets railed against the rich for their oppression of the poor. Yahweh demanded justice and righteousness and declared that nations would be judged by how they treated their poor. Right relationship to the Lord required the setting straight of all economic and social relationships.

Jesus is God made poor. His coming was prophesied to bring social revolution. His kingdom would turn things upside down: The mighty would be brought low, the rich sent empty away, the poor exalted, and the hungry satisfied. Jesus identified himself with the weak, the outcast, the downtrodden. He told us to look for him among the "least of these," and said our love for him would be tested by whether we fed the hungry, clothed the naked, sheltered the homeless, visited the sick and the prisoners. His kingdom undermines all economic systems which reward the rich and punish the poor.

The early Christians shared their goods with one another and with the poor. The Jubilee redistribution was fulfilled among them, no longer just at periodic intervals, but as a way of life. The apostles taught that one could not profess love for God while ignoring the needs of hungry neighbors.

Likewise, the biblical imperatives put a limit on the human propensity for violence. The biblical writers repeatedly attacked the roots of violence in greed, envy, hate, and self-righteousness.

Even the Old Testament outlaws the kind of militarism that governs the nations today: The Israelites were not to trust in their horses and chariots but were to rely on Yahweh for their protection. But it is the New Testament which reveals how God's purposes for reconciliation are made clear in Jesus Christ. No longer merely restrained in our violence, we are now taught to love our enemies and are "entrusted with the ministry of reconciliation." It is the peacemakers, says Jesus, who will be called the children of God.

There are Christians pursuing this biblical vision. They are heeding the Scriptures' call for simplicity of life, sharing of resources, stewardship of the earth, and fundamental redistribution of wealth and power which recognizes God's special concern for the poor. They have learned the biblical wisdom of finding security not in economic accumulation and armament stockpiling but in the pursuit of justice and reconciliation.

Something very significant is happening. In our own community and in other places around the country something has occurred that is so simple it could easily be missed.

Three things are now true of a growing number of Christians. First, we no longer believe that our worth and identity as human beings depends on our consumption and possession of things. We are ordinary people— single, married, adults, and children—who no longer believe the central lie of the economic system. We neither ignore nor shun material needs but meet them simply as we care for one another. There is no longer a financial incentive in our lives; economic success is no longer a goal. Material goods now have only instrumental value.

Second, we do not feel the need for a nuclear arsenal to protect us. I'm not speaking simply about our position on peace. I'm talking about what we feel. We are not secretly glad that nuclear weapons are there to protect us. We just don't accept the need for the arms race.

Third, a change has come about in the way we tend to look at the world. Social questions, political decisions, and newspaper headlines are now viewed from the vantage point of how they affect poor people. For most of us, that's an entirely new starting point, a whole new perspective for how we think politically. It is to view the world from the experience of those at the bottom, not the top. Now, our first impulse is to ask the question, "How does this affect those who are poor?"

These are most significant and hopeful things, because they demonstrate a disbelief in the two most basic assumptions of the present system. Today the fundamental problem economically is that people believe the myth that economic gain is the key to happiness. The fundamental problem militarily is the myth that security comes from more and more weapons. Those myths are dying among us. And to the extent they are no longer believed, the system has lost its legitimacy for us.

The success of the American economic system depends on people identifying themselves principally as consumers. If even a minority begins to define itself differently, the system is threatened. When the assumption that our value and worth is tied up in material things dies, it foretells the death of the whole system.

Similarly, when people no longer believe in the ruling assumptions of national security, that system is in jeopardy. When people fear the military arsenals more than they fear the things the arsenals claim to protect us from, the military system will lose its credibility. People begin to believe in peace more than war.

The power of a system is not finally in its wealth, military hardware, or technology. Its power is in the spiritual authority it has in people's lives. In other words, a system has power only to the extent that people believe in it. When people no longer believe the system is ultimate and permanent, the hope of change emerges. Undermining the belief in the system is therefore the first step toward defeating it.

Most of us were born and bred to be the managers and beneficiaries of this system, and now we no longer believe in its most basic assumptions. That is social change. It is a new social vision in the making based in religious faith.

Our society needs more than a new perspective. It needs a new social vision. We can see the possibility of the church providing such a vision through its life.

We can see the beginnings of a church living by biblical economics. It would be a community in which competition was replaced by sharing. Even in hard times, the community would see to it that the needs of every person were met. The needs of the poor would take priority in the economic decisions and ministry of the congregation. Living at a fraction of present lifestyle levels would become a natural way of life as compassion takes root in the community.

The presence of such a people would be significant. They would be ordinary people who broke with the "givens" of their society. They would be concrete proof that it is possible to live a different way. Theirs would be a clear and credible voice defending the poor and attacking the arrangements of wealth and power which oppress them. This community's very existence would indeed hold the promise of new social and economic possibilities.

We can also envision congregations of Christians all over the world who sense the urgency of peace in the face of nuclear war. Only those who have found their security elsewhere can effectively challenge their nations' misplaced security in weapons of ultimate destruction. Those who are reconciled together in Christ and drawn from all the world's warring factions are particularly well situated to show the way to peace, and can help fearful nations learn less destructive ways of resolving conflict. In communities of faith, where the war system has been renounced as spiritually idolatrous and politically suicidal, concrete initiatives could emerge to beat swords into plowshares.

Social disintegration should not simply be viewed with despair. It can be, in fact, a sign of hope as people lose their belief in the system. It is when distintegration leads only to despair that we are in danger. Despair breeds passivity and becomes yet another victory for the system.

The biblical understanding of hope is relevant here. Biblical hope comes from having a vision of the future that enables us to live even now in its promise. It means bringing the future into the present with power and authority. Hope in something new and better is always the greatest spark for change. Without that hope we are controlled by present realities, wandering between passivity and despair.

The crucial movement is from optimism through despair into hope. Hope cannot be limited to a better life in the next world but is born of the possibility of living differently in this one. Christians should know too much about the world to be optimistic; they also should know too much about the future to remain in despair.

We are witnessing a battle for the minds and hearts of people in the churches. Some would try to channel people's insecurity into a rigidly ideological agenda that reinforces the worst values and structures of the present system. Some are even seeking a power base for their own political aspirations.

It is the practice of a new social vision that will offer hope in the midst of a hopeless time. The situation need not improve to give rise to hope. All that is needed is a belief in the possibility of an alternative.

The key is to live the hope among us *now*. In so doing we can create new social, economic, and political possibilities. We must be firm in our belief that the biblical vision is socially relevant, first in defining a new shape for the church's life and then in reshaping our social structures. Such biblical living on the part of the church could also lead to persecution, but at least we would be living a life worth persecuting in an oppressive and disintegrating social order.

It is the responsibility of those who hold a vision for the future to provide hope, whether or not it is received. We must recognize the future in what we are believing now, and live it. Otherwise, we allow the system to close off the future.

Unless we're able to see the connection between what we do, even daily, and what we believe, we will become discouraged. Our understanding tends to be parochial and narrow. We become bogged down in our own work, feelings, and selves, and we become unable to see the relationship between what we're doing and the vision that motivates us. Without the biblical vision renewing our minds and hearts, we will perish.

Even a small group of people trying to live a new way can be a significant sign of hope. But we can take our life for granted and lose sight of its broader meaning. Preoccupied with how hard it is to live on the margins, outside the mainstream, we lose our vision. We feel all the deficits of minority status without the self-consciousness of a creative minority. At that point we lose hope in our own life, and cannot possibly be a sign of hope to the churches or to anyone else.

Only when belief in the system has died and has been replaced by faith in God will real change come. It is ultimately only our faith that can break the stranglehold of the system, create the possibility of living a different way, and offer the vision of new social possibilities.

# 2

# The Church's Response to Social Issues

It is one thing to speak of the response of individual Christians to the morality of the society; it is something else to speak of the church's response to moral and social issues. Within the church itself there is considerable difference of opinion whether the church as a corporate body (or denomination) can or should address itself in any official way to social issues. There are several reasons for this, two of which we will mention.

First, who really speaks for the church? Can bishops or presidents of churches be expected to reflect the thinking of all the membership? Is there even likely to be a consensus that they could express? Something becomes an "issue"—take preparation for nuclear warfare, for example—because there is a significant difference of opinion in the population concerning it. This division is as likely to be reflected among church members as among those outside the church. Because there is no clear-cut and obvious answer on which everyone agrees, the subject divides us and assumes the character of an issue. For anyone in authority to speak for the church on such a topic, there is a risk of further dividing the church by antagonizing those who disagree with what is said.

There is, furthermore, the question of expertise and adequate knowledge. Does a church official possess the necessary grasp of all the ramifications of an issue to speak a definitive word in behalf of the church? During the time of the Vietnam war this point was often raised: How could the church speak out when the public was in the dark concerning all the facts of the matter? Would it not take a staff of political and military scientists and large numbers of researchers to enable one to address this subject in a knowledgeable and relevant manner?

Those who are convinced that the church must address the issues of our day have answers to these objections. They say it is not necessary for a church official to find a consensus in his church in order to address a social issue. It is quite conceivable for any given social issue that the majority of church membership may not reflect a viewpoint that represents a careful and responsible application of Christian ideals. Church leadership always speaks *to* the church as well as *for* the church, helping to educate and sensitize the membership concerning the implications of Christian belief for a given social issue. The responsibility of church leadership is to know and understand the facts of the matter and then to draw out the implications of the Christian orientation to human life as they would apply to the particular issue. There may well be room for disagreement (and this disagreement should be expressed), but at least the Christian community is being stimulated to think about its convictions in relation to an important issue in the society. To say nothing is to say that the church is irrelevant in relation to the most important issues in human relationships. This would be a denial of all that the faith stands for.

In regard to the question of adequate knowledge, of course, it is true that a responsible moral judgment is only possible when all the relevant facts are known. But most issues do not involve factual material that is in principle inaccessible to the public. Often the dimensions of a moral issue do involve disagreements over just what the facts of the matter are; where this is the case it must be recognized and taken into one's consideration of the issue. The responsibility of church leadership clearly is to perceive the moral issue involved and to bring theological and ethical resources to bear. Again, in the case of military preparedness in an age of nuclear warfare, this would mean that the church has the obligation to make its judgment known on the acceptabliity or nonacceptability of nuclear warfare (which would certainly involve discussion on the viability of limited nuclear warfare), without attempting to address questions of strategy unless they affect the basic stance of the country on this issue.

As one looks at the history of North American church involvement in addressing social issues, there has been until recently a rather clear pattern in which most of the doctrinally and ideologically conservative churches have not invested much time and energy in addressing political and social issues. They have emphasized the church's message to the individual who stands in need of salvation. Churches generally characterized as liberal, on the other hand, have been more inclined to address the issues that arise from living in society. Christians in the first group often think that those in the latter are diluting, if not subverting, the Gospel by mixing it with social issues. They accuse the latter of using the message of the church to support social welfare programs that are far afield from the church's purpose to evangelize the masses. Those in the latter group are just as critical of those in the former, claiming that passivity in regard to social issues simply reinforces the status quo and leaves the church without a prophetic message.

One of the merits of the article by John C. Bennett is that it provides insight into why we have this split among the churches. The concerns of both sides are actually rooted in the message of Scripture. Bennett captures these concerns in the two words "comfort" and "challenge," and points out the incompleteness of each side when it fails to include the concern of the other. Those who concentrate on the church's role in promoting social change may miss the aspects of faith that provide personal comfort and support—grace in times of brokenness, healing in times of suffering, meaning in times of anxiety. Those who see only an individualistic gospel or a church whose only task is spiritual miss the element of God's judgment and the Gospel imperatives to minister to the oppressed and the powerless. These two dimensions of the church's message are necessary to each other.

The emergence of the so-called Christian New Right prompted the article by Peter L. Berger, but it leads him to some wider reflections on how the church should relate to political issues, and the dangers of the church becoming identified with a particular economic or social class. Berger is clearly more cautious than Bennett about the necessity of churches speaking out on social issues. Berger see mainline denominations as being as vulnerable to the influence of special interests (tending to left of center) as are the evangelical types who identified with right-wing interests in the 1980 elections. As a sociologist, Berger is particularly attentive to the sociological context within which churches live. To transcend the formational context is not possible in any absolute sense, but the church's calling certainly is to maintain a sense of self-criticism against its own national culture and its social class. This vigilance is integral to an authentic prophetic witness.

Many people would argue that at this point the Christian New Right raises a more serious issue than Berger may lead one to believe. One can group the interests of this movement under three headings: (1) the preservation of traditional moral values, which is expressed by the movement's opposition to abortion, the Equal Rights Amendment, and gay rights; (2) the strengthening of religion, which is expressed by the movement's opposition to the so-called secular humanists and its support of prayer and the teaching of creationism in the public schools; and (3) the movement's exaltation of the United States as the last hope of Christian civilization against "godless Communism," expressed in vigorous support of an aggressive foreign policy and increased military spending.

This last feature—the uncritical nationalism—in the stance of the Christian New Right probably disturbs their fellow Christians the most. To provide religious sanction for an all-out pursuit of military supremacy in the era of nuclear warfare is a sobering spectacle indeed. Flag waving may be more popular than flag burning, but somewhere in between must be a willingness to objectively evaluate the intentions and policies of our nation. This kind of self-critical activity is essential to the health of every nation, and the Christian community should be expected to carry it out in a vigorous and responsible way. Bennett's reference to U.S. Senator Mark Hatfield at a 1973 prayer breakfast gives us a stirring example of this kind of witness.

# Two Christianities

John C. Bennett

Journalists, historians, sociologists, and religious leaders are all agreed that the American churches are badly split. The division is partly theological, but it recognizes no traditional bounds of denomination, afflicting Roman Catholics as much as the various Protestants. The thesis of Dean Kelley's *Why Conservative Churches Are Growing* (New York, 1972) is suggested by the title he himself had chosen for the book: "Why *Strict* Churches Are *Strong*." Churches that are ecumenical in spirit and open to the wider world do not prosper like those that are highly authoritarian and exclusivistic. Strict authoritarianism responds to the desire for secure foundations in a badly shaken culture.

If one takes a global view of the theological differences among Christians, however, it is obvious that our ideas of what is "conservative" and what is "liberal" need some revising. Conservative theologies in some other countries are not so tied to conservative politics as is the case in the United States. Right-wing religious Americanism naturally has no appeal in other countries, and it is precisely that type of religious expression in America which so inflames the split in our churches.

Then too, those who project an indefinite trend toward the demise of "open" forms of Christianity tend to ignore a long trend to the contrary. Denominations that take theological scholarship seriously usually move over a period of a few decades from right to center, and frequently beyond that. Scholarship is not very compatible with absolutistic exclusivism and uncritical authoritarianism. Theological schools offer the clearest example of this pilgrimage in recent decades, and their influence upon the churches is inestimable.

I want to focus, however, on the split between those who want churches to seek fundamental change in society and those who espouse an individualistic gospel removed from involvement in progressive social or political action. This split is often most evident between members of local churches and the stance of their denominational or ecumenical officialdom. Frequently and unfortunately it appears as a conflict between clergy and laity.

Reprinted, with deletions, by permission from *Worldview* magazine, October, 1973. John C. Bennett is former president of Union Theological Seminary, New York, and author of numerous works on Christian ethics, including *The Radical Imperative* (1975).

A summary of two common attitudes toward the social responsibility of churches might be useful, not because it is a new issue, but because it has recently flared up in new ways. On one side are those who see their churches as agents of social change and thus give strategic priority to the cause of oppressed people both at home and in "the Third World." They stress the mission of the church to the outside world as much as, or even more than, its service to its own members. The church must engage in transforming institutions and structures, as well as caring for individuals and families. They are ready to risk involvements that will be regarded by their opponents as more "political" than "religious."

On the other side are those who would have the church stick to its traditional functions: the salvation of individual souls, often in an other-worldly context, and pastoral service to people in their private lives. Most of the social teaching and action of the churches is viewed as alien secular work. The belief is that converted individuals will do what needs to be done to change social structures. They seek to avoid controversy in the church, and have a special anxiety that some group within a denomination or local church may say or do something controversial that commits the denomination or local church as a whole. These are only the surface marks of the two types of Christianity.

Christianity, to say the obvious, is a manysided faith. It is embodied in a multiplicity of institutions and activities and belief systems which are legitimate expressions of the faith, though some of them, when isolated from others, appear as caricatures of what one may believe Christianity to be. *This manysidedness of Christianity is the source of its richness and also of our current controversies.* People become Christians and join churches for many different reasons. For some, of course, it is merely a matter of following family patterns or joining a church in order to become part of a community. But among those who make a real decision we can distinguish between those who have had an experience of God through Christ that has given them inner joy and peace and deliverance from a personal sense of lostness and those who are attracted to Chrisitanity and the church because they see in them resources for social change, for justice, and peace. Others see Christianity and churches chiefly as stabilizing forces. The last understand religion as giving sanction to the American way of life, to the so-called Protestant ethic and, in general, to American goals in the world.

*To Comfort and to Challenge* (by Glock, Ringer and Babbie, Berkeley, 1967), was a study of the Episcopal Church in the United States, but its findings as indicated by other studies probably reflect the experience of many other churches. Glock found that the dominant role of the church in the minds of most members is associated with the word *comfort,* while a minority see Christianity as a religion of prophetic *challenge.*

In fact, the words "comfort" and "challenge" both have solid ground-ings in the New Testament. "Come to me, all you who labor and are heavy laden, and I will give you rest" (Matt. 11:28–30). "I came to cast fire on the earth; and would that it were already kindled! . . . Do you think that I have come to give peace on earth? No, I tell you, but rather division" (Luke 12:49–53).

Professor Glock and his colleagues have been helpful in calling attention to this contrast within the church, but I very much doubt that the word "comfort" brings out the depth or range of the problem. I would substitute for the word "comfort" the phrase "the affirmative and supportive aspects of faith." These aspects are not only essential, but it is with them that Christianity begins and ends. Such affirmative and supportive aspects in-clude:

Praise—thanksgiving—celebration
Gospel or good news—the promise of Salvation
Grace—forgiveness—acceptance
A sense of meaning in the face of the mystery of existence, of massive evil, of personal pain, of frustration and death
Healing of spirit and what Paul Tillich called "the courage to be."

Comfort is really a consequence of all these elements in our faith. When isolated from this context it trivializes Christian experience, but comfort is not trivial. There would be neither Christian Gospel nor Christian wor-ship nor Christian faith nor Christian church without these affirmative and supportive aspects.

No doubt Dean Kelley is right in underscoring the great weakness of mainline churches that are open theologically and progressive socially, but whose members often feel they are not helped in finding meaning for their lives. Comfort, in any deep sense, results from the discovery of meaning. Meaning includes the elements of judgment and prophetic teaching, but if only these elements are emphasized the result is a Chris-tianity as distorted as when they are omitted. The omission is, of course, the more common distortion.

The faith in its wholeness witnesses to the God of judgment who tran-scends all nations and powers of the world. Judgment includes warning against the idolatries of one's nation or way of life, of power, security, success, and affluence. Judgment illuminates our period in history. It in-volves the imperative that churches should identify with the poor and oppressed majority of the human race. Religious interpreters today see the last point more clearly than most of their predecessors, not because they are more committed or more intelligent, but because they have listened, have been unable to avoid listening, to the articulate representatives of the poor and oppressed everywhere. In this country the articulate representatives of the black minority have been most instrumental in putting white churchmen on the moral defensive.

Anyone moved by this understanding of divine judgment and by these imperatives cannot avoid becoming political in the broad sense of the word. When these concerns are brought into churches, they disturb the peace and comfort of the congregations.

An event in Washington, D.C. illustrates the contrast between the perception of Christian faith as judgment and religion as the sanction for present uses of power. At a prayer breakfast in January 1973, attended by hundreds of notables, including President Nixon and Billy Graham, Senator Mark Hatfield of Oregon spoke in a way that no doubt seemed to some to be inappropriate to the spirit of the occasion. The Senator, a conservative evangelical theologically close to Billy Graham, said:

> If we as leaders appeal to the god of civil religion, our faith is in a small and exclusive deity, a loyal spiritual adviser to power, a defender of only the American nation, the object of a national folk religion devoid of moral content. But if we pray to the Biblical God of justice and righteousness, we fall under God's judgment for calling upon his name but failing to obey his commands. . . . We sit here today as the wealthy and the powerful. But let us not forget that those who follow Christ will more often find themselves not with comfortable majorities, but with miserable minorities. Today our prayers must begin with repentance. Individually, we must seek forgiveness for the exile of love from our hearts. And corporately, as a people, we must turn in repentance from the sin that has scarred our national soul.

Senator Hatfield is well known as a critic of American war policy, and his hearers did not have to guess at what "sin" he had in mind. Seldom is there such a dramatic and widely publicized confrontation between the two types of religion. . . .

The point is that both aspects of the faith are essential. When the churches are polarized over this contrast, both types of Christianity become serious distortions. As individuals we may be somewhat one-sided, but a church—any unit of the church—should in liturgy, teaching, and program strive to correct such one-sidedness. This is more difficult for a local church than for the larger unit. Local churches usually reflect the mindset of a rather homogeneous residential area that *by itself* cannot make judgments about large social questions. There simply is not enough real experience or diversity of perspectives.

There is an extraordinary global populism implied in the Christian view of God in the very fact that God identifies himself with humanity in Christ. The God whom we praise in church is the God of all the poor and hungry of the world. He speaks through Jeremiah to one of the corrupt sons of the good King Josiah and to us: "Woe to him who builds his house by unrighteousness, and his upper rooms by injustice; who makes his neighbor serve him for nothing, and does not give him his wages." And then Jeremiah underscores the unity of these two aspects of our faith: "Did not your father eat and drink and do justice and righteousness? Then it was well with him. He judged the cause of the poor and needy; then it was well. Is not this to know me? says the Lord" (Jer. 22:13–16). Our very knowledge of the God we praise in church cannot be separated from issues of justice. This belongs to the center of our Christian faith and not to some marginal element called "social action."

And of course all this touches on our understanding of Jesus the Christ. In the past fifty years there have been startling shifts in the way in which Jesus' teaching, life, and death as concrete historical events have been regarded. For the Social Gospel this history of identification with real people was the heart of the Christian revelation. It was later pushed aside, partly because of historical skepticism and partly because of preoccupation with the *kerygma,* or the Gospel about Christ's death and resurrection. One of those remarkable and almost unconscious changes in theology came about as theologians began to realize that the death and resurrection of a Christ about whom not much was known meant very little. Far stronger is the belief in significant affirmations about his life and mind and deeds as an historical person.

Recently the argument has begun again as to whether Jesus was a revolutionary. Perhaps it can be seen more surely than was the case twenty-five years ago that, though Jesus was probably not a political revolutionary, he does call his followers to social revolutions, which in many situations today must have political implications. One of the theologians who seemed to support the neglect of the historical Jesus, Karl Barth, drew more radical social implications from Jesus and his message than most so-called liberal Christians. . . .

Pope Paul VI in his encyclical *Populorum Progressio* puts his Christian responsibility in a global context. He speaks more cautiously, but the implications are far-reaching: "We must repeat once more that the superfluous wealth of rich countries should be placed at the service of poor nations. The rule which up to now held good for the benefit of those nearest to us, must today be applied to all the needy of this world." Then he adds: "Besides, the rich will be the first to benefit as a result. Otherwise their continued greed will certainly call down upon them the judgment of God and the wrath of the poor, with consequences no one can foretell." The Pope is not the first to link the judgment of God with the wrath of the poor, but when he relates it to the contrast between rich and poor nations, he is saying something we urgently need to hear, especially as it applies to relations between the United States and Latin America.

Jesus' parable about Dives and Lazarus assumes fresh meaning when we recognize the dominantly white nations as Dives and the majority of the human race as Lazarus. It also makes a vast difference if we understand that in the loved story of the last judgment in Matthew 25 the hungry and thirsty, the strangers (refugees), the naked, the sick and the imprisoned with whom Christ identifies himself are not a marginal assortment of individuals but represent more than a billion people in the world, including thirty million in our own country.

All this should be obvious, but why has there been such a widespread tendency to obscure this radical side of Christian teaching? And why, when the obvious is set forth in the churches, is there such divisive controversy? There are at least three answers. The first is the manysidedness of Christianity to which I have referred. People become Christians or members of churches for so many reasons in their most impressionable years, and they do not readily change their emphasis on those aspects of Christianity they have found most satisfying.

A second answer is that there is usually no unequivocal Christian teaching that settles questions relating to *specific* social policies or issues. This gives an excuse to avoid the larger social imperative itself. I believe that Christian teaching should help to establish parameters within which policies should be sought. Also, it should throw light on the human consequences of existing policies and institutions, creating an awareness that forces us out of ruts and helps us see that situations with which we have lived complacently are intolerable.

A third answer, and probably the most important, has to do with our place in the world. One of the ironies of Christian history is that aspects of Christianity proved to be dynamic forces of Western civilization; thus members of churches ended up on top of the wealthiest and most powerful nations of the world. This was the result of no evil conspiracy, but arose from the very success of some Christian influences. This very success helped to create the distortions from which we now suffer. Churches have less influence than in the heyday of "Christendom," but in Western, predominantly white nations they have not recovered from the tendency to see the world as it is viewed from the centers of power and privilege. This tendency is being overcome in considerable measure at the ecumenical level, but it still limits the vision of most white congregations, Protestant and Catholic, in the United States. I cannot accept the assumption that there is little hope of enabling people, especially the younger generation, to see how judgment and grace belong together. Nor do I doubt the power of the more comprehensive biblical message and of the experience of the larger units of the church to invade the local churches, which will in any case be shaken by events that reveal the onesidedness of much they have taken for granted.

In contemplating the two emphases on the affirmative and supportive aspects of the faith and on judgment and prophetic illumination, I see the need to take one more step. This step starts, in a sense, from the opposite point. If we take judgment and prophetic challenge seriously for more than a short period of commitment to a particular cause, we are likely to find that we need religious support, even comfort. Enthusiasm for a cause is not enough. There is a phase in a particular struggle when the cause may simplify one's life, make decisions clear, enable one to know with whom to stand. But complexities finally overtake such simplifications. One discovers there are no total solutions, that even successes create new and unanticipated problems, that actual alternatives call for new and troublesome decisions. Those who have been most political and activistic often find the people with whom they have worked split away over strategies and develop a shocking hostility toward one another. This has been a common and disillusioning experience in the struggle for racial justice and for peace in Indochina.

Many sensitive people are tempted to abandon political efforts, to conclude there is nothing to be done within what they call "the system." While they might support a "revolution" against the system, they generally discover that there are not the cadres to make revolution plausible in this country. In the end, they hope to have some leverage for change, or else escape from politics, as many are doing, and seek private forms of fulfillment.

It may be helpful to suggest that there have been darker times, times of far more oppression and far less resistance to it, times when intimidation of dissent was far more effective, as was the case as recently as the early 1950s. Also, there have been many periods in the life of the church when there was less hope than now of the emergence within it of countervailing minorities. There may not be many revolutionaries prepared to challenge the system, but the system includes elements of the press that have proved their courage in recent months, courts and Congress that have sometimes defied the power of an administration which, as we now know, is obsessed with what it calls "national security."

The general acknowledgment of failure in Vietnam may prevent other ideological interventions and free many nations from American pressure to preserve the *status quo*. The absolute enmity of the cold war has begun to dissolve, and new possibilities now appear for peaceful relations between East and West. There are still enormous global problems, especially those connected with nuclear armaments, pollution, world poverty, and the limits of resources, but these may cause lines to be drawn differently and modify some of the hardened divisions between people, driving a new generation to think quite new thoughts. Indeed there is hope in the fact that, while the spectacular student revolts have subsided, there seems to be among students, more pervasive than the revolts themselves, a humane spirit, freedom from nationalistic illusions, concern about racial injustice and about poverty, a disbelief in the doctrines of economic individualism, and disenchantment with material success as life's goal. I mention these factors not to encourage complacency but to offer solid reasons against despair.

Prophetic challenge may produce a paralyzing sense of guilt in some and a harsh self-righteousness in others. It may lead to an uncritical identification of Christian faith or the Kingdom of God with particular movements for liberation or revolutionary change. Those who stand on the side that stresses prophetic challenge will need to see themselves under judgment and mercy. They may need fresh sources of morale when they face baffling complexity or frustration. It will not suffice the needs of hope to calculate the secular forces which are on this side or that. The challengers need gospel as well as challenge. They need to be grasped by the reality of God's presence regardless of which way the tides currently flow; to be inspired and healed by the vision of God's ultimate rule without allowing that vision to undercut the sense of urgency in battling particular wrongs in order to achieve proximate goals; to see life, if only intermittently, under the signs of both cross and resurrection. Struggle for political ends can become a deeply personal pilgrimage.

# The Class Struggle in American Religion

Peter L. Berger

The fanatical mullahs have been let loose in the land, *this* land. They travel all across America in the flesh; even more alarmingly, they fill the air with the electronic projections of their presence. They are not a monolithic group, to be sure, and some seem more threatening than others. What they have in common is that unity of religious and political certitude which, despite all the ideological differences, is uncomfortably reminiscent of the fanaticism unleashed by Muslim fundamentalists.

Leave aside for the moment such endearing theological opinion as the one that God refuses to accept the prayers of those outside one particular

Copyright 1981 Christian Century Foundation. Reprinted by permission from the February 25, 1981 issue of *The Christian Century*. Peter L. Berger is Professor of Sociology at Boston College and author of numerous works relating to the social sciences and religious thought.

congregation of certitude—an expression not so much of anti-Semitism, one would guess, as of a peculiarly electronic conception of the divinity: "Sorry, sir, this number is unlisted." More relevant to the present considerations is the mind-blowing specificity of the messages received from the great switchboard in the sky by these people: God is against Salt II but for the MX missile. God is for prayer in the public schools but against ERA. And so on.

## FLAG-WAVERS AND FLAG-BURNERS

One does not have to believe that the country is about to be taken over by *enragé* Southern Baptists to be alarmed by the recent upsurge of the Christian right. Theologically, the terrible simplicities of this neofundamentalism must be disturbing to anyone with more complicated notions of God's interventions in the human condition. Politically, what is most troubling is the effortless linkage between reactionary religion and reactionary politics, especially in terms of an aggressive and at least potentially bellicose nationalism. Flag-waving preachers are always disturbing; they become truly frightening in an age of nuclear weapons. The alarm provoked by the Christian New Right, then, is not unreasonable.

Inevitably, however, the religiopolitical extravaganza on the right has reminded fair-minded observers of the comparable extravaganza on the left—a phenomenon which, far from having been laid to rest with the late 1960s, is still going full blast and has even been institutionalized in important agencies of mainline religion in this country. Inevitably, one must ask by what criteria one deems good the pronouncements of left-of-center geese while condemning the preachments of right-of-center ganders. This question is, of course, at least in part a constitutional one. If it was wrong for the Internal Revenue Service to make threatening noises against church groups opposing the Vietnam war, then it would be wrong for the Federal Communications Commission to start harassing broadcasters for airing the political views of another set of church groups. But the issue is much deeper than the proper relations of church and state in the American democracy, important though these are. The issue touches on fundamental questions about Christians acting in the world, and ultimately it touches on the central question as to the nature of the Kingdom of God announced in the gospel.

If it is wrong to sanctify Americanism in Christian terms, how about the virulent *anti*-Americanism that permeates Christian church agencies and seminaries? Why is flag-*waving* objectionable, while flag-*burning* was an admirable expression of the prophetic ministry of the church? After all, what is prophecy to one is a reprehensible misuse of Christian symbols to another. And the specificity with which the political implications of Christian faith are spelled out on the right can be matched, *pronunciamento* by *pronunciamento,* on the left. An individual with even a modicum of detachment from the contemporary American scene may wonder how Christians can be so sure that God is either for or against all these specific political and social positions, or how Christians make it plausible to themselves that Jesus was either a capitalist ("The Man Nobody Knows") or a socialist ("The Man Only Good Guerrillas Know").

Obviously, the degree of alarm with which one perceives these two sets of militant American mullahs will depend on one's own political convictions. It will also depend on just where one happens to live. A resident of, say, Texas will understandably be less alarmed by the mullahs on the right. If, on the other hand, one resides in, say, Boston, the left-of-center mullahs are much more real and consequently more likely to get on one's nerves.

Let it be assumed, though, that Christians can aspire to *some* freedom from these ideological and geographical determinations (if they cannot, there must be something wrong with their understanding of the gospel that sets us free). In that case it is possible—*should* be possible—to draw some lessons from what is currently going on in American religion. It might even be possible, then, that the advent of the Christian New Right may turn out to be a blessing in disguise, and not only for those with right-of-center political opinions.

## THE PRESENCE OF THE KINGDOM

Specifically, there is a theological and a sociological lesson to be learned. The theological lesson is an old one, but since it is periodically forgotten, it may now be in need of repetition: *It is not the purpose of the Christian church to sanctify political institutions or programs.* Further: *This applies to programs that would preserve the status quo as well as to those intending to replace it.*

The church is the presence of the Kingdom in this world (or, if one prefers, in this eon—for the present purpose, either formulation will do). Yet the Kingdom is not of this world; it is yet to come, in God's own time. As the Kingdom embodies a promise of justice, the church must be concerned with justice in this world, and it is inevitable that this concern will embroil Christians in the political realm. And, as Jesus proclaimed, the Kingdom must have a particular concern for the victims of every sort of oppression.

Probably most Christians, of whatever political persuasion, would assent to these basic propositions. And insofar as the concern for the oppressed means acts of compassion, there is hardly any controversy (one may think here, for example, about the work of the churches on behalf of refugees or in the alleviation of famine). The problems begin, of course, when the political involvement of Christians goes beyond this kind of *diakonia* to engagement in political action in the service of what some perceive as a quest for justice. And, needless to say, what to some Christians appears as such a quest for justice will appear to other Christians as an exercise in futility or even moral delusion.

It is not possible to say that the church must never legitimate any human endeavors whatever. For one thing, to say this would be to demand what is empirically unfeasible. Religion, for reasons that cannot be developed here, always gets into the business of legitimation in human society and history—that is part of its nature—and the Christian religion is no exception. The church itself, in its worldly shape, is an institution among others, subject like any other to social and political forces.

Also, however, it would be theologically inappropriate to say that the church must never legitimate anything, because that would imply a denial of the sacramental view of the world disclosed by Christian faith. Thus, for example, the Bible legitimates human parenthood by speaking of God in parental terms: the point here is not primarily that human symbolizations are employed to make God understandable (although that, of course, is the case), but that specific human acts or gestures come to be seen as adumbrations of a divine, metahuman reality. But it is the parent who shields a child from harm who adumbrates the sheltering love of God, *not* the parent who thrusts a child into danger or loneliness. By the same token, Christian faith legitimates loving parenthood—and, in so doing, cannot fail to legitimate institutions that embody the acts of loving parenthood, notably the family.

What is *not* included in this legitimation, however, is any specific sociological configuration—say, the bourgeois family as it developed in the modern West, or any modification thereof that someone may propose. In other words, the theologically appropriate legitimation must remain on a level of considerable generality, even abstraction, and will therefore be hard to apply to specific institutional concretizations.

## WHERE TO DRAW THE LINE

It will be objected here that such abstraction makes Christian faith a ready tool for anyone who wishes to employ it. Historically, no doubt, this has frequently been the case. Therein lies the vulnerability of the church in the world. It is all the more important that Christians know how to make distinctions—especially in the political realm, where ideological legitimations are always in demand. Christians must be engaged in the quest for justice. The church must affirm not only the quest as such but those human gestures that embody justice, such as the gesture of one who has power and shields the powerless.

To that extent, the church must even legitimate the state, which, at its best, institutionalizes the gestures of justice. *That* legitimation, however, is a long way from legitimating specific forms of government. Both a benevolent despot and a modern democracy may exercise power to shield the powerless, and the church can affirm the legitimacy of these uses of power. But the church was wrong when it drew out of this a doctrine of the divine right of kings, as the church would be wrong today in sanctifying the American form of government as the only one mandated by God. The same considerations pertain to all political institutions or programs.

Admittedly, it is often difficult to draw a line here. Perhaps different lines have to be drawn at different moments in history. In the late 1960s a very radical notion of how to draw the line was suggested by a man who is still one of the most interesting ecclesiastical figures in Latin America, Sergio Méndez Arcéo, the bishop of Cuernavaca. Méndez then took the position that, in the political realm, the church must never bless, only condemn. He since then changed his mind, at least for a while when he became convinced that the church must endorse socialism as the only way out of the human miseries of Latin America. The earlier position was not only more radical but also more persuasive. Thus, in 1968, after the Mexican army had fired on a student demonstration and killed a large number of people in the so-called Tlatelolco massacre, Méndez read a statement from the pulpit of his cathedral condemning the government for this act. He did this in his capacity as a bishop, speaking *ex cathedra* for the entire church.

In retrospect, there is no reason to question what he did. The facts were readily available, and their moral import was clear. No particular expertise was required to say that soldiers firing with machine guns on unarmed students were violating fundamental moral principles. Méndez, at that time, did not follow up his condemnation of the government with an endorsement of any specific program designed to reform the political system of Mexico. Wisely, he understood that this was not within his competence as a bishop. Unwisely, he assumed such competence when he endorsed socialism—a program for alleviating misery on which every conceivable category of experts has failed to reach agreement and concerning which the training of a bishop hardly bestows expertise. Again, *mutatis mutandis,* these observations pertain to political issues across the board, in the United States as much as in Latin America.

The church has every competence to condemn terror or starvation, or exploitation—more specifically, to condemn the specific political arrangements that allow these oppressions to take place in an institutionalized form. But the church does *not* have the competence to bless any particular political modality either practiced or proposed as an alternative. And it is precisely in failing to make this distinction that American churches have gone astray, on both sides of the political spectrum.

Thus it was right when, in the 1950s, many in the churches condemned communism for its violations of human rights and dignity; it was wrong to deduce from this an unquestioning legitimation of the foreign policy of the United States in that period. Similarly, in the 1960s, it was right to condemn atrocities committed by the United States and its allies in Indochina; it was wrong to go on from this stand to an endorsement of the political goals of the North Vietnamese regime.

As in the case of the bishop of Cuernavaca, the reasons for this distinction are not only theological but also eminently empirical. Those who speak for the church have, very commonly, a fine sense of what is morally unacceptable in particular human situations. It may even be said that such a sense of injustice or inhumanity is one of the fruits of the Spirit. But these same people have no more expertise than others (and usually less) in designing practicable programs for political action. Put simply, one has good reason to be respectful of a bishop who condemns a military atrocity; one usually has very little reason to be respectful of that bishop's opinions on the political dynamics of southeast Asia—especially when the bishop is an American who has never been there.

## INFLATIONARY PROPHECY

Quite apart from the preceding theological considerations (and even if one should disagree with these), the representatives of the church deceive the public if they lay claim to an expertise (political, economic, or what-have-you) which in fact they do not possess. The idea that moral sensitivity somehow bestows the competence to make policy recommendations on every subject under the sun is delusional. It is also an idea that seems to have deep roots in American church history (let the experts on the latter decide whether the Puritans are to be blamed for this, along with so much else they have been blamed for, or whether the causes should be sought elsewhere).

The consequence, repeatedly, has been what one might call *inflationary prophecy.* The prophet who solemnly tells people what they ought to do may get away with this once or twice, especially if the recommendations do not lead to immediate and highly visible disaster. The prophet who keeps on doing this soon loses credibility. It simply is not credible that God's will can be ongoingly specified in terms of the details of political life.

What is more, human beings seem to have a limited capacity for being inspired. The average person can psychologically cope with a couple of crusades in one lifetime. When every other day this or that political agenda is prophetically elevated to the status of a crusade, people get tired, bored, incredulous, or all of these. When prophecy (self-styled) is institutionalized in modern organizations, the end result is that the only people who are eagerly awaiting the next solemnly launched position of a particular church organization are the bureaucrats in the other organization down the block. This is what appears to have happened to mainline Protestant organizations already; there is every likelihood that, eventually, the same will happen to the evangelicals who are drawing all the attention now. After all, how many specific weapons systems can God be expected to endorse?

In all of this a distinction ought to be made between the church as the gathered community of the faith and individual Christians (including such individuals banded together for a particular political purpose). If the Christian concern for the world is to have any reality to it, it must, of course, express itself in concrete activity on behalf of specific purposes. Individuals and groups can do this, even in the name of their Christian faith, without identifying their activity with the church as such, and without insisting that the church endorse this activity with some modern variant of the formula "Thus saith the Lord." It is important to understand that, as soon as this distinction fails to be made, one of the most basic characteristics of the church is put in jeopardy—namely, its catholicity.

If one says of a particular political position that it and no other is the will of God, one is implicitly excommunicating those who disagree. Contemporary American Christians, presumably without acknowledging that this is what they are doing, have been widely engaged in this sort of mutual excommunication. If one believes that it is indeed God who wills the building of the MX missile, or the passage of the Equal Rights Amendment, or any other specific political purpose, then one cannot remain in communion with those who reject this view and thereby posit themselves in open rebellion against God. The formula "Thus saith the Lord" always implies the correlate "Anathema be the one who denies this."

Another way of saying this, in a lower key, is that the incorporation of specific political agendas into the public worship of the church makes it impossible for those who disagree to join in that worship. This may not be understood as excommunication by those who do it, but the empirical consequence is the same. The theological error is that political partisanship is now counted among the *notae ecclesiae*. The sociological effect is that the church ceases to be catholic and is broken up into ideological conventicles, each claiming the authority of the gospel for its respective program.

## A STRUGGLE BETWEEN TWO ELITES

This last point leads up to the sociological lesson that may be drawn from the current excitement about the new American fanatics: *It is not the purpose of the church in contemporary America to take sides in the current class struggle.*

This class struggle, let it quickly be said, is *not* the one that Marxists still fantasize about, proletariat pitted against bourgeoisie, the wretched of the earth rising against their oppressors. Rather, it is a struggle between two elites. On the one side is the old elite of business enterprise, on the other side a new elite composed of those whose livelihood derives from the manipulation of symbols—intellectuals, educators, media people, members of the "helping professions," and a miscellany of planners and bureaucrats. This latter grouping has of late been called the "new class" in America—a not wholly felicitous term that is likely to stick for a while.

It is not possible here to discuss what some people, a little generously, have called the theory of the new class. But the main features of the theory are not difficult to grasp. In modern technological societies a diminishing proportion of the labor force is occupied in the production and distribution of material goods—that activity which was the economic base of the old capitalist class or bourgeoisie. Instead, an increasing number of people are occupied in the production and distribution of symbolic knowledge; these are the people enumerated above, and, if a class is defined by a particular relation to the means of production (as Marx, for one, proposed), then indeed there is here a new class. Like other classes, it is stratified within itself. And like other classes, it develops its own subculture.

The current class struggle is between the new knowledge class and the old business class. As in all class struggles, this one is over power and privilege. The new class is a rising class, with its own very specific (and identifiable) vested interests. But, in the public rhetoric of democracy, vested interests are typically couched in terms of the general welfare. In this, the new class is no different from its current adversary. Just as the business class sincerely believed (presumably still believes) that what is good for business is good for America, the new class believes that its own interests are identical with the "public interest." It so happens that many of the vested interests of the new class depend on miscellaneous state interventions; indeed, a large portion of the new class is economically dependent on public-sector employment or subsidization.

Once this is seen, it comes as no surprise that the new class, if compared with the business class, is more "statist" in political orientation—or, in other words, is more on the "left." Many if not most of the great liberal programs since the New Deal have served to enhance the power and privilege (not to mention the prestige) of the new class; not surprisingly, its members are devoted to these programs.

## SYMBOLS OF CLASS CULTURE

It should be emphasized that to say this is *not* thereby to invalidate any particular claims made on behalf of the liberal agenda for the society—just as one does not invalidate a political program simply by pointing out that it may benefit the business community. The point is simply to be aware that political purposes, in contemporary America as elsewhere, are not concocted in some Platonic heaven of ideas divorced from class interests. What is essential is the perception that many if not most current political issues are directly related to class interests. This, for example, is eminently the case with the issues raised by the environmentalist movement—a virtually pristine new-class affair, which has created a plethora of organizations devoted to the alleged protection of the environment, providing numerous jobs for members of the new class.

Other current political issues are not so directly linked to class interests. They have a more symbolic character, but the symbolism too has a class component. An example is the abortion issue. Attitudes on abortion divide sharply along class lines, with the new class in the vanguard of the pro-abortion movement. It is not altogether clear why this should be in the class interest of this particular stratum; but, for whatever historical reasons, the issue has attained a symbolic nexus with this stratum, so that members of the new class do indeed strongly tend to be in favor of abortion, while their class adversaries tend to be against it.

Other examples could readily be enumerated. The symbols of class culture are important. They allow people to "sniff out" who belongs and who does not; they provide easily applied criteria of "soundness." Thus a young instructor applying for a job in an elite university is well advised to hide "unsound" views such as political allegiance to the right wing of the Republican party (perhaps even to the left wing), opposition to abortion or to other causes of the feminist movement, or a strong commitment to the virtues of the corporation. Conversely, a young business school graduate seeking a career with one of *Fortune* magazine's "500" had better not advertise his or her career in the new politics, or views associated with the environmentalist, antinuclear or consumer movements.

## A CLASS COMPONENT TO MORAL BELIEFS

What does all this have to do with the church? And, more specifically, what does it have to do with the current effervescence of the Christian right? The answer is: almost everything!

Precisely the issues on which Christians divide today are those that are part of the current class struggle and of the *Kulturkampf* that symbolizes it. One of the easiest empirical procedures to determine very quickly what the agenda of the new class is at any given moment is to look up the latest pronouncements of the National Council of Churches and, to a somewhat lesser extent, of the denominational organizations of mainline Protestantism.

Conversely, virtually point by point, the Christian New Right represents the agenda of the business class (and of other strata interested in material production) with which the new class is locked in battle. What is more, while undoubtedly there are religious reasons for the upsurge of right-leaning evangelicalism, much of it can in all likelihood be explained as a reaction against the power grab of the new class. In that, of course, evangelicals are part of a much wider reaction, the political crystallization of which (temporary or not—that remains to be seen) was the major event of the 1980 national elections. As to the reasons for this alignment of different religious bodies, they could not be simpler: the main reason, of course, is the class character of the respective constituencies of these bodies.

To repeat: the sociological disclosure of a class component to political or moral beliefs does not (and methodologically cannot) settle the question as to the justice of these beliefs. For example, historians have argued that antislavery sentiment was strong in the northern business class because this sentiment was in accord with the interests of that class. Maybe so. But, having duly noted this linkage, one may still affirm that the antislavery cause was morally just. More contemporaneously, it can be shown that the new class, probably more than any other group in the American population, has freed itself from the poisonous beliefs of racism. It can also be argued that there are class interests involved in this: the new class staffs the welfare-state and civil-rights institutions, the major putative beneficiaries of which are the racial minorities of America. This argument, if granted, still need not detract from one's moral approval of a group relatively free of racist superstitions. The same holds for every one of the issues about which Americans divide along class lines today.

## STRIVING FOR A MEASURE OF DISTANCE

That, however, is just the point that must be made here: no class has a monopoly on moral insights. From a Christian point of view, no class can claim, in its vested interests and symbols in the aggregate, to be closer to the Kingdom of God. Christian ethics, without a doubt, will have to *disaggregate*. Thus, one might conclude on grounds of Christian ethics that the new class is "more Christian" in its resolute antagonism to racism, but "less Christian" in its uncritical allegiance to the cause of abortion.

But for such reflective disaggregation to take place at all, the churches must cease from responding with Pavlovian automatism to their respective class cultures. They must instead, in the freedom of the gospel, strive for a measure of distance from the immediate pressures of class location and class struggle. This is certainly not going to be easy and, sociologically speaking, it can probably never be achieved fully. Unless it is tried, however, the class divisions between American denominations will become near-absolute. Prophecy, so-called, will be nothing but propaganda on behalf of the one or the other class. Each congregation will be the one or the other class gathered for prayer. And that, every Christian should be able to affirm unhesitantly, is *not* the will of God.

# SUGGESTIONS FOR FURTHER READING FOR PART ONE

Baum, Gregory. *Social Imperative: Essays on the Critical Issues that Confront the Christian Churches.* New York: Paulist Press, 1979.

Bellah, Robert N. *The Broken Covenant.* New York: Seabury Press, 1975.

Benne, Robert, and Hefner, Philip. *Defining America: A Christian Critique of the American Dream.* Philadelphia: Fortress Press, 1974.

Bennett, John C. *The Radical Imperative: From Theology to Social Ethics.* Philadelphia: Westminster Press, 1975.

Ellul, Jacques. *The Politics of God and the Politics of Man.* Grand Rapids, Mich.: Eerdmans, 1972.

Gladwin, John. *God's People in God's World: Biblical Motives for Social Involvement.* Downers Grove, Ill.: Inter Varsity Press, 1980.

Hauerwas, Stanley. *A Community of Character: Toward a Constructive Christian Social Ethic.* Notre Dame, Ind.: University of Notre Dame Press, 1980.

Jewett, Robert. *The Captain America Complex.* Philadelphia: Westminster Press, 1974.

Jorstad, Erling. *The Politics of Moralism: The New Christian Right in American Life.* Minneapolis: Augsburg Publishing House, 1981.

Maguire, Daniel C. *The New Subversives: Anti-Americanism of the Religious Right.* New York: Crossroad/Continuum, 1982.

Neuhaus, Richard John. *Time toward Home: The American Experiment as Revelation.* New York: Seabury Press, 1975.

Norman, Edward R. *Christianity and the World Order.* New York: Oxford University Press, 1979.

Richey, Russell E., and Donald G. Jones, eds. *American Civil Religion.* New York: Harper & Row, 1975.

Shriver, Peggy. *The Bible Vote: Religion and the New Right.* Princeton, N.J.: Pilgrim Press, 1981.

Wallis, Jim. *Agenda for Biblical People.* New York: Harper & Row, 1976.

# Part Two

## The Christian and Sex Ethics

# 3

# Perspectives on Sexuality

During the past few decades there has been an extensive reevaluation of Christian attitudes toward sexuality. Traditional perspectives have been challenged as being "anti-sexual," and considerable reeducating has occurred in developing a more positive attitude toward one's bodily self. The negative orientation toward sexuality is often traced to certain passages from the letters of Saint Paul or to the writings of Saint Augustine in the fifth century, both of whom have had a profound influence in shaping Christian anthropology. The negativism in the tradition is often noted in the fact that the two words "sex" and "sin" have been so closely united in our thinking that they are often regarded as synonymous.

Theologians generally agree that the "culprit" in this situation is the prevailing notion that humans are divided beings, consisting of a spiritual part (the "soul" or "self") and a physical part (the body). The soul has been identified with the essence of the human person, which bears the image of God and which is therefore good. The body, on the other hand, has been seen as the physical "garment" in which the self is clothed, and from which the evils of desire and passion emerge. Against this view, Christian writers today are stressing the fact that the human being is a psychosomatic unity, a bodily self who cannot be so neatly divided. Moreover, if our *whole* being is essential to who we are as creatures of God, then we have reason to thank God for our physical as well as our spiritual being. It follows that our sexuality is essential to our being, to be celebrated as God's gift rather than to be mortified as an instrument of the devil.

These insights have had a salutary impact on current Christian anthropology, but they have also resulted in a pendulum swing that some writers are in danger of riding too far. It is fair to say that a wholly positive or a wholly negative evaluation of our sexuality is a distortion which is neither true to our experience nor accurate in expressing a Christian perspective. We are too prone either to deify or demonize our sexuality. The Christian doctrines of creation and the fall point us to the fact that our sexuality is ambiguous, for it shares in both our promise as God's children and in our capacity for exploitation as self-centered, wayward children. As sexual beings we are capable of establishing beautiful relationships of mutual dependence and respect, but we are also capable of reducing another person to an extension of ourselves, creating excessive dependence because of our need to control. It is precisely as sexual beings that we are most vulnerable to the desire to possess another person and to reduce him or her to the object of our desire. An awareness of this fact would seem to be essential for any two persons who seek to establish a relationship that is personally liberating and contributes to the humanity of each.

To address the subject of sex ethics adequately, one has to begin with fundamental reflection on the nature of our sexuality. If we probe our sexual experience at all deeply, we are pushed back to such religious and moral questions as: What does it mean to be human? to be male and female? What is the relation of sexuality to our humanity? How can sex contribute to fully human lives? The articles in this chapter express some basic perspectives on the nature of our sexuality, and use these perspectives to arrive at certain conclusions.

Helmut Thielicke understands the human being as two-dimensional, with the totality of one's being expressed in one's personhood and one's *bios,* or physical life. This he expresses further in terms of being and function, but he wants to affirm the indivisibility of these two dimensions in the Christian understanding of sexuality. If seen only in terms of our personhood, our sexual life is spiritualized and thereby distorted. On the other hand, if regarded as simply a biological function, sexuality becomes no more than an animal activity and is again distorted. Thielicke's view of the self is based on an "orders of nature" argument for the differences between the sexes; his conclusions would be strongly opposed by contemporary feminists. His grounding of sex differences in nature also leads him to point out the logic, if not the validity, of the traditional "double standard" of sexual morality and to reject homosexuality as inauthentic to human nature.

Such a view has been challenged by those who contend that a society's perception of sexuality and sexual differences is more adequately explained by cultural conditioning, and that all sexual understandings continue to be altered by culture and history. Sexuality in its cultural setting is what Sidney Callahan is concerned about; she argues that the various myths of sexual paradise prevent a sensitive apprehension of sexual realities. Sexuality is one of the ways by which we gain personal identity and communicate with others. Where Thielicke sees sexuality partly in terms of a tension between male and female, Callahan sees the tension between the individual and the community. The contrast between a Christian ethic and that of the secular culture is just at this point, she contends, with the culture failing to affirm communal norms involving commitment, responsibility for others, and openness to the future. The traditional

Christian norms had these aspects in mind, but one's explanation of these norms is different today because it is based on the concrete situation of the community.

There are those who would accuse James B. Nelson of idealizing, if not deifying, the sexual act in his suggestion that it has a sacramental character. In this an extreme effort to make sex "holy" against the negativism of the past? The sexual drive is physical, meaning that desire for the other is at the same time desire for one's own self-gratification. Overlooking the two-sided character of the sexual act is what leads either to a spiritualized sexuality or to a purely physical and self-serving (demonic) view of sexuality. But Nelson recognizes that imputing mystical qualities to the sexual act per se would not give sex its sacramental character. Rather, it is within the context of commitment and mutuality over a period of time that the sexual act has its "special power to create the gracious communion of persons." The larger context of the whole commitment of two persons to each other would appear to be the prerequisite for the possibility of sexual intercourse becoming a sacramental act.

# The Crisis of Anthropology and Becoming One's Self

Helmut Thielicke

## THE CRISIS OF ANTHROPOLOGY

He who no longer knows what man is, also cannot know what it is on which his peculiarity as a sexual being is based. He who disregards this *anthropological* motif of sexuality degrades it to a mere biological question. (The decline of sexual morality and countless marriage breakdowns are connected with this.) Not that sexuality has no essential relation to the biological. Only a doctrinaire moralist could ignore or refuse to admit this. But the mystery of man consists in the interconnection of personhood and bios, not merely in the sense that bios affects and puts its stamp upon his personality—to say this is by now almost a commonplace—but also in the sense that bios is given its character by the personhood of the human being; this, however, is something that has not yet been appreciated to the same degree. But if it is true that the bios of man is not simply identical with the bios of the animal, then the sexuality of man, despite the parallelism in physiological processes, is also not simply identical with the sexuality of the animal. Therefore it is important that we should examine the relationship of person and bios in order by this means to discover the peculiar, unique nature of human sexuality.

Once we take into account the totality of man, which means his thinking, feeling, and willing, and also the products of these activities as they occur in his sexual existence, we find again and again that they resolve themselves into two main dimensions. Characterizing them somewhat abstractly to begin with, we may say that in one dimension it is a matter of man in his *being* and in the other of man in his *function.*

by man in his *being* we mean man as he is related to God, man insofar as he is the bearer of a responsibility and an infinite value and insofar as he thus has the dignity of being an "end in himself" (Kant), that is, never to be used as a means to an end. By man in his *function,* on the other hand,

From pp. 20–26 and 79–86 in *The Ethics of Sex* by Helmut Thielicke. Translated by John W. Doberstein. Copyright © 1964 by John W. Doberstein. Reprinted by permission of Harper and Row, Publishers, Inc. Helmut Thielicke has been for many years professor of theology at the University of Hamburg in West Germany. Many of his works in theology and ethics as well as his sermons have been translated into English.

we mean man as he actively steps out of himself, accomplishes and effects something, becomes, so to speak, "productive"—whether this has to do with things or with persons.

When we are dealing with man, no matter in what area, we are constantly meeting with these two dimensions. And this coordination of two dimensions is especially acute in the social area.

Karl Marx, for example, accused capitalist society of valuing the workingman merely in terms of his function, that is, his capacity as a labor force. It was therefore treating him as a means of production (and thus as a means to an end) and failing to respect him as a human being. In capitalist society the being of man was disregarded in favor of his function. But to regard man merely as the bearer of a function, a "functionary," is to dehumanize and make a thing of him, and therefore to enslave him. On the other hand, one might take a look at Goethe's *Werther,* for example, and ask how human society is to function at all, if man is to attribute such excessive importance to his being, for example his being as one who loves and is loved, and in this way cultivate his entelechy as an end in itself. We ask ourselves whether this Werther had no functions to perform (did he not have to have a student job or work as a candidate for a degree?) and, if he had been obliged to perform such functions, would he not have had far less trouble with his hypertrophied being and his lovesick sufferings and sorrows?

It becomes apparent that the being and the function of man are coordinated in a way that still needs to be defined, and that when the two are isolated from each other the immediate and inevitable result is the emergence of pathological conditions of a psychic or social kind. (Perhaps one could approach the whole social question as it affects us today from this point of view.)

One must immediately add, of course, that being and function can be related to each other in very different ways. In purely mechanical functions, for example, such as those performed on an assembly line or operating the controls of automatic processes, the person and the function become widely separated; these are "nonpersonal" forms of work. A poet, on the other hand, or a dedicated physician will be able to perform his function only as he becomes personally engaged and puts "his heart" into his functions.

Now, there can be no doubt that the extreme of immediacy in the interconnection of these two dimensions, that of being and that of function, the personal and—in this case—the biological-functional sphere, is to be found in the area of *sexuality.* The details of this interconnection we shall deal with more fully later. At this point we merely recognize that it exists. In order merely to indicate for our present purpose what this interconnection means, we may point out that it is present in the choice of the erotic partner, where the personal element is extremely different in different cases. We have only to think of the Platonic myth of a bisexual primordial man in the *Symposium* to see a symbol of how the being of two persons is correlated and therefore how both are involved in this their being. If sexuality were merely a matter of physiological function (and thus a glandular problem) or of the business of reproduction (and thus again of a function), it would be difficult to see why the partners should not be just as interchangeable as the bearers of any other biological or mechanical functions, such as draft animals, for example, or machines.

> Then it would be hard to see why Don Juan and Casanova should not be regarded as the typical, ideal representatives of *eros,* which, as a matter of fact, they are in the eyes of many. We propose to show that just the opposite is the case, namely, that despite their erotic artistry these very figures missed the mystery of *eros* and in the end were deserted by it. The aging "Casanova," the lover "in retirement," who, so to speak, no longer performs his "function" and is put out to pasture in the field of "beingless" senility after having exhausted his amorous promptings, is really a macabre figure. Can we believe that he was ever really in league with *eros,* if he is left in solitude even before death comes to fetch him?

So, once more, if sexuality were merely a function, we would hardly be able to understand why the partners should not be exchangeable at will and why promiscuity should not be legalized and made a social institution. The fact that this is not so, or that in any case it is felt that it is something which should not be, the fact that on the contrary we prefer to uphold monogamy and thus respect the uniqueness of the choice of partner and thus the uniqueness of the other person's being, makes it clear that we see something more and something other in sexuality than a mere function, that here we recognize that the being of the person is involved and engaged.

In the light of what we have said above, the fact that this individual character of choice of partner has been, not institutionally but yet *de facto,* largely lost in the modern world, and replaced by a certain discrimination in the sense of promiscuity, points to far deeper defects than mere moral laxity or unbridled passions. What is evident here is rather that the interconnection of person and bios, of personal being and biological function, is no longer realized. But where bios is taken by itself and given the monopoly, the bearers of the function of bios become interchangeable at will and the ability to perform the (erotic) function becomes the sole criterion of the exchange.

> This law of interchangeability of function-bearers can also be observed in other areas of life. One can actually state it as a formula that to the degree that this tendency to regard the person as a thing increases and the person is impugned at the point of his substantial being, men become stereotypes

which are interchangeable at will. In *economic* materialism man becomes an impersonal bearer of a labor force, and when his ability to work is gone he is "finished" (liquidated). The ant in the production process of the termite state can be replaced at any time with another member to perform the function. In *biological* materialism man becomes completely analogous to an impersonal bearer of a propagative apparatus and thus becomes mere raw material for population politics and biological selection. Laws, which are in this sense ideologically determined, then have a habit of decreeing that in cases where only one of the married partners is capable of procreation, and hence capable of performing a function in accord with the population policy, divorce is to be favored. Marriage which is viewed as being merely instrumental no longer binds the partners together at the level of being, but rather makes continuance or exchange of partners dependent upon the function. Only the "being" of a person is unique, irreplaceable, and unrepeatable.

Wherever sexual chaos, i.e., exchange of partners at will, prevails, we are confronted with a crisis, a breakdown of *personal* being, of person-hood. Therefore, it would be misleading to look for the causes of certain manifestations of sexual deterioration in the destruction of morality. Where such destruction is present it is itself the effect of this deeper crisis. Moreover, it is altogether possible that this crisis in the being of a person may evidence itself only partially. That is to say, the result may be a very specific loss of the ability to see the interconnection of bios and person and thus may lead one to degrade one's partner to the status of a mere function-bearer in this one area of sex. Experience teaches that this occurs frequently. People who are otherwise "ethically intact" and capable of friendship and fellow humanity may perpetrate this degradation of another human being in this *one* area of sex. When they do this, they are allying themselves (at least partially) with an anthropology which they certainly would not accept theoretically and generally, and they would be horrified if they were confronted with this consistent interpretation of their actions.

It is the task of pastoral care in this area to communicate this interpretation. That is to say, pastoral care must point out what one makes of his erotic partner when he isolates bios and person from each other (namely, a selfishly misused function-bearer); and inversely, it must show that he separates person and bios from each other when he allows certain forms of sex to have power over him. But pastoral care will move on *this* level of thought and interpretation in the positive sense too; it will not attempt to combat the insistent libido with the moral appeal: "You dare not do this"; because this appeal does not touch the root of the problem at all and is therefore fruitless. The Law reaches only the "outside of the cup and of the plate" (Matt. 23:26 ff.) and not always even this; but it certainly never reaches the "inside." The libido can be attacked only by the kind of pastoral care which is aware of the anthropological problem and challenges the person to engage in a particular kind of meditation or exercise of his own thinking. The aim of this meditation is to arrive at the conviction that the desired body belongs to the "being" of a human being who himself belongs to another; a human being, that is, who has been bought with a price (I Cor. 6:20; 7:23), and has a temporal and eternal destiny, a destiny in which one who claims this other person in his totality responsibly participates. Only through this meditation do we come to see that *whole* human being, who alone is capable of disclosing the full richness of sexuality. For among the conclusions of our study will be the realization that focusing one's intention upon the whole man, upon his indivisible unity, does not merely curb sex, but rather liberates it and brings it to its fullness. He who seeks only the partial—only the body, only the function, and again possibly only a part of this—remains unfulfilled even on the level of *eros*, because, having lost the wholeness of the other person, he also loses the other person's uniqueness. The general part of the functions, however, he shares with everybody. Hence there is something like a communism in the erotic. It evidences itself in the fact that that which evokes the peripheral manifestations of eroticism are present everywhere as public property in the form of sex appeal, revealing styles of clothing, and the illustrations and content of advertising in general.

The same uncertainty and reduction which evidence themselves in the loss of the wholeness of the person are also discernible in much of the "technical" literature dealing with sex knowledge and marriage, at least insofar as it is offered to the broad public as an aid. When we say this we are not even referring to the great mass of publications which are intended to be merely stimulants to erotic fantasy under the guise of aids to marriage. We are thinking rather of some of the serious literature in this field. To cite one which is representative of many others, we mention the well-known marriage manuals written by Th. van de Velde, without disparaging their importance for the physiological and technical side of sexual life.

Since sexual life requires an art of loving *(ars amandi)* and therefore has its techniques, it is justifiable and even necessary that prophylactic and therapeutic measures be taken against sexual crises from this angle too. This conclusion is fully consistent with our basic starting point, which was to emphasize and keep in view the whole person; for, since the psychophysical nexus is an indivisible whole, injuries in one sector inevitably have their effect upon the others. It would be pseudotheological onesidedness to think only in terms of primary injuries in the area of the person—such as disregard of the person of the other partner and merely making use of his bios function—without at the same time taking into account the opposite source of difficulty, namely, that something may be wrong in the elementary bios relationship, the physiology and technique of the sexual relationship. This too can threaten and undermine the person-relationship. Hence there are many marriage crises which are not primarily the province of the pastoral counselor, but rather the gynecologist or the neurologist or the psychotherapist. The subject matter dealt with by van de Velde therefore has its importance also from the standpoint of a theological anthropology which puts the emphasis upon the whole man; and it is an indication of a lack of openness to the whole realm of created life and vitality to regard van de Velde from this quarter with the reserve of prudery.

The difficulty, however, is that the total intention of van de Velde's books creates the fatal impression that in the sexual area it is all more or less only a problem of techniques and that all that it requires to stabilize a marriage is to give the partners erotic training in order to develop their ability to function properly. Therefore, what lies behind it may again be that functional idea of man in which the personal concept of *community* in marriage has no place. In view of this inadequacy, we ought to recommend with praise theological and medical works in our generation which stress the wholeness of man and the interconnection of bios and person, especially in the realm of sex, but also within the framework of an expanded medical anthropology....

## BECOMING ONE'S SELF

The meeting of two persons under the influence of *eros* momentarily throws them both off their usual track. Like two colliding billiard balls they are deflected from their previous course. This is exactly what Marguerite is referring to as she sings at the spinning wheel:

> My peace is gone,
> My heart is sore:
> I shall never find it,
> Ah, nevermore!
>
> My poor weak head
> Is racked and crazed;
> My thought is lost,
> My senses mazed.[1]

Ecstasy in the sense of being beside oneself also means being thrown off the track. This leads us to ask whether this is really a matter of being blindly shifted away from one's self or whether it is rather knowingly coming to one's self. The question could also be framed in this way: Is what happens in the *eros* encounter a "transformation" *[Umformung]* of one's essential nature or is it a forming of the self from within of itself *[Heraus-formung]*? In line with the verse on love in Goethe's *Orphic Sayings* we should have to say it is the latter. In other words, the solitary Robinson Crusoe does not, strictly speaking, come to himself.

Here again we come to the mystery of sexuality: just as the mystery of the person is enclosed in the husk of sexuality, so this person comes to himself only *in* sexuality and also becomes the object of its self-knowledge.

[1]Goethe, *Faust,* 1, 16, trans. by Bayard Taylor (New York: Random House, Modern Library, 1950), p. 129.

But since on the other hand sexuality points beyond its physical ingredients, we may say that *mutatis mutandis* this coming to oneself takes place not only in the erotic encounter but also in the *agape* encounter with other people (in diaconic love, for example, and many other sublimations into which the structure of love can change). We have intentionally said *mutatis mutandis,* for naturally in both kinds of relationship a self is formed in each case with a different center of gravity, and the one without the other generally leads to an actual self that has imperfect contours (even though some very significant exceptions do occur). It is as if a photographic plate with its still invisible picture were immersed in each case in a different developer containing different reagents, which then have their effect in the different way in which the picture "turns out." Therefore the real image of man emerges only in love of God, the magnitude which encompasses all I-Thou relationships. And connected with this is the fact that a living Christian is freed through his encounter with God to become an "original" person and that in the succession of more original—because they are closer to the Origin—Christians there actually are those persons whom we call "originals," because they are different from mere copies of everybody else *(das Man)* and functions of the *Zeitgeist.*

A woman reveals her essential image, as it "comes out" in the sexual encounter, more than does a man. The reason for this is that the woman is identified with her sexuality quite differently from the man. It is, so to speak, the "vocation" of the woman to be lover, companion, and mother. And even the unmarried woman fulfills her calling in accord with the essential image of herself only when these fundamental characteristics, which are designed for wifehood and motherhood, undergo a sublimating transformation, but still remain descernible, that is to say, when love and motherliness are the sustaining forces in her vocation.

The man, on the other hand, invests a much smaller quantum of the substance of his being in the sex community. He has totally different tasks and aims beyond the sex relationship, which cause him, to be sure, to come back to his companion, but only in the sense that he returns home from an outside world that claims a far larger part of his time. The peculiar nature of the man tends to emerge less exclusively in his sexuality; it comes out more strongly in confrontation with what Schiller called "hostile life," in which he must struggle, take risks, scheme, and hunt.

Therefore the wife gives her "self" when she gives herself sexually. She holds nothing back and precisely in doing this she comes to her self-realization. She gives away her mystery (and even—how powerfully symbolic this is!—her maiden name), whereas the husband brings in only a part, a very substantial, but still only a part, of himself. The consequence of this nontotality of the man's sexuality is that the man is not nearly so deeply stamped and molded by his sexual experience as is the case with the woman. And related to this again are three basic features which show the difference between the sexuality of the man and that of the woman.

First: We speak characteristically of the seduction of a girl, but not—at least in the same sense and certainly not with the same seriousness—of the seduction of a man. The meaning that underlies this usage is probably clear enough after what we have said: to seduce a girl means to bring her to self-abandonment; it means to characterize, to stamp her by sexual intercourse and thus to release her from a bond which was decisively constitutive of her essential image. In this way the seduction works against the self-realization which the sex community is meant to bring about.

This can be seen in the tragedy of Marguerite in *Faust:* it is not Faust who is ruined because of the seduction, but Marguerite. It becomes a tragedy of Faust only very indirectly, since Faust has wronged another person. Faust must come to ruin because he caused the ruin of Marguerite and because— and here again the mystery of the person appears—the man is bound to the personal fate of another person and thus is indirectly subjected to his own fate.

This fact that the woman must abandon herself when she gives herself sexually explains why it is that the term "harlot" is actually applied only to a woman and that we have no parallel term for a man even though we take into account the term "gigolo" *[Strichjunge]*. When a man who lives a promiscuous life is called a gay dog, a Casanova, a philanderer, or any other of the terms available in popular speech, even the most drastic of them have a different quality from that of the word "harlot." For while the term "harlot" is actually meant to express the real nature of a female individual, in the case of a man people tend at most to speak of an unfortunate "sector" of his life. We are capable of speaking of a weak "spot" in an otherwise serious life and of merely saying that a man's "private life" is questionable in order to set it apart from his professional and public activity. In the historians' books such references are usually relegated to the footnotes. Over against this the great hetaerae who have entered into history, from Cleopatra to Madame de Pompadour, are characterized, not primarily by what they actually accomplished, but rather by the fact that they acquired historical significance through being hetaerae.

Naturally, this phenomenological observation cannot mean that we attribute to it the normative force of a fact. And yet even though we hold that this general normative attitude and its evaluations are highly questionable and unjust, we cannot fail to recognize that underneath this Pharisaism which puts an unjust burden upon the woman there are certain characterizations which bring out the difference between the sex nature of man and woman.

Second: Connected with this difference is also the phenomenon of the so-called "double standard of morality." This means that general normative public opinion expects of the woman before marriage an abstention from sex in an altogether different way from what is expected of a man, and that the man, even though he himself may live by other standards, not infrequently demands virginity of his future wife. Perhaps we may say that this disparate evaluation of virginity in man and woman, in other words, this "double standard of morality," does have some basis—which we would not wish to be understood as a legitimation of it!—in the physiological structure of the sex organs: whereas the woman receives something into. herself, the male sex organ is directed outward, away from himself; it discharges. The *receiving* of something is contrasted with being *relieved* of something. From a purely physiological point of view, the woman receives something from the sexual encounter (and the medical men point out that this is important even though conception does not take place), whereas the man discharges and thus rids himself of something. The extraordinary force of the symbolism of this disparate physical structure can hardly be evaded.

Thus if we make the physiological element normative we do in fact arrive at the double standard. However, we have already been sufficiently warned to see the dubiousness of this absolutizing of the merely partial, physiological side and to know that it is untenable even in the realm of the purely sexual. In connection with the problem of monogamy we shall have to find out at what place the critical point and therefore the theological problem is to be sought.

Third: Connected with this basic physical structure is the fact that there is in the man a polygamous tendency but in the woman a monogamous.

In the light of our foregoing investigations we can no longer doubt the fact that woman is oriented monogamously and the reason why this is so: the woman, because she is the one who receives, the one who gives herself and participates with her whole being, is profoundly stamped by the sexual encounter. To this extent she is marked by the first man who "possesses" her. One must go even further and say that even the first meeting with this first man possesses the faculty of engraving and marking the woman's being, that it has, as it were, the character of a *monos* and thus tends toward monogamy. Kierkegaard was alluding to this when he said it would matter nothing to him to betray the whole world, but that he would shrink from betraying a pure maiden; for this would mean that one was violating the "self" of this maiden.

Numerous psychopathological symptoms are determined by this structure of feminine sexuality, which in turn bear witness to this structure. Thus a woman's frigidity as well as the vampire insatiability of the strumpet can be caused by a similar experience in youth (violation or brutality in her first sexual encounter). A case of frigidity with this provenience must then be interpreted psychologically: it can be unconsciously willed and used as a defensive weapon by means of which the woman shuts herself off from further invasions and, so to speak, "plays dead."

Here again the way in which such a defense occurs is characteristic of the interrelationship of the physical and the personal. We see this clearly when we observe the corresponding masculine parallel. We have such a case when a man is, for whatever reasons, a chronic antifeminist—like Schopenhauer, for example. Sexually, this results in his continuing—for simple physiological reasons—to make use of sexual intercourse, but the emphasis here is on "use." Thus Schopenhauer, with all his contempt for women, made use of prostitutes. Thus one refuses ever to allow the woman to enter the personal realm of one's own self in such a way that might result in real community or human partnership, but permits her only to come into the physical forefield of the self by using her for the purpose of an instinctive abreaction. It is therefore significant that the male nature *can* interpret, or rather misinterpret, the physical realm as this kind of forefield and thus is capable of interpreting sex as a mere accident of the person but not as something which is itself *permeated* with the personal. This indicates how the man is able to escape from being stamped and characterized by the sexual encounter and that it does not touch him at the core of his personality—or *seems* not to touch him. On the other hand, if the woman is determined by an anti-male attitude (for which there may be reasons other than those mentioned above), she defends herself against the invasion of sex by resorting to frigidity, in other words, to sexual anaesthesia. Accordingly, she does not think of the physical as a forefield in which she might receive at least a physical satisfaction. Rather in her the physical is so interfused and amalgamated with the personal that she can no longer experience orgasm and resists even the very idea of the physical. If she is married, she may tolerate cohabitation as a duty, but then she not only suffers it as something alien to her person which she must put up with, but also she merely endures it physically.

In the light of this peculiar integration of the physical and the personal in the woman and the consequent formative power of the first sexual encounter, we begin to understand why there is an innate tendency toward monogamy: out of the center of her nature the woman strives to make totality of her experience correspond to her total submission to the man. Her goal is to make not only the physical side of the man her own, not merely once or temporarily, but rather to own the man's very self. The motive of monogamy lies essentially in the very nature of feminine sexuality. It lies in the urge toward self-realization; whereas without this *monos-*bond she is threatened with being delivered up to a deep contradiction of her own nature, namely, the cleavage of that which in her is integrated and which as a unity she cannot give up without suffering a trauma at the center of her being. In her the incapability of separating the physical from the personal and ignoring the "person" of the man would promote loss of selfhood rather than effect the sought-for self-realization.

# Human Sexuality in a Time of Change

## Sidney Callahan

Asked whether I am pessimistic about the crisis in sexual mores, I find myself in a dilemma. I am not aware of any crisis in this area of modern life. I see change, yes—what might be called a sexual renaissance or even a sexual revolution, but no "crisis." And the change under way is certainly not ominous. Indeed, as I see it, human sexuality is the one aspect of life today which gives genuine ground for optimism and hope.

What, then, is the nature of this change in attitude toward sex? First of all, it appears to be an evolutionary, step-by-step advance rather than a sudden revolution. "Revolution," in fact, seems exactly the wrong word to describe what is happening sexually; that implies a violent, communal dash to the barricades, while actually we see a process of quiet, private relaxations, individual by individual. There is an increase in sexual receptivity now rather than in aggressive hostility for the sake of sexual liberation.

True, we do have a few fringe prophets of what might be called emancipated sexuality. Hugh Hefner of *Playboy* and Linda LeClair of Barnard College, for instance, while in some respects holding opposite views, are alike in taking themselves very seriously. Other equally earnest prophets are handing out birth control equipment, demanding the abolition of marriage, arguing the advantages of homosexuality, and so on. Then there is the angry young woman who founded the Society for Cutting Up Men (SCUM for short)—the same young woman who, a few months ago, got herself a gun and shot her former mentor, Andy Warhol of pop art and movie fame. Yet these apostles of sexual freedom are a definite minority; they get disproportionate attention because the hungry media must have news.

However, the news media play another, more important role on the sexual scene. Without them, the public could never have been so quickly and widely informed of medical discoveries relating to human sexuality. The general acceptance of contraception, in pill or mechanical form, is due in large measure to the media. The possibility of controlling human

Copyright 1968 Christian Century Foundation. Reprinted with revision, by permission from the August 28, 1968 issue of *The Christian Century*. Sidney Cornelia Callahan, author and columnist, has written several works in the area of sexuality and family life, including *Parenting: Principles and Politics of Parenthood* (1974).

fertility without resort to such ancient means as abortion or infanticide is a new and one of the most important elements in the sexual situation today. Such a new development makes us hesitate to label our cultural change a "sexual renaissance"; that implies that somewhere at some time a first birth occurred. But has man ever known a sexual flowering before? St. Thomas held that sexual pleasures would have been far greater before the Fall, but those who do not take the Garden of Eden into their calculations are unable to discover a primitive sexual paradise.

In culture after culture, sexuality seems distorted in very familiar ways —subordinated to economics, weighted down with taboos or sacral meaning, made a symbol of social status. Often the suppression of women militates against sexual reciprocity, or the emphasis on procreation divides pleasurable from respectable sexuality. So the romantic idea of a primitive paradise which civilization later ruined seems no more sturdy on analysis than other forms of nostalgia. The sophisticated images of untrammeled sexual primitivism created by writers like D. H. Lawrence are merely evidence of the malaise experienced by industrialized man. The notions of tribal sexuality advanced by today's hippies are equally naive. But such fantasies are a constant in civilized societies. Thus Marie Antoinette played shepherdess at Versailles and Gauguin took every man's dream flight to the South Seas. The myth of a primitive sexual paradise dies slowly.

Closely allied to this myth is the misunderstanding of animal as compared with human sexuality. It is supposedly the "beast in man" that rouses sexual passion in an otherwise rational being. In fact, however, copulation is a rather dull affair among animals (with the possible exception of birds). The seasonal cycles of instinctual patterns keep it brief and businesslike. The female great ape, for instance, is available to the male on only 3 percent of the days of her life. She alone signals her readiness, and, once pregnant, she becomes indifferent to the male's advances. Which means that in nature, sex serves procreation, period. And there is little evidence that sex is pleasurable for animals. *Homo sapiens,* however, is distinguished by a far greater and almost constant sexual capacity that can go well beyond what is required for procreation. Moreover, he generally finds sexual activity pleasurable.

But man, this most rational and most sexual of creatures, has got so far in the evolutionary race by being also the most emotional of beings. His capacity to feel deep and powerful emotions, including sexual desire, makes him peculiarly man. We all suffer from left-over stoic ideas that control and suppression of emotions raise man to a higher level. Yet the consciousness of intense suffering, joy, love, and hate distinguish man from either animal or computer. Strong emotions are an advantage in man's evolution simply because caring keeps men together and cooperating. Fear and aggression aid survival, but the bond of love creates the human couple and the human group who care for the helpless young and give the children the cultural tutelage which makes the difference. Inadvertent but horrible experiments in depriving the young of parental care have made it clear that loving nurture is necessary for full individual development in intellect, health, sexuality, conscience, and affect. The human self, including the sexual self, is a creation of others who care and who provide more than physiological support.

Indeed, man is such a complex whole whose emotions, reason, and physiology are so interwoven with a cultural context that it is all but impossible to analyze him into parts. Thus, human sexuality can be seen only as an involved and culturally influenced psycho-biological process. We who have been shaped by Western culture are slowly developing a human sexuality of the whole person who freely chooses genital communication as a form of personal communication.

Sex is indeed one of the very important ways in which we learn who we are, hence who others are and how we can communicate with them. Reason, language, work, and play are also ways of learning to know one's self and others, ways to inner and outer reality. In the infant and the child all these processes are relatively undifferentiated. Norman O. Brown's private myth of the primitive "polymorphously perverse" body supposes that at this earliest stage all the senses of life are alike, that there is not genital or other specialization. But research on newborn infants shows that a high degree of active organization exists from the start, and that selective attention and selective pleasure begin at birth. The process of selectivity, organization, and differentiation proceeds with amazing rapidity. Had man not developed as a highly organized differentiated organism he would not have been flexible enough to adapt, hence to survive, as a species.

Sex, then, is but one of the important ways in which we grow, adapt, and communicate. Yet it has special characteristics which tend to give it emotional precedence. Since it is so largely dependent upon touch, and touch is an intimate proprioceptor (as opposed to distant receptors like the eye), sex seems more "central" in the personality. Also, since the skin delimits the body, touch and identity become related. And, harking back as it does to early tactile and oral-anal-phallic pleasures, sex can express an integral unification of the body-person more easily than other less intimate activities. One can strive for an integrated experience of self and others in work or play or reasoning or language, but these activities are difficult to personalize in our specialized technological world. Undoubtedly, sex is so emphasized in our fragmented, dullish culture because so many people find in it their only experience of drama, fantasy, ecstasy, consummation. During sexual orgasm the human being at least feels alive and "in touch."

Because of its biological orientation to reproduction, sex can also involve a purposiveness that is missing in many other areas of life today. For example, who could view children as meaningless or fail to feel personal involvement in progeny and family? The procreative aspect of sexuality tends to foster consciousness of the community. Few couples, in fact, are so trapped in individualism that they lose all sense of past and future and openness to others. When there is misery in homosexuality or in a hopeless affair, it springs in part from the closure to the past, the future, and the social community. The logic of the *Liebestod* is impeccable: man cannot live by sex alone. The lovers in *Elvira Madigan* and other romantic fables bore us to death before they finally get around to suicide. To be bearable, the present must be open to others and to a past and a future; that is, the sexual partners need a community and other areas of reality.

Considering the potential of sexuality in our era, I think Christians present a norm for human sexuality which in modified form can still have general meaning. A Christian tradition freed of antisexual bias would declare sexuality the good gift of a good God in a good Creation. The allegory of the fall of man means that sexuality, like every other human faculty, may be used for ill, but is not in itself more dangerous or more sacred than any other. With Christian demythologization this is seen as such a free personal expressive activity that some persons can live and love for the sake of the Kingdom without full sexual expression. When sexual expression is freely chosen, the fully human norm will be a heterosexual genital relationship that involves sharing a present and future community of life. In such a relationship, neither the individual nor the community is subordinated to the couple; for male-female complementarity provides one means of growing, just as procreation provides one means of communal giving.

Can the non-Christian accept this Christian norm? On the whole, I would say Yes. Western secular culture has been so much influenced by the concept of the dignity of the person that there is little conflict with the Christian sexual norm, at least as an ideal. What conflict there is comes from Christians who emphasize a communal ideal. There is resistance to seeing children as gifts to and responsibilities of the community; there is resistance to celibacy for the sake of the community; there is resistance to abstaining from nonmarital sex for the sake of fidelity to marriage and family. In other words, Western secular culture affirms sexuality as a norm of personal communication expressing affection, but rejects the inhibitions that the Christian norm prescribes as necessary for the sake of freedom and the community.

Yet every group, every culture, must manage to deal with both sexual activity and sexual limitation. To survive, a community must get babies and get them reared, and at the same time it must set limits. At the most minimum of minimums, sexual aggression must be inhibited, and seduction of minors or family members must be curbed. Few champions of sexual freedom defend incest, condone homosexual seduction of the young or favor promiscuity. What they usually have in mind is the freedom of responsible adults ("responsible" enough to take precautions against pregnancy) to develop heterosexual genital relationships which express personal affection but need not be exclusive or permanent. If sex is a basically good form of loving communication, why should it be exclusive and why should it be inhibited?

I do not think a case for exclusiveness can be made on the basis of abstract logic. The ideal of complete physical reciprocity expressing complete reciprocity of life is purely aesthetic in its appeal. In fact, one might just as well embrace the ideal of pure communism—that is, complete reciprocity of life with all, complete sexual communication with all, regardless of sex and age. Abstractly speaking, love of one and love of many are not in conflict or contradiction. The Christian concept of love of neighbor includes this universalism. But though some of the early Christian sects carried communal love to a sexual conclusion, the usual Christian approach has been to distinguish between eros and agape. Sexual love is "physical," it is said, and therefore different. But surely this is an untenable distinction; at least it must seem untenable to anyone who takes the incarnation and the resurrection seriously or accepts the psychological concept of man as a subjective whole. The fact is that sexual love informs every other kind of loving and that all personal relationships are infused with sexuality. All loving is a gift or grace from beyond ourselves. Christians, like infants, love because they were first loved.

Indeed the great hope of sexual change in our culture is the realization of the oneness of loving. At last the vicious Platonic split in our view of man is being healed and sex is seen as an integral aspect of the human personality. The flowering of human sexuality that we witness today does not betoken a return to the primitive; rather, it is a step in the evolution to a synthesis of many functions into one complex patterning.

How, then, justify inhibition of sexual impulses? If we are to love all, why not make love with all? The answer is that abstract distinctions between kinds of love do not hold water. Instead, our concrete situation provides the only rationale for inhibition and limitation of personal acts of sexual loving.

Human speech serves well as an analogy for human sexual expression; for sex is not a new language, but an old language constantly changed and changing. The first limitation on both speech and sex is physical. Some sounds and combinations of sounds cannot be produced by the human vocal apparatus; and some sexual postures are physiologically impossible for the human organism (despite the great range of differing individuals within the species). The second limitation on both speech and sex is temporal: an infant cannot speak and a small child cannot perform the sexual act. Since the capacity for both speech and sexual expression derives from the care and stimulation of community, the community inculcates limitations. The individual learns the two kinds of language: what sounds and practices are permitted and what it is appropriate to express to whom. A private language and autistic sexuality prevent communication with others, therefore must be inhibited.

As the child grows, it enters into an ever more complicated communal context which requires that he select among the kinds of communication now opening to him. But because human beings live in space and time, one option precludes another; a child cannot walk and crawl simultaneously. Mastery of the self and effective communication involve exclusion and suppression of the diverting or irrelevant. On the sexual level, the narrowing of focus to full reproductive heterosexual genitality is compensated for by the expanding of attachment from one's self, to one's own sex, to the opposite sex, to children, and so to the wider future community. Happily, in mature sexuality a couple can regain through play and the wholistic sexual orgasm earlier stages of sexual development.

Of course, this process of selection and inhibition by which emotion and expression are channeled cannot motivate commitment to the Christian ideal of sexual fidelity, but it does serve to show what the ideal means. The No's necessary for an intense Yes to some one person and to the community can be seen as a function of integrity. The No to incest and other so-called perversions seems more "natural" and so easier to understand. The No to premarital and extramarital sexuality requires that man either look ahead to future commitment or be aware of a continuing commitment to mate and family. In limited time and limited space, the Yes to the mate is built upon and strengthened by the No to everyone else. Sexually, the ideal is not only to be fully genital and heterosexual, but also to have one's private sexual activity congruent with the rest of one's public social life.

It is well to heed those anthropologists who maintain that in any culture there is a transfer between learning in a sexual context and learning in other spheres of life. Each affects the other. Thus a laissez-faire business ethic geared to private consumption tends to produce a sexual ethic of extreme individualism which emphasizes private pleasure. The present-day attempt to place equal emphasis on individual and community is an eminently Christian enterprise, a move one step beyond either tribal communism or isolated individualism. Sexually, our culture can also move in this direction. Hope for the future springs from the conviction that as a people we can make the new synthesis of individual and communal values.

I see the function of Christians in this time of changing mores as that of the traditional leaven. They must encourage integration of sexuality into the whole personality and into communal life. For them to censure the trivialization of sex is probably a waste of energy. The adolescent phenomenon of the playboy cannot long survive the decline of Victorian prudery and the rise of the sexually mature woman. If Christians can witness to personal purposive sexuality within the community they can let the bunnies be.

Some Christians might witness to asceticism or celibacy. The society which finds it inconceivable that a person should live in sexual abstinence or on less than $10,000 a year is a society that hampers the individual's freedom to express himself; for, bound to comfort, the society is also bound to the comfortable status quo. The cozy domesticity of the premarital "arrangement" is far better than predatory or promiscuous sex; but it is a bad sign for the community when permanent commitment comes so hard to the young, and the strictures of self-sufficient sexual abstinence seem unbearable to them. How can the comfortable uncommitted ever make the sustained efforts needed for the reform of our society?

I must say, then, that my optimism over the outcome of our changing sexual mores is based on a nonsexual condition. If persons and community have lost purpose and a sense of identity, then healthy sexuality will not help matters. The sexual alone never degraded the human community; hence there can be no sexual salvation. Perhaps we can raise all our children in such a way that they are capable of freedom; but if the concept of the whole man with communal concern and purpose has no meaning, we are in trouble as a people. The outcome of the present encouraging changes in sexual mores will depend on the outcome of communal changes that are beyond sexuality. If, as we have said, communication and expression are the essence of sexuality, the question is what man will express and communicate. The problem of what we shall say remains. And there lies the crisis.

# The Church and the Sacramentality of Sex

James B. Nelson

Various groups and people have found various ways of orienting themselves to sex. Some, to be sure, have been primarily sex-negative. Among those who have valued sex, however, some have accented its pragmatic worth (procreation and enjoyment); some have valued its escapist possi-

Reprinted from *Embodiment* by James B. Nelson, copyright 1978. By permission of Augsburg Publishing House. James B. Nelson is Professor of Christian Ethics at United Theological Seminary of the Twin Cities, New Brighton, Minnesota, and the author of several books, including *Human Medicine: Ethical Perspectives on New Medical Issues* (1973).

bilities (release from boredom and frustration, the assertion of autonomy in the face of social restrictions); some have prized sex's romantic dimensions (its unitive possibilities and the value of desire). Still others, however, have seen sex as sacramental, bearing the power to link human and divine in cultic act.

Sex has been understood as sacred mystery by different groups with various levels of sophistication. In some primitive forms it was simply a powerful magic expression, appealing to the sacred generative power which brought fertility to crops and tribe, a fairly common understanding in certain earlier and more corporate cultures. But in ancient Greece and Rome where personal self-awareness began to emerge, sex in some cultic expressions became a vehicle for *communion* with deity.

It is easy to write this off as grossly pagan and obscene. Yet, historical studies also show positive elements. In one variation, intercourse at the temple with the priest or priestess was sacramental. G. Rattray Taylor comments: "This is the temple prostitution which has so often scandalized Christian observers. But the term prostitution, with its connotations of sordid commercialism and . . . lust, wholly misrepresents the sacred and uplifting character of the experience as it was experienced by those who took part. It was nothing less than an act of communion with God. . . ."[1] True, such cultic sex always bore the danger of deteriorating into simple lust and gross distortion, and this sometimes happened. But in its more ordered forms certain values appeared which cannot be written off lightly.

In the Greek worship of Dionysus there was not only communion with the deity but also an approved cathartic medium for releasing various tensions, unrelieved in daily existence. In a subsistence economy where there was unending heavy work, little leisure, and scant economic or psychic security for most people, such a Dionysiac festival, as Rosemary Haughton comments, "however disgusting it may appear to us, was in fact a healing and peace-bringing act."[2] Further, the Greeks recognized the presense of the divine in all beauty. Their unashamedly open and delicate appreciation of the human body flowered in the superb artistic creations of that age, and it is not surprising that they found beauty in the sexual act in a religious context and hence divine meaning in that situation.

Significantly, however, the Greeks did not appear to associate "ordinary everyday sex" with divine union. Ordinary sex was pleasurable and necessary for proceation, but it was undignified and not sacramental. Even the approved and celebrated male homosexual relationship between an adult and a youth was, in its ideal form, devoid of intercourse. Sacramental sex appeared only in the cultic context.

As far as I am aware, one voice in the ancient world boldly asserted that ordinary married intercourse was sacramental—the apostle Paul. If later

[1] G. Rattray Taylor, *Sex in History* (New York: Harper & Row, 1970), p. 229.
[2] Rosemary Haughton, *Love* (London: Watts, 1970), p. 77.

Christians spiritualized his words, Paul's original intent seems clear. And this, perhaps, is one of the great surprises of sexual history: that this apostle, who himself was so ambivalent about sexuality in many ways, should raise the possibility that the intercourse of wife and husband could have divine meaning and could celebrate the divine mystery. This possibility was submerged for centuries of Christian history. Hints of it emerged much later in Shakespeare and John Donne, and still later in D. H. Lawrence.

While I have spoken of spirit-body dualism in completely negative terms to this point, it did have a positive result at an earlier stage of human history. In some ways it nurtured the growth of the notion of a distinctly human personality. The spirit separated from the body was also the spirit released from total earth-boundedness into the possibilities of self-transcendence, future-orientation, and transformation of the environment. Thus, in an ironic way, the very dualism which saw sexuality as deeply suspect if not outright evil contributed to the personalization of the sex drive and its fusion with self-transcending love and commitment. And, in its unintended way, spiritualistic dualism has paved the road to the possibility of sexual love as sacramental.

But what, more specifically, might the sacramentality of sexual loving mean? Christian tradition has insisted in its wiser moments that a sacrament is not simply a *sign* of grace, as if grace were experienced quite apart from the sacrament itself. Rather, it is a *means* of grace. One can experience God's wholeness-creating love in the sacrament itself and through it become receptive to that same love elsewhere in life. By this functional definition, it would seem that sexual love is sacramental. Yet, should it be considered a *Christian* sacrament and identified as such by the church?

Instructive parallels can be drawn between Baptism and the Eucharist, on the one hand, and sexual love, on the other.[3] Like Baptism, a loving act of sexual intercourse is a reenactment of dying and rising. Orgasm's "little death" occurs in temporary sense of loss of self-conscious individuality, but with this comes the self's death in surrender to the other. Then the self is received back with new life, joyful and replenished from the divine plenitude itself.

With the Eucharist, there are even more sacramental parallels. The Eucharist's body language is obvious. Its promised unity is not a unification which erases individuality but rather a union or communion which bonds together deeply unique individuals. The appropriate mood of participation in the Eucharist is that of joyful gratitude to God. There is in the sacrament an eschatological dimension: it is an earthly experience of the ultimate unity promised to all in the kingdom. All of these things also characterize acts of true sexual love.

[3]William Phipps, *Recovering Biblical Sensuousness* (Philadelphia: Westminster, 1975), pp. 86ff.

Both Baptism and the Eucharist are rituals for communicating something that cannot adequately be expressed in words alone. The experience itself is intrinsic to the communication. And both sacraments can be misused. With improper understanding of their intention and significance, with distorted motivation for their use, the sacraments do not function in a sacramental way at all, but rather can harm the individuals so participating in them. And all of these things can be said of genital sexual activity.

Theologians from more sacramental traditions of the church have been quicker to recognize this potential of sex. Thus, Evgueny Lampert writes of sexual intercourse as "the mystery of the breaking down of all the limits and limitations of human life and isolated human existence . . . It is the mystery of a sudden merging and union into a single indivisible being of flesh and spirit, of heaven and earth, of human and divine love."[4] Likewise, Philip Sherrard contends: "It may be concluded therefore that this sacramental form of sexual love is not simply a human emotion or impulse or even a created cosmic or elemental force. Still less is it to be identified simply with a bodily or psychosomatic energy. It is, in its origins, a spiritual energy. . . . Hence, to be united in this love is to find oneself returned to oneself, to one's full being, and primal condition. In this sense, it is not simply to be born in beauty. It is also to be regenerated in God and to have the divine Paradise revealed to one."[5] In a very real way, this mystery of sexual love is also the place where many of today's young adults find their most real sense of the sacred. Beyond society's acquisitiveness and pragmatism, here there is honesty, intimacy, tenderness, and mutual surrender. Many find here the occasion where awe and religious language are once more meaningful.[6]

If we grant the capacity of sexual love to break the self open to the true meaning of divine-human communion, still the question remains: should it be considered a Christian sacrament, and if so, how? Perhaps, as John W. Dixon, Jr., has argued, the wisest course is to affirm sexual love as sacramental or, in the tradition of some churches, "a sacramental," without attempting to identify it as a sacrament as such.[7] In the historic Christian community, sexual intercourse has not been seen as a carrier of the image of Christ in the ways that a true Christian sacrament must be. Part of this reason, undoubtedly, has been the antisex dualism which infected the church. But it is also due to the fact that Jesus, while blessing married sexuality, did not single out either marriage or sexual love as such for unique status in the new community.

[4]Evgueny Lampert, *The Divine Realm: Towards a Theology of the Sacraments* (London: Faber & Faber, 1943), p. 97.

[5]Phillip Sherrard, *Christianity and Eros* (London: SPCK, 1976), p. 3.

[6]See Michael Novak, as quoted in Phipps, pp. 95ff.

[7]See John W. Dixon, Jr., "The Sacramentality of Sex," in Ruth Tiffany Barnhouse and Urban T. Holmes, III (eds.), *Male and Female: Christian Approaches to Sexuality* (New York: Seabury, 1976). I am indebted to his interpretation at this point.

At the same time, to consider sexual intercourse as no more than a natural good of human life is to underestimate its power. Its power to create and to destroy, to give utter ecstasy and to produce brokenness, goes beyond many of God's other "good gifts" of the natural life which are far less central to personhood. Even the language of sex testifies to its potency—it can be used as curse, as magical incantation, or as invitation to passion.

Where then is the sacramentality of sex? It lies in its power to invite wholeness through relationship. Dixon says it splendidly: "In this is the reality of the sacramentality of sex. We are not whole persons [by ourselves] and cannot be. Our sexuality is not only a paradigm of our completion but a paradigm of our humanity as well. Nowhere in our life are we so remorselessly taught our creaturehood, the earthiness of our origin. Nowhere are we so subject to the powers of nature, to the terrible passions of our flesh. . . . Nowhere is failure so abjectly humiliating or power so personal and destructive. Nowhere is pleasure so joyful, delight so satisfying. Nowhere are the possibilities so endless: for charity and forgiveness, for patience and understanding, for an infinite range of patterns of dominations and submissions, for exorcising evil by turning it into a game, for balancing ecstasy with the sweaty realities of the flesh, for power and gentleness, for giving and receiving, for glory and patience.[8]

In this particular discussion I have drawn heavily upon insights from the theologians of the Anglican and Catholic traditions wherein sacramental life is so central. Those of us from other Christian traditions can be enriched by this emphasis even if we do not give it such primacy. Nevertheless, it is a mistake to accord inherent mystical qualities to sexual intercourse *per se*, as some of the sacramental writers tend to do. As a physical act, intercourse is susceptible of many and varied meanings. What it means, what it communicates—in short, its language—is not "biologically constant" nor is there anything automatically sacramental about it. Indeed, it would seem that it is sexuality in a broader sense that is much more gracebearing than any particular sexual act. It is physical intimacy over a period of time, in the context of loving commitment and mutual growth, and in the context of many other dimensions of shared intimacy that has the special power to create the gracious communion of persons. But in precisely *this* kind of setting an act of sexual intercourse *can* be a sacramental act. Again and again it can teach us the secret of human wholeness and be an authentic means of divine grace. And, if liturgists are imaginative, sensitive, and careful, appropriate language might be found to celebrate this in public worship. By doing so, perhaps its sacramental power could be celebrated even more fully by Christian people in the privacies of their own committed relationships.

[8]*Ibid.*, pp. 254f.

# 4

# The Morality of Sexual Relationships

Our discussion of sexuality inevitably leads us to consider our relationships with others, for we know ourselves as sexual beings in relation to others. The word "relationships" is apt not only because it is descriptive (sexual activity usually involves two people) but also because it is value laden. It points to an aspect of what it means to be human, namely, to be in relationship with others in a way that respects and honors them, rather than exploits or oppresses them. Human life is characterized by the varied perceptions people have of their living in community. No person is an island; no child grows to maturity without receiving nurture from others or without being dependent on others. The absence of meaningful relationships leads to loneliness, which can lead to depression and even to suicide, the ultimate denial of the person and the meaning of life. "Love," "fidelity," and "covenant" are terms that express ideals for human interaction. The substance of these terms in any relationship is grounded in a combination of words and action. Language, which is itself relational, is the articulation of the commitments of the person to others; action confirms one's word and demonstrates that it is not just "talk." This is where the moral dimensions enter. Despite the legal implications of the term, "illicit sex" is not illicit primarily because it is against the law, but because the experience has an absence of human relationships or because it breaks an existing relationship. Rape, for example, inspires moral revulsion because it is an exploitation of one person by another; the victim's personhood is violated, and society ponders whether the rapist is "sick" and whether a society in which this behavior consistently occurs is not also morally "sick."

Determining what is moral and what is immoral in sexual relationships is increasingly difficult in a pluralistic society. We see various ideals placed against each other as people argue their case. The "Playboy" image exalts freedom and independence from norms that are thought to be restrictive of full human expression. A simplistic emphasis on individuality and autonomy, however, implicitly discounts the value of human relationships with consequences that go far beyond the realm of sexual activity. What understanding of the human person lies behind the view that justifies sex without love? Other moral ideals affirm a certain kind of community by attacking a larger, possibly more abstract, ideal of human community. For example, some lesbian sexual relationships in recent years have implied either a hatred of males or anti-establishment, radical politics.

The two articles in this chapter have been selected because they provide clear expressions of an ethical method, and they differ in their use of rules—a critical issue in ethics, which is apparent in discussions of sex outside marriage. No sharper conflict has developed between the canons of the new freedom and the moral absolutes of the Christian tradition than on the point of premarital sex. One of the significant events in the development of this conflict was the publication of the Kinsey reports on male and female sexual behavior. Though not uncriticized, Kinsey's scientific account of the incidence of premarital sexual activity made it plain that traditional norms were being honored more in the breach than in reality. Although the reports did not draw moral conclusions from the statistics, it was easy for others to conclude that what was taking place was what ought to take place. Additional attacks on the negative ethic of legalism have come from several fronts, including those who advocate the *Playboy* philosophy, those who reject any moral implications in sexual activity, and those who operate under the banner of "situation ethics." The latter view is certainly not restricted to sexual ethics, but many of its most prominent illustrations have to do with the interrelationship of sex, love, and rules.

The older, objectivist morality has tended to evaluate deeds only; thus, what would be morally right after the wedding ceremony would be morally wrong before it. This method is clearly oriented toward maintaining institutional sanctions supported by both state and church. The "new morality" looks beyond the acts to the persons involved, their relationship, and their motivations. Furthermore, the new morality recognizes an element of ambiguity in virtually every ethical situation, a factor unaccounted for in absolute rules. Denying the existence of any codifiable universal moral order, the new moralists usually affirm only one absolute: the biblical command to love.

Such discussion has raised with new vigor some perennial questions relating to sexuality. What, for example, does love mean? One of the most elusive English words, "love" refers to a great variety of responses. Many ethicists, including some in the previous chapter, choose the Greek words for love (*agape,* selfless love; *eros,* physical love; *philia,* friendship) in order to be more precise in their discussion. Further, how does love operate? Does it function as a homing device, directing the individual intuitively toward moral action? Or does love use rules of conduct or ethical principles that somehow embody its essence? And what does marriage mean? What, precisely, is the meaning of premarital sex? Does it refer to the status of the persons involved (they are not married), or does it refer to their relationship (they are on the way to being married)? The failure of most ethical reflection to deal substantively with the ethics of marriage has meant that most discussions of premarital sex are sidetracked by trivial questions.

It should be obvious from the following selections that there is no disagreement among these ethicists about the primacy of love. Although they disagree about the proper moral relationship between sex and marriage, both would oppose the point of view that it is proper to separate sex and love. And although their ethical methods differ, these authors' differences on this specific issue seem more subtle than one would have anticipated from the methods themselves. Joseph Fletcher, the most prominent defender of situation ethics, is not opposed to delineating such ethical principles as "The integrity of persons is inviolable," and "We ought to love people and use things." In his own categorization of other ethical positions, however, he places all those concerned with developing more specific ethical principles together with the defenders of fixed absolutes, a categorization that misrepresents what persons such as Joseph C. Hough, Jr., are trying to do.

Hough's article represents the kind of thinking that accepts Fletcher's concern for a person-centered ethic, but also recognizes that self-deception and exploitation may be as much a part of a sexual experience as love and the desire that no one get hurt. Rules are not absolutes, but guidelines for humanization. Thus, rules for Hough are not arbitrary prohibitions, but reflect the wisdom of the society in its attempt to maintain responsible relationships between people. Where rules do not effectively serve this purpose, they need to be rethought. Though Hough and Fletcher basically agree on this point, Hough reveals a deeper appreciation of the fact that our sexual activity takes place in a social environment to which we are responsible. Whenever Fletcher finds a justifiable exception to a rule, he tends to think that the exception invalidates the rule, while Hough expects that an exception will continue to be an exception.

# Ethics and Unmarried Sex

## Joseph Fletcher

Ever since birth control separated lovemaking and baby-making the resistance movement, principally in our Christian churches, has warned us that sooner or later "they" would be recommending it for "everybody"—even the unmarried. The time has come—*der Tag* is here.

Before the Second World War, Lewis Terman predicted that premarital sex would be accepted in the near future.[1] Now, in 1966, the press is picking up and publishing news that several universities and coeducational colleges are being faced with a policy question by their health services: Should unmarried students be informed, supplied, and guided in the use of fertility control devices upon request? Last year a report of the Group for the Advancement of Psychiatry, entitled "Sex and the College Student," gave its support to the principle of privacy and accordingly challenged the theory that an institution of higher learning should try to be in *loco parentis*. The psychiatrists concluded that "sexual activity privately practiced with appropriate regard to the sensitivities of other people should not be the direct concern of the administration."[2]

However, in this matter as in most, the usual distance between the conventional wisdom and critical reflection separates town and gown. Going to bed unwed is not regarded favorably in the sidewalk debate or at the coffee klatches after church. A Gallup poll in October 1965 showed that 74 percent of American adults disapproved of allowing college or university women to have oral contraceptives, or at least of *giving* them to them. This means, logically, an equal disapproval of making mechanical means such as diaphragms or intrauterine devices available to undergraduates, as well as other nonsteroid pharmaceutical methods. Elements of psychodynamics and cultural taboo are strong in the general public's opposition; it is far from being simply an informed and critical opposition

From *The 99th Hour: The Population Crisis in the United States,* edited by Daniel O. Price. Copyright 1967. The University of North Carolina Press. Reprinted by permission of the publisher. Joseph Fletcher is the well-known exponent of situation ethics, who in his later years has given particular attention to issues in bioethics.
[1]Lewis H. Terman, *et al., Psychological Factors in Marital Happiness* (McGraw-Hill Book Company, Inc., 1938).

[2]*Sex and the College Student,* Group for the Advancement of Psychiatry, Report 60, 104 E. 25th Street, N.Y., 1965, p. 98.

to a proposed ethical innovation. The "ancient good" is stubbornly grasped no matter how "uncouth" it may be alleged to have become. Shakespeare put the grass-roots temper very neatly in *The Tempest*, where he had Prospero warn Ferdinand:

> If thou dost break her virgin-knot before
> All sanctimonious ceremonies may
> With full and holy rite be minist'red,
> No sweet aspersion shall the heavens let fall
> To make this contract grow; but barren Hate,
> Sour-eyed Disdain and Discord, shall bestrew
> The union of your bed with weeds so loathly
> That you shall hate it both.

But Shakespeare did his thinking in a very different milieu. Approximately forty percent of the sexually mature population are unmarried. Just in terms of statistical weight this shows, therefore, how many people are affected by our question, and we can also make a good guess as to the extent of the hypocrisy which surrounds it. Social competition penalizes early marriage, and the postponement required by a lengthening period of training for career roles and functions pushes marriage farther and farther away from the biological pressure following puberty. Physical maturity far outstrips our mental, cultural, and emotional development. It is said that menstruation in girls starts in this epoch on the average at the age of thirteen and a half years, compared to seventeen a century ago.[3] No human culture in past history ever levied as much tension and strain on the human psychological structure as ours does. And since the Kinsey reports, it is an open secret that male virility is greatest in the late teens —when young men used to marry and rear families. But now they go to high school and become college freshmen!

Just as Herman Kahn's *Thinking about the Unthinkable* has forced us to come to grips with such "unthinkable" possibilities as a nuclear decimation of people by the millions, so the "sexplosion" of the modern era is forcing us to do some thinking about the "unthinkable" in sex ethics. If we had to check off a point in modern times when the sex revolution started, first in practice but only slowly and reluctantly in thought, I would set it at the First World War. Since then there has been a phenomenal increase of aphrodisiac literature, visual and verbal, as well as more informational materials. We have seen an unprecedented freedom of expression orally as well as in print, both in ordinary conversation and in the mass media which glamorize sex—the movies, TV, radio, slick-paper magazines.

All of this reflects a new temper about sexual concerns. It is a new mental and emotional attitude, based on a new knowledge and a new

---

[3] *Newsweek,* April 6, 1964.

frankness. Hollywood personalities are cultural heroes, and they lose none of their popularity or charismatic appeal when they openly engage in sexual adventures apart from the ring and the license. In the movie *The Sandpiper*, even a minister is portrayed as improved and uplifted by a sex affair with an unmarried woman (played by the sexnik, Elizabeth Taylor). The radical psychic ambivalence of the old discredited antisexual tradition, in which women were seen as prostitutes (sexual and bad) or madonnas (angelic, nonsexual, and pure), is not gone yet but its cure is well on the way.

In the great universities of our times, described by Clark Kerr as "multiversities," there is a pluralism or multiplicity of sexual practices and of ethical opinions. We have a sexual diversity that is in keeping with our principles of individual liberty and intellectual freedom. Some of us are quite archaic, some are extremely *avant-garde*, most of us are curious, critical, still cogitating. Undergraduates are often insecure in their sexual views and activities—as in most other areas of responsibility. They tend to despise the hypocrisy with which their elders deal with the "sex question" or evade it. Many of them, of course, profess to be far more confident in their prosex affirmations than they really are. In any case, the older generation has turned them loose, young men and women together in great coeducational communities, with only a few parietal rules to separate them. In the nineteenth century, middle-class parents protected their daughters' virginity with all kinds of chaperonage; in the mobile twentieth century, they've turned it over to the boys and girls themselves.

In what follows we shall focus our attention sharply on one form of unmarried sex—*pre*marital. "Unmarried sex" is a term that covers a wide range of human and infrahuman sexuality, as we know. Homosexuality is a part of it, as well as ethical issues about noncoital sex problems such as abortion and sterilization. (For example, few states are as enlightened as North Carolina, which provides voluntary sterilizations and "pills" for unmarried mothers who request them.)

## THE SITUATION

Back in 1960, Professor Leo Koch of the University of Illinois, a biologist, was fired for saying that it was ethically justifiable to approve of premarital intercourse. His offending statement was: "With modern contraceptives and medical advice readily available at the nearest drugstore, or at least a family physician, there is no valid reason why sexual intercourse should not be condoned among those sufficiently mature to engage in it without social consequences and without violating their own codes of morality and ethics."[4] With due regard for his three qualifying factors—maturity, social

[4]*Time*, April 18, 1960, p. 48.

concern, and integrity—we can say that Professor Koch's position is the one at which this position paper will arrive. We shall try, incidentally, to demonstrate that the fear of honest discussion revealed by Koch's dismissal is at least not universal. (Professor Koch shared the earlier opinion of Professor George Murdock of Yale that premarital intercourse would prepare young people for more successful marriages.[5] But this paper will not offer any analysis favoring or opposing the Murdock-Koch thesis about marriage preparation.)

The American Bar Association has lately urged the different states to review and revise their civil and criminal laws regulating sex acts. Few have done so—except for Illinois. Serious efforts are under way in California and New York, in the face of strong opposition in the churches. A model code committee of the American Law Institute in 1956 reported some important proposed changes in existing law, all in the direction of greater personal freedom sexually, and calling for a lowering of the age of consent to eliminate unjust convictions for statutory rape. Fornication is a criminal offense in thirty-six of our fifty states, the penalty running from $10 in Rhode Island to $500 plus two years in jail in Alaska. Fourteen states have no law against it, but in six of these states "cohabitation" (nonmarital intercourse consistently with the same person) is a criminal offense.

This is a typical anomaly of our sex laws. It makes the punishment for cohabitation heavier than for promiscuity, thus creating the absurd situation in which a measure of interpersonal commitment between such sexual partners is penalized and promiscuity or *casual* fornication is preferred! In Massachusetts, for example, the penalty for fornication is $30 or ninety days in jail, but for cohabitation it is $300 or as much as three years. On the other hand, while many states outlaw adultery, there are others that allow extramarital sex—as in wife-swapping clubs. California is one, for example.

A great deal of both clinical and taxonomic evidence has been gathered showing that sexual activity, or at least sexual exploration, occurs before marriage—unrecognized by the conventional wisdom. The Kinsey findings were that 67 percent of college males are involved, 84 percent of males who go as far as high school, and 98 percent of those who only finish grade school. We can raise these figures for the intervening fifteen years or more, but very probably it is still true that there is a reverse correlation between education levels and nonmarital intercourse. With females the opposite is the case—the higher the school level the greater their frequency of fornication. College women rated 60 percent in Kinsey's studies (1953), but the rate would be discernibly higher for 1966.

In recent years there has been a considerable black market in oral contraceptives. They can be had from "a man on the corner" or from

[5]*Time,* Feb. 13, 1950, p. 57.

drugstores that just don't ask for a prescription. Five million pills were hijacked in Philadelphia not long ago. Incidentally, local investigators have learned that more pills are sold in the vicinity of colleges than elsewhere. Doctors give unmarried girls and women prescriptions for them even when they do not personally approve of their patients' use of them. They rarely refuse them to applicants, and practically never when the young woman is engaged to be married. A year's prescription costs from $5 to $25 as the fee. In some college health services the medical staff make this distinction, giving to the engaged and refusing the unengaged. Soon we will have injections and vaccines that immunize against ovulation for several months at a time, making things easier than ever. It is even likely that a morning-after pill is coming, an abortifacient.

This will be a blessing because of the increase of unintended pregnancies and venereal diseases, due to the new sexual freedom. The surgeon general has said that fifteen hundred people get a venereal disease every day in the year.[6] Syphilis has increased by 200 percent from 1965 to 1966, among persons under twenty.[7] The rate of illegitimate pregnancies among teenagers doubled from 1940 to 1961, and it quadrupled among women in the age level twenty to twenty-five. The highest incidence of pregnancy is among those least promiscuous, i.e., those who are least competent sexually. Yet the risks do not deter them anymore. Fifty percent of teenage girls who marry are pregnant; and 80 percent of those marry teenage boys. It is estimated that nearly 200,000 teenagers are aborted every year.

Sociologists, psychologists, and psychiatrists give us many reasons for the spread of premarital sex. Popularity seeking, the need for a secure companion and dater, the prestige value of full sexual performance, the notion that it achieves personal self-identity, even—but rather rarely—the need for physical satisfaction: these are among the things most mentioned. It is probably still the case that the majority of young women, and some young men, ordinarily and except for an occasional lapse, stop short of coitus, practicing petting to the point of orgasm instead of actual intercourse. Yet from the moral standpoint, it is doubtful that there is any real difference between a technical virgin and a person who goes "all the way." And as for the old double standard for masculine and feminine behavior, it is clearly on its way out in favor of a more honest and undiscriminatory sex ethic.

These changes in attitude are going on even among Christians. The Sycamore Community at Penn State made a survey anonymously of 150 men and women, mostly ministers or professors and their wives, and found that while 33 percent were opposed to premarital sex, 40 percent favored it selectively. Forty percent of their male respondents reported that they had themselves engaged in it (a low percentage compared to the

[6] *Saturday Review,* Dec. 12, 1964, p. 61.
[7] *The New York Times,* Sept. 2, 1965, p. 1.

whole population), and 35 percent of the women so reported. Fifteen percent reported that they had or had had premarital coitus frequently or regularly. Of the married respondents, 18 percent of the husbands and 15 percent of the wives reported extramarital sex acts, although one-third of them said they had petted short of coitus. Yet 40 percent felt it might be justifiable in certain situations.[8]

In order, however, to get a sharp focus on the ethical problem and a possible solution, let us agree to stay with *pre*marital sex. And let us agree that this term covers both casual sexual congress and more personalized experience with dating partners, "steadies," and a "shack-up" friend.

## THE PROBLEM

In terms of ethical analysis we have, so to speak, *two* problem areas. The first one is the problem of premarital sex for those whose moral standards are in the classical religious tradition, based on a faith commitment to a divine sanction—usually, in America, some persuasion or other of the Judeo-Christian kind. The second area is the "secular" one, in which people's moral standards are broadly humanistic, based on a value commitment to human welfare and happiness. It is difficult, if not impossible, to say what proportion of our people falls in either area, but they exist certainly, and the "secular" area is growing all the time.

As a matter of fact, there is by no means a set or unchanging viewpoint in the religious camp. Some Christians are challenging the old morality of the marital monopoly of sex. The Sycamore report declares that "there are no distinctively Christian patterns of sexual behavior which can be characterized by the absence or presence of specific acts." Their report favors a more situational, less legalistic approach to sex ethics. "Let Christians," they say, "face squarely the fact that what the body of authoritative Christian thought passed off as God's revealed truth was in fact human error with a Pauline flavor. Let us remeber this fact every time we hear a solemn assertion about this or that being God's will or *the* Christian ethic."

Over against this situation ethics or religious relativism stands the legalistic ethics of universal absolutes (usually negatives and prohibitions), condemning every form of sexual expression except horizontal coitus eyeball-to-eyeball solely between the parties to a monogamous marriage contract. Thus one editorial writer in a semifundamentalist magazine said recently, and correctly enough: "The new moralists do not believe that the biblical moral laws are really given by God. Moral laws are not regarded

[8] *Sex Ethics: A Study By and For Adult Christians,* The Sycamore Community, P.O. Box 72, State College, Pa., 1965.

as the products of revelation."[9] A growing company of church people are challenging fixed moral principles or rules about sex or anything else.

The idea in the past has been that the ideal fulfillment of our sex potential lies in a monogamous marriage. But there is no reason to regard this ideal as a legal absolute. For example, if the sex ratio were to be overthrown by disaster, polygamy could well become the ideal or standard. Jesus showed more concern about pride and hypocrisy than about sex. In the story of the woman taken in adultery, her accusers were guiltier than she. Among the seven deadly sins, lust is listed but not sex, and lust can exist in marriage as well as out. But even so, lust is not so grave a sin as pride. As Dorothy Sayers points our scornfully, "A man may be greedy and selfish; spiteful, cruel, jealous and unjust; violent and brutal; grasping, unscrupulous and a liar; stubborn and arrogant; stupid, morose and dead to every noble instinct" and yet, if he practices his sinfulness within the marriage bond, he is not thought by some Christians to be immoral![10]

The Bible clearly affirms sex as a high order value, at the same time sanctioning marriage (although not always monogamy), but any claim that the Bible requires that sex be expressed solely within marriage is only an inference. There is nothing explicitly forbidding premarital acts. Only extramarital acts, i.e., adultery, are forbidden. Those Christians who are situational, refusing to absolutize any moral principle except "love thy neighbor," cannot absolutize Paul's one flesh (*henosis*) theory of marriage in I Cor., ch. 6.[11] Paul Ramsey of Princeton has tried to defend premarital intercourse by engaged couples on the ground that they become married thereby. But marriages are not made by the act itself; sexual congress doesn't create a marriage. Marriage is a mutual commitment, willed and purposed interpersonally. Besides, all such "ontological" or "naturalistic" reasoning fails completely to meet the moral question of nonmarital sex acts between unengaged couples, since it presumably condemns them all universally as unjustifiable simply because they are nonmarital. It is still the old marital monopoly theory, only one step relaxed.[12]

The humanists in our "secular" society draw close to the nonlegalists, the nonabsolutists among Christians, when they choose concern for personal values as their ethical norm, for this is very close to the Biblical "love thy neighbor as thyself." Professor Lester Kirkendall, in a privately circulated position paper, "Searching for the Roots of Moral Judgments," puts the humanist position well:

[9] *Christianity Today*, Oct. 8, 1965.

[10] Dorothy Sayers, *The Other Six Deadly Sins* (London: Hodder & Stoughton, Ltd., 1961).

[11] I Cor. 6:16: "Do you not know that he who joins himself to a prostitute becomes one body with her? For, as it is written, 'The two shall become one.'"

[12] See also *Consultation on Sex Ethics*, World Council of Churches, Founex, Switzerland, July 6–10, 1964.

The essence of morality lies in the quality of the interrelationships which can be established among people. Moral conduct is that kind of behavior which enables people in their relationships with each other to experience a greater sense of trust, and appreciation for others; which increases the capacity of people to work together; which reduces social distance and continually furthers one's outreach to other persons and groups, which increases one's sense of self-respect and produces a greater measure of personal harmony.

Immoral behavior is just the converse. Behavior which creates distrust destroys appreciation for others; decreases the capacity for cooperation; lessens concern for others; causes persons or groups to shut themselves off or be shut off from others; and which decreases an individual's sense of self-respect is immoral behavior.

This is, of course, nothing new. The concept has been implicit in religions for ages. The injunction "love thy neighbor as thyself" is a case in point.[13]

On this view, sarcasm and graft are immoral, but not sexual intercourse unless it is malicious or callous or cruel. On this basis, an act is not wrong because of the act itself but because of its *meaning*—its motive and message. Therefore, as Professor Kirkendall explains, the question "Should we ever spank a child?" can only be answered, "It depends upon the situation, on why it is done and how the child understands it."

In the same way, as a *Christian* humanist, Professor John Macmurray declares: "The integrity of persons is inviolable. You shall not use a person for your own ends, or indeed for any ends, individual or social. To use another person is to violate his personality by making an object of him; and in violating the integrity of another, you violate your own.[14] This one of Kant's maxims, at least, has survived the ravages of time. Recalling Henry Miller's book titles, we might paraphrase Kant and Macmurray by saying, "The plexus of the sexus is the nexus."

Both religious and secular moralists, in America's plural society, need to remember that freedom *of* religion includes freedom *from* religion. There is no ethical basis for compelling noncreedalists to follow any creedal codes of behavior, Christian or non-Christian. A "sin" is an act against God's will, but if the agent does not believe in God he cannot commit sin, and even those who do believe in God disagree radically as to what God's will is. Speaking to the issue over birth control law, Cardinal Cushing of Boston says, "Catholics do not need the support of civil law to be faithful to their own religious convictions, and they do not need to impose their moral views on other members of society. . . ." What the cardinal says about birth control applies just as much to premarital intercourse.

[13]See Lester Kirkendall, *Premarital Intercourse and Interpersonal Relations* (Julian Press, Inc., 1961).

[14]John Macmurray, *Reason and Emotion* (Barnes & Noble, Inc., 1962), p. 39.

Harking back to the report of the Group for the Advancement of Psychiatry in its support of sexual *laissez faire* on college campuses, we could offer an ethical proposition of our own: Nothing we do is truly moral unless we are free to do otherwise. We must be free to decide what to do before any of our actions even begin to be moral. No discipline but self-discipline has any moral significance. This applies to sex, politics, or anything else. A moral act is a free act, done because we want to.

Incidentally, but not insignificantly, let me remark that this freedom which is so essential to moral acts can mean freedom *from* premarital sex as well as freedom for it. Not everybody would choose to engage in it. Some will not because it would endanger the sense of personal integrity. Value sentiments or "morals" may be changing (they *are*, obviously), but we are still "living in the overlap" and a sensitive, imaginative person might both well and wisely decide against it. As Dr. Mary Calderone points, out, very young men and women are not always motivated in the same way: "The girl plays at sex, for which she is not ready, because fundamentally what she wants is love; and the boy plays at love, for which he is not ready, because what he wants is sex."[15]

Many will oppose premarital sex for reasons of the social welfare, others for relationship reasons, and some for simple egoistic reasons. We may rate these reasons differently in our ethical value systems, but the main point morally is to respect the freedom to choose. And short of coitus, young couples can pet each other at all levels up to orgasm, just so they are honest enough to recognize that merely technical virgins are no better morally than those who go the whole way. In John Hersey's recent novel, the boy and girl go to bed finally but end up sleeping curled up at arm's length.[16] It is ethically possible, that is to say, to be undecided, conflicted, and immobilized. What counts is being honest. In some cases, decisions can be mistaken. Let honesty reign then too. Bryan Green, the evangelist, once said that the engaged but unmarried should thank God for the "experience" and ask for forgiveness for a lack of discipline.[17]

## THE SOLUTION

Just as there are two ethical orientations, theistic and humanistic, so there are two distinct questions to ask ourselves. One is: Should we prohibit and condemn premarital sex? The other is: Should we approve of it? To the

[15]Mary Calderone, in *Redbook Magazine*, July 1965.
[16]John Hersey, *Too Far to Walk* (Alfred A. Knopf, Inc., 1966).
[17]Quoted in R. F. Hettlinger, *Living with Sex: The Student's Dilemma* (The Seabury Press, Inc., 1966), p. 139.

first one I promptly reply in the negative. To the second I propose an equivocal answer, "Yes and no—depending on each particular situation."

The most solid basis for any ethical approach is on the ground common to both the religiously oriented and the humanistically oriented—namely, the concern both feel for persons. They are alike *personalistically* oriented. For example, both Christians and non-Christians can accept the normative principle, "We ought to love people and use things; immorality only occurs when we love things and use people." They can agree also on a companion maxim: "We ought to love people, not rules or principles; what counts is not any hard and fast moral law but doing what we can for the good of others in every situation."

The first principle means that no sexual act is ethical if it hurts or exploits others. This is the difference between lust and love: lust treats a sexual partner as an object, love as a subject. Charity is more important than chastity, but there is no such thing as "free love." There must be some care and commitment in premarital sex acts or they are immoral. Hugh Hefner, the whipping boy of the stuffies, has readily acknowledged in *Playboy* that "personal" sex relations are to be preferred to impersonal.[18] Even though he denies that mutual commitment needs to go the radical lengths of marriage, he sees at least the difference between casual sex and straight callous congress.

The second principle is one of situation ethics—making a moral decision hangs on the particular case. How, here and now, can I act with the most certain concern for the happiness and welfare of those involved—myself and others? Legalistic moralism, with its absolutes and universals, always thou-shalt-nots, cuts out the middle ground between being a virgin and a sexual profligate.[19] This is an absurd failure to see that morality has to be acted out on a continuum of relativity, like life itself, from situation to situation.

The only independent variable is concern for people; love thy neighbor as thyself. Christians, whether legalistic or situational about their ethics, are agreed that the *ideal* sexually is the combination of marriage and sex. But the ideal gives no reason to demand that others should adopt that ideal or to try to impose it by law, nor is it even any reason to absolutize the ideal in practice for all Christians in all situations. Sex is not always wrong outside marriage, even for Christians; as Paul said, "I know ... that nothing is unclean in itself" (Rom. 14:14). Another way to put it is to say that character shapes sex conduct, sex does not shape character.

As I proposed some years ago in a paper in *Law and Contemporary Problems,* the Duke University law journal, there are only three proper

[18]Hugh Hefner, in *Playboy,* December 1964.
[19]See Harvey Cox, *The Secular City* (Crowell-Collier and Macmillan, Inc., 1965), p. 212.

limitations to guide both the civil law and morality on sexual acts.[20] No sexual act between persons competent to give mutual consent should be prohibited, except when it involves either the seduction of minors or an offense against the public order. These are the principles of the Wolfenden Report to the English Parliament, adopted by that body and endorsed by the Anglican and Roman Catholic archbishops. It is time we acknowledged the difference between "sins" (a private judgment) and "crimes" against the public conscience and social consensus.

Therefore, we can welcome the recent decision of the federal Department of Health, Education, and Welfare to provide birth control assistance to unmarried women who desire it. It is a policy that puts into effect the principles of the President's Health Message to Congress of March 1, 1966. If the motive is a truly moral one, it will be concerned not only with relief budgets but with the welfare of the women and a concern to prevent unwanted babies. Why wait for even *one* illegitimate child to be born?

Dr. Ruth Adams, new president of Wellesley College, has said that the college's role is to give information about birth control educationally, but no medical assistance. Actually, birth control for unmarried students, she thinks, is "the function of the student's private physician rather than the college."[21] This is the strategy being followed by most universities and colleges to separate knowledge and assistance, relegating to off-campus doctors the responsibility of protecting the unmarried from unwanted pregnancies. As a strategy, it obviously avoids a clash with those who bitterly oppose sexual freedom; it is therefore primarily a public relations posture. It bows the neck to people whose attitude is that if premarital sex can't be prevented, then the next thing is to prevent the prevention of tragic consequences—a curiously sadistic kind of pseudo-morality.

But surely this policy of information but no personal help is an ethical evasion by the universities. If they accept a flat fee for watching over the student's health, is not contraceptive care included? If college health services have treatment to prescribe which is better than students can get in a drug store, they *ought* to provide it. They should give *all* the medical service needed except what is too elaborate or technical for their facilities. Nobody is suggesting that pills or IUD's or diaphragms should be sold in the campus bookstore, but they ought to be regarded as a medical resource *owed* to the student as needed and requested. This is the opinion of most physicians on college health services, and I would support it for ethical reasons—chiefly out of respect for personal freedom.

[20]Joseph Fletcher, "Sex Offenses: An Ethical View," *Law and Contemporary Problems,* Spring 1960, pp. 244–257.
    [21]Ruth Adams, in *The New York Times,* March 22, 1966.

# Rules and the Ethics of Sex

## Joseph C. Hough, Jr.

One of the important issues raised by the so-called "new morality" is the role of rules in the ethics of sex. For example, the majority of the illustrations in Joseph Fletcher's *Situation Ethics* call into question the traditional rules of sexual behavior. The same is true of Bishop Robinson's chapter on "new morality" in *Honest to God* and his pamphlet *Christian Morals Today.*

Fletcher in particular gives the impression that when one confronts a rule-challenging situation the only course open is to suspend the rules and rely on love. He is deeply concerned about the rigidity and the restrictiveness of rule ethics, and rightly so, but the cure of "love" alone may well be worse than the disease. What is called for is not abandonment of rules but rather fresh deliberation about the kind of rules that are appropriate for sexual behavior and a clear understanding of the role rules play in moral decision-making.

First, however, several things need to be said about the role of rules in the Christian moral life. For one thing, no one with any common sense has ever thought that rules always apply in the same way to every situation. Thomas Aquinas knew that "natural law," when applied to civil law, would have to take account of local conditions and peculiarities. Kant of course is the favorite whipping boy of the situationists. He made the mistake of insisting on truth-telling as the universal obligation, and ever since moralists have harped on his example. The example goes something like this: One of Kant's friends who is being sought by a murderer is hiding in Kant's house. The would-be murderer comes along and asks, "Where is Sam Jones?" Kant argues that the host must tell the truth, for to do otherwise would be to will that lying be a universal law, a form of the categorical imperative. The problem with this example resides in the fact that there is also a universal obligation to preserve life—especially to preserve the life of another person. What Kant failed to see was that when two universals conflict, one has to deliberate on the priorities. Surely the preservation of human life is a higher priority than simple truth-telling. This is not to say that lying is right. In this case, however, it is surely more right to lie about the friend's whereabouts than to sacrifice him to the

Copyright 1969 Christian Century Foundation. Reprinted by permission from the January 29, 1969 issue of *The Christian Century.* Joseph C. Hough, Jr., is Chairman of the Faculty of Religion at Claremont Graduate School, where he teaches Christian ethics.

purity of one's lips. Many of us can recall such extreme cases of moral ambiguity.

What is important, however, is to realize that moral rules do not govern extreme cases only. And this is my second point about moral rules. Moral rules are the guidelines for ordinary behavior. I do not have to decide every day whether or not I shall steal a loaf of bread from the food market. Conceivably a time might come when I would entertain that possibility —if my family were starving and there was no other way for them to live. But ordinarily I shall not steal because I think it is wrong to steal. Or again, ordinarily when I give my word I expect to keep it. I will not intentionally deceive another by making a promise I do not intend to keep. Conceivably, circumstances might arise that would render this rule inappropriate, but these would be exceptional cases, and not for one moment would they invalidate the rule I recognize.

A third characteristic of rules in the Christian moral life is that they provide guidelines for what I want to *be*. Because God calls men to *be* truly human, they reflect upon the kinds of rules that describe how one acts in a truly human way. Therefore, when we state the rules of moral behavior, we are not stating absolute laws inscribed on tablets of stone; we are citing the deliberations of men about what constitutes a truly human response of man to man in light of some kind of understanding of a covenant with God or a moral ideal. For example, The Ten Commandments were not given as direct pronouncements from God Almighty; they were the deliberations of a very brilliant man on the question, "Given our covenant with Yahweh, what constitutes some guidelines for the behavior of covenant man?" Or look at Paul's letter to the Romans. The first eight chapters are a hymn to the glory of God's mighty action upon men. Then, in chapter 12, Paul turns to a very simple question, "In light of these mercies of God, what should the Christian man do?" There follows some excellent instruction about the kind of behavior that is appropriate to the Christian. In both cases, moral rules, rather than being a burden to men, illumine their choices.

When we talk about moral rules, then, we do not necessarily mean moral restriction. We can mean the shaping of man's moral freedom so that it becomes clear to him just what he wants to do in light of certain basic commitments. This is the personal function of moral rules. They play the role of enabling me to decide upon the course of my own moral integrity. They help me to answer the question, "What will I do?" Not what ought I to do, for the obligation to do anything is not contained in the rule; but rather what *will* I do, granted that I am determined to be a certain kind of person.

Professor Fletcher argues that the Christian is armed only with love, and Bishop Robinson says that this is enough, for like a homing pigeon love will find the good thing to do without the pressure or structure of rules. This may be true for Bishop Robinson, but if it is, he is different from most men I know. Most of us find that our consciences, whether possessed by the love pigeon or some other chicken, more often than not come home to roost on pure and simple impulsiveness and selfishness—unless we have given some thought to the rules we regard as important and to the general pattern of moral behavior we shall follow.

A fourth characteristic of rules is their social function. Put simply: rules form the public document by which others learn what to expect of us. Thou shalt not steal, for example, is a declaration of honest intention. But it is also an invitation to trust. I am saying of myself that I will not steal, and I am saying to you that you need not worry about my stealing from you. I am also saying that I do not expect you to steal from me. Since all of us are related to others—that is, since we are incurably social—rules like this have the very important function of providing the informal structures that help to order our lives.

It is precisely here that all "pop existentialism" comes to ruin. The truth of the matter is that no one can live his life humanly when, to use Sartre's words, "hell is other people." The very possibility of human life is other people. All the truly human needs and experiences are social. We begin, continue and end in a social matrix from which we cannot extricate ourselves, and even if we could, to do so would be to destroy our true humanness.

Further, no single pair of people can live alone in this world. What other people do and expect of us always impinges on me and on the "one other" even in our utmost privacy. And what we do has broad social effects, whether we acknowledge as much or not. In the rapture of an automobile back seat or in the privacy of one's own little pad, the world may seem to be encompassed in the hopes and passion of just two of us. But it is not so. Every little nest for two opens inevitably into the world of wider relations. The world of our own private affairs is a dream world, and failure to realize that has shattered many people over many centuries. Ironically, some trips into the depth of human reality may result in the dehumanizing of those who love us very much.

So much for the way rules function in the Christian life. What about rules that might apply to the specific act of sexual intercourse?

The "new moralists" have given us two very important insights into this problem. In the first place, they are calling attention to the fact that the rule "don't have sexual intercourse outside marriage" does not adequately state the conditions for moral sexual intercourse. The problem has been that once a rule is stated, people too often interpret it to mean that any sexual intercourse within marriage is good. It is important to realize that rape and prostitution can occur in marriage. The man who uses threats or abuse to force his wife to assent to sexual intercourse is committing rape, and the woman who uses sex to manipulate her husband is committing prostitution—even if her price is only a new hat instead of the $25 or $50 a night demanded by the "professional." I might add that anyone who tries to force a partner to "prove" his or her love by sex is simply demonstrating that there is no love in him for the other.

A second point made by the new moralists is that the reasons we have been giving for limiting sexual intercourse to marriage no longer hold up. The pill and penicillin have ended both the long-used lines of argument for continence. A teacher I once had cautioned us about sexual intercourse because of the danger of disease and of "getting the girl in trouble." The dire consequences he pictured rivaled the medieval concepts of hell— although his hell, like the medieval one, deterred only those who were too fainthearted to sin anyway. At any rate, we must find better reasons than these if we are to support the moral rule for sexual intercourse.

Where, then do we start in setting up rules for sexual behavior that are based on deeper understanding of morality? Necessarily, with some understanding of what it is to be truly human. For the sexual behavior of human beings may be the part of their behavior that is most distinctly human. Certainly a good case can be made for the assertion that the sexual act is the act in which the human being is more totally involved than in any other kind of act. Here all of us is present—our emotions, our mind, our past and present, and our expectations for the future. Do we not indeed say of sexual intercourse that the woman "gave herself" to the man? Yet the fact is that sex is human and no more. In our understanding of sex we must avoid two extremes. On the one hand, sex is not bad; it isn't the "apple" Eve ate that resulted in the downfall of us all. On the other hand—and this is perhaps more important today—sex is not the main purpose of life either. It is important, to be sure, but it is not ultimately so—contrary not only to the *Playboy* style but also to the typical campus Christian movement style of several years ago. Some Christian writers would have us believe that sex is so high and holy that we should have a communion cup and bread right on the nightstand by the bed.

Sex is neither the worst nor the best, but it is fully and completely human. If we think, however, that the desire for or the mere repetition of copulation can cement a relationship between a man and a woman, we are deluding ourselves. There is nothing more disappointing than ordinariness when one expects the ultimate; hence there is nothing more fruitless than the quest for meaning in sexual intercourse that is dehumanized.

What, then, is the rule for human sexual intercourse? If it is to be truly human, it must be entered on in full respect for the freedom of the partner. No force, either psychological or physical, must be involved; it must be an act in which both parties freely give themselves to each other.

But, as I have said, sexual intercourse is not merely one human activity among others. It is a total experience, a total giving of all of one's selfhood.

It is not to be taken lightly, as if it were insignificant. Therefore intercourse is not morally appropriate unless there is a history to the relationship between two persons involved. How can one give one's self in response to the self of another unless there has been time for mutual understanding to develop? And mutual understanding means mutual speech and mutual hearing of one another. Thus, to be truly human, the act of sexual intercourse must flower out of a history of common interest and true mutuality.

Further, if sexual intercourse means giving oneself to another, it means that there is a breadth of common interest in the present. Giving of oneself is completed only when one is received, and true receiving is completed only in full acceptance and giving in return. Such giving and receiving cannot be compassed by the excitement of an orgasm; they are a giving and a receiving of common interests and common hopes.

This points to a third aspect of the proper moral context for sexual intercourse: the anticipation of a common future. One cannot give himself without including his past, and one cannot give his present in fullness unless that present points to a fulfillment in the continued mutuality of a common future. I am not fully myself in the present unless my past is included, and unless I can honestly face my future and affirm what I am now as genuinely moving toward the future. In other words, giving oneself to the other points to a future when our mutual giving and receiving will take on dimensions that we have not yet explored. As we become more fully one with each other, we can share more fully in mutual giving— which means that the present act of giving has a prophetic dimension. The proper context of human sexual intercourse is the willingness, even the eagerness, to take responsibility for the other's future as my own future and his own future.

This is the proper moral context of sexual intercourse. It neither deifies nor demonizes sex, but simply humanizes it. And that is exactly what is required for action to be truly moral—that it be truly human. This certainly means two things: (1) there can be sexual intercourse outside of marriage that is more meaningful than some sexual intercourse within marriage; and (2) there can be premarital sexual activity stopping short of intercourse that may be less moral than some premarital sexual intercourse.

But there is a further consideration. Granted that the highest criterion for moral action is its true humanness, and granted that humanity is not fully defined by the marraige ceremony, we must ask what the *moral* meaning of the marriage ceremony is. Here I refer back to what I suggested above: No act on the part of any two persons can be isolated from the social nexus. True humanity is social, and as such it involves the obligation not only to be human in interpersonal relationships but also to honor those structures by which we try to provide the possibility for true humanity by protecting each other from the abuses that result from immoral actions. For example, while the laws against discrimination and segregation do not ensure moral actions between blacks and whites, they do remove certain barriers by limiting the excesses of immorality and by defining the expectations that are our norms.

Now, if we agree that human life is social and if we accept the criterion of true humanity as the proper moral context for sexual intercourse, what is the social sign that a man and a woman have a common past and a common present and are committed to a common future? Marriage. That is precisely how marriage functions in our society—at least ideally. It is a public announcement of the fruition of a human relationship in which sexual intercourse is part of the ongoing development of that relationship as the full giving of oneself to the other and the full receiving of the other to oneself. In rather crass terms, marriage is the step whereby the partners legally "put the talk on the line." They say in effect: Not only are we emotionally tied to each other, but the evidence of our good faith is that we want the world to share in the knowledge of our life together and to hold us responsible within our common social existence for the vows we make to each other. Moreover, the marriage ceremony informs others that there is between these two persons a special relationship, unique and exclusive, which now defines the expectation of other men and women in other relationships.

Ideally, then, marriage is the social sign of the truly human relationship that must be the moral context for sexual intercourse. As such it should precede the consummation of the act itself. But the significance of this moral rule, like that of all other moral rules, is twofold. It is both a direction for my own moral action and a declaration of my intentions to the other persons to whom I am related.

How strictly should we adhere to this rule? As I noted above, there may be extreme cases where it would not apply. The rule *alone* does not define the morality that is at stake; it is only the rule interpreted as the sign of truly human action that has force. So interpreted, however, it has validity in most cases. Perhaps the matter can be best put by way of an analogy. In constitutional law, questions about the extent of the freedoms guaranteed in the Bill of Rights come up now and again. For example, Justice Black has argued that the rule of freedom of speech should be honored in all cases. To be sure, some qualifications of the rule have been developed the "clear and present danger" proviso, for instance. But what is important is that the burden of proof lies upon the one who would make an exception to the free speech rule. It is not the keeper of the rule but the breaker of it who is on trial. Analogously, then, the rule is that sexual intercourse ought to be done only in the context of a truly human marriage. The burden of proof lies upon those who would break it.

# 5

# Marriage and the Family

In a recent *New York Times* article a well-known educator was quoted as saying that traditional, lifelong marriage and the family as we have known them are in a state of "desperate decline." This point of view has been expressed so often in recent years that we have become used to words such as "crisis" and "revolution" and even "death" to describe the present state of marriage and the family. In some areas of our country the number of divorces is beginning to equal the number of marriages. The situation is worsened by the conclusion of a research project, involving 601 couples, that over half of all married couples stay together not because they love each other, but because divorce is too painful or expensive.

Social scientists list several reasons for the weakening of monogamous marriage; some are noted in the article by Donna Schaper. One can speak of certain values that have emerged in recent decades which work against marriage as it has traditionally existed. The human potential movement, for example, has stressed the independence and the freedom of the individual and the justified quest for one's own self-actualization. This quest has accented the preferences of the individual over any obligations one might have to people or institutions, for the individual self is the measure of all values. Self-growth as an absolute ideal has been understood in such a way that responsibility to others is not integral to its realization. The well-known "Gestalt Prayer" by Fritz Perls expresses this idea:

I do my thing and you do your thing. I am not in this world to live up to your expectations and you are not in this world to live up to mine. You are you and I am I, and if by chance we find each other, it's beautiful.

To a person who is burdened by excessive expectations on the part of others, this statement might be liberating and helpful; but as summary of a general orientation toward life, one could well question its adequacy.

Whatever the gamut of reasons for the weakening of marriage, it appears that the Christian understanding of marriage as commitment and mutual lifelong fidelity is increasingly being replaced by the view that marriage is an arrangement of convenience. This means that marriage is to serve the needs of the two individuals entering into it; and if it is no longer perceived as doing so by one or both of the partners, then it should be dissolved. Since children can complicate such dissolution, it is best to get one's divorce early or to refrain from having children. With this understanding, the nature of marriage as a promise of two persons to each other is removed in favor of a basically self-centered approach that is concerned primarily, if not solely, with the question "What good will this relationship do for me?"

How should Christians respond to this situation? The Christian religion has sanctified monogamous marriage; and more than any other institution today, the church provides the undergirding and support for maintaining the ideal of marriage as a lifelong commitment. Have we entered a cultural situation that has transformed this ideal into a hopeless anachronism? Should Christians give serious consideration to the alternative forms of marriage now being proposed? One example which is being discussed in several state legislatures is "contract marriage," where two persons would sign a contract to get married for a specific period of time, say three or five years, at the conclusion of which the marriage could be dissolved without court action. This would be a significant step beyond "no fault" divorce laws, which have served to get rid of much of the ugliness of divorce suits, but which have also encouraged couples to turn to divorce as a way of "solving" their marital problems.

Not much is said about marriage in the Bible, but the Apostle Paul does address the subject several times in his letters. He works with the notion of a hierarchy in which the man is the head of the family; yet Paul is ahead of his time in making clear the obligations of the man to his wife and children. With the contemporary model of marriage as a partnership of equals rather than a hierarchy, Christian theologians have generally concluded that Paul's model should be understood as culturally conditioned and in need of adaptation to our situation. Donna Schaper notes that it is precisely the current egalitarian model of marriage that accentuates the difficulty—even the impossibility—of the marriage commitment according to the Christian conception. The very demand of such a commitment gets at our deepest selves and raises the larger questions of life's meaning and destiny. When spiritual malaise afflicts society, and faith and hope lose their vitality, this most intimate and demanding of human relationships must also suffer. Schaper's reflections lead one to self-examination and raise the question whether a secularized society can maintain an institution that ultimately rests upon a religious vision.

Raymond Lawrence agrees that traditional monogamy is in deep trouble. His response is to suggest a change which he believes would enable monogamous marriage to survive. He sees permanence and exclusiveness as the two major aspects of the marriage relationship. Where a marriage partner has had an extramarital affair, the offended partner's decision to divorce him or her expresses the exclusiveness of marriage and results in the destruction of its intended permanence. Lawrence would turn this around, advocating marriage that does not insist on exclusiveness but retains permanence. This would allow for extramarital affairs, and Lawrence believes that they can be "integrated into a marriage with creative and positive results." This proposal is based on an ethic of compromise that many would be inclined to challenge, but at least Lawrence moves beyond handwringing to make a concrete suggestion. He obviously disagrees with Sidney Callahan's statement in Chapter 3 that "the Yes to the mate is built upon and strengthened by the No to everyone else."

Closely related to the state of marriage in our society is the state of the family. Sufficient concern has been generated on this topic to prompt the proposal of the Family Protection Act in the United States Senate. The deliberations of the White House Conference on Families, summoned by President Carter, revealed how basic the problems have become, with extended debate over the fundamental question "What is a family?" Some would address the issue by turning the clock back to a time when social relationships were simpler and the family more secure. Others have greeted the "death" of the family and urge a departure from outmoded familial forms and expectations of the past.

Herbert Anderson would avoid either of those extremes as he seeks to locate the nature of the crisis in the contemporary family. He sees the fundamental problem as a crisis in the purpose of the family, which has increasingly lost its traditional roles of economic production and socialization of the young. Consequently, the family has withdrawn into a privatized existence and no longer exerts the stabilizing influence that it once had in society. Anderson maintains that the task of the family that cannot be usurped by the rest of society is the "individuation" of each of its members—the nourishing of individual growth. In this process of growing up so that we become "separate together," the principal purpose of the family is to provide a setting in which both individual autonomy and community are mutually strengthened. This is clearly not a matter that can be solved by passing a law, but calls for a continuing and growing concern on the part of our society over family nurture and the responsibility of the family to each of its members.

# Marriage: The Impossible Commitment?

## Donna Schaper

The causal explanations for the rise in the divorce rate are as numerous as the breakfast cereals on the supermarket shelf.

# I

**Extended Adolescence.** Young people grow up more slowly, find employment later, depend on parents longer but marry too early. Before the adolescent becomes an adult, he or she makes an adult commitment. Thus the theory develops that the first marriage is only prelude to second marriage and a greater maturity.

**Women's Liberation.** The entry of women into the job market, their demand for freedom, their interest in being cared for as well as caring for others all place a strain on marriage as we have known it. If these were not legitimate interests on the part of women, blame could be placed. The tragedy is the price women are paying for their "liberation" and the price men are paying for their refusal to engage in systemic change. Women suspect that career success is incompatible with two things: marriage and motherhood. Men have structured their lives in appreciation of that view for years. Systemic change would equalize both the burdens and the advantages of marriage and career.

**Masculine Shortcomings.** Men, it is said, don't know how to relate to strong women; therefore, as women grow stronger, men withdraw. Centuries of mothering have prepared them for this choice. The ego-protecting chauvinism of those who prefer the relationship they were taught as boys to expect combines with the women's movement theory like fire to dynamite.

**Economic Issues.** The need for two incomes in many American families removes the woman from the home, by her choice or not. The family needs a "wife," once man and woman both take on a job. Nurture and housekeeping are the tasks left undone by dual-career couples. Inflationary pressures mount, rising consumer expectations join them, and income takes priority over relationship, marriage, and family.

Copyright 1979 Christian Century Foundation. Reprinted by permission from the June 20–27, 1979 issue of *The Christian Century*. Donna Schaper is Associate Chaplain at Yale University.

**The Genetic Explanation.** Now that reproduction is possible without sexual union, some say that men and women no longer biologically need each other. According to this theory, our conflicted state is reflective of an evolutionary determinism to which technology has educated our psyches.

**Lack of Commitment.** Both the right and the left indulge in charges here. From the left comes a self-righteousness about the capability for intimacy ("You *have* been to Esalen, haven't you—or at least been analyzed?"). The right displays the stiff upper lip, the assumption that suffering builds character and that marriage involves a legitimate suffering. The issue, however, is not one's capacity to make a commitment but rather the question of whether one is committed to the self's agenda or the selfless agenda. Moralisms grow in the fertile soil of difficulty. A "tsk, tsk" attitude only exacerbates the problem, applying a veneer of legalism over a tangled human ambiguity.

**A Rise in Sexual Expectation.** Birth control having liberated sex from procreation, recreation substitutes as the goal. We are told that it is wrong *not* to pleasure ourselves (what a switch!), and so we righteously insist on pleasure. For those who married before the advent of this compulsive liberation, another pattern had been established; the discovery of sex as an end in itself has caused many individuals to search for greener pastures.

**The Apocalyptic Interpretation.** The culture is dying or dead, we have lost faith in ourselves and our institutions, and therefore we experiment desperately with new forms. Is the institution of marriage in worse shape than the schools? In the cry that all have sinned and fallen short, there is a small comfort. At least we are doing no better or worse as married individuals than we are doing in our other social roles. Nothing is more absolving of personal responsibility than the apocalyptic theory.

**Peer Pressures.** Covenantal relationships are fragile. Without social support for the institution of marriage, with the sense that "everybody's doing it"—that is, divorcing—marriage becomes a minority behavior and suffers all the pressures thereof.

**The Turner Thesis of American History.** "Go west, young man:" The sad and ridiculous procession of older men leaving their wives for younger women would support this thesis. We would be fools to assume that the great American escape would restrict itself to the continental landscape. Escape/avoidance is the archetypal American response to difficulty.

## II

I would give all these theories some credence, and then add one more. Carl Jung talks about the psychology of marriage as essentially that of the container and the contained, the paradigmatic structure of male and female. One must envelop and structure the other; relationship requires hierarchy. The church historically has understood marriage as a sacrament, an adventure into impossible commitment which has divine sanction, encouragement, and blessing.

The rhetoric of equality between men and women has disallowed Jung's hierarchical model, and the cultural if not actual death of God has made the pursuit of impossibilities meaningless. We've had enough of exciting adventures in the secular scene. There being no bottom line to failure, we simply fall through to the bottom.

I think marriage, particularly of the exalted, egalitarian model now being pursued, *is* impossible. One cannot do it alone, nor can two. With the aid of neither transcendence nor forgiveness—a bottom line on the freedom to try again after failure—relationships are thwarted. And marriage being the primary relationship, it becomes the first to evidence the signs of an unredeemed and unredeemable brokenness.

Do I argue for God out of desperation, out of the profound experience of human failure and brokenness? Not at all. Surely at the limits of our own experience we do reach out for something more. But that search is damned by its own dependent origin. God's gifts are hard enough to receive even when they come to *successful* human beings.

Rather, I argue that the profound and seemingly unmanageable pressures which marriage faces are a spiritual and not a psychosocial matter, one having to do with questions of human destiny: are we to live for ourselves, or for others, or for both in some yet undiscovered dialectic of being? Can we deny ourselves pleasure, care or stimulation and avoid the Freudian trap of destructive unconscious resignation? If we give up, is there any comfort beyond our own selves? If we hang in, is there any support beyond what we ourselves can muster or our friends provide? Just how ultimate are our personal decisions? To questions of destiny, questions of nature adhere.

## III

The question of purpose intersects that of nature and destiny. Is marriage an end in itself—or is it part of a nurture fitting us more ably for larger purposes? Until the spiritual condition of modern persons is addressed, marriage will continue to be a victim of a larger malaise.

To those struggling with marital decision and to those living with the consequences of their decision—whether commitment or separation, marriage or divorce—the same words can be spoken. Human relationships are not carried out in a human vacuum. Persons unresponsive to issues of nature and destiny, the recourse when suffering comes, the purpose of their life and times, will find relationships difficult. Without commitments in these areas, the self is not formed concretely enough to include an other. Emptiness encounters emptiness, and confusion reigns.

Persons uncertain about themselves and their faith dare not engage in an intimate relationship unless all they expect are psychosocial benefits, of which there are some. But to get married for these reasons and to expect to stay clear of more ultimate issues is to beg the sanity and sanctity of human experience.

Few are able to live close to another and, at the same time, live with such aridity. Few can resist their own urge to understand levels above and below the superficial. Marriage is a covenant involving our deepest selves —our sexuality, fertility, generativity, talent, inadequacy and death. It is our link to past (parents) and future (children). Its very nature is intolerant of superficiality. Until the larger questions of destiny, nature and purpose are grasped coherently and communally, marriage will continue to be the victim of a formerly Christian culture that has lost its identity and therefore is incapable of maintaining its institutions.

Intimate relationships maintain their victim status so long as psychosocial explanations dominate. The myth of no connections, implying culture's demonic power and otherness, is a stranger to reality. Reality demands that we own the culture we have permitted to exist, and that we accept complicity if not responsibility.

## IV

The church can aid the married and the unmarried only by refusing the victim posture and by incarnationally addressing the questions of nature, purpose, and destiny. All the "marriage encounter" weekends in the world will not save what theology has relinquished.

The church's message is primarily neither psychological nor economic. It is the good news that speaks a word of freedom to these and all other factors. The good news is not that the God of love delivered us from difficulty and failure but rather that he permitted, by his own death and resurrection, our entry into these experiences with hope. Herein lies the power we have to risk the impossible—namely, fulfilling an intimate relationship. We are not condemned to a life of petty and possible dreams; rather, we are free to lift our sights to the humanly impossible and there to wager the accompaniment of God. More than failure, we fear the petty dream and the absence of engagement in human reality.

What do we ourselves deeply want? Do we prefer the script of unredeemable failure to the drama of God? With what degree of freedom do we acquiesce or claim a destiny? Which vision of our nature will claim us? How much suffering will we tolerate or choose, and for what purposes? Precisely to what extent are we able to repress and avoid the question of creation? Did we, in fact, make ourselves? Are we the pride and pinnacle of it all? Can we bear that loneliness? Are we here for a reason?

God, after all, in an eschatological yet primitive promise named our life as *good*. Then God claimed it in new covenant and named it *saved*. We are the ones damned by and desirous of the alternate options—the script of unredeemable failure, the purposelessness, the assumptions of impossibility.

Perspective soon becomes the issue. Marriage is not the only stage on which we act. I see nothing in the Word itself that elevates matrimony to the level of salvation. If anything, celibacy is the preferred state, biblically speaking. In the land of ultimate questions, our fidelity to one partner is a small region. That we choose safety or hope, possibility or impossibility, love or hate is a matter of another order. It's a matter of the spine in the soul, the lust in our heart rather than the lust in our behavior.

What is not penultimate is the basis for our decision. Do we love beyond our own capacity, give beyond our own capacity, or hope beyond our own capacity? Once the energy conversions occur, we are responsible for our decisions and live beyond continual regret over consequences in a knowledge of hope. These are the points at which we take our marriage vows seriously—where we accept the help of God. If brokenness occurs following that release to larger power, then we move into that brokenness in hope. God will call us to love again, or in another way. We will risk brokenness again, or in another way. These risks mark our journey, our nature, and destiny.

Some hurts will never go away, nor should they. But they are not the final word about us or God. We may have failed; we may have failed another; another may have failed us. Or these sins may tangle with each other in an unmanageable web. Trust can be irreparably broken between people.

# V

The stakes are obviously high. If small homogeneous communities can't work, then what chance is there for larger heterogeneous communities? If we cannot acknowledge our personal failure with one partner, on what basis do we risk future encounters? But we risk the truth of the gospel by living as though its promise were already here. I know of no other way to appropriate it save in the risking. Possibility is the stone we throw at the Goliath of impossibility.

The issue of hope is confronted in our faith about our capacity to change and in our faith about the other's capacity to change. The faith is not a duty but rather an attraction to the deeper self within us whom we wait to know as one that confronts and goes beyond brokenness. In both instances, by our own power we will fail. In the power available to us in the incarnation, we find another situation. It is not necessarily the power to "save a marriage" but the power to assure that love and justice are motivating factors, that they be both the means and the ends of our action.

The gospel provides few answers about how we should live or what decisions we should make. It is not a recipe for right living. The gospel transcends the law only to name a more difficult law—that of love, first of God and then of each other, even ourselves. There is no provision in the Word which avoids on our behalf human ambiguity. We make our own decisions and live with their consequences. But in a love that will not let us go, God provides the clue to our purpose, nature, and destiny. We are, quite simply, called and empowered to the task of love and to its consequent justice. We are called simultaneously to provide each other with the sanctuary of love and the challenge of justice, and to expect the other to provide the same for us. This expectation is not private or individualistic; it is the mission of humanity, not only of spouses.

To the extent that our marriages are based in and led by those purposes, we are responsive to our created image. To the extent that they are not, whether by pursuit of law's safe moralism or in rebellion against it, we miss the mark. In Paul's words, we sin. And then, and only then, do we move from the power and presence of God.

We can never know whether we have loved enough or hoped enough. That is a luxury denied to us, and which we deny by the safety of self-deception. We can go only so far in those directions and then relax in the love that knows no limits and the hope that has no bounds. And there at the edge of our own limits, I believe, we are surprised by the transformation of impossibility into possibility.

# TOWARD A MORE FLEXIBLE MONOGAMY

Raymond Lawrence

There is no denying that traditional marriage is in trouble. It is an institution that has been asked to carry more weight than it can bear. Persons have been reared to expect that such a marriage will satisfy all their needs for deep intimacy in human relationships. But these expectations do not

Reprinted by permission from the March 18, 1974 issue of *Christianity and Crisis.* Copyright © 1974 by Christianity and Crisis, Inc. Raymond Lawrence is Chaplain and Director of Clinical Pastoral Education at St. Luke's Episcopal Hospital in Houston.

seem to be met in the vast majority of marriages. Furthermore, the prime values of traditional marriage are security and predictability. But we are living at a time when the need to realize one's full possibilities as a person is being rediscovered. Openness to one's potential often involves spontaneity and the stimulation of a variety of human relationships. For many today the security and predictability that traditional marriage provides hinder this openness.

The time has come to begin serious public conversation about the validity of the popular and traditional notions of marriage. Permanence and sexual exclusiveness—for generations the hallmarks of the institution of marriage—have in recent decades been challenged openly and publicly. The divorce rate is escalating and the aura of shame that in the past surrounded divorce and remarriage is evaporating rapidly. . . .

So we are living in a time when alternatives to traditional monogamy are shaping up. The most prevalent alternative is the increasing practice of serial polygamy, the contracting of one marriage after another. Here one's needs for stimulation and variety can be met. But what is lost is the value of a continuing lifelong relationship.

My own theoretical bias is that the *permanence* of marriage is to be more greatly valued than its exclusiveness. This runs counter to the popular wisdom that generally attaches more shame to an affair than to a separation. Nevertheless, my clinical impression from years of working professionally with troubled marriages leads me to conclude that people with nonexclusive marriages generally are more successful in maintaining a variety of relationships than those who choose a life of serial polygamy. An affair brings people together. Divorce separates. In the long run it is better that people come together, although for certain seasons separation is an important value too. It is my conclusion that the permanence of some relationships can be enhanced by the abandonment of their exclusive character.

## ENLARGING COMMITMENT

One form of marriage today attempts to hold to both the value of lifelong commitment between two persons and the value of the stimulation that can come from a variety of multiple intimate relationships. Dr. Robert Francoeur of Fairleigh-Dickinson University suggests that this new marital form be called flexible monogamy.

Flexible monogamy is different from traditional monogamy on one main issue. The latter is an *exclusive* genital sexual relationship, while the former is a *primary* genital sexual relationship. Exclusive relationships do have advantages. They provide a measure of security and predictability that cannot be achieved any other way. But in so doing they sacrifice the stimulation of the new. A primary relationship, on the other hand, is one in which two persons give to each other their first loyalty, while permitting each other the relative freedom to search for and explore other relationships, even to the point of genital sexual intimacy.

On one level flexible monogamy is not new. When I began my career as a clergyman 14 years ago, my most startling task, and the one for which I felt least prepared by my training, was that of working with married persons struggling with the problem of extramarital relationships. However, though extramarital sex is not new, what is new is the increasing evidence that extramarital sex may be openly and contractually integrated into a marriage with creative and positive results. So integrated, it becomes both legitimized and less threatening because it holds a subordinate position to the marriage.

Within traditional monogamy extramarital sex is usually experienced as a bid to supplant the existing marriage with a new one. Statistically, however, an affair that disrupts a marriage does not usually develop into a marriage. Nevertheless, the threat of being supplanted is often experienced because a relationship that contracts to be total or exclusive cannot, by definition, incorporate the competition of even a minor satellite. It must remain total or be disrupted. I have heard many a spouse complain that his or her marriage partner could not tolerate gracefully any appreciation of another person. On the other hand, a marriage contract that espouses a primary loyalty rather than an exclusive allegiance will permit a satellite relationship, so long as the primacy of the original relationship is maintained. Even though we might not want to project a subordinate-primary model as ideal, flexible monogamy provides at least a strategy for loosening some of the binds of traditional marriage.

I have seen numerous affairs that have been largely destructive, either in their intent or in their results. I have known women who got themselves pregnant in order to take revenge against their husbands. I have known men who sought to estrange a lover from her husband just to prove their masculine prowess.

Much has been written by therapists and ministers about the ways in which extramarital sex is used as a destructive device. But if we are going to be faithful to human life and experience, it is incumbent upon us to make something more than a categorical response to those choosing a more flexible marriage contract. It is time that we establish the bench marks for extramarital sex.

An affair engaged in for an ulterior purpose, for example, to "do something to one's spouse," whether or not he or she becomes aware of it, is an unfaithful act. It is a relationship engaged in not for its own sake but for an ulterior purpose, and as such it is not authentic. A faithful affair is one engaged in for its own sake, where one seeks neither to hurt nor to please any other person but rather to participate in the existence and being of oneself and the other.

Just as the decision in favor of an affair may be made for inappropriate reasons, so may the refusal of an affair. Many persons avoid an affair out of a desire for innocence, others because of extreme dependency feelings or a failure to achieve autonomy. These attitudes are appropriate to young children, and obviously many adults remain children in their psychosexual development.

## THE LONGING FOR INNOCENCE

The need to feel innocent may be the most underestimated intrapersonal dynamic in human relationships. Relatively immature persons need to feel innocent in direct proportion to their lack of maturity. The process of fulfilling one's sexual potential is for many a continuing story of the loss of "innocence." I recall an adolescent boy named Roger who felt the necessity of confessing his acts of masturbation to his parents. His parents at first thought that this was commendable. But, in fact, it was dynamically a regressive development.

Roger's confession was a striving to regain his lost "innocence" in relation to his parental world. It was a step backwards in his psychosexual development. In counseling Roger I tried to help him develop more independence, or even an interim counterdependence. My hope was that he would become autonomous enough to bear his own guilt feelings rather than to take flight to a childlike "innocence." The more spiritually mature one is, the more one is capable of embracing "alien" elements.

Many married persons struggle with their own sexuality in ways similar to Roger. For many the principal deterrent to an affair is the overriding need to feel "innocent." What surprises me is the frequency with which this dynamic is at work in a marriage even when the "other" has already revealed an affair.

The need to feel "innocent," then, is not necessarily lessened by the revealed "guilt" of one's spouse. I have often met a husband or wife who quite sincerely, but secretly, wished his or her spouse would have an affair in order to reset a balance of power or in order to equalize the relationship. Few interpersonal problems are more difficult to resolve than the negotiation between the "innocent" and the "guilty" partner. The clinging to "innocence" may be childishness, and "innocence" itself may even be a "filthy rag," but "innocent" persons cling to their supposed virtue with great tenacity.

The need to feel "innocent" often creates another common problem: the compulsion to confess abruptly one's sexual adventures. What typically happens in such cases is that the one who confesses becomes the target of anger or hostility or feels ashamed. He or she may then experience punishment and as a result feel "cleansed" and, in a sense, restored to "innocence."

This is a neurotic pattern derived from the failure to experience enough grace to enable one to bear the responsibility of choice. We may choose to suffer and perhaps even to die in order to pay for the necessity to choose. Or we may find at the heart of life enough grace to accept our responsibility. In this world the fall of Man (Adam) is a fall upward. The land east of Eden where Man lives may be full of sorrow and toil, but joys are to be found there too. And who would return to the land of innocence? A sign of the spiritually mature person is that he or she no longer needs to pay for his or her loss of "innocence." Such a person is the second Adam. It is to this that we are called.

## THE FAILURE TO ACHIEVE AUTONOMY

A common misconception in marriage folklore is that real intimacy means full disclosure of one's thoughts, feelings, and actions. I contend that total openness is a naive form of dependency and not a true form of intimacy. It is also an oppressive and smothering goal. Real intimacy is experienced in the rhythmical movement toward and away from another person. It is experienced only when persons have the capacity and wisdom both to give and to withhold. One who cannot be distant destroys the value of his or her being close. One who cannot be close negates the value of his or her distance. Most marriages need both more closeness and more distance, each in its own time.

One dynamic of those who have affairs is that they are no longer in the comfortable position of being able to "tell all." Full disclosure to one's spouse becomes much more problematic than among the traditionally monogamous. A satellite relationship does not lend itself to supper-table conversation or pillow talk. I have found it to be almost invariably true that married persons do not want to hear any of the details of their spouse's exploits. An unusually articulate counselee of mine put it this way:

> Just before Jackie and I were married, I told her about all the sexual experiences I had had before I met her. Of course I was young then, and there wasn't a lot to tell, but I somehow felt like I owed it to her to tell her everything. It was sort of like cleaning the slate. . . . It kind of surprised me several years later when I found out from her that these revelations made her angry. . . . Now in the past year, after having gotten involved with Barbara, I still sometimes feel the need of telling Jackie everything. It's sort of like I want her to know everything I have done. I am not sure whether this is because I am seeking her approval or whether I simply want to share with her everything that is important to me. Perhaps both. But since I have been talking to you, I think I have finally discovered that it is okay to have

secrets..., secrets are necessary to my being a man. It is like they are part of my manhood. And I think to tell her everything is sort of like treating her as if she is my mother.

One limitation of an affair is that the joy of it usually does not lend itself to sharing with one's spouse.

An inhibiting dynamic to extramarital sex for many, then, lies in the distaste for the distance or the withholding that is necessary in relation to one's spouse. It goes without saying that these same persons likely lack genuine intimacy in their marriages as well. In fact, it is certainly true that a significant number of marriages today could be described as mutually oppressive and clinging dependency relationships.

I remember one counselee complaining that he was becoming impotent with his wife. He had developed an inability to maintain an erection. In the course of our conversation it emerged that he had developed some very deep feelings for a colleague. He had never touched his new friend, but nevertheless his conflicted feelings were quite powerful. He felt terribly guilty even for having such feelings, particularly when he was about to have intercourse with his wife. This illustrates a rather extreme example of clinging dependency.

## FLEXIBLE MONOGAMY: A CASE HISTORY

Ed and Marjorie have been married for 16 years, since they were 20 and in college. Ed is a successful attorney; Marjorie has worked only in the past five years—as a receptionist. They have four children, the oldest is 15 and the youngest seven. Both are gregarious people who mix well and like to socialize. They are significantly involved in many social, religious, artistic, and political activities. Their 16 years of marriage can be separated into four phases.

### Phase 1

Both Ed and Majorie are cautious, thoughtful people by disposition and upbringing; in many respects they might even be described as conservative. Both went into marriage as technical "virgins," though both had had considerable foreplay experience both together and with others. The first seven years of marriage were quite traditional. Each felt attracted to numerous other persons along the way, sometimes even feeling almost "driven crazy" by desire, and each of them confessed to a rather active fantasy life. But they contained these fantasies.

During this period Marjorie experienced considerably more anxiety about her desire for other experiences than Ed did. A typical pattern of events would find Marjorie angry with Ed on the way home from a cocktail party because of his flirtatious behavior toward women at the party. Though she had usually drawn ample attention herself, she was less tolerant and accepting of her own sexual feelings than was Ed, and she focused her anger on him. These years were marked by a repetitious pattern of open flirting by Ed and of Marjorie's jealousy and accusation, followed by periods of reconciliation.

## Phase 2

Marjorie's anger tended to accumulate during phase one. As a result, in the 8th year she entered into an affair. This man eventually asked her to leave Ed and marry him. Though she came close to making such a decision, she was never able to abandon her marriage. Marjorie's affair seems to have been designed largely to pay Ed back for his overtures toward other women. Predictably, she managed to be discovered by leaving an implicating note where Ed was bound to find it.

The next four years were critical ones. Marjorie was forced to choose between Ed and her new lover. Ed demanded this either/or decision, and Marjorie decided to recommit herself to her marriage. But she experienced a considerable amount of grief over the loss of her friend. She often wondered if she had made the best choice, and she frequently found herself hating Ed for forcing such a decision.

Ed did not retaliate by involving himself sexually with anyone else. This was a period of shock and defeat for him, and he did not have enough confidence during this period to manage an affair. His predominant feeling was that he had failed as a man. As a result, the relationship deteriorated. Marjorie had two more affairs and was again tempted to dissolve her marriage. Ed became aware of one of them and felt even more like a failure and became more depressed. At times he bordered on being suicidal.

## Phase 3

During the 12th year of marriage Ed met and fell in love with Cheryl, a young divorcee with one child. They developed a deeply personal and intimate relationship, which they maintained rather intensely for about 18 months. Cheryl was willing to marry should Ed abandon his marriage, and he seriously considered it. But he decided to continue to work at his marriage because he still loved his wife also. The deciding factor was his expectation of having to face the same issues of intimacy, fidelity, and the meaning of a marriage contract with Cheryl, and there did not seem to be enough of a difference between the two women to make a divorce and remarriage worthwhile.

Ed's involvement with Cheryl was a major turning point. Though he did not enter the affair to reestablish his sense of self-esteem, that was a major by-product. He put it this way:

It was like a whole new life was open to me. You know, I fought against sexual intimacy with any other woman for so long, even though I knew my wife had cheated on me a couple of times. . . . I think I was afraid to risk losing my marriage, and that's why I never got involved in spite of all that she had done. I was simply scared of losing her, to tell you the truth. But once I had cut the cord, so to speak, once I did it, I really felt like I was a new man.

## Phase 4

From this point on I observed the end of gradual deterioration and the beginning of a healing process. Ed was now ready to negotiate a new contract with Marjorie, who had been ready to do this for some time. As they sat down with me to do so, several significant matters emerged:

1. Both wanted the freedom to have other, including sexual, relationships. And each wanted the other to have this freedom.
2. Both seemed to love and respect the other deeply. Each expressed a strong need to be held in primacy. In other words, each wanted to be considered the primary friend of the other. And each had some very concrete notions about what a primary loyalty would mean.
3. Both insisted that they not be accountable to each other for all of their time, nor for all their outside relationships. Up to this point Ed had always made excuses about going to the office, for example, whenever he wanted to see Cheryl in the evening. Now each was willing to grant the other the prerogative of "going out" in the evening or "being away" over a week-end.
4. Both agreed not to dissimulate to cover their activities.
5. Neither desired to hear about the other's activities, although each of them did want to know generally about the persons with whom the other was having a relationship.

## HARBINGER OF NEW MARRIAGE PATTERNS

In agreeing to these five points, Ed and Marjorie contracted a form of flexible monogamy. How has it worked? After more than three years, they claim to be happier than ever before.

"We could never go back to traditional monogamy, nor would we ever want to," said Marjorie. There have been difficult times, however. Inviting some of Ed's friends to dinner, Marjorie would sometimes find herself fantasizing about the possibility of one of the women as a sexual partner to Ed. And it is more difficult for Ed to accept Marjorie's "going out" in the evening or "being away" than it is for Marjorie to accept his. Ed's fears of abandonment seems more deeply rooted than Marjorie's. I suspect that this is, at least in part, a cultural product, a result of the double standard.

I am favorably impressed with the contract Ed and Marjorie made for themselves. I am also favorably impressed with the quality of their relationship. The evidence of respect and love they have for each other is substantial. Although they seem to share a high degree of intimacy, there is a relative absence of the possessiveness and clinging dependency that characterizes so many marriages. Their marriage is no longer an exclusive relationship, but they seem to have a strong primary loyalty to each other. And this is the cornerstone of their marriage. They have chosen an unorthodox form of marriage, to be sure. Those who think that orthodox patterns are adequate for anyone who attempts to live fully will find their flexible monogamy a spurious venture. But it is my hunch that their unorthodoxy will be for some a harbinger of a more satisfactory way of understanding marriage in the years ahead.

There is no question that something serious is happening to the institution of marriage. Traditional monogamy has lost its credibility as the only way for heterosexual social organization. It is by no means about to disappear, but it will most certainly have to compete with other forms. The challenge that faces clergymen and others who counsel persons struggling with the issues of human existence is that of evaluating these emerging patterns of life with an open mind. It is not enough to parrot the orthodoxy of the past. It is a more complex task to struggle with the present and attempt to test the value of new and unanticipated social phenomena.

# The Family Under Stress: A Crisis of Purpose

## Herbert Anderson

### THE FAMILY: AN INSTITUTION UNDER STRESS

In January of 1970, Russell Baker entitled one of his columns "The State of the Family Message." In that essay, Baker outlined issues facing the family. He began this way:

Herbert Anderson is Associate Professor of Pastoral Theology and Counseling at Wartburg Theological Seminary in Dubuque, Iowa. He has published several articles in the areas of human sexuality, loss and grief, and family systems theory.

The family being all assembled in the parlor for the annual occasion, Great Mortgaged Father entered the chamber, took his place at the hearth and spoke as follows:

"Madam Wife, Minister Grandfather, members of the Younger generation, distinguished cats and tropical fish:

Occasionally there comes a time when profound and far-reaching events command a break with tradition in the style of the State of the Family Address. This is such a time.

I say this not only because 1970 marks the beginning of a decade in which the entire family may well die of its own environment unless visionary measures are taken. I say it because the most casual glance about the house as well as hard experience argue persuasively that both our programs and our habits need to be reformed.

Quiet air, clean bathrooms, uncluttered hallways, neatly packed garbage cans, these should once again be the birthright of every member of this family. Accordingly, the program I propose today is the most comprehensive design for improving family environment that I have ever put before you."[1]

The address goes on to call for an end to clusters of dog hair on clothes, hotdogs with everything in the glove compartment, mashed bananas and peanut butter on the television screen, and aging grease behind the stove. It is a delightful spoof on how family environment is polluted.

We are all aware of more complicated issues facing the family today than dog hair, hotdogs in the glove compartment, or fungus on the phonograph. Changing social patterns prompted by industrialization, urbanization, increased mobility, inflationary economics, mass media, and new work habits have deeply affected the family. Traditional roles and values that previously undergirded family life continue to be in ferment. Wife-beating and child abuse are more evident. So are violent acts of children against their parents. The rate of divorce continues to increase. Illegitimacy has more than doubled in the past three decades. One out of every six children lives with a single parent. Every year at least one million children run away from home. The topic of conversation in social gatherings often concerns troubled adolescents or underachieving children of unfulfilled wives or bewildered husbands or a letter from a friend announcing one more surprising divorce or aging parents unwilling to let their children go. This familiar litany of family struggle and tragedy is not limited to the poor and the nonwhite. It involves families of all social strata.

It is often said that living in a family is difficult these days. But then it has never been easy, human nature being what it is. We like to think that our crises are unique and that the family has never been under such stress. We romanticize the time when the stress came from outside rather than inside the family. We think we would rather deal with raiding Indians or

[1]Russell Baker, "The State of the Family Message." *The New York Times,* January 25, 1970.

plagues of locusts than peanut butter on the television screen or aging grease behind the stove. Nonetheless, internal stress, delinquency, and familial disaffection have always been present in the family. One only needs to read the Bible to discover that marital deceit, sibling rivalry, incest, abusive husbands and parents, and family violence are not inventions of the twentieth century. The family has always been an institution under stress.

If this is so, then it is more important for us to determine the particular crises of our time. It is relatively easy to think about those crises simply in terms of the frequency of divorce or the disintegration of family structure. While the statistical evidence related to divorce and other signs of particular family distress seem overwhelming, there are four more fundamental ways of identifying stress on the family today: the crises of values, of competence, of perspective, and of purpose. While each of these crises is significant, it is my judgment that the crisis of purpose is critical for the survival of the family and the future of generations.

## The Crisis of Values

One of the factors contributing to family stress is the crisis of *values.* There is a great deal of turmoil and change in every corner of society. The 60s and 70s have been a time of unmistakable transition in values. Social "anomie" or normlessness are common. In one sense, the family's trouble in our time is a microcosm of a larger cultural malaise. This confusion of values and the absence of a moral consensus in the larger society have created uncertainty in the family. Parents who are bewildered by the disjunction between their values and those of their children are often tentative in discipline.

At other times they become rigid and inflexible out of impotence and fear, insisting on their own moral standards in a way that renders them even more ineffective with their children. Parents often give inordinate power to their children in order to avoid painful confrontations. As a result, they feel powerless in the face of peer pressure and the pluralism of values. They cannot count on the support of a common system of values and common institutions which provide meaning and support personal significance. And so the family is overburdened by the weight of a moral and spiritual load it simply cannot bear alone.

## The Crisis of Competence

The family is also facing a crisis of *competence.* With industrialization, production was removed from the household, collectivized, and then put under the supervision of the factory. The emergence of the factory system has meant that childrearing functions have also become the task of the larger society rather than the family. We have gradually transferred the responsibility for raising our children from the family to such social agencies as school, church, and recreation groups.

This shift has in part been accomplished by well-meaning social experts who have declared parents incompetent to raise their offspring without professional help.[2] As a result, parents who would like to do what is best for their children have lost confidence in their ability to perform ordinary functions of childrearing. They cannot determine and maintain consistent curfew schedules. They feel powerless to assign their children household tasks or responsibilities. They are insecure and therefore ineffective in simple parenting tasks.

It is difficult to determine whether the crisis of competence began because parents abdicated their responsibilities or because social technologists assumed parental tasks. No doubt both are true. Adults who are bewildered by parenting tasks and terrified by their own children are sometimes desperate for help. Undoubtedly, many families have learned techniques from programs such as Parent Effectiveness Training that have been helpful in childrearing. Moreover, it is neither possible nor desirable to turn back the clock, shut off the TV, close down the public schools, disband the scout troops, and eliminate all agencies of health or welfare that work for the improvement of human life. And yet we need to ask whether the cure is worse than the disease. We need to be cautious about developing a technology of parenting and a cadre of experts who market those techniques that diminish a family's sense of competence under the guise of humanizing the family.

The crisis of competence raises serious ethical questions of responsibility for childrearing. The sex education of children illustrates the complexity of the problem. Anxieties and taboos about sex have silenced centuries of parents. Educators and family planners filled that gap created by parental awkwardness and ignorance, and they did it with the blessing of parents. Now parents are claiming that sex experts and Planned Parenthood professionals have developed programs and fostered values that undermine the family.

It is a delicate sequence. On the matter of sex education, experts did not just usurp the parental role. Parents gave it up, thus initiating what has become a destructive cycle. Parents do not meet their own expectations for parenting. The social technology that emerges because of that failure further erodes confidence and leads families to be even more tentative about childrearing. And this in turn confirms the assessment of social scientists that parents are not competent. And that in turn generates more programs and agencies intent on helping the family.

[2]Christopher Lasch, *Haven in a Heartless World* (New York: Basic Books, Inc., 1977), p. 18.

## The Crisis of Perspective

The third crisis in the family is one of *perspective.* Since it is increasingly society rather than the family that has primary responsibility for the socialization of its young, the family has no inherent reason to give much attention to the needs of the next generation. Guaranteeing the wellbeing of another generation is regarded as the responsibility of the larger society. As a result of this shift, the forecast of Bertrand Russell has proven accurate: "Sexual love has become trivial, there is a shallowness in personal relations, and it is far more difficult to take an interest in anything after one's death."[3] The absence of a perspective that orients toward the future is a fundamental crisis for the family.

It is not difficult to see how this absence of interest in the future has made it possible for the family to regard itself as a refuge from the world. Because the family is not responsible for future generations, it can be preoccupied with the immediate gratification of emotional needs. No longer needed for production and socialized by the larger society, children are considered an intrusion into the family. The evidence for this loss of future perspective is considerable. "The modern parent's attempt to make children feel loved and wanted does not conceal an underlying coolness—the remoteness of those who have little to pass on to the next generation and who in any case give priority to their own right to selffulfillment."[4] There is a growing segment of society that not only neglects and fears children, but regards them as a nuisance to personal freedom and satisfaction. Such lack of future-orientedness and absence of responsibility for the sequence of generations is what prompts the bizarre action of the couple who attempted to trade their baby for a sports car.

A recently married couple, neither of whom had custody of their chidren from a previous marriage, sought counseling because they could not manage their children when they came every other weekend for a visit. They scheduled those visits together so they could have two weekends per month "for themselves." Both partners wanted to create a new merged family when their children visited and yet both of them treated their own children (all under the age of 11) as guests rather than as their children. Each parent was angry because his or her children were not appropriately grateful. The resentment this couple felt toward their own children for not responding properly to being entertained illustrates this thinly veiled parental detachment. Any recovery of a future perspective will require an emotional commitment on the part of parents to their children, which Urie Bronfenbrenner has called "being crazy about kids."

[3]Bertrand Russell, quoted in *Culture of Narcissism,* by Christopher Lasch (New York: W. W. Norton & Company, 1979), p. 187.

[4]Christopher Lasch, "Narcissist America," *New York Review of Books,* XXIII, 115 (September 30, 1976), p. 12.

## The Crisis of Purpose

This crisis of perspective is linked to an erosion of *purpose,* the fourth and most fundamental crisis facing the family today. The family's purpose is no longer manifestly clear. Stripped of its responsibility for production and for reproduction, the family has made itself into a private shelter, a place of refuge from the world. This privatization of the family is a self-defeating effort to discover a purpose for the family in the face of a highly urbanized, highly industrialized, highly technologized society. It is self-defeating because if the family continues to turn inward on itself, it may very well "die of its own environment," as Russell Baker has suggested. It does not have a way out of itself. The privatization of the family can only lead to an emotional incest that is self-destructive.

This crisis of purpose makes it difficult to be critical of all the well-meaning programs available in the marketplace of both church and society that promise to save the family. However, most of these programs do not address the question, "For what purpose shall the family be saved?" Either they assume a self-evident purpose or endorse a traditional design. Therefore it is necessary that the question of purpose be addressed so that efforts to rescue the family do not resemble saving the baseball team in order to keep the hotdog concession going. I mention this not to foreclose exploration of genuine alternatives for the family's future but to caution against running after simplistic solutions. The bumper-sticker approach to saving the family is not enough.

Reconsidering the purpose of the family is at the same time a complex process today because defining the family has become a highly charged political issue. The ideal family of two parents, two kids and one wage earner is still sacrosanct. It conjures up visions of God, stability and apple pie. The ideal, however, is less and less the norm. Therefore, the definition of family needs to be flexible enough to allow for the variety of familial forms and relationships without rendering the concept meaningless. For our purposes, the family is understood as a kinship system of two or more persons involving a commitment in time. It should be remembered that we are presupposing a society in which industrialization has occurred and in which the family as a unit is not confronted with physical survival as its immediate, fundamental task.

## LEARNING TO BE SEPARATE TOGETHER: THE PRIMARY PURPOSE OF THE FAMILY

Despite the erosion of its authority, influence and competence, there are still people who regard the family as the fundamental cell in society. The purpose of the family is to maintain social stability. Proponents of this position argue that whatever strengthens the family strengthens society.

If all is well with the family, then life in the society is worth living because the family is the most potent moral, intellectual, and political unit in the body politic.

There is truth in this position, but it should not be overstated because the place of family in the larger society has become more ambiguous. Although in many ways the family continues to have social significance, it is a bulwark of society more in memory than in fact. It is no longer the seat of civic virtue. The privatization of the family and its isolation from society has diminished its centrality in the social order. Because the family has become a refuge *from* society rather than a fundamental unit *in* society its role as social stabilizer is diminished.

Another traditional understanding of the purpose of the family is that of socializing its young. It is generally agreed that socialization has been a primary function of the family and to a less exclusive degree still is. It is the place where we learn to live with others. The family is to be a laboratory for life and a schoolhouse for society. It is the context in which we are first schooled in the art of group living. We learn about sharing and responsibility and are exposed to the rules and roles that sustain community.

However, church and school have participated in this process for some time. More recently other agencies or institutions in society have emerged that share in that process of learning to live in community. Because other agencies in society have been given and have assumed responsibility for socialization, it can no longer be regarded as the central purpose of the family. Even though for some the family is still the primary agent of socialization, it is not enough to determine the family's purpose.

Despite the changes that have occurred in society diminishing the family's influence, social stabilization and socialization *are* necessary purposes. Future generations depend on a stable social order that is supported by stable subunits within society such as the church and the family. Individuals do need to learn how to participate in larger communities and structures. The family is usually an individual's primary experience of community life. Social stabilization and socialization are both necessary purposes of the family for maintaining a dependable society but they are not enough. For our time it is also important to consider that the family exists for the individual as well as the larger community. The purpose of the family is to provide a context for individual growth in the midst of community. In order to keep a balance between individual and community, between individuation and socialization, it seems best to define the purpose of the family as enabling people *to be separate together*. Being separate together means that personal distinctiveness and selfhood are preserved in family interaction. Being separate together means maintaining the tension between developing one's individual uniqueness and participating in significant human community. Being separate together has as its goal autonomous individuals who are commited to participation in family and in larger social units in order to create new settings in which individual growth might continue to flourish. Being separate together means that one can stand to be alone even in the midst of others. Being separate selves capable of being together with other separate selves is necessary for a vital society that celebrates diversity and honors community.

This process of self-definition, or claiming our own unique personhood, is called individuation. It has to do with developing autonomy, becoming free to differ, valuing one's own worth, claiming that my thoughts, feelings, wishes, fantasies are valid because they are my own. Individuation means that I am comfortable with "I-statements." It means that my body is my own, to cherish, nourish, and use responsibly.

Becoming a separate and distinct person, capable of autonomous action —capable of having feelings, ideas, thoughts, dreams that are one's own —is the goal of individuation. And being individuated is necessary for community. To be an autonomous person is not the same as being independent. Identity precedes community. At the same time, becoming a separate and distinct person can only occur in the context of communities that love and let go. Whatever other changes have occurred in terms of the structure and purpose of the family in relation to the larger society, the family remains the primary locus of individuation.

Becoming a separate person capable of participation with others is ordinarily a life-long task. As we grow up our physical survival depends less and less on our parents. We learn to walk, cross the street, talk, go to school, take care of ourselves more and more. If, however, we continue to depend on our parents for self-definition and self-esteem, the process of individuation is tarnished. We spend time and energy seeking their approval, living up to their expectations, worrying whether our feelings are acceptable or the decision we made was right, and failing through it all to gain a sense of our autonomy. We may reach physical maturity well socialized and eager to accommodate others and still not be individuated. Cutting loose from the emotional mooring of our infancy is a life-long process that is in the interest of self-definition. That process of separation is inescapable to the beginning of life. The family is the primary context in which separation occurs in the interest of individuation.

Being separate together in family requires delicate balancing of being together in community and being separate as individuals. This dialectic has been summarized well by Napier and Whitaker in *The Family Crucible:*

> The family's capacity to be intimate and caring and their capacity to be separate and divergent increase in careful synchrony. People can't risk being close unless they have the ability to be separate. It's too frightening to be

deeply involved if you aren't sure you can be separate and stand on your own. They also can't risk being truly divergent and separate if they are unable to count on a residual warmth and caring to keep them together. The more forceful and independent they become, the easier it is to risk being intimate and close. The more closeness, the easier it is to risk independence.[5]

Personhood presupposes community. This means that to become a separate individual one must first be connected with others. And at the same time, the possibility of community presupposes being separate. There is no intimacy without identity. Separateness and togetherness are organically interrelated.

## ANTHROPOLOGY AND ETHICS: THE INDIVIDUAL AND THE FAMILY

There are several implications of this paradigm of being separate together. First of all, the family is not always more important than the individual. If social stabilization were indeed the sole purpose of the family, then accommodation should be from the individual to the family and from the family to the larger society. That has been a common pattern in the past. It is not so long ago that the decision of a grown child to leave home to go to school or get married was largely determined by the needs of the family as a unit of production. We have generally regarded such necessary action as sacrificial when in fact it was frequently based on economic necessity.

Being separate together assumes that each person is a unique creature of God and therefore it is important for everyone to have freedom to develop his or her gifts. Most of the time, commitment to community does not exclude freedom for personal growth. As a matter of fact, the community benefits from the growth of its members. Sometimes the conflict between the individual and family is more perceived than real. At other times, however, there are agonizing choices that people must make between personal development and belonging to a community like the family. Acknowledging the work of individuals means that the larger unit of family or society does not always have primacy over individual needs. Rather it means that autonomy and one's community are both valued.

The second assumption challenged by the paradigm of being separate together in family is an anthropological one. The understanding of human nature which seems to undergird socialization as the family's primary purpose is that we are naturally anti-social creatures bent on "looking out

[5]Augustus Napier and Carl Whitaker, *The Family Crucible* (New York: Harper & Row, 1978), p. 93.

for number one." Given this presupposition it is not surprising that we have regarded the tasks of the family as the primary childrearing agency to curtail egocentrism, socialize the impulsive savage, and help solidify the structures that keep our self-oriented impulses in line. Under this rubric the family has the responsibility of breaking down self-centeredness so that we will be sufficiently committed to community.

The focus on individuation within the family presupposes that human beings are also naturally disposed toward community. From the beginning of life, we are fragile, dependent creatures. Early attachments that make our survival possible are so long and so powerful that being connected together is as natural as being separate. Attachment is more than survival. Alfred Adler is not too optimistic when he suggests that human beings are by nature community-minded (*Gemeinschaftsgefühl*). The fear that any promotion of individual uniqueness and worth will lead to rampant self-centeredness and denial of community is based on a narrow anthropology. Being alive means being connected. Being together is as natural as being separate. The difficulty arises in keeping those two foci in balance.

## The Sin of Too Much Togetherness

The reality of selfishness in human life is indeed one manifestation of sin. It is personally destructive and socially disruptive for an individual not to outgrow the necessary self-mindedness of infancy. Being preoccupied with one's self is neither socially desirable nor ethically responsible. However, the failure to claim one's own distinctiveness in favor of excessive togetherness is also sin. Always choosing for the community or denying the necessary process of individuation for the sake of being together is an inappropriate denial of self. This duality of sin as self-assertion and self-negation is parallel to the struggle within the family for ways to be separate together.

Being too separate ends in self-deification. From that perspective, self-justification, alienation, or dominating self-assertion are the central images of sin. If social stabilization and socialization are regarded as the primary purposes of the family, then self-assertion is the dominant image for sin. Being too much together, however, ends in deification of the family and self-negation. The self is underdeveloped and personal gifts are not fully actualized. Triviality, distractibility, diffusiveness, lack of an organizing center, dependence on others for self-definition are all sins of self-negation. Commonly they are the consequence of too much togetherness and not enough separateness. I am suggesting that inadequate individuation is as sinful as faulty socialization. Being separate together is an image of the family that may provide a hedge against both self-deification and self-negation.

Individuation leads to self-definition rather than self-deification. It has to do with developing autonomy, becoming free to differ, valuing one's own work, claiming the validity of thoughts, feelings, wishes, and fantasies because they are one's own. The question of autonomy is at the heart of all struggle for human dignity. In response to a growing sense of powerlessness and helplessness in a faceless technologized society, Christian theology needs to find new ways of respecting human agency. Fostering individuation toward autonomy may be one way. That would include recognizing that the central purpose of the family is to create the context in which that growth toward autonomy might best occur.

## SUMMARY

The suggestion that "being separate together" is the central purpose of the family does not immediately resolve the crises of the family today. It will continue to be difficult for families to promote their own values because of the absence of a moral consensus. There will still be a gap between generations. If, however, families could learn to live with the diversity that is an inevitable result of promoting individual growth, then finding ways to live with pluralism would be enhanced. In order to survive, any family needs to be adaptable. The crisis of competence is not readily resolved because it is in part a consequence of unrealistic expectations of the family. Because there are so many agencies in society concerned about fostering social stability and implementing the socialization process, the family may always regard itself as incompetent unless its purpose is clear. Individuation remains the one task allotted to the family that is not done by any other social institution. It is therefore mandatory that the family at least be a community that nourishes individual growth.

The crises of purpose and perspective are interwoven. Ultimately the family's purpose must be linked to the continuation of the species. The family does not exist for its own sake. People do not live together merely to be together. They live together to do something by themselves or together. Even the family's purpose of fostering individuation is qualified by a perspective that is committed to the future. At least until some other arrangement is determined, no other agency of society is responsible for the future of generations. Privatizing or even glorifying the family strips it of its moral function. At minimum the family is responsible for teaching people how to live individually together in order that another generation will be prepared for the ongoing care and nurture of the human species.

# SUGGESTIONS FOR FURTHER READING FOR PART TWO

## Chapter 3: Perspectives on Sexuality

Barnhouse, Ruth Tiffany, and Urban T. Holmes, eds. *Male and Female: Christian Approaches to Sexuality*. New York: Seabury Press, 1976.

Francoeur, Anna K., and Robert T. Francoeuer. *Hot and Cool Sex: Cultures in Conflict*. New York: Harcourt Brace Jovanovich, 1974.

Kosnik, Anthony, *et al. Human Sexuality: New Directions in American Catholic Thought*. New York: Paulist Press, 1977.

Morrison, Eleanor S., and Vera Borosage, eds. *Human Sexuality: Contemporary Perspectives* (2nd ed.). Palo Alto, Calif.: Mayfield, 1977.

Nelson, James B. *Embodiment: An Approach to Sexuality and Christian Theology*. Minneapolis: Augsburg Publishing House, 1979.

Phipps, William E. *Recovering Biblical Sensuousness*. Philadelphia: Westminster Press, 1975.

Small, Dwight Hervey. *Christian, Celebrate Your Sexuality*. Old Tappan, N. J.: Revell, 1974.

## Chapter 4: The Morality of Sexual Relationships

Francoeur, Anna K., and Robert T. Francoeur, eds. *The Future of Sexual Relations*. Englewood Cliffs, N.J.: Prentice-Hall, 1974.

Hettlinger, Richard F. *Sex Isn't That Simple*. New York: Seabury Press, 1974.

Masters, William H., and Virginia E. Johnson, with Robert J. Levin. *The Pleasure Bond: A New Look at Sexuality and Commitment*. Boston: Little, Brown, 1975.

Gordon, Sol, and Roger W. Libby, eds. *Sexuality, Today and Tomorrow: Contemporary Issues in Human Sexuality*. North Scituate, Mass.: Duxbury Press, 1976.

Smedes, Lewis B. *Sex for Christians: The Limits and Liberties of Sexual Living*. Grand Rapids, Mich.: Eerdmans, 1976.

## Chapter 5: Marriage and the Family

Fullerton, Gail Pritney. *Survival in Marriage* (2nd ed.). New York: Holt, Rinehart and Winston, 1977.

Greeley, Andrew, ed. *The Family in Crisis or in Transition: A Sociological and Theological Perspective* (Concilium, 121). New York: Seabury Press, 1979.

Lasch, Christopher. *Haven in a Heartless World*. New York: Basic Books, 1979.

O'Neill, George, and Nena O'Neill. *Open Marriage: A New Life Style for Couples*. New York: M. Evans, 1972.

Smith, James R., and Lynn G. Smith, eds. *Beyond Monogamy: Recent Studies of Sexual Alternatives in Marriage*. Baltimore: The Johns Hopkins Press, 1974.

Thamm, Robert. *Beyond Marriage and the Nuclear Family*. New York: Canfield Press, 1975.

Voth, Harold M. *The Castrated Family*. Kansas City, Kans.: Sheed Andrews and McMeel, 1977.

# Part Three

# The Christian and Liberation Movements

# 6

# Racism: The Continuing Struggle

The importance of power in intergroup relationships has become increasingly apparent in recent decades. The civil rights movement of the 1950s and early 1960s attempted through legislative and judicial action to establish and safeguard the legal rights of minority groups. It became apparent, however, that such measures—important and necessary as they were and continue to be—could not guarantee to deliver what they promised. Even in a land proud of its government "of, by, and for the people," the stark fact is that if a group of people has no political and economic muscle of its own, its concerns and goals are very unlikely to be achieved. Recognition of the importance of power resulted in growing militancy on the part of minority groups. The "Black Power" movement was most obvious to white America because of the size and visibility of the Black minority and its consequent impact upon the life of the nation; but other minorities—notably Native Americans and Hispanic Americans—have also embarked on the quest for power.

By the end of the 1970s many white Americans—even those in progressive circles—were inclined to believe that major barriers in the struggle of minorities for their civil rights had been removed. The struggle against discrimination in housing, education, and employment had been essentially won through legislation and enforcement in the courts. While not denying that discrimination still occurs, many today feel that the substantive problems are economic rather than racist in origin. That is, minorities today are more likely to feel oppressed because of the structure and functioning of the American economy than because of systematic exploitation by white racism. The Black "underclass," it is maintained, is now suffering from socioeconomic factors, while the Black middle class has been liberated from this oppressive existence. This point of view has been most notably expressed by the University of Chicago sociologist William

127

Julius Wilson in his book *The Declining Significance of Race: Blacks and Chang- ing American Institutions* (1978).

This viewpoint is challenged by those who argue that in spite of the impressive gains, the status of a growing number of poorly trained minorities is actually worsening. The idea that racist attitudes are no longer a paramount factor is countered by reference to the present resurgence of hate groups such as the Ku Klux Klan. Even though many educated whites are too sophisticated to express blatantly racist attitudes, not far below the surface are prejudices that easily emerge in times of social stress. Thus, it is argued, racism is a continuing factor at every level of our society and should never be minimized. It leads to persistent resistance to the legal progress made in behalf of minority rights. With the current resurgence of conservatism and economic retrenchment, even members of the minority middle class find little reason to be optimistic.

In the selections in this chapter, attention is not focused on the moral and legal issues that have been in the forefront of the minority quest for equal rights, such as affirmative action or open housing. The concern here is rather to address the nature of racism as an individual and social phenomenon, to address it further from a Christian perspective, and to ask what can be done about it. The first selection is part of a document prepared by a Consultation to the World Council of Churches. It consisted of 19 participants from 11 different countries, with a variety of races represented. Racism is here regarded as a fact of deep and universal dimensions, calling for a concerted and sustained effort to combat it. The document is not defensive in behalf of the Christian church, but acknowl- edges significant Christian involvement in the problem and the need for repen- tance and action. It provides a good example of the self-critical spirit that many regard as inherent to Christian faith. The redefinition of discipleship in light of the pervasiveness of racism is particularly powerful—the constant effort of the church "to reconstitute itself in situations of real suffering, where suffering is the deepest expression of the struggle for human freedom and reconciliation."

This struggle for "freedom and reconciliation" is linked with the concept of power in the statement of the National Committee of Negro Churchmen (later to become the National Committee of Black Churchmen). Formulated in 1966, this statement stands as a classic document expressing a Christian response to the struggle for power on the part of the Black community. The statement was triggered by a concern over the growing polarization of Blacks and Whites in our society, and seeks to interpret power for Blacks in terms of their quest for identity, self-respect, and equality. If these elements are absent, then the goal of an integrated society will never be achieved.

These churchmen provide a theological and humanistic meaning for power; the "empowered" person can stand on his or her own feet, with the self-respect necessary to live a rewarding life. Historically, Christians have had difficulties in giving theological sanction to the concept of power, but in this statement a group of Christians whose life experience has been marked by the scars of prejudice and discrimination has provided us with a positive concept of power with obvious social implications. Black Power, for these clergy, is the power to be free from social bondage, which suffocates the spirit and threatens the avenues of human self-fulfillment. Their statement is marked by a desire to understand and reconcile the differences between persons of goodwill who seek to resolve the tensions among themselves. The ultimate goal of Black Power is an integrated society in which Blacks can participate as equals.

Will D. Campbell's article is eloquent in his portrayal of one of the most maligned groups in recent decades: the "poor whites," or "rednecks," of the South. These persons have been identified with racial bigotry, but Campbell argues that their powerlessness has made their impact on Black destiny less racist than the influence of the rest of us. A brief look at the rednecks' history provides us with some understanding of the attitudes we associate with them and reminds us that every graceless posture we see in various ethnic groups has its historical warrant—a fact that encourages our understanding rather than a judgment of simple rejection. One of the fascinating dimensions of this article is its depiction of the redneck mentality within the expression of biblical religion. The term "redneck" becomes a symbol for a life orientation that cannot be restricted to poor whites of the South. Campbell succeeds in holding up the redneck as a mirror: We look at him and see ourselves. All persons display attitudes shaped by the interests of the ethnic group of which they are members, and these attitudes can be destructive in their exclusiveness. Can liberation from narrow group interest and from the closed and bigoted outlook shaped by one's own self-interest occur? If so, how does it happen?

# Racism in Theology, Theology Against Racism

World Council of Churches

## THE UBIQUITY OF RACISM

Racism pervades our world today. Racial notions, prejudices, and fears are deeply rooted in the hearts and minds of human beings. In order to assess the full weight of these phenomena a brief look at the historical dimensions of racism is necessary. The history of racism in modern times begins with the African slave trade of the 16th and 17th centuries and the systematic extermination of the aboriginal people of the New World that accompanied it. At one period or another almost every nation in Europe profited from the traffic in African slaves and in North America chattel slavery became a basic institution of a powerful Protestant Christian society.

Following the suppression of the Atlantic slave trade in the 19th century the nations of Europe divided up Africa among themselves and by subterfuge and military conquest colonized the people and proceeded to exploit their land and labor to benefit the metropolitan centers of Europe. The people of India, Indonesia, and South-Eastern Asia were similarly dominated and exploited for European and American markets in the 19th and early 20th centuries.

In order to justify this massive expropriation of the wealth of black, brown, and yellow people, the myth of the superiority of the white race was used, sometimes explicitly, sometimes as a tacit presupposition. According to this myth the darker races of the world were held to be subhuman or innately inferior to all white people. They were divinely ordained to be "hewers of wood and drawers of water" for the Christian nations of Europe and America.

White skin colour, therefore, became the accepted standard of human beauty and all people were judged to be worthy of respect, civil rights, and dignity in accordance with the affinity of their complexion to that standard. Even the oppressed peoples themselves accepted this standard and stratified their communities along color lines.

Reprinted with permission. Extract from "Racism in Theology, Theology Against Racism," Commission on Faith and Order and the Programme to Combat Racism of the World Council of Churches, Geneva, Switzerland, 1975.

The consequence of this development, which climaxed in Europe and America in the 19th century, continues to affect the whole world. White racism and its consequences is ubiquitous. But its deepest and most harmful penetration is in Western Europe, the United States, and Southern Africa. Almost every aspect of civilization—science, religion, law, economics, politics, etiquette, and art—have been infected with white racism. All the institutions of Western culture, including the church, are inheritors of the racism that flourished for more than 300 years in Europe and America and continues today in many manifest and latent forms.

In summing up these reflections we would say:

**Racism is present** whenever persons, even before they are born, because of their race, are assigned to a group severely limited in their freedom of movement, their choice of work, their places of residence and so on.

**Racism is present** whenever groups of people, because of their race, are denied effective participation in the political process, and so are compelled (often by force) to obey the edicts of governments that they were allowed to have no part in choosing.

**Racism is present** whenever racial groups within a nation are excluded from the normal channels available for gaining economic power, through denial of educational opportunities and entry into occupational groups.

**Racism is present** whenever the policies of a nation-state ensure benefits for that nation from the labor of racial groups (migrant or otherwise), while at the same time denying to such groups commensurate participation in the affairs of the nation-state.

**Racism is present** whenever the identity of persons is denigrated through stereotyping of racial and ethnic groups in textbooks, cinema, mass media, interpersonal relations and other ways.

**Racism is present** whenever people are denied equal protection of the law, because of race, and when constituted authorities of the state use their powers to protect the interests of the dominant group at the expense of the powerless.

**Racism is present** whenever groups of nations continue to profit from regional and global structures that are historically related to racist presuppositions and actions. . . .

As the churches began to discover the real breadth and depth of the evil of racism and the close relation between reflection and praxis, the involvement of church and theology became more and more apparent. Western theology, not least during the last two centuries, has been deeply imbedded in Western culture. It has been shaped by the claims and assumptions of the superiority of white people over against other races and it has in turn influenced and undergirded some of these assumptions. However, as we learn to listen to the experience of oppressed and suffering people we begin to see in a new way the shortcomings and, for the most part unconscious, the racist implications in the manner in which theology has been done traditionally. We feel that, perhaps to a differing degree, the great

traditions of Orthodox churches share in the same predicament. Therefore, as all our theological approaches have to become more ecumenical,
we also see the great task of reevaluating and rethinking theological notions. In order to explain what we have in mind we offer the following
brief examples:

A.   The concepts of the "People of God" and the notions of elec-
     tion and pre-destination which are closely linked to them have
     been used to justify the expansionism and privileges of the
     white races. The migration of white people into North Ameri-
     ca or Africa have been associated with the migration of the
     people of Israel into their promised land. By virtue of such
     a typological identification the people already living in these
     lands were supposed to be the new Canaanites who were
     divinely condemned to subjection and servitude by white
     Christians.

B.   This concept was further undergirded by a certain literal under-
     standing of some Biblical ideas—the Hamitic hypothesis, for in-
     stance, which was used to read back the basic inequality of the
     human races into the stories of Genesis and the Ur-Geschichte
     (Gen. 1–12). A static understanding of Creation made it possible
     to regard this assumed inequality as something given, as a natu-
     ral law. The eschatological aspect of the belief that women and
     men are created in God's image in order to become truly hu-
     man, has been lost.

C.   The understanding of Jesus of Nazareth has been strongly in-
     fluenced by the image of the Western man. Accordingly, in
     artistic depictions of Jesus and in assumptions about his personal-
     ity and behavior much has been read into the New Testament
     that was derived from European and American culture. He
     became the white Jesus, alien and unrecognizable for the peo-
     ples in Africa, Asia, and elsewhere.

D.   The understanding of the Bible has been distorted by the heavy
     emphasis on the individual person and his/her spiritual needs.
     This led to the development of Christianity as a private religion.
     The movements of awakening and conversion focussed largely
     on the individual person and the eternal salvation of his or her
     soul. The Church became the assembly of reconciled individu-
     als. Consequently the ethical teaching underlined the individual
     righteousness and became largely concerned with personal eth-
     ics. The corporateness of the Christian community and its com-
     mon witness and service as the salt and leaven of this world
     receded into the background. Accordingly there developed an
     inability to see and to deal with the structural and institutional
     elements of the life of the churches.

Yet the roots of racism are still deeper. Even when these and other implicitly racist concepts in theology are no longer explicitly promoted or defended they remain in the minds of many Christian people as unspoken, perhaps unrecognized, assumptions. They therefore continue to operate on the subconscious level and help to confirm racial prejudices. In this area of the subconscious the insights of depth psychology prove valuable in enabling us to understand the psychological mechanisms of racism. Our fears of the unknown, our guilt, shame, anger, etc. are suppressed into the unconscious, what some would call the dark shadow of our conscious existence. As a result we project our guilt and fear, both individually and collectively, onto other human beings or groups. The dark races in particular have often become the scape-goats of unacknowledged and repressed fears of white societies. As a result of all this racism was able to become a normal and usually unnoticed element not only in the behavior but also in the beliefs of Christians. It appears that the help of depth psychology should be sought more widely not only to understand but to heal the situation in which both oppressors and oppressed find themselves today.

Incomplete though it is, our description of some of the more obvious features of racism gives some idea of how far-reaching the problem of racism is. Its causes are complex, since they are to be found in all areas of life, not least in our personal histories. In racism we are confronted with a powerful force which induces a profound sense of perplexity, hopelessness, and even despair in many people. How can we be set free to renew our struggle against the evil of racism?

## CHRISTIAN WITNESS AGAINST RACISM: COLLECTIVE REPENTANCE IN CORPORATE ACTION AND REFLECTION

Some of us hold that it will only be possible to sustain the fight against racism if we start with the Gospel of grace and forgiveness. Our faith is in Jesus Christ who suffered on the Cross and through the Cross won the victory. He is the victorious victim. Out of the depth of his suffering he is the Lord of history, a history undercutting the histories of demonic oppression and of the evil revolt against God.

It is in this story that forgiveness and grace are always available and that new beginnings can be made. The witness of the foregoing grace in Jesus Christ must be the starting point. Others are convinced that to begin with the Gospel of grace would leave us with the danger of belittling the sin of racism. The first emphasis ought to be on confession. The Gospel of grace comes to those who truly repent. We must be aware of the fact that the word forgiveness can and has been used in an all too easy way: both asking and offering forgiveness can become an escape from the task of facing the depth of sin and the need for renewing action. There has been much cheap preaching of forgiveness which makes the term almost unbearable for many who have suffered from racist persecution.

We would affirm that it is essential to link both the Gospel of grace and the confession of sin very closely together. Because of the costly grace of Christ we are enabled to confess that racism is a sin which separates us from God and from our fellow human beings. Without it racism could be regarded as a disastrous fate which leaves us with despair or apathy.

We are obliged to confess that racism is a sin not only of individual Christians, but of churches and societies at large. To see the ubiquity of racism makes it mandatory to say that churches and peoples have become guilty of this sin.

The term "collective sin" is appropriate because it indicates that racism has so permeated the churches and the societies in which they are set that it has become part of the structure of ordinary life. People have become accustomed to patterns of neglect of and contempt for others, of injustice and prejudice, of degradation and exploitation, and now regard them as "normal." In the same way, churches have come to take for granted separations along lines of color, to accept as "given" the divisions and barriers between people of different races. This demonic pervasiveness of racism compels us to speak of collective sin. "None is righteous, no not one" (Rom. 3:10). We are thrown together in a solidarity of sin. We are not free to dissociate ourselves self-righteously from this evil.

But even when we speak of collective sin with its evil ramifications, we are still within the sphere of Christ's sovereignty. Christ makes us free to repent. And we need indeed to repent. We dare not brand racism as sin without at once responding to it with real and practical penitence.

This response involves repentance both at the individual level and at the corporate level, and repentance commits us to action. The two elements are intimately connected, which is why we prefer to speak of repentance-action or penitent action. But what is the appropriate action?

Some we know, define repentance in terms of compensatory action. We hesitate to adopt this solution, however, mainly because no material compensation could possibly repair all the immeasurable harm done in the past. To call for compensation in this sense would only be to belittle the suffering which has been caused. There is also the danger that such compensation would lead groups in the Third World to perpetuate their dependence on white churches. Moreover, compensatory action leads us to look backwards, whereas repentance, we are convinced, moves forward, and is concerned not to restore the past but to seek a new and more just future. We have tried, therefore, to establish certain criteria for a forward looking active repentance which would do more justice to the still more radical imperatives of the Gospel.

a) Ideally the *action* should not be unilateral but *decided by both parties,* oppressors and oppressed, *together.*
b) It should open up the possibility of *real community in the future.*
c) It should be *related to the wider area of racism in the secular and political field.*
d) Adherence to these criteria will *be costly.*

This means that repentance-action must be part of a deliberate effort to achieve a new kind of community, an effort which will call for radical changes not only in the administrative structures of the churches but also in society.

The political and economic implications will need to be spelled out and realistically faced, since privileged groups will inevitably have to forego some of their privileges.

In suggesting this idea of repentance-action, it is not supposed that such measures will eliminate all racist sins in the future. That is not within our power. What we envisage is action which can point effectively both to the reality of the sin we repent of and the new life we believe in. Repentance-action of this kind will not be unambiguous nor safe from misinterpretation. We could wish it were otherwise but the sad fact is that all our actions will inevitably bear the mark of the histories and structures in which we live and will therefore still sometimes have racist elements. There will always be a risk of making ourselves vulnerable on all sides.

Discovering the sin of racism with all its implications and choosing the risky road of repentance-action, these are two aspects of one and the same process. It is a process which involves individuals and groups in the whole of their life and challenges their entire pattern of behavior. But it is also a process which involves and challenges the Church of Christ in a preeminent way since there the message of forgiveness is spelled out and articulated as explicitly as possible. In this process we are driven to rethink our ideas as to the nature of the Church and to recover the meaning and implications of its original mission.

We have tried to set out some criteria for repentance-action. Basically, these criteria reflect an attempt to find a new understanding and new forms of discipleship, but not simply in view of the need to combat racism. It is a more radical challenge than that which confronts the churches. We have to go back to the roots and try to restate the real meaning of discipleship. The criteria we found all point to one thing, namely the need to reestablish community in situations where there is suffering. This should be our starting point for redefining discipleship.

In many churches and groups around the world, people are experiencing today this process of redefinition and although much still remains obscure here, this experience provides us with our main clue. The link between our knowledge of Jesus Christ, victorious as victim and regnant as suffering servant on the one hand and our understanding and experience of racism on the other is such that "suffering" is the concrete reference point for the Church. The issue of racism gives renewed force to the words of Jesus: "Whosoever will save his life shall lose it, but whosoever shall lose his life for my sake and the Gospel's shall save it" (Mark 8:35).

Seen in this light, discipleship could mean the Church's constant effort to regroup and reconstitute itself in situations of real suffering, where suffering is the deepest expression of the struggle for human freedom and reconciliation. Without this constant effort, all declarations of faith, even anti-racist ones, are empty words, and even our active repentance remains arbitrary and haphazard.

In saying such things, none of us has any right to sit in judgement on others. Of that we are painfully aware. We also realize the difficulty of asserting that the Church is defective so long as it evades the radical significance of actual suffering for its own self-understanding and self-expression. Yet we are driven to assert this. Not to do so would be to close our eyes to the real implications of the Gospel and to the real dimensions of our situation. The cost of discipleship is high and each church has to reckon with this at every level of its life. . . .

## CONSIDERATIONS AND RECOMMENDATIONS FOR FURTHER ACTION

In the light of the reflection set out in this paper we want to draw special attention to the programs and activities in which various churches are already involved in their particular contexts. The suggestions listed below should be regarded neither as exhaustive nor as competing with those already put forward by various groups and agencies in the churches and the ecumenical movement.

The Church's task of fighting racism within its own ranks is concerned not only with the education of the clergy and laity but also involves conducting a relentless inquiry into the life of the Church in order to identify and eliminate both institutional and personal racism. The call for discipleship and discipline within the Church is implemented in the conversion of its own structures and of its theological methods and educational policies. For it is only by being authentic at the very center of its ministry that the Church can fulfil the prophetic role to which it is called in society at large.

1. In the field of theology and education we are confronted with the following tasks:
   a) To organize programs to conscientize members of church and society to enable them to discover their direct and indirect support for racism at all levels in the past and in the present.

b) To conduct investigations into the curricula of schools at all levels, i.e. in primary, secondary and university education (particularly of mission-schools and theological seminaries) in order to discover their possible contribution to ethnocentric views and their lack of information on intercultural and interracial dialogue.

c) To revise textbooks—e.g., catechisms, hymns and prayer-books, Bible-translations, books on the history of churches and missions, descriptions of other faiths—with respect to their possible support of racial and cultural imperialism.

d) To inquire into the methodology of theological education especially with regard to communication between literary and oral cultures as mainly identical with the cultures of the rich and the poor, the oppressor and the oppressed.

e) To sponsor programs of training for minority-groups to permit the maximal fulfilment of their educational potentials and for their basic recognition within the common life of the churches.

2. In living a disciplined life of unity and solidarity we are asked to be ready for changes in order to:

a) Be prepared to go where the victims of racism are, to become engaged with them in the struggle against oppression and in situations of crisis.

b) Help those who have been unconsciously ignored by, or deliberately discriminated against, to have access to real power in the decision-making bodies which control and deploy the human and material resources of the church.

c) Give support to indigenous churches which act as identity-groups for the social and spiritual survival of their members and for the preservation and re-awakening of their dignity as human beings and values of their communities.

d) Contribute to groups which are prepared to share in worship, fellowship and service in their respective multi-racial communities and so help to create the new atmosphere of mutual trust, healing and co-operation.

e) Help to create living liturgies in the context of racial tensions and encourage the inter-communication of liturgies from different geographical, cultural and denominational backgrounds.

f) Support solidarity with minority-churches by inviting them into local and national church-councils on the basis of Christian fellowship rather than of technical or statistical requirements.

3. In our ministry to society we need to work in the following ways:

a) By exposing, through documentation and the mass-media, the interrelation between racism and international economic structures of exploitation and disclosing factors which contribute to personal and institutional racism.

b) By supporting groups involved in the struggle against exploitation and oppression and by supporting their claim for access to equal power-sharing, education and employment.

    c)  By giving financial, legal and medical support to victims of oppression and assisting them by prayer and meditation so that they may be enabled to stand for themselves and to make their own decisions in their particular situations.

# Black Power

## National Committee of Negro Churchmen

We, an informal group of Negro churchmen in America, are deeply disturbed about the crisis brought upon our country by historic distortions of important human realities in the controversy about "black power." What we see shining through the variety of rhetoric is not anything new but the same old problem of power and race which has faced our beloved country since 1619.

We realize that neither the term "power" nor the term "Christian Conscience" is an easy matter to talk about, especially in the context of race relations in America. The fundamental distortion facing us in the controversy about "black power" is rooted in a gross imbalance of power and conscience between Negroes and white Americans. It is the distortion, mainly, which is responsible for the widespread, though often inarticulate, assumption that white people are justified in getting what they want through the use of power, but that Negro Americans must, either by nature or by circumstances, make their appeal only through conscience. As a result, the power of white men and the conscience of black men have both been corrupted. The power of white men is corrupted because it meets little meaningful resistance from Negroes to temper it and keep white men from aping God. The conscience of black men is corrupted because, having no power to implement the demands of conscience, the concern for justice is transmuted into a distorted form of love, which, in the absence of justice, becomes chaotic self-surrender. Powerlessness breeds a race of beggars. We are faced now with a situation where conscienceless power meets powerless conscience, threatening the very foundations of our nation.

Therefore, we are impelled by conscience to address at least four groups of people in areas where clarification of the controversy is of the most urgent necessity. We do not claim to present the final word. It is our hope,

From the *New York Times*, July 31, 1966.

however, to communicate meanings from our experience regarding power and certain elements of conscience to help interpret more adequately the dilemma in which we are all involved.

## TO THE LEADERS OF AMERICA: POWER AND FREEDOM

It is of critical importance that the leaders of this nation listen to a voice which says that the principal source of the threat to our nation comes neither from the riots erupting in our big cities, nor from the disagreements among the leaders of the civil rights movement, nor even from mere raising of the cry for "black power." These events, we believe, are but the expression of the judgment of God upon our nation for its failure to use its abundant resources to serve the real well-being of people, at home and abroad.

We give our full support to all civil rights leaders as they seek for basically American goals, for we are not convinced that their mutual reinforcement of one another in the past is bound to end in the future. We would hope that the public power of our nation will be used to strengthen the civil rights movement and not to manipulate or further fracture it.

We deplore the overt violence of riots, but we believe it is more important to focus on the real sources of these eruptions. These sources may be abetted inside the ghetto, but their basic causes lie in the silent and covert violence which white middle-class America inflicts upon the victims of the inner city. The hidden, smooth and often smiling decisions of American leaders which tie a white noose of suburbia around the necks, and which pin the backs of the masses of Negroes against the steaming ghetto walls —without jobs in a booming economy; with dilapidated and segregated educational systems in the full view of unenforced laws against it; in short: the failure of American leaders to use American power to create equal opportunity in *life as well as in law*—this is the real problem and not the anguished cry for "black power."

From the point of view of the Christian faith, there is nothing necessarily wrong with concern for power. At the heart of the Protestant reformation is the belief that ultimate power belongs to God alone and that men become most inhuman when concentrations of power lead to the conviction—overt or covert—that any nation, race or organization can rival God in this regard. At issue in the relations between whites and Negroes in America is the problem of inequality of power. Out of this imbalance grows the disrespect of white men for the Negro personality and community, and the disrespect of Negroes for themselves. This is a fundamental root of human injustice in America. In one sense, the concept of "black power" reminds us of the need for and the possibility of authentic democracy in America.

We do *not* agree with those who say that we must cease expressing concern for the acquisition of power lest we endanger the "gains" already made by the civil rights movement. The fact of the matter is, there have been few substantive gains since about 1950 in this area. The gap has constantly widened between the incomes of nonwhites relative to the whites. Since the Supreme Court decision of 1954, de facto segregation in every major city in our land has increased rather than decreased. Since the middle of the 1950s unemployment among Negroes has gone up rather than down while unemployment has decreased in the white community.

These are the hard facts that we must all face together. Therefore, we must not take the position that we can continue in the same old paths.

When American leaders decide to serve the real welfare of people instead of war and destruction; when American leaders are forced to make the rebuilding of our cities first priority on the nation's agenda; when American leaders are forced by the American people to quit misusing and abusing American power; then will the cry for "black power" become inaudible, for the framework in which all power in America operates would include the power and experience of black men as well as those of white men. In that way, the fear of the power of each group would be removed. America is our beloved homeland. But, America is not God. Only God can do everything. America and the other nations of the world must decide which among a number of alternatives they will choose.

## TO WHITE CHURCHMEN: POWER AND LOVE

As black men who were long ago forced out of the white church to create and to wield "black power," we fail to understand the emotional quality of the outcry of some clergy against the use of the term today. It is not enough to answer that "integration" is the solution. For it is precisely the nature of the operation of power under some forms of integration which is being challenged. The Negro church was created as a result of the refusal to submit to the indignities of a false kind of "integration" in which all power was in the hands of white people. A more equal sharing of power is precisely what is required as the precondition of authentic human interaction. We understand the growing demand of Negro and white youth for a more honest kind of integration; one which increases rather than decreases the capacity of the disinherited to participate with power in all of the structures of our common life. Without this capacity to *participate with power*—i.e., to have some organized political and economic strength to really influence people with whom one interacts—integration is not meaningful. For the issue is not one of racial balance but of honest interracial interaction.

For this kind of interaction to take place, all people need power, whether black or white. We regard as sheer hypocrisy or as a blind and dangerous illusion the view that opposes love to power. Love should be a controlling element in power, but what love opposes is precisely the misuse and abuse of power, not power itself. So long as white churchmen continue to moralize and misinterpret Christian love, so long will justice continue to be subverted in this land.

## TO NEGRO CITIZENS: POWER AND JUSTICE

Both the anguished cry for "black power" and the confused emotional response to it can be understood if the whole controversy is put in the context of American history. Especially must we understand the irony involved in the pride of Americans regarding their ability to act as individuals on the one hand, and their tendency to act as members of ethnic groups on the other hand. In the tensions of this part of our history is revealed both the tragedy and hope of human redemption in America.

America has asked its Negro citizens to fight for opportunity as *individuals* whereas at certain points in our history what we have needed most has been opportunity for the whole group, not just for selected and approved Negroes. Thus in 1863, the slaves were made legally free, as individuals, but the real question regarding personal and group power to maintain that freedom was pushed aside. Power at that time for a mainly rural people meant land and tools to work the land. In the words of Thaddeus Stevens, power meant "40 acres and a mule." But this power was not made available to the slaves and we see the results today in the pushing of a landless peasantry off the farms into big cities where they come in search mainly of the power to be free. What they find are only the formalities of unenforced legal freedom. So we must ask, "What is the nature of the power which we seek and need today?" Power today is essentially organizational power. It is not a thing lying about in the streets to be fought over. It is a thing which, in some measure, already belongs to Negroes and which must be developed by Negroes in relationship with the great resources of this nation.

Getting power necessarily involves reconciliation. We must first be reconciled to ourselves lest we fail to recognize the resources we already have and upon which we can build. We must be reconciled to ourselves as persons and to ourselves as an historical group. This means we must find our way to a new self-image in which we can feel a normal sense of pride in self, including our variety of skin color and the manifold textures of our hair. As long as we are filled with hatred for ourselves we will be unable to respect others.

At the same time, if we are seriously concerned about power then we must build upon that which we already have. "Black power" is already present to some extent in the Negro church, in Negro fraternities and sororities, in our professional associations, and in the opportunities afforded to Negroes who make decisions in some of the integrated organizations of our society.

We understand the reasons by which these limited forms of "black power" have been rejected by some of our people. Too often the Negro church has stirred its members away from the reign of God in *this world* to a distorted and complacent view of *an otherworldly* conception of God's power. We commit ourselves as churchmen to make more meaningful in the life of our institution our conviction that Jesus Christ reigns in the "here" and "now" as well as in the future he brings in upon us. We shall, therefore, use more of the resources of our churches in working for human justice in the places of social change and upheaval where our Master is already at work.

At the same time, we would urge that Negro social and professional organizations develop new roles for engaging the problem of equal opportunity and put less time into the frivolity of idle chatter and social waste.

We must not apologize for the existence of this form of group power, for we have been oppressed as a group, not as individuals. We will not find our way out of that oppression until both we and America accept the need for Negro Americans as well as for Jews, Italians, Poles, and white Anglo-Saxon Protestants, among others, to have and to wield group power.

However, if power is sought merely as an end in itself, it tends to turn upon those who seek it. Negroes need power in order to participate more effectively at all levels of the life of our nation. We are glad that none of those civil rights leaders who have asked for "black power" have suggested that it means a new form of isolationism or a foolish effort at domination. But we must be clear about why we need to be reconciled with the white majority. It is *not* because we are only one-tenth of the population in America; for we do not need to be reminded of the awesome power wielded by the 90% majority. We see and feel that power every day in the destructions heaped upon our families and upon the nation's cities. We do not need to be threatened by such cold and heartless statements. For we are men, not children, and we are growing out of our fear of that power, which can hardly hurt us any more in the future than it does in the present or has in the past. Moreover, those bare figures conceal the potential political strength which is ours if we organize properly in the big cities and establish effective alliances.

Neither must we rest our concern for reconciliation with our white brothers on the fear that failure to do so would damage gains already made by the civil rights movement. If those gains are in fact real, they will withstand the claims of our people for power and justice, not just a few select Negroes here and there, but for the masses of our citizens. We must rather rest our concern for reconciliation on the firm ground that we and all other Americans *are* one. Our history and destiny are indissolubly linked. If the future is to belong to any of us, it must be prepared for all of us whatever our racial or religious background. For in the final analysis, we are *persons* and the power of all groups must be wielded to make visible our common humanity.

The future of America will belong to neither white nor black unless all Americans work together at the task of rebuilding our cities. We must organize not only among ourselves but with other groups in order that we can, together, gain power sufficient to change this nation's sense of what is *now* important and what must be done *now*. We must work with the remainder of the nation to organize whole cities for the task of making the rebuilding of our cities first priority in the use of our resources. This is more important than who gets to the moon first or the war in Vietnam.

To accomplish this task we cannot expend our energies in spastic or ill-tempered explosions without meaningful goals. We must move from the politics of philanthropy to the politics of metropolitan development for equal opportunity. We must relate all groups of the city together in new ways in order that the truth of our cities might be laid bare and in order that, together, we can lay claim to the great resources of our nation to make truth more human.

## TO THE MASS MEDIA: POWER AND TRUTH

The ability or inability of all people in America to understand the upheavals of our day depends greatly on the way power and truth operate in the mass media. During the Southern demonstrations for civil rights, you men of the communications industry performed an invaluable service for the entire country by revealing plainly to our ears and eyes, the ugly truth of a brutalizing system of overt discrimination and segregation. Many of you were mauled and injured, and it took courage for you to stick with the task. You were instruments of change and not merely purveyors of unrelated facts. You were able to do this by dint of personal courage and by reason of the power of national news agencies which supported you.

Today, however, your task and ours is more difficult. The truth that needs revealing today is not so clear-cut in its outlines, nor is there a national consensus to help you form relevant points of view. Therefore, nothing is now more important than that you look for a variety of sources of truth in order that the limited perspectives of all of us might be corrected. Just as you related to a broad spectrum of people in Mississippi instead of relying only on police records and establishment figures, so must you operate in New York City, Chicago, and Cleveland.

The power to support you in this endeavor *is present* in our country. It must be searched out. We desire to use our limited influence to help relate you to the variety of experience in the Negro community so that limited controversies are not blown up into the final truth about us. The fate of this country is, to no small extent, dependent upon how you interpret the crises upon us, so that human truth is disclosed and human needs are met.

# The World of the Redneck

## Will D. Campbell

Bowed by the weight of centuries,
He leans upon his hoe and gazes on the ground.

Not long ago I was on a program at a leading Southern university where journalists were gathered to discuss the South and its people, their religion, their racial attitudes. The morning was given over to the subject "The Black Church Today." The speaker was a black man, a former professor of philosophy, holder of earned and honorary degrees, author of several books, a man highly respected in the academic world. His presentation was brilliant and entertaining. It was also filled with the dialect of his heritage and numerous racial anecdotes. (Perhaps this was what made it so entertaining to his all-white audience.) Whatever the reason, he was well received.

The afternoon topic was: "Redneck Religion." I was to be the leader of that discussion. I began by noting that the two titles ranged from one of extreme sophistication to one of extreme vulgarity.

"The Black Church Today" was a title filled with dignity, intellectual sophistication and liberal, academic acceptance. But the other title, "Redneck Religion," was just the opposite. I wondered aloud what the response would have been if the morning subject had been "Nigger Religion," and the afternoon had been given over to a discussion of "The Church of the Culturally Deprived and Increasingly Alienated Caucasian Minority." Of course, I knew already that the response would have been one of offense

Reprinted, with deletions, by permission of the author from *Katallagete,* Spring 1974. Will D. Campbell is Director of the Committee of Southern Churchmen and publisher of their magazine, *Katallagete* ("Be Reconciled").

at this poor taste, this uncouth verbiage, this insult to a struggling minority, despite the fact that the term "redneck" is as filled with emotional intensity as the word "nigger"—though originally "redneck" was used in all good sport. Likewise, the term "nigger" was originally in all sport, with no harm meant at all. No harm, except that in both cases the words were, and are, used to describe a powerless, and to the user, unattractive group. Nevertheless, I had accepted the title assigned to me and proceeded with the discussion.

Like the morning speaker, I spoke often in the idiom of my people, the rednecks. But instead of being applauded, I was roundly attacked by the chairman as a fraud, posing as a "know-nothing" because he knew that I had graduated from an Ivy League school and "knows better than to use that kind of grammar." Needless to say, he also knew that the morning speaker had attended some of the world's finest universities and that his degrees and academic accomplishments far exceeded my own.

More recently someone I know quite well was doing a Coffee House Performance before a refined, ecclesiastical group of Episcopalians. He opened the gig with a currently popular country song called "Rednecks, White Socks, and Blue Ribbon Beer." It was received with much hand clapping, foot stomping, and cheering. But the House grew silent with hostility when he announced that his next song would be, "Niggers, Mudguards, and Red Ripple Wine." Moral: *Let's don't make fun of one another's favorite minorities.*

The point of the anecdote is that both subjects in the symposium and both song titles had to do with two proud and tragic peoples. To argue now as to which is the more proud or tragic—redneck or nigger— would be futile. But a discussion of the origins of the tragedy of each is appropriate.

Much has been said and written of the tragedy of black people. Serious consideration of the origin of the tragedy of the "redneck" is both lacking and long overdue. (Note that I freely use the term "redneck" when referring to economically poor whites of the South. But note also something that black people have always known: that the camaraderie of the ghetto is camaraderie *only in the ghetto* and the outsider had best not try to join in.)

My colleague on the university program said that he loved his people more than he loved my people. He is a wise and honest man. For one who says he loves another's people more than he loves his own is either sick or lying. Blood is for a fact thicker than water. He said that he was proud of his people. Only the worst bigot would question his right to be proud of his black ancestors. To cite the reasons justifying his pride at this point would be a boring redundancy. But for quite similar reasons I am also proud of my people. I am proud because I know that historically they too were the victims of the seeds of time, seeds which they did not plant, but the harvest of which has been thrust upon them and that they could have done worse. And because I know that without the incessant manipulation by the politics of the privileged they would have done better.

> He leans upon his hoe
> And gazes on the ground.

And as he so leaned and so gazed his posture left that cervical area from the temporal bones to the first dorsal vetebra exposed to the searing, shrivelling, parching rays of the mid-day Southern sun.

And we named him "redneck."

As one who has been through the romance and drama of participation in the Civil Rights Movement of the 'fifties and 'sixties I know how easy it was, and is, to identify with the most obvious minority—in this case the Blacks—and dismiss a less obvious minority—the rednecks, woolhats, peckerwoods, po' whites—as "The Enemy." But there is a real sense in which the redneck has been victimized one step beyond the Black.

It is bad to have your back and your blood taken as happened to the Blacks. But there is a sense in which it is worse to have your *head* taken away. Through it all the Blacks knew what was happening, that they were suffering, and why, and who was causing it. And early in the game they set about the task of doing something about it. But we whites never got their head. The job on the redneck was more extensive because he had his *head* taken away. He still hasn't identified his "enemy."

Perhaps one reason why he hasn't identified the enemy is that he too, historically, was a slave. It was a more sneaky kind of slavery, so the redneck never had to acknowledge it. His was an indentured slavery: "Serve me for seven years and I will set you free." But freedom to what and in what context? Most often it was a freedom to flounder, to drift, to wander westward in frustrating search of what had been promised him but never delivered—a secure life in a land of plenty.

Certainly I am not saying that all redneck history can be traced back to an indentured servanthood. The fact is that today very little of it can be so traced historically, because white scholars have never dwelt on it. By contrast, blacks created a culture out of their slavery, a history, art, music, literature. The white servant, ashamed to admit that his progenitors had been brought to these shores in almost the same fashion as the Blacks, would be more apt to tell his grandchild that his fathers landed at Plymouth Rock. Such deception was bound to result in a schizophrenia which may account for more of the deepest hostilities, bigotries, and prejudices of the redneck than any other historical factor. If he were to conceal successfully and deny his own slavery, then the redneck had to dwell heavily on the slavery of others and justify it in some fashion, whether by fact or by fiction.

Who made the redneck

> ... dead to rapture and despair,
> A thing that grieves not and never hopes?

No one, Mr. Markham. Though many have tried, they were never completely successful. For our redneck is alive to both rapture and despair. He is capable of deep grief and from one generation to the next he builds hope and passes it on. For the most part, politics has been seeped in his bones and sinew by those whose "politics" brought him over to the New World as indentured servants, and so his hopes have been pinned on many stars —from Shiloh to Tom Watson, From Robert E. Lee to Huey Long, and from General Nathan Bedford Forest to General MacArthur, Franklin Roosevelt, and George Wallace. But each time his hopes have been appropriated by the gentry class and he has been left yet again stranded

> ... stolid and stunned,
> A brother to the ox.

What forces of history have left him so is a matter of speculation. That speculation has ranged from hookworms which sapped his energy and ambition, to Thaddeus Stephens who gave him Jim Crow, and from the Anopheles mosquito which gave him malaria to Jefferson Davis who gave him his confederate cause. But stranded he has been.

I believe that the South stands where she stands today—neither integrated nor segregated, neither bussed nor unbussed, neither an integral part of the nation nor a nation unto herself—because the redneck has never been a party to any of the alliances which have been formed or the truces which have been written. Maybe this is because he steadfastly clings to the Baal worship of Politics as Messiah to deliver him from his infirmities, or maybe it is because he has been deliberately manipulated and used by the very persons upon whom he has depended for deliverance. But whatever the reason, the redneck, not the Black, has been largely the unseen and unacknowledged factor when it comes to the solution of what we seem to believe is our most pressing social problem: poverty/race/war. Moreover he has been used by us all as a whipping post. When we think *bigot* it comes out *redneck*. When we think *racist* we think *redneck*.

Yet it is my bias that the redneck is probably the *least* racist of any group in white American society. This is so because racism is not an attitude, a prejudice, a matter of bigotry. Attitudes can and have been changed and many of us have seen them change within ourselves. And though the vestiges of raw, naked prejudice remain in us all, we have somehow been delivered from the agony of it in its most primitive form. *Yet if we are white we are racist.* For *racism* is the condition in and under which we live. It is the structures in which we live and move and have our being. And we are, or seem to be, powerless to change them. By the accident of my white birth I could have become President, Governor, manager of a major league baseball team or pastor of the Roswell Street Baptist Church in Atlanta, Georgia. I can and do live where I want to. I can and do participate in a society every facet of which has afforded me the edge. I can change my attitudes. I can be educated out of a mind filled with hate and bigotry. But I cannot stop being a racist. It has nothing to do with how liberal, or radical, or enlightened, or educated or good I am. Nor does it have to do with how reactionary, conservative, ignorant or bad I am. It just has to do with *being white within these structures.* This fact subconsciously threatens us, so we must go on equating racism with redneckism. Yet there continues to be less real racism in redneckism because the redneck participates in the society from a base of considerably less power than the rest of us. Until and unless he is somehow brought in as a party to the truce, there will be no truce.

True, many alliances have been formed. First come to mind the old paternalism, the *noblesse oblige,* which has now fallen into such disfavor as surely to be gone forever. But it was more than just paternalism. It was a working relationship between two groups, the aristocratic whites and the Blacks. But it failed. The alleged religion of the South was Judaeo-Christian, but the alliance between the upper-class white and Black failed because the ethics of the Southern aristocracy was not Judaeo-Christian, but Greek and Roman; their politics was not democratic, but Stoic. By that is meant that among the Stoics ran the political conviction that sovereignty inheres *naturally* in the best man. The novelist and essayist Walker Percy put it so well nearly twenty years ago in an article on Southern Stoicism in *The Commonwealth.* He reminded us that if this notion of the right to rule were well suited to the Empire of the First Century it was remarkably suited to the agrarian South of the last century. And he also reminded us of William Faulkner's Colonel Sartoris, who made himself responsible for his helpless freedmen, and Lucas Beauchamp, who accepted this leadership. This arrangement formed between them a bond which remains even today in a strange and violent sequence of cross currents. The nobility and graciousness which James McBride Dabbs so linked to describe in the "manners" of the South, had its roots, not in Christianity, says Percy, but in the Stoic notion of a hierarchy of creation whereby those at the top behaved justly, decently, and gentlemanly toward those at the bottom they ruled. "Not because they were made in the image of God and were therefore lovable in themselves," Percy insisted, "but because to do them an injustice would be to defile the inner fortress which was oneself."

The Christian doctrine is that God is sovereign, creates no hierarchy and that original sin will not allow those who grab the reigns of governorship and power to rule very long without doing it sooner or later for their own sake. But in the Stoic notion of a hierarchy there was no place for the rednecks. The Blacks had been owned as property. The obligation to them was apparent to the noble Stoic. The upper-class white took care of his own as duty demanded. The notion of *noblesse oblige* was more than a myth created by historical novelists. Whatever we might say of it today, it was a fact of the time. The black Uncle Tom, also a man of dignity and manners like unto the dignity and manners of the upper-class white, interpreted the kindness and generosity of the aristocratic white to his people, and interpreted the demands of his people, meager though they were, to the white gentry. And between these two groups a sort of truce, which lasted for more than half a century, was drawn. There was peace. There was also stagnation because it was an uneasy peace, caused, I believe, by the fact that a large segment of society was not a factor in the truce—that is, the lower-class white masses, the rednecks.

It is generally assumed that this truce failed because the Blacks were not considered. They were considered, if for no other reason than that they were still useful to the gentry. But the poor white was not even needed and thus there was no Stoic obligation toward him. So several things happened. The white masses got restless. They stood in their cabin doors and watched Colonel Sartoris as he passed out the necessities of life to the Blacks, a house to live in, food, medicine, churches, a piece of land to farm, run money to make the year's crop, help when [they] got in trouble, while [the redneck] was left destitute and alone, despite the fact that he might have been on the front lines at Chickamauga, and he resented what he saw. He had no one to help him with his physical needs, no one to help him meet his psychological needs. So he turned to hating. And it was a religious hate. His religion was not the educated and well-tutored Stoicism of the aristocracy. His was a vague, varying and ill-defined folk religion, a combination of old wives' tales, Indian lore, and half-remembered biblical passages passed around between visits from the circuit riding Methodist or Baptist preachers who came through on their way from Philadelphia to Natchez. Added to this was what he learned during the Civil War years.

The gentry still had a problem. The Black could not vote, at least not after President Rutherford B. Hayes came on the scene. Voting was not a part of the alliance. Nor, for the most part, was school a part of the alliance. While the redneck did not have those other things the alliance provided, he did have the vote. Since the Black could not vote, he did not need to be feared. Because the redneck could vote he was always a potential threat to the alliance between the Colonel and Uncle Lucas. A trump card was needed. There was one available and it was freely used.

The trump card was the Black male, the poll tax, and disenfranchised women. Again in the Stoic tradition, women were no more apt to see the mantle of rulership fall on them than were slaves. They too were at the bottom in the hierarchy of creation. (While Christianity has had its problems with equal rights for women it has been at least ambivalent whereas the Stoic was of a single mind. In the time and place where he said it St. Paul's statement, "In Christ there is neither male nor female," was so controversial and so against the mainstream that we can almost forgive him for saying, "Let women be quiet in church.") But the point is that politics was man's business. And over liquors and cigars after dinner, or at the plantation commissary or crossroads store, it was an easy matter to figure out a system whereby the voting redneck could be convinced that if he insisted on the egalitarian activities of the Populist movement or the Farmer's Alliance, his daughters would be ravished, in mass, by Black Bucks. In that wise the one advantage the poor white had, the vote, was negated and turned against him, by his own markings at the ballot box.

But this uneasy truce between the white aristocracy and the Negro had to crack, and it did. The two parties of the truce went their separate ways, the Uncle Tom to the Courts and the Civil Rights Movement, the Aristocracy to sit tight-lipped and watch his world crumble around him.

What does all that have to do with the religion of the redneck? Everything. His religion has been and still is virtually synonymous with his politics and economics. There seems to be little doubt that it was "Christian" leadership which provided the morale which sustained the Civil War. Without that "Christian" leadership the War would have been a lost cause years before Appomattox. And one of the most tragic things about the institutional religion of the redneck is that it developed *as an institution* during the years of a defensive self-consciousness about slavery when the South was living under the cloud of the threat and then the reality of war. Previously, the aristocracy possessed the ever so respectable steeples of Calvin and Henry VIII to preside over their altar fires and tea parties. So the Blacks who were "converted" received their instruction in the faith out of a sophisticated brand of orthodoxy. The poor white, scattered up and down the hollows and eddies of the rural South, most often had the quarterly or semi-annual visit of the circuit riders who were in fact cultured and well-educated gentlemen. But between their visits, their religious experience was based largely on the half-remembered Bible verses, old wives' tales, mixed with the Indian and other folklore mentioned above.

Nothing has been so grossly exaggerated as the religiosity of the nineteenth century rural South. It simply did not exist. The climb to identify with the institutionalizing of *that* religion began and largely ended during the latter years of that century and the early decades of the twentieth.

Later, the brush arbors gave way to white-frame Baptist and Methodist buildings at virtually every crossroad, and steeples began to emerge in every town announcing to the world that redneck religion was on the way. In the towns, the peckerwoods, ridgerunners and woolhats and rednecks became what Faulkner made into a chronicle in his saga of Snopes. The Snopes' became the storekeepers and bankers and landlords and church leaders in the fashion so well described by Faulkner, and like that Empire of the First Christian Century, it began to erode and rot away.

The rednecks built their towns in the manner described by Faulkner in one of his novels about the Snopes':

> Ours a town established and decreed by people neither Catholics nor Protestants nor even atheists but incorrigible nonconformists. Nonconformists, not just to everybody else, but to each other in mutual accord. A nonconformism defended and preserved by descendants whose ancestors hadn't quitted home and security for a wilderness in which to find freedom of thought as they claimed and oh yes, believed, but to find freedom in which to be incorrigible and unreconstructable Baptists and Methodists, not to escape from tyranny, as they claimed and believed, *but to establish one.*

But before the rednecks of the mid-nineteenth century became the Snopes of the twentieth a lot of things had to happen. We should also note at this point that there are now *two* definitions of redneck. The one I have been discussing is the underprivileged white of mill town and rural South. But there now emerges into power the middle-class redneck of William Faulkner's stories about Snopes. These are the ones the sophisticates use today to identify anyone with "hick" characteristics, or who doesn't behave according to liberal, educated and middle-class norms. The guy who drives a Grand Prix with lots of chrome to the country club, and burps or crepitates at a seated dinner party. Or a President of the United States who toys with his partner's undergarments on the White House dance floor, as recounted by Robert Sherrill. I would insist upon a distinction between my honest-to-God poverty-stricken brothers and sisters in the boondocks and hollers and the "successful" Snopes' described by William Faulkner or the political slob described by Robert Sherrill, and I am willing to admit that not all rednecks are financially poor. But the religion of both groups has the same basic root. And that root which provided the branch and arose to steepled heights went deeply into the soil of slavery and war. In short, it was a religion founded on violence.

Because the South had limited industrial resources the success of the Confederacy depended on the degree of intestinal fortitude developed by the man up the creek from the plantation owner's mansion, or by the overseer who was raising a regiment—that is, the poor white. For the first time since indentured servanthood the redneck was needed. But he had first to be convinced that he was a member of God's chosen people. So the church of the aristocracy went to work.

Already that church had settled the rightness of slavery. Now they had to create a religious community based on war in order to keep the war going. The Church has always had trouble distinguishing between nationalism and faithfulness to God so all wars have had their priests to preside over the killings. Usually the religious community is established already and sides with Caesar without question. In the case of the redneck his religious community was not yet established. Since it was not, the recruitment for war and the imparting of religious instruction were simultaneous. . . .

I believe the point can be made that the *original* redneck was not the southern farmer leaning against his hoe, was not the French peasant or painter or poet. The original redneck from a religious standpoint was the sects and cults among Old Testament Judaism. (I am well aware that the term "Old Testament Jews" covers a lot of territory. One cannot generalize much about Old Testament Jews any more than he can about rednecks, or Blacks, or contemporary Jews or Southern Baptists or Catholics.) The religious expression of our redneck historically was mingled with piety and with hate. The two have gone hand in hand, piety and hate. The same thing is true of a large segment of Old Testament Judaism. And there were adequate historical reasons in both cases.

Have you ever been to a Klan rally and heard the mournful sounds of "The Old Rugged Cross" sung by ten thousand voices as the faithful march around the thirty-foot cross, hurling their personal little lighted torches at the base, soaked with gasoline and diesel fuel until it is lapping its tongues of fire to the very sky above? And have you heard their prayers, "Give us men, strong men, of courage and devotion to resist the Devil and His advocates"? And have you heard such spirited psalms as:

> You niggers listen now,
>   I'm gonna tell you how
> To keep from being tortured
>   When the Klan is on the prowl.
> Stay at home at night,
>   Lock your door up tight,
> Don't go outside or you will find
>   Them crosses a-burning bright.

Or the equally spirited singing of:

> Move them niggers north.
>   Move them niggers north.
> If they don't like our Southern ways,
> Move them niggers north.

Perhaps you have never had that experience. But most of us have heard these words:

> If I forget you, Oh Jerusalem, let my right hand whither away. Let my tongue cling to the roof of my mouth if I do not remember you, if I do not set Jerusalem above my highest joy. Remember, Oh Lord, against the people of Edom, the day of Jerusalem's fall when they said, "Down with it, down to its very foundation." Oh Babylon, Babylon, the destroyer. Happy is the man who repays you for all you did to us. Happy is he who shall seize your children and dash them against the rocks.

No. That is not part of a Klan ritual. It is part of the 137th Psalm. And the fall which the Psalmist was lamenting was so very important as to be affecting the lives of all of us today. The hate and piety of the Psalmist was not without reason.

Likewise:

> If I forget you, Oh Atlanta, Vicksburg, Oxford, Donelson, remember, Oh Lord against the Yankees, the night they drove old Dixie down! when Sherman said, "Raze it, raze it, burn it down to the ground!" Happy shall be he who takes your little Yankee babies and slams them against Stone Mountain.

The subject under discussion at this point is not right, wrong; justice, injustice; good, bad. The subject under discussion is human tragedy. Because of the nature of tragedy, the subject of the latter Psalm also continues to affect the lives of all of us.

Perhaps no book ever written is filled with more potential anti-Semitic material than the Old Testament, because it is an honest book, written by and about themselves. Perhaps the Assyrians were just as bad, but it isn't expressed. It doesn't come through. The very people who wrote the books were the elect, the "called of God," yet make themselves out to be true rednecks—contentious, forever murmuring, grumbling, hating, never satisfied. And in their acts of worship it often came through.

Especially was it true of some of their cults and sects, what might be called the Pentecostals of Israel. The Recabites, for example, described in Jeremiah 35: real stand-offs: have nothing to do with anything new; don't drink wine; don't build houses, plant fields and vineyards. Real kooks, oddballs. And the mainstream of their society saw them as the rednecks they were. Yet they really did *believe* something, and they were faithful to it and Jeremiah quoted the Lord as saying, "Because you have kept the command of your ancestors, and obeyed all his instructions," stupid though they might have been, "you will be blessed." And the Nazarites, defended by Amos, likewise standoffish but devout in what they believed; again, the Pentecostals of Israel, the rednecks. All part of Israel, called of God, nontheless suspicious, contentious, distrustful, grumbling.

But the point is important enough to repeat that in both cases, the redneck of Israel and the redneck of Dixie, there was adequate historical reason for their discontent. They believed something enough to hate and kill about. They were not lukewarm, a quality described by the writer of Revelation as being worthy only of being spewed out of the mouth of God.

But a more important point still is that it was from them came the Messiah. It was through the likes of them, the most unlikely of all, that God brought forth the Christ. We think, "how interesting it is that our Lord was born in poverty, in such humble circumstances, not in a motif befitting a king!" A more interesting thing is that he was born among this family of haters.

Most of us suspect that if Christ came back today he would once again be born among the lowly—Black or hippie. But wouldn't it shake us up a bit if he came today and was born into a Klan family!

"Hey man, Jesus is back."

"Yeah? Who'd he look like? Ralph Abernathy or Abbie Hoffman?"

"He looked like Robert Shelton. He's wearing a robe and a hood!"

Surely now, you are not reading words glorifying the Ku Klux Klan. What you are reading is an affirmation of the absolute sovereignty of God.

How quickly we make heroes. And how quickly we choose enemies. And how slow we are to see the tragedy of history and to come to terms with that part of it which is ours.

We are again in a time of ridicule against the redneck for starting what he calls his "Christian Academies" in the South—the little frame buildings dotted about the countryside or located in church houses to avoid integration. How we look down our liberal noses at such blatant bigotry! But dare we liberal, educated, cultured whites—dare we, talk about Christian academies? Who founded Emory and Vanderbilt and Mercer and Duke and Sewanee, or Yale and Harvard? Here are the *Christian* academies. And what have they stood for historically? It is they who have trained and *educated* the managers, the owners, the soldiers and the rulers of this present world. If there is any logic and truth at all in the earlier paragraph of this essay which says the redneck is less racist because he operates from a base of little power then it takes no genius to see that these Christian academies are more racist, teach and carry out more violence and repression in one day than all the pitiful little "Christian academies" springing up in cow-pastures will in a generation.

What then shall we say of our redneck brothers and sisters? Again, I hope that you do not judge this a simple glorification or romanticizing of either the redneck or the Klan. What I am trying to say is that the alleged redneck is a crucial factor to the social problem of race/poverty/war. I am trying to say that he, too, has been manipulated, used and abused, and that what makes a man like George Wallace so dangerous is that about ninety percent of what he says is true, factually and historically accurate. I am also trying to say that the redneck, even in this post-industrial, technological age, has hung on to a scrap of individualism. In this commitment, this dogged determination, this recalcitrant, complaining, murmuring, seething hostility and seeming helplessness, there may yet emerge deliverance from that body of death in the race and poverty which stalks and haunts and infects our land. If not, not; and death's shroud will blanket us all. What form the potential deliverance could take I have no notion. No predictions. Only the sign of Jonah.

So I leave you these words of the poet with which we began:

> How will the future reckon with this man?
> How answer his brute question in that hour
> When whirlwinds of rebellion shake all shores?
> How will it be with kingdom and with kings,
> With those who shaped him to the thing he is,
> When this dumb terror shall rise to judge the world?

And judge it, my brothers and sisters, he will. More precisely, perhaps he is judging it at this very hour.

# 7

# The Women's Movement

Among the many liberation movements that began in the 1960s the one which is most far-reaching and affects our whole society most directly is the women's movement. In terms of numbers alone, the reason is obvious enough. This movement has raised profound questions concerning the nature of male and female and the place of the family in our society; it has compelled a male-dominated society to examine the assumptions of masculine superiority that are implicit in most forms of social organization. As with every movement intent on changing society, there is a fundamental moral character to "Women's Liberation" in its protestation of inequality and injustice and its vision of a society in which women are better able to arrive at autonomy and self-realization.

However, when we turn from generalities to specifics, we find that the meaning of Women's Liberation is not universally agreed on by women themselves. Such matters as economic equality (equal pay for equal work) are generally endorsed, but a conservative reaction sets in when some advocates of the movement speak of fundamental changes in family structure and reject the customary child-rearing role of the mother. An extreme example of this controversial thinking is the observation of the ardent feminist Ti-Grace Atkinson that medical science should perfect the artificial womb and provide asexual reproduction as "a truly optional method, at the very least," to liberate women from their traditional sexual and family roles. Counterorganizations to the movement have been formed by women who argue that the goals of Women's Liberation actually deny the inherent distinctiveness of being feminine. They maintain that the women's movement glorifies the "male world"—that is, the world of economic production—as the ultimate place for feminine achievement as well. Much of the opposition to the Equal Rights Amendment has reflected this concern that women may lose more than they may gain in their quest for equality.

Some historical perspective is helpful in understanding a contemporary issue; Marianne H. Micks provides this background with a brief look at some nineteenth-century developments. She brings out the conflict in female goals in terms of the biblical images of Exodus and Eden, the former symbolizing a moving out from restrictive roles to new paths which promise a larger life; the latter symbolizing hearth and home as the proper domain of the woman, whose destiny is to provide a haven for husband and children. The tone of Micks's article is irenic; she does not want to polarize the sexes, nor to place an impassable gulf between the Exodus and Eden models in the life of a woman. Most important, as Micks points out, is that women have the opportunity to take the path that most appeals to them, perhaps also to live in the conflict that may arise in combining these images in one's life. Ultimately, Micks is moved to affirm the importance of the Exodus image over an Edenic image that too often expresses an abdication of that openness to the world which is the mark of human personhood.

The next two selections are written by two women who have achieved considerable prominence, one as an opponent and the other as an advocate of the women's movement. Phyllis Schlafly, one of the more vociferous antagonists of the movement, presents the "Positive Woman" as her answer to the negative image of woman she perceives among liberationists. By this term, she means that the women's movement is actually denying the God-given uniqueness of woman as it places her in competition with men and makes her dissatisfied with or even ashamed of her maternal destiny. Where liberationists would ascribe psychological and sociological differences between male and female to cultural conditioning, Schlafly argues that these differences reflect the distinctive natures of male and female and cannot be erased by social engineering. In this respect Schlafly's thinking is in line with the observations of Helmut Thielicke (see Chapter 3).

While Schlafly's selection tends to polarize, making accusations that feminists would regard as unfair, Betty Friedan confesses in her proposal of a "second stage" that the movement has in fact not been fair to those who resisted it in the name of home and family. Rather than placing the feminist and Schlafly's Positive Woman at opposite poles, Friedan recognizes that most women find themselves in sympathy with the concerns of both. The task is to work for economic structures that will allow men and women to share more fully in both worlds and allow women to avoid the burden of playing "super-woman"—working full-time outside the home and returning to take full responsibility for care of home and family. It is clearly a revolution of momentous proportions that is being called for, with business and labor being asked to change their expectations of the working force from management executive to blue-collar worker. Where Friedan would not want to give up the gains made for women in the working world, Schlafly seems to regard these gains as subversive of the true role and purpose of woman. While both Micks and Friedan see the need of maintaining a harmony (not without tension!) between the images of Exodus and Eden, Schlafly would make it an either/or.

The Christian tradition has often been blamed for supporting the notion of male superiority—usually reference is made to Saint Paul, who clearly makes the husband the head of the house and gives theological sanction to his authority over the wife. For many Christians the issue concerning the Equal Rights Amendment (ERA) is shaped precisely by such material from Scripture. ERA appears to them to be an assault on a divinely ordered social structure in which the woman is a "helpmate" whose place is in the home. Usually the more conservative churches take this stance, while many of the mainline denominations have gone on record in support of ERA. The latter argue that one should look at the merits of this amendment in light of our situation today, rather than reject it out of hand on the basis of Scripture.

It is noted, furthermore, that insights from Scripture should be expected to enhance and support whatever humane developments have taken place in the evolution of the family and the place of women in society. The message of Saint Paul should not be used to exalt the social order of ancient times as the model for today. It is clear from these observations that the problems in interpreting Scripture can be quite pronounced in view of the profound social and cultural distance between ancient and modern society.

As Micks observes, Women's Liberation is as capable as any other movement of appearing self-righteous and excessively serious. But the gathering of women in Mexico City in 1975 to mark International Women's Year constituted a powerful expression of what the women's movement can mean for the whole world in humanizing the structures of society. One point often made at Mexico City was that women in the West cannot isolate themselves from the burdens borne by women in the countries of the Third World. The worldwide power of sisterhood may be increasingly felt in coming years as global efforts are made to elevate the social status of women. In recognizing and affirming the mutuality and interdependence of men and women, the results of these efforts should be beneficial to the health of every society.

# Exodus or Eden?: A Battle of Images

Marianne H. Micks

American women are at war with themselves. The reborn feminist movement has issued a clear call for a new Exodus in American society. Over half of the population is being urged to come out of privatism into the public arena, out of what has been called the inner space of womanhood into that outer space where political decisions are made and new cities are built. Across the nation women are hearing the demand to become Miriams, sisters of Moses.

Nevertheless, many women reject the call completely. Already some have organized a militant counter-movement in support of the old self-image. The role of women, they believe, is to plant and tend a garden of domestic tranquility where the really important human relationships can best flourish. They view the home as an American version of Eden-Paradise. Yet the self-styled homemaker appears to picture herself not so much as Eve but as a combination of Mary and Martha, devoting herself to spiritual matters as well as to cooking her lord's supper in the suburbs of the holy city.

These two conflicting ideas of what it means to be a woman in our society have come into sharper focus in the last few years. Indeed, they are making daily headlines. They are not a new thing in American life, however. Each picture has long hung in the national gallery. Since the days of Abigail Adams some women have seen themselves called to fight for freedom. Since the days of Barbara Fritchie others have beheld themselves chiefly as creators and protectors of home and family. By looking more closely at each image not only in its 1970s costume but also in the perspective of the last 150 years, we should be able to see the present issues more clearly, and thus to take a critical second look at the war between them.

Copyright © Anglican Theological Review, 600 Haven St., Evanston, IL 60201. Reprinted, with deletions, by permission from *Anglican Theological Review,* July, 1973. Marianne H. Micks is Professor of Biblical and Historical Theology at the Protestant Episcopal Theological Seminary in Alexandria, Virginia, and author of several works in the areas of Christian worship and anthropology.

I

The literature of our revived feminism invokes, in fact, two levels of the Exodus theme. As everyone knows, it rejects the notion that women are properly subject to male domination, in order to urge them to share fully in the risky business of human freedom. It also rejects the notion that women are constitutionally more suited for a private world, in order to urge their full participation in the wilderness struggle for a better society. The outcry against "slavery" and for individual freedom captures more column inches and inspires more cartoons; but the second level of thought promises to have as great, if not greater, social consequences.

Women seeking individual liberation are giving the Eden myth a hard time. They see the biblical Eve as part of a "cosmic sexist conspiracy," as one liberationist put it. The "old, oppressive myth" of the fractured rib has turned many churchwomen back to Genesis 1, where God creates mankind in his own image, male and female. Some go beyond the Bible in search of the legends about the other first woman, Lilith. It is a deliberate search for alternative ways of thinking about oneself. Lilly Rivlin, for example, writing on Lilith in the *MS.* magazine for December, 1972, said, "My personal images were not of an infantile paradise, a protected garden of Eden, but of rough yellow and brown deserts, of iron gray molten rock, of golden thistles and thorned brambles."[1] Perhaps unwittingly, she was describing the biblical landscape through which the children of Israel marched en route to the promised land after they were delivered from bondage in Egypt.

Stereotyped thinking about sexual roles, such women realize, is not easily overcome. Even those who do not use the rhetoric of political activists, or ascribe the continuing subordination of women to subtle manoeuvres on the part of "the male power structure," are aware of the all-persuasive power of the feminine mystique. One of the the most insidious images of woman, the feminists argue, is that buttressed by arguments from biological differences. If she cannot any longer be thought of as chattel, in good medieval tradition, she can still be pictured as "naturally" passive, created primarily to receive love and give nurture.

The noted psychoanalyst, Erik H. Erikson, developed this argument almost ten years ago for a special 1964 issue of *Daedalus*, the journal of the American Academy of Arts and Sciences, devoted to "The Woman in America." In the eyes of analysts of the new feminism, Erikson's article, "Inner and Outer Space: Reflections on Womanhood," must be classified as prehistoric. Anything published before 1968 is put in that category. Yet it is still subject to serious feminist rebuttal, partly because Erikson's acknowledged stature in his field lends such weight to his words, and partly

[1]Lilly Rivlin, "Lilith," *MS.,* December, 1972, 93.

because of the nature of the evidence he adduces in support of his speculations.

Erikson presented there a variation on the familiar Freudian theme that anatomy is destiny. He spoke of "feminine development and outlook" in terms of woman's emphasis on inner space as it related to the "ground-plan" of her body. To document his theories of "uterine glorification" (as Kate Millet has termed it), he reported observed differences in the play behavior of boys and girls aged ten, eleven, and twelve. From the point of view of a feminist critic, children of that age are already so thoroughly conditioned to play their culturally determined roles that their behavior cannot properly be used to defend arguments of biological destiny. A girl's preference for the indoors, for static and peaceful domestic scenes, rather than for dynamic exploration of outer space, need not rest chiefly on her somatic construction.

In fairness to Erikson, it should be noted that his article stressed the interplay of psychic, somatic, and social forces, and included the recognition that women do have a role to play in the political realm as well as their own "unique job" to do in producing and rearing children. To a feminist reader, however, that appears a grudging concession. The total impression one gets from his views on womanhood is that male mammals are better equipped, biologically and psychologically, for outdoor work in the life of the city. And this is precisely the idea that today's liberationists emphatically reject. Women, if they are to claim their full human responsibility as well as their full human freedom, must risk the out-of-doors.

The commitment of the new feminist movement to social action became clear in early 1973 at the convention of the National Women's Political Caucus, the first national women's political convention since 1872. The debate before the election of the first national chairman of the new organization centered, in effect, on the question of whether the caucus was to work primarily for the special concerns of women or for broader social reforms. The vote was four to one for the candidate whose campaign platform emphasized what women can do to help bring needed changes to our whole society. "Sisterhood does not mean the end of brotherhood," the newly elected chairman said.

Not all of the sisters of Moses label their self-understanding in terms of the biblical Exodus, of course. But the theme is explicit in the writings of such theologians as Mary Daly, author of *The Church and the Second Sex.* Along with many other women in the churches who have begun to think seriously about their roles within the life of that institution, Daly is sharply critical of the patriarchal theology and ethics which have always dominated Christianity. She believes that women have too long accepted and internalized the role assigned to them, that of being eternally feminine, instead of seeking to become whole human beings dedicated to the struggle against all types of oppression. The churches have reinforced the sexual caste in such a fashion that they have been impotent either to play their proper prophetic role in criticism of the culture, or to create the community of human freedom which they proclaim.

Thus the sisterhood of the women's liberation movement, as Daly sees it, has become an exodus community. It is an exodus community because it has "left home on the basis of a promise. The promise is within women's minds, in newfound potentialities that point toward future fulfillment. The journey which is begun on the basis of this promise involves leaving behind the false self-imposed from within." The journey of such women is not just toward new selfhood, however, but toward a renewed society including a renewed church. As exodus community, the sisterhood seeks to release values in the religious tradition which, she believes, are now suffocated by sexist symbols and power structures. "As exodus community, it is suggesting to organized religion that it should also 'go away' from the culture in which it is immersed and from the traditions which hinder liberation."[2]

Modern-dress proponents of the Edenic image of women publish less than their sisters of the liberation movement. Their voice is clearest, at this point in our history, in state hearings on the 27th Amendment to the Constitution, the Equal Rights Amendment (ERA). The acronyms which the militants of the Mary-Martha stripe have chosen summarize with alphabetical economy the positions they have taken. One group calls itself HOW, for Happiness of Women, in conscious opposition to the feminist counterpart NOW. Another styles itself AWARE, American Women Already Richly Endowed. A third has taken the name Restore Our American Republic, with the consequent promise to speak out loudly in behalf of national tradition.

Representatives of such groups recently gave their state legislators loaves of homemade bread as encouragement to vote against ratification of the Equal Rights Amendment. According to a reporter riding with one group (in this case, HOW members and those belonging to the "House-wives and Motherhood Anti-Lib Movement") on their bus trip to the state capitol, the trip was enlivened by singing "God Bless America," "Onward Christian Soldiers," and "The Battle Hymn of the Republic."

Press reports of their testimony in the public hearing make it clear that what is at stake in the debate over this Constitutional Amendment is a self-definition supported by ideas of the divinely-given order of creation. The issues, as seen by some women in the midwest at any rate, are clearly theological.

The state chairman of AWARE, for example, is quoted as saying, "We believe that God made man to be the protector and leader and provider

---

[2]"The Spiritual Revolution: Women's Liberation as Theological Re-education," *Andover Newton Quarterly*, 12 (March, 1972), 163–176.

for the family. They're trying to take away the rights women enjoy. God gave those rights, not the government. I think God and one make a majority, and I think we've got God on our side." Another woman told the legislators "The cry is to get out of the house and fulfill yourselves. That's fine. But who will raise the babies? God created woman to be a helpmate to man, not be in competition with him." Or yet again, the wife of a Protestant clergyman said, "ERA is contrary to God's plan for women. Women were granted equality by God long ago. You can read it in Genesis. And in Proverbs, it says that a husband safely trusts his wife and she fulfills his needs. That is an opportunity to fulfill our potential."

Minor issues like desegregation of public restrooms came in for their share of emotional debate in these hearings, but the real threat in the proposed legislation was seen over and over again as the threat to home and family. In an address to a local chapter of the National Council of Catholic Women, a leader of the "Housewives and Motherhood Anti-Lib Movement" put it very simply. "What we're doing," she said, "is protecting our daughters, preserving their right to make a choice about their lives. With the ERA in effect, it will no longer be considered acceptable to stay home and be a wife and mother." She was echoed by the president of AWARE, commenting on the gifts of goodies to the legislators, "We hope legislators enjoy our homemade bread and defeat the ERA so those of us who want can stay home and bake bread for our families."

## II

... I have selected just two spokesmen for the earlier tradition of woman's liberation—Margaret Fuller and Sarah Grimké. Each of them has been acclaimed as the first American defender of the rights of women. Both of them criticized the religious institutions of their day in a way strikingly similar to Mary Daly last year. And both of them drew positive support for their ideas from the same biblical fountain.

Margaret Fuller is undoubtedly the better known of the two. It is she who was considered the high priestess of New England Transcendentalism, she who exchanged ideas with Ralph Waldo Emerson and Bronson Alcott, she who left her native Boston at the invitation of Horace Greeley to become the first woman editor of a major New York newspaper. As the editor of a valuable anthology of historical writings on American feminism put it, the 1840s were a time when many women were "beginning to move outside the confines of their domestic province."[3]

[3]Miriam Schneir, ed., *Feminism: The Essential Historical Writings* (Vintage Books, 1972), p. 62. The following quotations from Fuller and Grimké are taken from this collection.

Margaret Fuller's *Woman in the Nineteenth Century*, published in 1845, is said to have shocked and irritated contemporary readers much as the Englishwoman Mary Wollstonecroft's *Vindication of the Rights of Women (with Strictures on Political and Moral Subjects)* had fifty years earlier, or as Betty Friedan's *The Feminine Mystique* did well over a century later. Indeed, it was denounced at its publication as immoral and silly; and until the resurgence of interest in "woman studies" prompted a new paperback edition recently, it had largely been forgotten even by those students of American literature who consider Margaret Fuller part of the great flowering of New England.

The first thing that strikes today's reader of Fuller's 130-year-old tract is its use of the headlines. Women were in the news. She picks up her *Boston Mail* and finds a poem entitled "Dignity of Woman." She opens another periodical and finds an article on the emancipation of women in Hungary. The Rhode Island legislature has just acted to secure property rights for married women. These casually collected items, Fuller comments, are symptoms of the times. There appears to be "a growing liberality" on the subject of women. In 1845.

For our present purposes, however, two features of Margaret Fuller's writing about nineteenth-century women deserve special attention. The first is her deliberate stress on going outside the home to lead "a true life," to become a full human being. The second is her criticism of the current religious institutions which fostered women's continued exclusion from the public sphere, together with her appeal to biblical themes in support of her vision of women fully engaged in this "many-chorded world."

An irritated tradesman is Fuller's imagined adversary. Against the exodus she is advocating, he cries, "Is it not enough that you have done all you could to break up the national union and thus destroy the prosperity of our country, but now you must be trying to take my wife away from the cradle and the kitchen-hearth to vote at polls, and preach from a pulpit? Of course, if she does such things, she cannot attend to those of her own sphere."

The allusion to the work of the Abolitionists in the first part of this question is noteworthy; both the nineteenth- and twentieth-century outbreaks against the oppression of women have had close ties with social protest against the oppression of Blacks. So it is no coincidence that Fuller makes her rejoinder in these terms: "Those who think the physical circumstances of Women would make a part in the affairs of national government unsuitable, are by no means those who think it impossible for negresses to endure fieldwork. . . ."

The lesser-known pioneer in behalf of women's rights, Sarah Grimké, was more directly engaged in the battle for freedom about which she, too, wrote. Her early feminist tract, *The Equality of the Sexes and the Condition of Woman,* was published in 1838, some six years before Fuller's. By that time she had left her South Carolina plantation home to fight against slavery, left the Episcopal Church in which she had been brought up to don the sober dress of a Quaker, and left the reticence expected of a Southern lady to speak out against the bigotry of New England churchmen.

Sarah Grimké and her sister Angelina were apparently very effective public speakers. First in New York and later in Boston their lectures on the evils of slavery attracted such audiences of women that they had to move from church parlors into the church itself in order to accommodate the crowds. Shortly men began to attend also, so that the Grimkés were speaking before mixed audiences. Public morality was outraged. The General Association of Congregational Ministers of Massachusetts issued a Pastoral Letter, said to have been read from every Congregational pulpit in the state.

The ministers called the public appearance of women in the work of social reform contrary both to Christian faith and to nature. "We appreciate," they said, "the unostentatious prayers of woman in advancing the cause of religion at home and abroad ... but when she assumes the place and tone of man as a public reformer ... she yields the power which God has given her for protection, and her character becomes unnatural." The God-given power of woman, the letter insisted, was to exercise a softening influence on man's opinions, unobtrusively and in private. Her duties, it said, were clearly spelled out in the New Testament. She was made to be a vine leaning on a trellis. (The metaphor was actually used.) If she presumed to think she was an elm tree she would "fall in shame and dishonor into the dust."

In response to this extraordinary document, Sarah Grimké commented that it would one day evoke as much astonishment as Cotton Mather's ideas on witchcraft; and she was right. Her reasoned rebuttal was published originally in letter form in *The New England Spectator* before being issued as a pamphlet. She tackles the biblical argument head on. As she reads Genesis, man and woman are given coregency over the earth. She does not think that Adam's easy acquiescence to his wife's proposal says much for his intellectual superiority.

What of the New Testament evidence, which the ministers found so clear? Her copy (which she notes had had to be translated by men since women were not taught Hebrew and Greek) did not say anything about women being vines made to cling to a trellis. The Sermon on the Mount, she argues, does not distinguish between the moral responsibility of men and of women. The Lord Jesus defines the duties of his followers without reference to sex or condition. No one is to hide his light under a bushel.

Men as well as women are commanded to bring forth the fruits of the Spirit—love, meekness, gentleness. Women as well as men should be "engaged in the great work of public reformation" for they are equally responsible moral beings.

The whole series of letters has as its unifying idea the duty of women to act for the welfare of the world. Grimké is disturbed because women are not given the educational opportunities to help them do this. Since they are educated from early childhood to regard themselves as inferior creatures, they lack self-respect. Because of the training they get, she believes, women come to think of themselves as "a kind of machinery, necessary to keep the domestic engine in order."

While Grimké was commenting on the feminine self-image in such terms, other women were busily at work trying to inculcate in young girls precisely the notion of domestic engineer which she deplored. But with a conviction that the calling of women was superior to that of men, being the calling to build a Christian home. What the Grimké sisters thought of themselves and their society must be set alongside the conflicting ideas of what their contemporaries thought to be the proper role of the daughters of Eve. The Beecher sisters will serve as a typical example.

Catherine Beecher has been called one of the chief architects of the cult of domesticity which grew rampantly, along with the cult of "true womanhood" throughout the nineteenth century. Together with her famous sister, Harriet, she published in 1869 *The American Woman's Home: or, Principles of Domestic Science*, a vast compendium of information on how to make the domestic engine run more efficiently. Along with advice on how to minister to the earthly needs of the family, however, the Beecher sisters presented their theories of ministry to spiritual needs too. The Christian home was for them the most important sphere of activity for anyone, male or female. Jesus, they believed, chose to be a carpenter in order to emphasize the priority of homebuilding.

The Beecher sisters rejected the Calvinist theology, New Haven variety, of their distinguished father, Lyman; but their childhood life in his rural parsonage in Litchfield, Connecticut apparently provided them with the model for all American life. According to one social historian, the cult of the idyllic home exemplified in the Beechers' book must be understood in terms of the tremendous changes taking place in American society in the middle decades of the century. The rapid changes of the economic and social order, especially the fast growth of cities with their immigrants, slums, saloons, and gambling dens, helped make the symbol of the ideal country home doubly attractive. He quotes the Beechers as evidence: "Each and all of the family, some part of the day, should take exercise in the pure air, under the magnetic and healthful rays of the sun. Every head of a family should seek a soil and climate which will afford such opportunities. Railroads, enabling men toiling in cities to rear families in the country, are on this account a special blessing."[4] Catherine and Harriet did not yet have to worry about pollution or the problems of commuter trains.

For whatever reasons, the Beechers and dozens of other "scribbling women" (to use Melville's contemptuous phrase) pounded into middle-class readers of *Godey's Lady's Book, Ladies' Magazine,* and other fore-runners of *House and Garden,* an exalted notion of their own calling and a self-image impossible to fulfill. The woman's job, in brief, was to create Eden. Here her husband might retreat from the struggles and temptations of his work in the city. Here her children might be nurtured in an atmo-sphere of peace and harmony. Here she must provide a spiritual climate pervaded by her own purity and goodness.

It is difficult to read the cotton candy produced by some of these women writers with appropriate detachment, and almost impossible not to char-acterize their high aspirations as hubris. Undoubtedly there were unfortu-nate side-effects. The vague physical malaises which came to be termed "female diseases" were not the least of these, and no modern psychothera-pist would attribute them, as the Beecher sisters were wont to do, simply to the effects of wearing a Victorian corset. In the seventy-five years after the founding of our republic, those women who defined themselves as "the pious, pure keepers of the hearthside" suffered a "notable decline in autonomy and morals."[5] Life on a pedestal, even a pedestal largely of one's own choosing, is at best uncomfortable.

A lot of people helped to keep woman propped up there, of course. Shortly after the turn of the century, Congress and the clergy both rallied notably in support of sanctified images of Home and Motherhood. In a splendid study, "The Feminine Mystique: 1890–1910,"[6] Dorothy Bass Fraser cites works by the Social Gospel theologians Walter Rauschenbusch and Lyman Abbott as prime expressions of the prevalent picture of the ideal woman. Abbott, incidentally, succeeded the Beechers' brother as minister of the influential Plymouth Congregational Church in Brooklyn. His word picture of the proper attitudes for a bride, in his 1908 book *The Home Builder,* demands requotation:

She wishes, not to submit a reluctant will to his, but to make his will her own. She wishes a sovereign and is glad to have found him—no! to have been found

---

[4]*The American Woman's Home,* pp. 24–25, as quoted by Kirk Jeffrey, "The Family as Utopian Retreat from the City: the Nineteenth-Century Contribution," *Soundings,* LV (Spring 1972), 25.

[5]Jeffrey, *op. cit.,* p. 34.

[6]Dorothy Bass Fraser, "The Feminine Mystique: 1890–1910," *Union Seminary Quarterly Review,* XXVII (Summer, 1972), 225–239.

by him. . . . To give up her home, abandon her name, merge her personality in his keeping—this is her glad ambition, and it swallows up all other ambitions.[7]

That same year Mother's Day was first celebrated in this country, to be endorsed by the Presbyterian General Assembly the following year and by Act of Congress in 1914. By that time women who believed that their place was in the home had organized nationally against the 19th Amendment to the Constitution, against the amendment to the American way of life which would have permitted them to go to the polls.

## III

The battle of images which has been part of the life of American women for almost 200 years has comic overtones and tragic undertones. We have been listening chiefly to the voices of extremists, militants at one pole or the other for whom the self-image is clear and unequivocal. Yet most American women looking into their mirrors on a cloudy morning [today] would, I suspect, see there at least two images. Is it necessary to choose between them? And, if so, on what grounds?

A conflict of self-images may be a very healthy phenomenon. Many observers of our current social scene think we may be in excessive danger of polarizing everything, demanding that everyone wear either a white hat or a black one as if we were all actors in a daytime television show. We must learn instead to affirm our cultural pluralism. HOW and NOW and a host of other positions between the two may all have a proper place in a pluralistic society.

Much as all of us would prefer to have simple answers for the complexities of our lives, we are increasingly having to learn to cope with ambiguity. Perhaps for a woman to affirm both the Mary-Martha and the Miriam image of herself would be a healthy exercise in being human. No single self-image is adequate to express the many dimensions of full personal being.

The image of oneself as builder of Eden, for example, may offer a good basis for becoming an active environmentalist. Catherine Beecher's vision of women as duty-bound to provide fresh air and rural beauty for their families was curiously fulfilled a century later in Ladybird Johnson's roadside beautification program. There may be a causative relationship between an Edenic view of home life and a positive view of nature. If the

[7]Abbott, *op. cit.*, p. 25 as quoted *ibid.*, p. 235.

utopian retreat from the city postponed urban renewal grievously, it may nevertheless have contributed directly to emerging awareness that the earth will not remain a garden unless it is tended.

Seen in historic perspective, however, the Eden mythology has at least three major drawbacks which should make any modern woman hesitate a long time before including it in her own gallery of images. If the choice is between Eden and Exodus, I must agree with NOW. It is time for women unambiguously to join the Exodus community.

Perhaps the most obvious flaw in the Edenic view of womanhood, one noted frequently by social historians who have no feminist axe to grind, is that it belongs almost exclusively to white middle-class Americans. For the mid-nineteeth century, the word "Protestant" should be added. It is a WASP product. Only in a relatively affluent family, then or now, can the woman afford to stay home. The women who most enthusiastically enshrined themselves by the hearth were not the mill hands, the cotton pickers, or the garment workers. Nor were they women living in the city tenements or frontier cabins. The picture has always had a romanticism about it, a luxury possible only for the well-fed and the well-housed.

A second clear and present danger in thinking of oneself as made for a dependent but all-important role in the bosom of the nuclear family is that abdication, or at least limitation, of moral responsibility to which Sarah Grimké and Margaret Fuller pointed, each in her own way, so long ago. The members of AWARE, HOW, ROAR, and all their unorganized sisters appear to prefer the feminine mystique of the vine-and-trellis type to responsible coregency in the affairs of the Lord's world. They appear to prefer to tighten the silver cord on the circumference of their love.

But perhaps the most serious weakness of this imagery in theological terms is its realized eschatology, its presupposition that the Kingdom of God has already fully arrived in our midst, with little left to hope, pray, or work for. American women are already richly endowed, they say. It is intriguing to learn that such women en route to testify against ERA chose to sing "The Battle Hymn of the Republic." The first line of that hymn is almost a textbook definition of what is meant by the term "realized eschatology," dissolving all tension over the coming of the Kingdom and oversimplifying the facts of Christian experience. "Mine eyes have seen the glory of the coming of the Lord"? Yes and no; already but not yet. Julia Ward Howe, the woman who wrote those words in 1862, it should be noted, later became an active and prestige-lending convert to the suffrage movement.

The image of oneself as a Miriam, called to be part of the Exodus community, on the other hand, commends itself on many counts. Its strong emphasis on the common human fight against oppression wherever it is found; its recognition that we have not yet arrived at the promised land, do not yet live fully in the Kingdom of God; its view of life as involving responsible struggle in the wilderness—all are authentic biblical motifs from the story of the bondage in Egypt through to the vision of the New Jerusalem at the end of the Apocalypse.

Free and full participation of all Americans in the marketplaces and the halls of government, in all of the arenas of our public life, seemed a reasonable proposition to Abigail Adams when she wrote to her husband John about the new code of laws he was making for the nation in March, 1776. It still seems to be so. If I read them correctly, few of our latter-day feminists would go so far as Mrs. Adams did when she said that, unless particular care and attention were paid to the ladies, they were determined to foment a rebellion. But all of them would agree with her that men of sense in all ages abhor those customs which treat women only as vassals, and prefer for the title tyrant the name of friend. Provided, of course, that the rhetoric were better up-dated. Our founding mothers did not speak the idiom of today's liberationists.

Present-day advocates of liberation, on the other hand, often seem to lack the sense of humor so conspicuous in the letters of such women as Abigail Adams. They seem often to have an overly grim notion of what it means to be in an Exodus community. They sometimes sound almost as self-righteous as that anti-liberation woman who was sure that she and God made a majority.

It might be well for all of us who hear the call to come out of inner space into that outer space of public action, out of bondage into full human personhood, to reread the biblical account of our prototypes. Miriam and her sisters, it tells us, took with them their timbrels. Their music led the whole community in singing and dancing and rejoicing over their common freedom, the gift of God.

# Understanding the Difference

Phyllis Schlafly

The first requirement for the acquisition of power by the Positive Woman is to understand the differences between men and women. Your outlook on life, your faith, your behavior, your potential for fulfillment, all are determined by the parameters of your original premise. The Positive

Reprinted by permission of Arlington House Publishers, Westport, Connecticut. Copyright © 1977 by Phyllis Schlafly. Phyllis Schlafly, lawyer and author, is National Chairperson of Stop ERA and author of *The Power of the Positive Woman,* from which this selection is taken.

Woman starts with the assumption that the world is her oyster. She rejoices in the creative capability within her body and the power potential of her mind and spirit. She understands that men and women are different, and that those very differences provide the key to her success as a person and fulfillment as a woman.

The women's liberationist, on the other hand, is imprisoned by her own negative view of herself and of her place in the world around her. This view of women was most succinctly expressed in an advertisement designed by the principal women's liberationist organization, the National Organization for Women (NOW), and run in many magazines and newspapers and as spot announcements on many television stations. The advertisement showed a darling curlyheaded girl with the caption: "This healthy, normal baby has a handicap. She was born female."

This is the self-articulated dog-in-the-manger, chip-on-the-shoulder, fundamental dogma of the women's liberation movement. Someone—it is not clear who, perhaps God, perhaps the "Establishment," perhaps a conspiracy of male chauvinist pigs—dealt women a foul blow by making them female. It becomes necessary, therefore, for women to agitate and demonstrate and hurl demands on society in order to wrest from an oppressive male-dominated social structure the status that has been wrongfully denied to women through the centuries.

By its very nature, therefore, the women's liberation movement precipitates a series of conflict situations—in the legislatures, in the courts, in the schools, in industry—with man targeted as the enemy. Confrontation replaces cooperation as the watchword of all relationships. Women and men become adversaries instead of partners.

The second dogma of the women's liberationists is that, of all the injustices perpetrated upon women through the centuries, the most oppressive is the cruel fact that women have babies and men do not. Within the confines of the women's liberationist ideology, therefore, the abolition of this overriding inequality of women becomes the primary goal. This goal must be achieved at any and all costs—to the woman herself, to the baby, to the family, and to society. Women must be made equal to men in their ability *not* to become pregnant and *not* to be expected to care for babies they may bring into the world.

This is why women's liberationists are compulsively involved in the drive to make abortion and child-care centers for all women, regardless of religion or income, both socially acceptable and government-financed. Former Congresswoman Bella Abzug has defined the goal: "to enforce the constitutional right of females to terminate pregnancies that they do not wish to continue."

If man is targeted as the enemy, and the ultimate goal of women's liberation is independence from men and the avoidance of pregnancy and its consequences, then lesbianism is logically the highest form in the ritual of women's liberation. Many, such as Kate Millett, come to this conclusion, although many others do not.

The Positive Woman will never travel that dead-end road. It is self-evident to the Positive Woman that the female body with its baby-producing organs was not designed by a conspiracy of men but by the Divine Architect of the human race. Those who think it is unfair that women have babies, whereas men cannot, will have to take up their complaint with God because no other power is capable of changing that fundamental fact. On some college campuses, I have been assured that other methods of reproduction will be developed. But most of us must deal with the real world rather than with the imagination of dreamers.

Another feature of the woman's natural role is the obvious fact that women can breast-feed babies and men cannot. This functional role was not imposed by conspiratorial males seeking to burden women with confining chores, but must be recognized as part of the plan of the Divine Architect for the survival of the human race through the centuries and in the countries that know no pasteurization of milk or sterilization of bottles.

The Positive Woman looks upon her femaleness and her fertility as part of her purpose, her potential, and her power. She rejoices that she has a capability for creativity that men can never have.

The third basic dogma of the women's liberation movement is that there is no difference between male and female except the sex organs, and that all those physical, cognitive, and emotional differences you *think* are there, are merely the result of centuries of restraints imposed by a male-dominated society and sex-stereotyped schooling. The role imposed on women is, by definition, inferior, according to the women's liberationists.

The Positive Woman knows that, while there are some physical competitions in which women are better (and can command more money) than men, including those that put a premium on grace and beauty, such as figure skating, the superior physical strength of males over females in competitions of strength, speed, and short-term endurance is beyond rational dispute.

In the Olympic Games, women not only cannot win any medals in competition with men, the gulf between them is so great that they cannot even qualify for the contests with men. No amount of training from infancy can enable women to throw the discus as far as men, or to match men in push-ups or in lifting weights. In track and field events, individual male records surpass those of women by 10 to 20 percent.

Female swimmers today are beating Johnny Weissmuller's records, but today's male swimmers are better still. Chris Evert can never win a tennis match against Jimmy Connors. If we removed lady's tees from golf courses, women would be out of the game. Putting women in football or wrestling matches can only be an exercise in laughs.

The Olympic Games, whose rules require strict verification to ascertain that no male enters a female contest and, with his masculine advantage, unfairly captures a woman's medal, formerly insisted on a visual inspection of the contestants' bodies. Science, however, has discovered that men and women are so innately different physically that their maleness/femaleness can be conclusively established by means of a simple skin test of fully clothed persons.

If there is *anyone* who should oppose enforced sex-equality, it is the women athletes. Babe Didrickson, who played and defeated some of the great male athletes of her time, is unique in the history of sports.

If sex equality were enforced in professional sports, it would mean that men could enter the women's tournaments and win most of the money. Bobby Riggs has already threatened: "I think that men 55 years and over should be allowed to play women's tournaments—like the Virginia Slims. Everybody ought to know there's no sex after 55 anyway."

The Positive Woman remembers the essential validity of the old prayer: "Lord, give me the strength to change what I can change, the serenity to accept what I cannot change, and the wisdom to discern the difference." The women's liberationists are expending their time and energies erecting a make-believe world in which they hypothesize that *if* schooling were gender-free, and *if* the same money were spent on male and female sports programs, and *if* women were permitted to compete on equal terms, *then* they would prove themselves to be physically equal. Meanwhile, the Positive Woman has put the ineradicable physical differences into her mental computer, programmed her plan of action, and is already on the way to personal achievement.

Thus, while some militant women spend their time demanding more money for professional sports, ice skater Janet Lynn, a truly Positive Woman, quietly signed the most profitable financial contract in the history of women's athletics. It was not the strident demands of the women's liberationists that brought high prizes to women's tennis, but the discovery by sports promoters that beautiful female legs gracefully moving around the court made women's tennis a highly marketable television production to delight male audiences.

Many people thought that the remarkable filly named Ruffian would prove that a female race horse could compete equally with a male. Even with the handicap of extra weights placed on the male horse, the race was a disaster for the female. The gallant Ruffian gave her all in a noble effort to compete, but broke a leg in the race and, despite the immediate attention of top veterinarians, had to be put away.

Despite the claims of the women's liberation movement, there are countless physical differences between men and women. The female body is 50 to 60 percent water, the male 60 to 70 percent water, which explains why males can dilute alcohol better than women and delay its effect. The average woman is about 25 percent fatty tissue, while the male is 15 percent, making women more buoyant in water and able to swim with less effort. Males have a tendency to color blindness. Only 5 percent of persons who get gout are female. Boys are born bigger. Women live longer in most countries of the world, not only in the United States where we have a hard-driving competitive pace. Women excel in manual dexterity, verbal skills, and memory recall.

Arianna Stassinopoulos in her book *The Female Woman* has done a good job of spelling out the many specific physical differences that are so innate and so all-pervasive that

> even if Women's Lib was given a hundred, a thousand, ten thousand years in which to eradicate *all* the differences between the sexes, it would still be an impossible undertaking. . . .
>
> It is inconceivable that millions of years of evolutionary selection during a period of marked sexual division of labor have not left pronounced traces on the innate character of men and women. Aggressiveness, and mechanical and spatial skills, a sense of direction, and physical strength—all masculine characteristics—are the qualities essential for a hunter; even food gatherers need these same qualities for defense and exploration. The prolonged period of dependence of human children, the difficulty of carrying the peculiarly heavy and inert human baby—a much heavier, clumsier burden than the monkey infant and much less able to cling on for safety—meant that women could not both look after their children and be hunters and explorers. Early humans learned to take advantage of this period of dependence to transmit rules, knowledge and skills to their offspring—women needed to develop verbal skills, a talent for personal relationships, and a predilection for nurturing going even beyond the maternal instinct.[1]

Does the physical advantage of men doom women to a life of servility and subservience? The Positive Woman knows that she has a complementary advantage which is at least as great—and, in the hands of a skillful woman, far greater. The Divine Architect who gave men a superior strength to lift weights also gave women a different kind of superior strength.

The women's liberationists and their dupes who try to tell each other that the sexual drive of men and women is really the same, and that it is only societal restraints that inhibit women from an equal desire, and equal enjoyment, and an equal freedom from the consequences, are doomed to frustration forever. It just isn't so, and pretending cannot make it so. The differences are not a woman's weakness but her strength.

Dr. Robert Collins, who has had ten years' experience in listening to and advising young women at a large eastern university, put his finger on the reason why casual "sexual activity" is such a cheat on women:

> A basic flaw in this new morality is the assumption that males and females are the same sexually. The simplicity of the male anatomy and its operation

[1]Ariana Stassinopoulos, *The Female Woman* (New York: Random House, 1973), p. 30–31.

suggest that to a man, sex can be an activity apart from his whole being, a drive related to the organs themselves.

In a woman, the complex internal organization, correlated with her other hormonal systems, indicates her sexuality must involve her total self. On the other hand, the man is orgasm-oriented with a drive that ignores most other aspects of the relationship. The woman is almost totally different. She is engulfed in romanticism and tries to find and express her total feeling for her partner.

A study at a midwestern school shows that 80 percent of the women who had intercourse hoped to marry their partner. Only 12 percent of the men expected the same.

Women say that soft, warm promises and tender touches are delightful, but that the act itself usually leads to a "Is that all there is to it?" reaction. . . .

[A typical reaction is]: "It sure wasn't worth it. It was no fun at the time. I've been worried ever since. . . .

The new morality is a fad. It ignores history, it denies the physical and mental composition of human beings, it is intolerant, exploitative, and is oriented toward intercourse, not love.[2]

The new generation can brag all it wants about the new liberation of the new morality, but it is still the woman who is hurt the most. The new morality isn't just a "fad"—it is a cheat and a thief. It robs the woman of her virtue, her youth, her beauty, and her love—for nothing, just nothing. It has produced a generation of young women searching for their identity, bored with sexual freedom, and despondent from the loneliness of living a life without commitment. They have abandoned the old commandments, but they can't find any new rules that work.

The Positive Woman recognizes the fact that, when it comes to sex, women are simply not the equal of men. The sexual drive of men is much stronger than that of women. That is how the human race was designed in order that it might perpetuate itself. The other side of the coin is that it is easier for women to control their sexual appetites. A Positive Woman cannot defeat a man in a wrestling or boxing match, but she can motivate him, inspire him, encourage him, teach him, restrain him, reward him, and have power over him that he can never achieve over her with all his muscle. How or whether a Positive Woman uses her power is determined solely by the way she alone defines her goals and develops her skills.

The differences between men and women are also emotional and psychological. Without woman's innate maternal instinct, the human race would have died out centuries ago. There is nothing so helpless in all earthly life as the newborn infant. It will die within hours if not cared for. Even in the most primitive, uneducated societies, women have always cared for their newborn babies. They didn't need any schooling to teach

[2]*Chicago Tribune,* August 17, 1975.

them how. They didn't need any welfare workers to tell them it is their social obligation. Even in societies to whom such concepts as "ought," "social responsibility," and "compassion for the helpless" were unknown, mothers cared for their new babies.

Why? Because caring for a baby serves the natural maternal need of a woman. Although not nearly so total as the baby's need, the woman's need is nonetheless real.

The overriding psychological need of a woman is to love something alive. A baby fulfills this need in the lives of most women. If a baby is not available to fill that need, women search for a baby-substitute. This is the reason why women have traditionally gone into teaching and nursing careers. They are doing what comes naturally to the female psyche. The schoolchild or the patient of any age provides an outlet for a woman to express her natural maternal need.

This maternal need in women is the reason why mothers whose children have grown up and flown from the nest are sometimes cut loose from their psychological moorings. The maternal need in women can show itself in love for grandchildren, nieces, nephews, or even neighbors' children. The maternal need in some women has even manifested itself in an extraordinary affection lavished on a dog, a cat, or a parakeet.

This is not to say that every woman must have a baby in order to be fulfilled. But it is to say that fulfillment for most women involves expressing their natural maternal urge by loving and caring for someone.

The women's liberation movement complains that traditional stereotyped roles assume that women are "passive" and that men are "aggressive." The anomaly is that a woman's most fundamental emotional need is not passive at all, but active. A woman naturally seeks to love affirmatively and to show that love in an active way by caring for the object of her affections.

The Positive Woman finds somebody on whom she can lavish her maternal love so that it doesn't well up inside her and cause psychological frustrations. Surely no woman is so isolated by geography or insulated by spirt that she cannot find someone worthy of her maternal love. All persons, men and women, gain by sharing something of themselves with their fellow humans, but women profit most of all because it is part of their very nature.

One of the strangest quirks of women's liberationists is their complaint that societal restraints prevent men from crying in public or showing their emotions, but permit women to do so, and that therefore we should "liberate" men to enable them, too, to cry in public. The public display of fear, sorrow, anger, and irritation reveals a lack of self-discipline that should be avoided by the Positive Woman just as much as by the Positive Man. Maternal love, however, is not a weakness but a manifestation of strength and service, and it should be nurtured by the Positive Woman.

Most women's organizations, recognizing the preference of most women to avoid hard-driving competition, handle the matter of succession of officers by the device of a nominating committee. This eliminates the unpleasantness and the tension of a competitive confrontation every year or two. Many women's organizations customarily use a prayer attributed to Mary, Queen of Scots, which is an excellent analysis by a woman of women's faults:

> Keep us, O God, from pettiness; let us be large in thought, in word, in deed. Let us be done with fault-finding and leave off self-seeking. . . . Grant that we may realize it is the little things that create differences, that in the big things of life we are at one.

Another silliness of the women's liberationists is their frenetic desire to force all women to accept the title *Ms* in place of *Miss* or *Mrs.* If Gloria Steinem and Betty Friedan want to call themselves *Ms* in order to conceal their marital status, their wishes should be respected.

But that doesn't satisfy the women's liberationists. They want all women to be compelled to use *Ms* whether they like it or not. The women's liberation movement has been waging a persistent campaign to browbeat the media into using *Ms* as the standard title for all women. The women's liberationists have already succeeded in getting the Department of Health, Education and Welfare to forbid schools and colleges from identifying women students as *Miss* or *Mrs.*[3]

All polls show that the majority of women do not care to be called *Ms.* A Roper poll indicated that 81 percent of the women questioned said they prefer *Miss* or *Mrs.* to *Ms.* Most married women feel they worked hard for the *r* in their names, and they don't care to be gratuitously deprived of it. Most single women don't care to have their name changed to an unfamiliar title that at best conveys overtones of feminist ideology and is polemical in meaning, and at worst connotes misery instead of joy. Thus, Kate Smith, a very Positive Woman, proudly proclaimed on television that she is "Miss Kate Smith, not Ms." Like other Positive Women, she has been succeeding while negative women have been complaining.

Finally, women are different from men in dealing with the fundamentals of life itself. Men are philosophers, women are practical, and 'twas ever thus. Men may philosophize about how life began and where we are heading; women are concerned about feeding the kids today. No woman would ever, as Karl Marx did, spend years reading political philosophy in the British Museum while her child starved to death. Women don't take naturally to a search for the intangible and the abstract. The Positive Woman knows who she is and where she is going, and she will reach her goal because the longest journey starts with a very practical first step.

Amaury de Riencourt, in his book *Sex and Power in History,* shows that a successful society depends on a delicate balancing of different male and

[3]HEW Regulation on Sex Discrimination in Schools and Colleges, effective July 18, 1975, 86.21(C)(4).

female factors, and that the women's liberation movement, which promotes unisexual values and androgyny, contains within it "a social and cultural death wish and the end of the civilization that endorses it."

One of the few scholarly works dealing with woman's role, *Sex and Power in History*, synthesizes research from a variety of disciplines—sociology, biology, history, anthropology, religion, philosophy, and psychology. De Riencourt traces distinguishable types of women in different periods in history, from prehistoric to modern times. The "liberated" Roman matron, who is most similar to the present-day feminist, helped bring about the fall of Rome through her unnatural emulation of masculine qualities, which resulted in a large-scale breakdown of the family and ultimately of the empire.

De Riencourt examines the fundamental, inherent differences between men and women. He argues that man is the more aggressive, rational, mentally creative, analytical-minded sex because of his early biological role as hunter and provider. Woman, on the other hand, represents stability, flexibility, reliance on intuition, and harmony with nature, stemming from her procreative function.

Where man is discursive, logical, abstract, or philosophical, woman tends to be emotional, personal, practical, or mystical. Each set of qualities is vital and complements the other. Among the many differences explained in de Riencourt's book are the following:

> Women tend more toward conformity than men—which is why they often excel in such disciplines as spelling and punctuation where there is only one correct answer, determined by social authority. Higher intellectual activities, however, require a mental independence and power of abstraction that they usually lack, not to mention a certain form of aggressive boldness of the imagination which can only exist in a sex that is basically aggressive for biological reasons.
>
> To sum up: The masculine proclivity in problem solving is analytical and categorical; the feminine, synthetic and contextual. . . . Deep down, man tends to focus on the object, on external results and achievements; woman focuses on subjective motives and feelings. If life can be compared to a play, man focuses on the theme and structure of the play, woman on the innermost feelings displayed by the actors.[4]

De Riencourt provides impressive refutation of two of the basic errors of the women's liberation movement: (1) that there are no emotional or cognitive differences between the sexes, and (2) that women should strive to be like men.

A more colloquial way of expressing the de Riencourt conclusion that men are more analytical and women more personal and practical is in the

[4]Amaury de Riencourt, *Sex and Power in History* (New York: David McKay Co., Inc., 1974), p. 56.

different answers that one is likely to get to the question, "Where did you get that steak?" A man will reply, "At the corner market," or wherever he bought it. A woman will usually answer, "Why? What's the matter with it?"

An effort to eliminate the differences by social engineering or legislative or constitutional tinkering cannot succeed, which is fortunate, but social relationships and spiritual values can be ruptured in the attempt. Thus the role reversals being forced upon high-school students, under which guidance counselors urge reluctant girls to take "shop" and boys to take "home economics," further confuse a generation already unsure about its identity. They are as wrong as efforts to make a left-handed child right-handed.

# The Second Stage

## Betty Friedan

"The women's movement is over," said my friend, a usually confident executive, who is also a wife and a feminist. "At least," she continued in a grim tone, "it is in my shop. The men are making jokes about bimbos again. It doesn't matter if we get mad; they act as if we aren't there. When a new job opens up, all they look for now is men. It's as if the word has gone out that we've lost our case; there won't be any Equal Rights Amendment [ERA], so they don't need to worry anymore about lawsuits over sex discrimination, even though laws against it are still on the books. They figure they can do what they want about women now, like the old days."

The women's movement in some form will never be over. But the rights that women have struggled to win in the last decade are in deadly danger, with right-wing groups in Congress determined to gut laws against sex discrimination and to abolish legal abortion, and a conservative Supreme Court already backtracking on equality. . . . If ERA does not become part of the Constitution by June 30, 1982, it may not come up again in this century.[1]

Copyright © 1981 by Betty Friedan. Reprinted by permission of Summit Books, a Simon and Schuster division of Gulf and Western Corporation. Betty Friedan has written several works of consequence in the feminist movement, the most recent being *The Second Stage* (1981), from which this selection is taken.
[1] This deadline has been extended by a congressional vote.

Listening to my own daughter and others of her generation, I sense something off, out of focus, going wrong. From the daughters, working so hard at their new careers, determined not to be trapped as their mothers were, expecting so much and taking for granted the opportunities we fought for, I've begun to hear undertones of pain and puzzlement, almost a bitterness that they hardly dare admit. As if, with all those opportunities that we won for them, they are reluctant to speak out loud about certain other needs some of us rebelled against—needs for love, security, men, children, family, home.

I sense a frustration in women not so young, about those careers they're lucky to have, facing agonizing conflicts over having children. Can they have it all? How?

I sense a desperation in divorced women and men and an unspoken fear of divorce in those still married, which is being twisted into a backlash against equal rights that are more essential than ever for the divorced.

I sense a sullen impatience among some of those women who entered the workforce in unprecedented millions over the last 10 years, who are in fact earning 59 cents for every dollar men earn because the only jobs available to most women are still in the low-paying clerical and service fields. Even among the few who have broken through to the executive suite, I sense the exhilaration of trying to be superwomen giving way to disillusionment with the tokens of power.

What is going wrong? Why this uneasy sense of battles won, only to be fought again, of battles that should have been won and yet are not, of battles that suddenly one does not really want to win, and the weariness of battle altogether—how many feel it?

I, and other feminists, dread to discuss these troubling symptoms because the women's movement has been the source and focus of so much of our energy, strength and security for so long. We cannot conceive that it will not go on forever the same way it has for nearly 20 years. But we cannot go on denying these puzzling symptoms of distress.

I believe that it is over, the first stage. We must now move into the second stage of the sex-role revolution that the women's movement set off.

In the first stage, our aim was full participation, power and voice in the mainstream—inside the party, the political process, the professions, the business world. But we were diverted from our dream by a sexual politics that cast man as enemy and seemed to repudiate the traditional values of the family.

In reaction against the feminine mystique, which defined women solely in terms of their relation to men as wives, mothers and homemakers, we insidiously fell into a feminist mystique, which denied that core of women's personhood that is fulfilled through love, nurture, home. We seemed to create a polarization between feminists and those women who still looked to the family for their very identity, not only among the dwindling numbers who were still full-time housewives, but also among women who do not get as much sense of worth or security from their jobs as they get —or wish they could get—from being someone's wife or mother.

The very terms in which we fought for abortion, or against rape, or in opposition to pornography seemed to express a hatred for men and a lack of reverence for childbearing that threatened those women profoundly. That focus on sexual battles also took energy away from the fight for the ERA and kept us from moving to restructure work and home so that women could have real choices. We fought for equality in terms of male power, without asking what equality really means between women and men.

I believe that we have to break through our own feminist mystique now and move into the second stage—no longer against, but with men. In the second stage we have to transcend that polarization between feminism and the family. We have to free ourselves from male power traps, understand the limits of women's power as a separate interest group and grasp the possibility of generating a new kind of power, which was the real promise of the women's movement.

For the second stage is not so much a fixed agenda as it is a process, a mode that will put a new value on qualities once considered—and denigrated as—special to women, feminine qualities that will be liberated in men as they share experiences like child care.

The true potential of women's power can be realized only by transcending the false polarization between feminism and the family. It is an abstract polarization that does not exist in real life.

New research shows that virtually all women today share a basic core of commitment to the family and to their own equality within and beyond it, as long as family and equality are not seen to be in conflict.

One such study, "Juggling Contradictions: Women's Ideas About Families," was conducted by the Social Research Community at the University of Michigan in 1979. The 33 women in this study were between the ages of 28 and 45, white, with children, living in small and medium-size Michigan cities. A third of the women had some college education, most of the families had an income between $15,000 and $30,000, and more than half of the women were employed, most of those part time.

The researchers admitted that their preconceptions and practically everything they had read had prepared them to put the women they interviewed into two categories—familial or individualistic. The "familial ideology" places a tremendous value on the family and on motherhood, both as an activity and as a source of identity. It holds that family— husband and children—should be the primary focus of a woman's life and that the needs of the family should be placed above all else. In contrast, the "individualistic ideology" places the individual on an equal level with the family—mothers have needs and goals to meet as persons apart from the family.

The researchers reported: "Instead of finding categories of women, we found categories of ideas . . . bits and pieces of two distinct belief systems—familial and individualistic ideologies. None of the women we spoke with subscribed completely to one ideology or the other; they all expressed some combination of the two, in their words and in their lives."

The tension between the two ideologies—woman-as-individual and woman-serving-her-family—looked irreconcilable in the abstract, but was, in fact, reconciled in the women's lives. They worked, usually part time or on different shifts from their husbands, shared child care with husbands or grandmothers or others, and approved of child-care centers.

There are not two kinds of women in America. The political polarization between feminism and the family was preached and manipulated by extremists on the right—and colluded in, perhaps unconsciously, by feminist and liberal or radical leaders—to extend or defend their own political power.

Politically, for the women's movement to continue to promote issues like ERA, abortion and child care solely in individualistic terms subverts our own moral majority. Economic necessity and the very survival of the family now force the increasing majority of women to work and to make painful choices about having more children.

The women's movement has appealed to women as individualists; the Moral Majority has played to—and elicited an explosive, defensive reaction on behalf of—women as upholders of the family. Perhaps the reactionary preachers of the Moral Majority who decry women's moves to equality as threats to the family are merely using the family to limit women's real political power. In a similar vein, feminists intent on mobilizing women's political power are, in fact, defeating their own purpose by denying the importance of the family.

That Michigan study showed something very important. All the women believed in equality and all of them believed in the family—from the same [base] of converging needs for security, identity, and some control over their lives.

"Family" is not just a buzz word for reactionaries; for women, as for men, it is the symbol of that last area where one has any hope of control over one's destiny, of meeting one's most basic human needs, of nourishing that core of personhood threatened now by vast impersonal institutions and uncontrollable corporate and government bureaucracies.

Against these menaces, the family may be as crucial for survival as it used to be against the untamed wilderness and the raging elements, and the old, simple kinds of despotism.

For the family, all psychological science tells us, is the nutrient of our humanness, of all our individuality. The Michigan women, and all the others they exemplify, may show great political wisdom as well as personal survival skills in holding on to the family as the base of their identity and human control.

It is time to start thinking of the movement in new terms. It is very important indeed that the daughters—and the sons—hold on to the dream of equality in the years ahead and move consciously to the second stage of the sex-role revolution.

There is a quiet movement of American men that is converging on the women's movement, though it is masked at the moment by a resurgence of machismo. This movement of men for self-fulfillment beyond the rat race for success and for a role in the family beyond breadwinner makes it seem that women are seeking power in terms men are leaving behind. Even those women who have made it on such terms are forfeiting the quality of life, exchanging their old martyred service of home and children for harassed, passive service of corporation.

In the second stage, women have to say "No" to standards of success on the job set in terms of men who had wives to take care of all the details of life, and standards at home set in terms of women whose whole sense of worth and power had to come from that perfectly run house, those perfectly controlled children.

Instead of accepting that double burden, women will realize that they can and must give up some of that power in the home and the family when they are carrying part of the breadwinning burden and some beginnings of power on the job. Instead of those rigid contracts that seemed the feminist ideal in the first stage, there will be in the second stage an easy flow as man and woman share the chores of home and children—sometimes 50–50, sometimes 20–80 or 60–40, according to their abilities and needs.

In the second stage, the woman will find and use her own strength and style at work, instead of trying so hard to do it men's way, and she will not feel she has to be more independent than any man for fear that she will fall back into that abject dependence that she sometimes secretly yearns for.

Politically, instead of focusing on woman as victim and on sexual battles that don't really change anything, like those marches against pornography, feminists in the second stage will forge new alliances with men from unions, church and corporation that are essential if we are to restructure jobs and home on a human basis.

Above all, the second stage involves not a retreat to the family, but embracing the family in new terms of equality and diversity. The choice to have children—and the joys and burdens of raising them—will be so costly and precious that it will have to be shared more equally by mother, father and others from, or in place of, the larger family.

It will probably not be possible economically for most women to have a real choice to be just a housewife, full-time or lifelong. But men as well as women will be demanding parental leave or reduced schedules for those few years—or in early, middle or later life for their own rebirth.

In the second stage, unions and companies will begin to give priority to restructuring hours of work—flextime and flexible benefit packages—not just to help women but because men will be demanding them and because improved quality of work will not only cost less but yield greater results in terms of reduced absenteeism, increased productivity and profit than the conventional package.

But in the second stage, when we talk about "family" we will no longer mean just Mom and Dad and the kids. We will be more keenly a-ware of how the needs of both women and men for love and intimacy and emotional and economic sharing and support change over time, and of the new shapes family can take. In the second stage, we will need new forms of homes and apartments that don't depend on the full-time service of the housewife, and new shared housing for single parents and people living alone, who are the largest new group in the population.

The common interests of all these kinds of families will create the basis for a new political alliance for the second stage that may not be a women's movement. Men may be—must be—at the cutting edge of the second stage. Women were reborn in effect, merely by moving across into man's world. In the first stage, it almost seemed as if women and men were moving in opposite directions, reversing roles, or exchanging one half-life for another.

In the second stage, we will go beyond the either/or of "superwoman" or "total woman" and "house husband" or "urban cowboy" to a new wholeness: an integration, in our personal lives, of the masculine and feminine in each of us in all our infinite personal variety—not unisex but new human sex.

If we can move beyond the false polarities and single-issue battles, and appreciate the limits and true potential of women's power, we will be able to join with men—follow or lead—in the new human politics that must emerge beyond reaction.

I know that equality, the personhood we fought for, is truly necessary for women—and opens new life for men. But I hear now what I could not hear before: the fears and feelings of some who have fought against our movement. It is not just a conspiracy of reactionary forces, though such forces surely play upon and manipulate those fears.

There is no going back. The women's movement was necessary. But the liberation that began with the women's movement isn't finished. The equality we fought for isn't livable, isn't workable, isn't comfortable in the terms that structured our battle.

How do we surmount the reaction that threatens to destroy the very gains we thought we had already won in the first stage of the women's movement? How do we surmount our own reaction, which shadows our feminism and our femininity (we blush even to use that word now)? How do we transcend the polarization between women and women and between women and men to achieve the new human wholeness that is the promise of feminism, and get on with solving the concrete, practical, everyday problems of living, working and loving as equal persons? This is the personal and political business of the second stage.

# 8

# Gay Liberation

Activities on several fronts in recent years have helped to bring the topic of homosexuality from the nether reaches of whisper and myth into the open air of rational discussion. When local police are gradually ending their surveillance of public restrooms and when various laws for the criminal punishment of convicted (although most likely consenting) homosexuals are critically scrutinized and gradually repealed, some progress is being made. The homosexual, long harassed and condemned by society, is now visible in a way never before seen in American life; homosexual drama, "gay" bars and dances, and demonstrations on behalf of "Gay Power," which have led to substantive claims for "Gay Liberation," have all contributed to this. There are now churches, chiefly the network of Metropolitan Community Churches, whose main constituency is homosexual and which demonstrate in their organization the neglect or rejection of the homosexual by the established religious communities. But the questions remain: What is the nature of homosexuality? What should be the response of morally sensitive persons and of the society at large to the homosexual?

The contemporary discussion of homosexuality by Christian theologians and ethicists reveals several rather clearly discernible positions on the nature of homosexuality. Some maintain what can be called the "traditional" view, in which homosexuality is regarded as a perversion that warrants a clear judgment from the church. More recent writers who reflect this position are often careful about expressing condemnation; yet they emphasize the "natural" or God-ordained character of heterosexuality and the consequent aberration that is inherent to homosexual activity. Our creatureliness involves our heterosexuality, and it is in knowing the opposite sex that we come to know ourselves. The homosexual person, for whatever reason, is caught in a deviant orientation that prevents him or her from attaining the self-knowledge that belongs to our very being as heterosexual creatures.

Another approach is intent on beginning with the empirical evidence concerning the nature of homosexuality. It is not at ease with the way in which the above position makes such a firm distinction between hetero- and homosexuality, for the evidence would indicate that our maleness–femaleness is a continuum in each of us, rather than an exclusive duality. Thus, the picture is too ambiguous for us to make clear and decisive judgments. Representatives of this second group do regard a heterosexual orientation as preferable, at the same time as they are willing to acknowledge that homosexual persons can and do maintain meaningful and life-building relationships with each other. Rather than pronouncing judgment, these writers see a need for understanding and support in order to enable homosexual persons to make as satisfying an adjustment as possible in a world that is hostile to them.

A third viewpoint maintains that homosexuality is as acceptable an orientation as heterosexuality. Human beings display a prodigious variety of sexual expression and needs, and any normative judgment must be limited to the rejection of exploitative sexual activity, whether heterosexual or homosexual. This is the position of the well-known English Quaker statement of 1963, which declared that homosexuality is no more to be deplored than left-handedness. Rather than emphasis on the division between hetero- and homosexuality, the question to be asked is whether persons can be loving and selfless in their sexual activity. Since there appears to be ample evidence that homosexual persons can be (a point disputed by others, however), their sexual activity should not be regarded as morally worse just because it expresses a homophile orientation, according to this third viewpoint.

One of the continuing arguments over the nature of homosexuality centers on its origin. How does one become a homosexual person? It is commonly recognized now that one must make a distinction between orientation and behavior. A young person may become involved in homosexual activity for a period of time because of peculiar circumstances, moving away from it as these circumstances change. The behavior in such instances does not reflect a homosexual orientation, which refers to a condition that is constant and apparently not subject to change. For those who see the homosexual orientation as an aberration or worse, its origin is often traced to a psychosocial cause rooted in the child's relation to its parents. A "malformation" of some kind has occurred. Those who accept homosexuality as a viable option are more inclined to regard it as a predisposition with which one is born—a genetic origin. Some have argued that a hormonal imbalance is the cause. Given the empirical evidence on this subject, the only viable conclusion is that we still have much to learn.

The unsettled state of the scientific community concerning the nature of homosexuality is also worth noting. In 1955 a committee of the Group for the Advancement of Psychiatry called the persistent, preferential emotional and physical attraction to members of the same sex "a severe emotional disorder" and stated that the homosexual "is an emotionally immature individual who has not acquired a normal capacity to develop satisfying heterosexual relationships, which will eventuate in marriage and parenthood." But in 1973 the American Psychiatric Association deleted homosexuality from its list of psychiatric disorders, since homosexuality could not be shown regularly to cause emotional distress or regularly to be associated with general impairment of social functioning. In 1975 a similar resolution was adopted by the governing body of the American Psychological Association, which also urged "all mental health professionals to take the lead in removing the stigma of mental illness that has long been associated with homosexual orientations."

For Christians one important source to consider in arriving at a perspective on this subject is the witness of Scripture and the tradition. This raises the problem of how to interpret what these sources are saying, since they reflect a cultural setting far removed from our own. John McNeill argues that we must reconsider aspects of the biblical and historical tradition which people have often thought gave definitive answers to the question of homosexuality. McNeill indicates that the record is not nearly so definitive, for biblical views were often colored by cultural needs that are no longer applicable; New Testament references have been misunderstood; and the Stoic emphasis on unemotional love in much of the tradition has been significantly qualified by the church over time. When these points are established, McNeill argues, the biblical and Western Christian ideal for personal and sexual development can be more clearly and accurately determined as "the free, mature human person living in a mature interpersonal community." This ideal includes homosexuals, who are as capable as heterosexuals of living in love with others and with God without promiscuity and depersonalization. Recognition of this ideal, furthermore, enables homosexuals to contribute to the growth of others by challenging dehumanization, opposing culturally determined images of sexual identity, and evincing a capacity for friendship and service to others.

A viewpoint clearly opposing McNeill's is found in the article by William Muehl. He deplores the attitude that regards homosexuality as particularly depraved or reprehensible, but he sees no justifiable reason for changing the church's traditional position, which refuses to acknowledge that homosexuality can be a viable or acceptable mode of sexual relationship. Even if homosexual persons are capable of establishing stable relationships marked by love and selfless concern, Muehl argues that there is an order or design to human relationships that simply makes some sexual activity inherently wrong or ultimately destructive (incest, for example). Whether or not love is present in this kind of sexual activity is beside the point, for love is legitimated only within human relationships which Christian wisdom has recognized as serving the ultimate good of the human family.

# The Homosexual and the Church

John McNeill

It should be obvious to all of us in the Christian community by now that our culture is in the throes of a serious revolt against the standards, forms and values of Western Christian tradition concerning human sexuality. The revolt takes many forms: the women's liberation movement, the gay liberation movement, the prohibition of premarital sex, the ideal of exclusive sexual fidelity within marriage and the charge that the Christian tradition is puritanical and basically opposed to sexual pleasure and fulfillment.

There is a real danger that the revolutionaries in their frequently legitimate revolt against traditional cultural attitudes concerning sexual behavior will destroy the real human values which these cultural attitudes both preserved and at times distorted. The sexual revolution places a difficult task on the shoulders of the Christian theologian and pastor, the task of separating the true ideals and implications of Christian belief from an overlay of purely human traditions, which, while they may have helped to preserve true Christian values in the past, no longer do so.

The church must continue its divinely appointed task of upholding moral ideals for the truly human use of sex; however, it must not continue to confuse moral ideals with cultural stereotypes and purely formal rules. As [20th-century Protestant theologian] Helmut Thielicke observes:

> The primary moral problem in sexual relations is not sex within marriage versus sex outside of marriage, or sex within a heterosexual versus sex within a homosexual relationship. The problem is sex as a depersonalizing force versus sex as a fulfillment of human relationship.

Consequently, there is a serious need for the Christian community to make a critical return to its sources in Scripture and tradition in the process of dialogue with the parties concerned. It would be well for the church to frankly face the fact that rationalization of sexual prejudice, animated by false notions of sexual privilege, has played no inconsiderable

Reprinted by permission of the author. From the October 5, 1973 issue of *The National Catholic Reporter,* excerpted from a keynote address at the first national convention of Dignity, an organization for Catholic homosexuals. John McNeill, S. J., is the author of *The Church and the Homosexual* (1976).

part in forming the traditions we have inherited and probably control public opinion and policy today in sexual matters to a greater extent than is commonly realized.

## SCRIPTURE AND THE HOMOSEXUAL

Christian ethics is a reflection on human reality within the context of Christian revelation. Obviously scriptural sources have a role to play. Biblical ethics constitutes data, but it is only one aspect, even if privileged, of the total data of ethical theology. There is a serious limitation to the use of Scripture in ethics. The Scriptures themselves are historically and culturally limited.

Perhaps no other text in Scripture has influenced Christian sexual ethics and the traditional attitude toward homosexuality as the creation account in Genesis. Some theologians interpret that text as expressing as God-willed the so-called natural state of heterosexuality. They assume that sexual differentiation is not only normative for human relations, but constitutes the very essence of what is human. To be human is to be purely male or female, and only in marriage desirous of reproduction is that essential duality kept in balance. Human sexuality derives its meaning exclusively in terms of the relation of male and female in a procreative union.

Some theologians even maintain that the likeness to God in man is precisely in terms of that sexuality by which men and women are able to enter into a covenant of love with one another. The problem is to understand to what extent the image of human sexuality recorded in Genesis is to be understood as a revelation of God's will or merely a reflection of the needs of the primitive human community.

We cannot expect that an entirely new sexual ethics should have arisen at once from the relation of God to his people. Belief in God did not instantly change social life; it did not immediately have far-reaching consequences on the horizontal plane of social-interpersonal relationships. In fact some biblical theologians suggest a new perspective from which we should read Genesis. The Garden of Eden in which man found himself perfectly at one with himself and his sexuality, his fellow man, nature and God represents primitive man's primordial dream of what ought to be in the future which he projected into the past as a state he once possessed and lost and now must work to regain.

From this perspective, ideal human sexual relations are not to be sought in the past, but must be created for the future. And the key to that future is man's ideal human nature which represents not so much a static given from the past but a dynamic ideal process of growth and development.

Underlying the documents that have come to us from the past there are various deep-rooted socio-psychological factors of which we have achieved conscious awareness only in recent times and which still await full and careful examination.

Thus, in reading Genesis we must enter into a corrective process by delving into the rather late time when the Genesis tradition was formed in order to appreciate the cultural needs of the then monogamous agrarian family unit.

One of the needs of that paternalistic society was to establish male superiority. Human nature and maleness were identified emotionally if not consciously in the popular mind. There was a real tension between the cultural need to establish male superiority and the revealed message that woman was man's equal and that there could be a real personal bond of love between man and woman.

Another historical factor which must be kept in mind in interpreting the Old Testament on sexuality is the real fear of Canaanite and other idolatrous sexual practices. The Old Testament always dealt with sexual sins in the context of idolatry. The idolators connected human sexuality with physical nature and the rhythms of biological life.

As a result sex was depersonalized and deprived of human value as in the sacred orgies and prostitution of the Canaanite fertility worship. The message of the Old Testament was that Yahweh works through the freedom of human history. Sex and fertility are not mysterious powers which man out of fear must dedicate to a deity; rather, sex belongs entirely to man as a free person.

Another cultural circumstance which concerns homosexual activities in particular was the common practice in the Middle East to submit a captured foe to sodomy as an expression of domination, contempt and scorn. The Jewish male population undoubtedly suffered this indignity during their captivity both in Egypt and in Babylon. Obviously, homosexual activity as long as it was understood as necessarily expressing hatred and contempt, was morally unacceptable. In a society where the dignity of the male was a primary consideration any activity necessarily associated with the degradation of the male was a serious offense.

It is interesting to note that in the Code of Leviticus it is not homosexual activity as such but only male homosexual activity that is condemned under the penalty of death on the grounds that it involves using a man as if he were a woman. There is no explicit condemnation of lesbian activity.

But what about the texts in the Old Testament which explicitly refer to homosexual activity? The church traditionally believed that homosexual activity is contrary to the will of God as expressed in the Scriptures.

Before we begin to examine that belief we must attempt to define what we mean by homosexuality. It can be argued that what is referred to in Scripture as homosexuality is either not the same reality at all or that the biblical authors did not manifest the same understanding of that reality as we have today. Therefore, it can be seriously questioned whether what is understood today as the true homosexual and his activity is ever the object of explicit moral condemnation in the Scriptures.

For the sake of definition we must first distinguish the homosexual condition or psychic orientation from homosexual activity. Most humans are capable of either hetero- or homosexual activity. Thus, there is no necessary connection between homosexual activity and the homosexual condition.

However, there is an important distinction to be made in the moral judgment to be passed on a heterosexual indulging in homosexual activities and a true homosexual involved in the same activities. Since knowledge of homosexuality as a psychic condition is a rather recent acquisition, it should be obvious that the biblical authors know nothing of the homosexual condition as such, but refer exclusively to homosexual activity undertaken by those they presume to be heterosexually inclined by nature.

For centuries the church taught and people generally believed that the sin for which God destroyed the cities of Sodom and Gomorrah was homosexual activity. However, recent studies by biblical scholars maintain that the principal sin of Sodom and Gomorrah and the reason for its destruction was the sin of inhospitality. . . . We are probably dealing here with one of the supremely ironic paradoxes of history. For centuries in the Christian West homosexuals have been victims of extreme inhospitality and persecution. In the name of a mistaken interpretation of the true crime of Sodom and Gomorrah, that crime has been repeated over and over.

## THE NEW TESTAMENT AND HOMOSEXUALITY

There is an important difference in the treatment of human sexuality between the Old and New Testament. In the Old Testament contact with God was connected with being the people of God, because in this chosen people alone God dealt with man. Therefore, it was imperative for every man and woman in Israel to receive this life and pass it on in marriage; sexual activity was closely linked with the covenant and the handing down of the promise from generation to generation.

In the New Testament, however, the new people of God are no longer bound together by blood relationship. Membership in the people of God is no longer a question of human descent. In Christ's words: "I can raise up children to Abraham from these stones!" One can be reborn into the new community of love through baptism. Thus, marriage no longer need occupy the central place it had under the old covenant. In the new covenant it is given to anyone to be fertile in the new community through a love which surpasses even marital love in value and, therefore, in fertility.

This new understanding of human love lies at the origin in the early Christian community of other vocational choices besides marriage and other forms of human community besides the family, for example, the celibate community. One can no longer identify the love between men which makes them the likeness of God exclusively with the heterosexual relationship in marriage.

Nowhere is that new attitude on human sexuality more evident than in the account of the baptism of the Ethiopian eunuch in the Acts of the Apostles [8:26–39]. The Lucan author depicts the work of the Spirit in forming the Christian community. He stresses that persons who were considered outcasts by Israel, to be "cut off from the assembly of the Lord" [Deut. 23:1], were fully acceptable in the new people of God. Just as the Spirit led Philip to his encounter with the eunuch, so the Spirit is leading [the organization] Dignity to win acceptance of the sexual outcasts in the church.

There are no references to homosexual activity in the four Gospels. There are only three references in the New Testament, all three in Paul's epistles. The first epistle to the Cor. 6:9 and 1 Tim. 1:10 are frequently translated as including homosexuals among the list of those who are excluded from the kingdom of God and outside the law of God. The two Greek words sometimes translated as referring to homosexuals are *malakoi* and *arsenokoitai*. The King James version translates these terms as the "effeminate" and "the abusers of themselves with mankind."

The Revised Standard Version translated both terms as "homosexuals." This translation is certainly at fault, since it fails to distinguish the homosexual condition, which is morally neutral, from homosexual activities. However, there is serious reason to doubt that either term necessarily refers to homosexual activity as such. *Malakos* literally means soft, and in a moral context, the morally debauched. *Arsenokoitai* is a more difficult term to translate. The Greeks in Paul's time had many terms, such as *paiderastes,* which clearly refer to homosexual activity, but this is not one of them. Later Christian writers sometimes used the term to refer to those involved in anal intercourse, which is not necessarily or exclusively a homosexual activity; more often the term is used to refer to male prostitution. This is the meaning Jerome attributes to it in the Vulgate translation: *Masculi concubitores,* male concubines.

The only remaining text in the New Testament is Romans 1:26. Here homosexual activities are referred to as *para phusin,* i.e. contrary to nature. The first question we must ask is what Paul meant by nature. In the seven uses Paul makes of this word he does not make a sharp distinction between custom and nature. He speaks, for example, of the Jews as circumcised by nature, whereas the Gentiles are uncircumcised by nature. He even writes: "Does not nature teach you that, if a man has long hair, it is a shame."

Obviously, Paul was shocked by the contrast between Jewish and Greek customs in sexual matters. He speaks of those men "who give up their natural relations with women"; the use of the active aorist participle "aphentes" indicated that Paul understood the Greeks who indulged in homosexual activity as heterosexuals involved in homosexual activity contrary to their own sexual orientation.

Paul's main point in the Romans text is that he understood homosexual practices to be the result of idolatry and, thus, a sign of alienation from God. Consequently, he dealt with homosexual activities in the same context as the Old Testament, the context of idolatry.

Biblical scholars point out that the primary message of the Old Testament concerning human sexuality was that love, including sexual love, requires respect for the other as a person. The sin which man can commit in his sexual conduct with another consists in dishonoring the person of a fellow human being.

The basic message was: If one does not acknowledge the only true personal God, it follows unavoidably that one also will not acknowledge one's fellow man as a person who has a value of his own. The positive ideal of the New Testament is the need every human being is under to struggle to integrate his sexual powers into his total personality so that his sexual drive can be totally at the disposition of his drive to achieve union in love with his fellow man and with God.

In the Old Testament an attempt was made to desacralize human sexuality by removing it from the realm of the mysterious impersonal forces of nature. In the New Testament an effort was made to resacralize sexuality by connecting it to the ideal context of free interpersonal love. There is strong empirical evidence that many true homosexuals have escaped the traps of promiscuity and depersonalized sex by entering into mature homosexual relationships with one partner with the intention of fidelity and mutual support.

By means of this relationship they have grown as human beings; they have learned to integrate their sexual powers in a positive way into their personality with the result that these powers are no longer a negative, compulsive and destructive force, but an instrument within their command for the expression of genuine human love. There is certainly no clear condemnation of such a relationship in Scripture; yet under these circumstances such a relationship can be interpreted as fulfilling the positive ideals of Scripture.

## TRADITION AND HOMOSEXUALITY

The New Testament ideal was not immediately assimilated, nor did it immediately change social or interpersonal relations. The primary influence on early Western Christian tradition was not the New Testament but popular Stoic philosophy of the community in which early Christianity flourished. The Stoic central message was "live according to nature." Nature was identified with reason. To conform to reason as it expressed itself in the objective physical laws of the universe was at the same time to achieve union with the divine. The principal virtue of the wise man was understood as *ataraxy,* or apathy, a life of indifference.

Moral life became a fight against all passions and affections such as pleasure, fear, and love as essentially irrational and, therefore, unnatural. One must eliminate the influence of all affections on human behavior and submit it totally to the control of reason. The principal value held by the Stoics was triumph over all fears, especially the fear of death.

Since the Stoics held an impersonal rational determinism, they denied the personal immortality of the individual; only impersonal reason was eternal. Consequently, the only rational response to death was to become detached from life and indifferent to one's personal survival.

In order to preserve this indifference the Stoic philosophers exhorted their followers never to fall in love. In fact Seneca urges husbands never to love their wives since all such love is "shameful." To fall in love is necessarily to open oneself to all misery and to lose all tranquility of soul. For the lover necessarily desires immortality for himself and his loved one, but such a desire is irrational.

The Stoic message of indifference met the needs of the early Christian community, since it was essentially a community of martyrs expecting the imminent coming of Christ who had to be ready daily to meet death. In dealing with sexual behavior the Stoics gave no consideration to the interpersonal love which might exist between the partners. Rather, stress was placed on the impersonal rational end of sexuality as that could be read in objective biological laws. Consequently, the only rational end and, therefore, moral motive for sexual intercourse was procreation. As [church father] Justin Martyr put it: "We Christians do not enter marriage for any other reason but procreation."

Stoicism entered deeply into Christian sexual ethics. As a result it placed all emphasis on the biological and physical aspects of sexual activities and tended to ignore the personal context in which that activity took place. Procreation became the exclusive end and motive of moral sexual activity. Thus, in dealing with homosexuality Thomas Aquinas argued that the motive for sexual intercourse must be either lust or procreation. Since procreation cannot be the motive in homosexual activities, lust must be the motive. There is no mention in Aquinas of a third possibility, namely, an expression of love.

The church's attitude toward the ends of sexual activity within marriage has undergone a definite development over the centuries. Beginning with an early insistence on the exclusive end of procreation, at a later stage the church began to stress procreation as the primary end, but granted the existence of secondary ends, namely, the mutual love and fulfillment of the marriage partners.

The church has traditionally recognized the moral goodness of the heterosexual relation between a married couple incapable of having children. From the moment the church granted the morality of the rhythm method as a natural form of birth control and justified sexual activity as still fulfilling the secondary aims of mutual love and fulfillment, there was a serious reason to reconsider the traditional position that all homosexual activity is necessarily wrong on the grounds that it cannot lead to procreation.

In their treatment of marriage the council fathers at Vatican II went a step further in this development, dropping all reference to primary and secondary ends and stressing the importance of conjugal love. The church continues to condemn any voluntary separation of the coequal purposes of procreation and mutual love. However, an argument against voluntary separation would be applicable to the true homosexual condition and persists in viewing all those who involve themselves in homosexual practices as remaining free to choose heterosexual relationships.

The genuine homosexual's situation is more comparable to that of a heterosexual couple incapable of having children than, for example, to those who practice birth control, since it is not by means of a free choice within his control that he eliminates the possibility of procreation from his sexual life.

Yet there is a considerable body of evidence that those homosexuals who have limited their sexual expression in an ethically responsible way have by that means achieved what Pius XI indicated in *Casti Connubii* as the "chief reason and purpose" of sexual love within marriage "as the blending of life as a whole and the mutual interchange and sharing thereof."

## HUMAN NATURE AND HUMAN FREEDOM

The idea that we can learn the purposes of nature by an impersonal and objective reading of the biological laws governing sexual operations of human procreation represents a rejection of what is unique in human nature, the personal realm. It negates any possibility of understanding human sexuality within the specific human dimension of interpersonal love. Man emerges from the impersonal forces of nature precisely as self-aware and free. What is specific about human nature is not some quality which is common to all the species such as reason, but the fact that every individual is more than the species. The personal uniqueness of every individual forms the necessary basis for the possibility of human love. A loving action, even if it takes the form of a sexual gesture, must be directed to the other as unique, as end in himself or herself. To treat another person merely as a means to an end that lies outside him or herself represents a failure to love that person as unique.

From this personalist viewpoint an overemphasis on procreation can be seen as leading potentially to a seriously immoral and dehumanizing form of sexuality in conflict with the gospel emphasis on the respect and love due to one's fellow human as person. There is something more to the question of the moral quality of sexual behavior than purely the objective legal question of marriage or the objective rational question of openness to procreation—that something else is love.

We have become progressively aware that human sexuality, like all human reality, precisely as human participates in the radical freedom of man. Many theologians ignore the rather obvious fact that human sexuality is not a totally instinctive determined phenomenon. Whatever participates in human freedom cannot receive its total explanation in terms of causal determinacy. Rather, it can be adequately understood only in terms of ideal goals and purposes. Man is freed from a deterministic push from the rear precisely because he is able to project out ideal goals and allow these ideals to be the ultimate determining factor in his behavior.

We do not believe that it is contrary to nature that man uses his hands, given him by nature as grasping instruments, for the ideal creative pursuits of wielding pen or brush—nor that he uses his mouth, obviously intended by nature for eating, in order to communicate his innermost sentiments. Therefore, it is no less according to nature if man chooses to use his sexual organs, designed by nature for procreation, in order to give the most intimate personal expression of his drive for union in love with a fellow human.

Since the sexual identity images which concretize heterosexual relationships at any point in human history are a human and not a divine creation, theologians who absolutize the man-woman relationship as given in contemporary culture as a divine image in man are potentially guilty of raising a human creation to the level of idolatry.

The task of the theologian, true to the spirit of the new covenant, should be to liberate humanity to the glorious liberty of the sons and daughters of God by undertaking a critical theological investigation of sexual identity images. We must become aware of the frequently dehumanizing and depersonalizing role that prevailing sexual identity images play in our culture. Men are supposed to be strong, tough, unsentimental, assertive and aggressive, whereas women are supposed to be weak, passive, receptive, emotional, etc.

These images have the serious consequence that if we assume that they constitute the total mature content of the human personality, the result would be that we would tend to understand the human individual as essentially partial and incomplete. No human person could be seen as complete in himself or herself, but essentially dependent on the other for his or her completion. We have all been rendered sensitive to the frequently depersonalized and unequal status of women in our culture. And since man usually achieves his identity in his relation to woman, he in turn also suffers a depersonalized and partial self-image.

Thus, the consequence of identifying with the heterosexual identity images proferred by our culture is that the only type of heterosexual relation that remains possible is a type of master-slave relation in which the male seeks to dominate and the female seeks to be dominated. No need to detail here the inevitable frustration and dependence that results from these images, leaving modern man open to all forms of exploitation.

Ideal Christian love, even married love, can only exist between persons who see themselves as somehow total and equal. Christian love must be love out of fullness and not exclusively out of need. It is not only the complementariness of the other sex that attracts, it is also the fact that while I sense that complementarity I can at the same time sense that here is a being whole and entire in him or herself and, although endowed differently than myself, worthy of standing beside me and entering my life as an equal. It should be obvious that the stereotypes mentioned earlier negate any possibility of such a personal relation for any heterosexual who takes them seriously.

The primary ideal goal of human sexual development is that we should fashion cultural identity images that make it possible for human beings to achieve the fullness of a true personal relationship in the process of conforming to the images provided by society. Paul made the claim that there was a seed planted by Christ, the seed of the spirit, whose eventual fruit would be the overcoming of all the divisions that separate man from man and, thus, separate each of us from the totality of ourselves.

The final and most difficult of those divisions he identified as the division between male and female. Obviously, Paul is not referring to the elimination of the biological differences but to the learned cultural distinctions which render women inferior to man, deny them full status as persons and, thus, prevent a true interpersonal encounter of love between men and women.

In Paul's mind ideal human nature lies in the future, not in the past. It is up to the creative freedom of man with God's grace and the models presented us by Christ to direct his development toward that ideal. The ideal is the free, mature human person living in a mature interpersonal community.

## THE ROLE OF THE HOMOSEXUAL IN THE HUMAN COMMUNITY

The greater part of moral thinking about homosexuality, as we have seen, tended to be vitiated at its source because it began with the presupposition that the culturally conditioned heterosexuality is the very essence of the human and at the very core of the mature human personality.

This assumption blinds its holder to any evidence that a homosexual relationship can be a truly constructive and mature expression of human love. However, one begins to detect the beginnings of a totally different and more helpful orientation of theological insight concerning the homosexual condition.

The earlier search for causes has proved a relatively useless enterprise. Some moral theologians have seized on the opinion that the homosexuality of a child is due to faulty parental relations in order to place an unproven burden of guilt on the parents. There are no necessary grounds for judging parents somehow guilty for their son's or daughter's homosexual condition; but there may well be grounds for seeing them responsible for the disturbed or neurotic condition that frequently accompanies homosexuality.

The real moral problem that exists for parents of a homosexual son or daughter is one of loving acceptance. Parents of a homosexual have no reason to assume guilt for his condition; but parents of a psychologically healthy homosexual have good reason to believe that they have done their difficult task well.

The truly useful question, then, is not from whence the homosexual comes, but why he is here. If the homosexual condition is not necessarily contrary to the will of God, nor necessarily a deviation from human nature, then, we can ask for what purpose does the homosexual exist? In what sense can he be seen as part of the divine plan? What intrinsic role is he to play in the development of human society?

From this viewpoint not only is it possible for homosexuality to be seen as of equal value with heterosexuality in individual cases, but it can be seen as having an overall significance and a special role to play in the general economy of human relations.

No more urgent task faces the moral theologian than the difficult and complex task of determining that finality. For on its discovery depends both the ability of the homosexual to accept him or herself with true self-love and understanding, as well as the ability of heterosexual society to accept a homosexual minority, not just as objects of pity and tolerance, but as their equals capable of collaborating in the mutual task of building a more humane society.

What, then, is the collective role that the homosexual community can play in human society and under what circumstances can that potential contribution become a reality? We have already talked about the depersonalizing effect heterosexual identity images can have. The homosexual community has, perhaps, a special role to play in liberating the heterosexual community to a fuller understanding of themselves as persons by being an organic challenge within society to the partial and dehumanizing aspects of these sexual identity images.

The psychologist C. G. Jung gives us a hint of what that role may be: "If we remove homosexuality from a narrow psychopathological setting and give it a wider connotation," Jung tells us, "it has many positive aspects as well." Among others Jung mentions that "homosexuality gives the individual a great capacity for friendship, which often creates ties of astonishing tenderness between men, and may even rescue friendship between the sexes from its limbo of the impossible."

Rather than continuing to play their present frequently negative role of undermining the married relationship by being forced into it in order to escape detection, the homosexual community, granted it were allowed to play its role in society with full acceptance, could potentially be a help in leading society to a new and better understanding of interpersonal love between equals as the foundation for the married relationship, rather than the role-playing of tradition.

Contemporary psychiatrist Dr. George Weinberg in his [1972] book, *Society and the Healthy Homosexual* observes perhaps the real illness in our culture is homophobia. This homophobia has many crippling effects on the development of the heterosexual's personality. In the objective act of allowing the homosexual community to be itself and live out its own life-style in peace, the heterosexual community would be in reality liberating itself. . . .

This same homophobia underlies the need of the male to reject all passivity and gentleness and establish his identity through aggressiveness and violence. Author Norman Mailer speaks of American culture as "cursed by the complex and hidden relations between repression, dread of homosexuality and violence." Every generation needs its war in order for the young to gain assurance of their virility. By liberating the heterosexual male to be able to recognize and accept his own homosexual impulses without repression, the homosexual community could make a decisive contribution to bringing violence under control in our society.

Another possible contribution is that of liberating the male to play service roles in the community. Traditionally these roles, such as caring for the young and the aged, education, nursing and social work have been seen as primarily feminine roles and not fit occupations for the true male.

As Jung observes frequently, the homosexual is "surprisingly gifted as a teacher" and Thielicke speaks of a "remarkable pedagogical eros, a heightened sense of empathy." By allowing the homosexual to be himself, the heterosexual male could realize his own liberation to be able to play service roles in the community without feeling guilty about betraying his male identity.

Jung mentions other positive characteristics, such as a developed aesthetic sense and a feeling for history, a tendency to be conservative in the best sense and to cherish the values of the past. Unfortunately we don't have time to develop these characteristics at this time. However, Jung's final observation has to do with the potential contribution the homosexual community can make to the spiritual development of humanity.

The homosexual, he tells us, "often is endowed with a wealth of religious feelings, which help him bring the *ecclesia spiritualis* into reality, and a spiritual receptivity which makes him responsive to revelation." The components of this particular gift have already been recognized.

We have noted that the homosexual community enjoys potentially a special freedom which could allow it to escape a hyperactive, aggressive attitude and allow it to be passive and receptive; attitudes which are essential to an attitude of prayer and the reception of revelation. It is no accident that in those cultures where a "machismo" image reigns, religious prayer and worship are considered activities only fit for women. The homosexual can be free from a need of violence and dedicated to a quest for peace. He can have a special sensitivity to the value of the person, especially those of the opposite sex. He is free to dedicate himself to a life of service to his fellow human.

There is an ideal identity image of what it means to be a full human person proferred to us by God in the New Testament; that image is given us in the person of Jesus Christ. Each of the special qualities Jung attributes to the homosexual community is usually considered as a striking characteristic of Christ—the qualities which distinguished him from the ordinary man. The ability to meet the individual as a person apart from stereotypes and cultural prejudices, the refusal to establish his identity and accomplish his mission by means of violence, the image of himself as the loving servant of all humanity.

The point I am trying to make here is obviously not that Christ was a homosexual, any more than he was a heterosexual in the usual significance that the cultural context gives that designation; but, rather, that he was an extraordinarily full human person and an extraordinarily free human being. The true fact is that there is no such person as a homosexual; no more than there is such a being as a heterosexual. There are human persons who happen to be relatively heterosexually or homosexually inclined.

We must be prepared to meet every individual person on his or her own merits without the falsification of the encounter that comes from stereotypes. Homosexuality as such can never be an ideal. However, heterosexuality as such can never be an ideal either. The only ideals involved in all questions of sexual orientation are the great transcendent values of justice, fidelity and love.

# Some Words of Caution

## William Muehl

We know very little about the causes and nature of homosexuality. Some psychotherapists treat it as an illness. Others refuse to do so. There appear to be people who are born into a physiological sexual ambiguity. And there are obviously many who adopt it either in response to abnormal social isolation such as imprisonment, or to provide outré thrills and stimulate a jaded appetite. There are homosexuals who long to become heterosexuals, while others profess to be quite content with their lot. As a psychological phenomenon homosexuality still seems to be a profound mystery.

There is nothing unclear, however, about the attitude of the Christian community toward sexual relations between persons of the same gender. They have been consistently proscribed and their practitioners often cruelly persecuted by ecclesiastical authorities. Both Old and New Testaments condemn homosexuality. Any effort to make a case to the contrary involves the kind of torturing of Scripture by which racists seek to defend segregation, and martial spirits to justify preemptive strikes. Whether the motives of those who want to blur the hard edges of the truth are compassionate or self-serving, the facts of history cannot be disputed. Genital homosexuality has been regarded as immoral by responsible Christians. Any discussion of the subject which begins with another basic assumption is doomed to futility.

To make the statements I have just made about the past and present attitude of Christians, even to propose that this attitude is right and ought to be perpetuated within the community of faith, does not imply any justification for the way in which homosexual people are treated by secular society today. Our society has encouraged the most flagrant exploitation of sexuality. It has allowed our appetites to be titillated in a great variety of ways by experts in the business; and the relevant moral standards of the past are being abandoned with shouts of liberation by those who first reflect and then shape the prevailing mood of Western society.

Statesmen and politicians are only mildly embarrassed when they are reported accurately to be womanizers. Business enterprises use commercial lovemaking to lure customers and clinch deals. Colleges virtually

From *Male and Female,* edited by Ruth Tiffany Barnhouse and Urban T. Holmes. Copyright © 1976 by The Seabury Press, Inc. Used by permission of the publisher. William Muehl is Professor of Practical Theology at the Yale Divinity School and author of *All the Damned Angels* (1972).

subsidize fornication by their dormitory arrangements. And those newspaper columnists who have become the arbiters of ethics urge prudent parents to put their teenage daughters on the pill.

It is both hypocritical and grossly unjust, therefore, for secular institutions to persecute and prosecute those whose sexual irresponsibility is somewhat more adventurous than average. A society cannot make free sex the national hobby and then penalize those who show creative imagination in the way they play the game.

It seems clear to me, as to many others, that when they act as citizens, Christians have a serious obligation to support basic civil rights for homosexuals. It is unthinkable that men and women should lose jobs, be denied housing, and suffer police harassment for refusing to be bound by rules which most of their neighbors have for all practical purposes abandoned long since. If we argue that what happens in bedrooms is not the public business, we cannot in good conscience keep peeking through keyholes. If we hold that what happens in bedrooms *is* the public business, we have far more pressing problems to solve than those presented by Gay Liberation.

Does the logic of this position require that Christians abandon their historic stand on homosexuality and declare to be good what they have in the past condemned? Obviously not. What is required is a firm reassertion of the time-honored distinction between toleration on the one hand and approval on the other. Or to put it in more familiar religious terms, adherence to the principle that one must love the sinner while hating the sin.

The appropriate Christian answer to the increase of sexual irresponsibility in society is neither to adopt that irresponsibility as its own mode of behavior nor to expel from its midst those who fall victim to it. It is, rather, to see all abuses of human sexuality as manifestations of that sinfulness which plagues our common existence; and to define homosexuality as one more symptom of a general problem rather than the outward and visible sign of a special depravity.

This is not an easy thing to do; partly because homosexuality has been so consistently condemned by religion that it has come to be regarded with special distaste. But more important for this discussion is the fact that homosexuals themselves show so little interest in being tolerated and seem determined to equate *acceptance* of themselves as persons with *approval* of their peculiar life style. As one informed colleague puts it, "The gays don't really want the right to privacy in their sexual activities. They want to act out their fantasies in public and force the rest of us to applaud."

The demand of militant homosexuals today is for social and religious endorsement of gay relationships, the recognition of same-gender sex as an appropriate expression of Christian love, the accrediting of gay persons as instructors, interpreters, and exemplars of the faith, and the solemnization of their unions by the church. They are asking, in short, that the religious community reverse its strongly held position on genital homosexuality and declare it to be fully consistent with a viable Christian commitment. And when anyone presumes to suggest that this proposal requires careful examination and the review of a number of substantive theological issues, he or she is very likely to be accused of loveless bigotry and charged with causing great pain to some very sensitive people.

A central feature of Gay Liberation strategy in the churches is to call attention to the unhappiness of homosexual men and women in our society and to demand that, as an expression of acceptance and love, compassionate Christians redefine homosexuality and call it good. You cannot really love us, they argue, unless you love our sexual preferences. And they have had an amazing success in getting otherwise intelligent human beings to accept this fallacy.

Yet if anything is central to Christian ethics it is the need always to distinguish between the doer and the deed. One need not embrace Marxism in order to acknowledge the humanity of Communists or adopt the social statics of Herbert Spencer out of regard for Republicans. If an alcoholic were to declare that we could not accept him as a person unless we endorsed alcoholism as a desirable life-style, we should suppose him to be well into his cups. When the Christian community is faithful to its calling, its doors and hearts will be open to all people. But it cannot be expected to deny its convictions and consecrate what it has steadfastly condemned in order to make any of us sinners feel more at home in the pews.

In a recent panel discussion of this topic I used the analogy with alcoholism and was immediately and angrily pounced upon by one of the other panelists. "What a cheap shot," he declared, "to compare homosexuality with alcoholism. Alcoholism prevents one from functioning as a viable human being. Homosexuality doesn't."

Well, that is precisely the issue involved in the Christian consideration of homosexuality, is it not? Does genital homosexuality impair one's ability to function in truly human fashion? Obviously it does not interfere with basic physical activity, any more than most alcoholism does. Thousands of alcoholics perform their daily jobs adequately, even impressively, then go home and drink themselves into a stupor. Undoubtedly an equal number of gay persons, perhaps many more, play out their economic and social roles efficiently all around us from nine to five.

The viability with which the Christian must be concerned, however, has far deeper and more complex dimensions than can be measured by a well-earned pay check. It is with this profound viability that moral statements are intended to deal. The panelist who wanted to make a qualitative distinction between homosexuality and alcoholism was guilty of a classic form of question-begging. He *defined* the gay life as "viable," and therefore good, and he casually brushed aside the great weight of Christian opinion to the contrary.

This is a problem which cannot be solved by definition. One must bore in relentlessly in a search for some responsible answer to the question which my fellow panelist sought to beg. Do homosexual relationships harm the persons involved in them?

Those who reply in the negative tend to rely on relatively gross standards in measuring the damage done to human beings by particular modes of behavior. (And they delight in finding damaging contrasts between the position of the church on homosexuality on the one hand and war on the other.) Homosexual activity does not kill, cripple, or shed blood; it probably causes no more incidental pain than heterosexual coupling. Ergo, it does no damage to those who participate in it.

There is only a superficial plausibility to such reasoning. And in any other area of debate those who champion the gay cause would be among the first to point this out. The human psyche is a very fragile thing and can be wounded in ways that leave no obvious scars. There is something called "dignity" that can wither and die without ever uttering a cry of pain or shedding a drop of blood. Why do Christians oppose the treatment of criminals by brain surgery or electrode implants? Surely such remedies are more humane than lifelong imprisonment. Why do we waste the bodies of our dead on cemetery grass when their decaying flesh could be used as fertilizer to ease the world food shortage? They are beyond the reach of pain and embarrassment, and the living would be greatly served by such a policy. Why do we prevent people from exposing themselves in school playgrounds? There is some reason to suppose that the kiddies find the performance highly amusing.

The answer to such questions cannot be given in measurable units of harm to personality. We can only affirm that there are ways of hurting people which break no bones and may even provide the victim with a moment of pleasure. And there seems to have been a clear consensus among Christian thinkers over the ages that genital homosexuality assaults human dignity in some such subtle fashion. That view may be in error. But it cannot be defined away or refuted by the absence of scars on homosexual partners.

Even if one were to grant the unsubstantiated premise that gay relationships do no damage to those individuals most immediately engaged in them, questions inevitably arise about the social consequences of giving religious sanction to genital homosexuality. What will happen to the concept of the Christian family in a society which *endorses* same-gender sexual coupling? Will the painful sexual ambivalences of adolescence be made more difficult and more likely to be resolved in favor of a homosexual orientation if the local rectory is occupied by the pastor and his or her "lover"? Can the battered institution of Christian marriage stand the sight of gay unions being solemnized at the altar? What will be the effect upon all sexual relationships of the consecration of what are essentially sterile unions characterized by a very high degree of instability?

It is the multitude of such legitimate questions and the scarcity of persuasive answers which argues strongly that the Christian attitude toward gay relationships be one of toleration rather than approval. Centuries of ruthless repression—one indication of how strongly the traditional opinion has been held—have forced gay people to live their lives furtively and have made it almost impossible even for sophisticated analysts to evaluate the impact of homosexuality upon persons and society. It is altogether possible that much of what seems essentially destructive in the gay life style is really the neurotic consequence of a hostile environment. Once legal bans on same-gender sex have been removed and its practitioners allowed to live without harassment, we shall be in a far better position to see the implications and consequences of any change in the basic position of the churches on this difficult subject.

I wish it were possible to stop at this point and assume that I have made the case for great caution in responding to the demands of gay militants for full approval of their way of life by the Christian community. Some experience in this area, however, has convinced me that those who wish to give serious thought to the place of homosexuals in the churches will find themselves under considerable pressure to throw caution to the winds in the name of something loosely called "love."

"God is love"—so runs the argument. Anything that is an expression of love is good. Since same-gender sex is an expression of love, it should be blessed by the church. This is another classic example of question-begging, an effort to define homosexuality into a state of grace. As such it needs very careful examination.

One of the most popular errors in the realm of Christian ethics has been the effort to make love an omnipotent spiritual quality which has the power to sanctify anything that is done in its name. The Inquisition tortured people's bodies in order to save their souls and sought to justify this action in the name of love. For centuries white Christians imposed patterns of paternalism upon blacks as an expression of their love for the sons of Ham. Employers once professed to love their employees too much to let them fall into the evil clutches of labor organizers. Parents tend to dominate their children's lives in the name of this same love. And generations of male chauvinists have counseled their sisters, wives, and daughters to eschew power and find their dignity and security in the love of their menfolk.

It is fashionable to interpret all such claims as sheer hypocrisy, as many of them were. But far more often than we care to admit, acts of exploitation and even brutality have been committed by people who honestly believed they were expressing disinterested love for their victims. It was the recognition of this hard fact of life which led Reinhold Niebuhr to say that we human beings are "never as dangerous as when we act in love." When we are motivated by anger or aggression, he pointed out, we arm our own consciences, alert our critics, and put our intended victims on their guard. But when we act in love, we disarm conscience, critic, and victim in one act and can do our worst unimpeded.

This was Niebuhr's characteristically dramatic way of saying that love does not empower anyone to transcend fully the structures of responsibility in human relating, and must always be expressed in ways that are appropriate to particular historical contexts and specific human associations. Love does not hallow the inquisitor's cruelty; the white's oppression; the employer's, parent's, and male's domination of others. It condemns such inhumanity and bids it cease. Love *establishes* the modes of interpersonal relating. It does not simply consecrate those that we find pleasant or profitable.

Thus, love does not always justify sexual union. It frequently makes it clear that sexual union is grossly inappropriate to a relationship. It is wrong for fathers to act out their love for their daughters in coition, for mothers to take their sons to bed, for brothers and sisters to copulate. Only the sickest minds would hold otherwise. And once we have established that fact the argument that homosexual union is good simply because it is motivated by love falls of its own weight. It is every bit as likely that the love of man for man or woman for woman bids them refrain from sexual intercourse as that it urges them into it.

For the purpose of making such statements about the argument that same-gender sex is an expression, however inappropriate, of love, I have assumed that some form of affection is, indeed, the driving force in gay relationships. This is by no means incontrovertibly established. A number of authorities in the field argue that the dynamic of homosexuality is not love for the same sex but hatred of the opposite sex. Men who take other men to bed, they suggest, may be less interested in expressing affection for their partners than in displaying contempt for women. And the same would be true, *mutatis mutandis,* for lesbians.

Still other psychologists hold that homosexuality is the result of a less sexually focused anger and reflects a more general aggression against people of both sexes. And there are obviously additional interpretations of the phenomenon for which there is no space here. While I am not qualified to evaluate such analyses, their net effect is to cast even more doubt upon the proposition that Christians ought to reverse their historic position against genital homosexuality and accept it as a manifestation of interpersonal affection. One needs to be very cautious about sacramentalizing what may well be a ritual of hatred or aggression.

In all discussions of this topic it seems crucially important to insist upon adequate time for full consideration of what is at stake. Too rapid a rate of change in critical areas of human relating can be dehumanizing in itself. But the Christian community has an understandably uneasy conscience on this point. It has often dragged its feet when it should have been leading the parade. And in consequence its leadership is somewhat inclined to suppose that in any proposal for change the burden of proof rests upon those supporting the status quo.

Some of the more militant gay leaders have been quick to seize the opportunity which this guilt syndrome offers. No more delays!—they cry. And link their cause with crusades on behalf of blacks, poor people, anti-war programs, and women. But there is a very important distinction between the proposals of Gay Liberation and such other appeals for changes in the attitudes of Christian churches. Most of the confrontations with which Christians are being called upon to deal these days reflect the demand that they bring their practice into line with their principles, that they more fully live up to what they have long been preaching.

The appeals of Gay Liberation, on the other hand, represent a proposal that the churches reverse their position on a moral issue of great importance to both themselves and society. This is not a question of bringing practice up to the level of principle but of revising principle in order to accommodate a particular and somewhat exotic practice. It is critical that Christians bear this distinction in mind and not allow their guilt feelings to push them into premature and ill-advised responses toward homosexuality. To allow themselves to be stampeded on this issue by emotional appeals and the fear of hurting someone's feelings will set a precedent which cannot help returning to haunt the churches often in the years ahead.

Let us end where we began. Homosexuality ought not to be treated as the manifestation of some special depravity whose practitioners should be driven from the church and harassed at law. But neither can it be defined as an appropriate expression of Christian love in interpersonal terms. The gay relationship is one form of sexual irresponsibility among many and no more reprehensible than most. Those involved in it have as much place in the pews as all the rest of us sinners. And as long as they recognize it as a problem and are prepared to seek help in dealing with it, there should be no arbitrary limits placed upon their full participation as leaders in the Christian fellowship.

When gay people claim, however, that their way of life is a morally healthy one, insist upon their intention to affirm it publicly, and ask that it be consecrated in some way by the church, they put themselves in contempt of Christian conscience. Under such circumstances it is not only the right but the duty of other Christians to express grave misgivings about the seriousness of their faith and to challenge the wisdom of admitting homosexuals to positions of leadership in the churches.

# SUGGESTIONS FOR FURTHER READING FOR PART THREE

## Chapter 6: Racism: The Continuing Struggle

Boxill, Bernard R. *Blacks and Social Justice.* Totowa, N.J.: Rowan and Littlefield, 1981.

Cone, James H. *Black Theology and Black Power.* New York: Seabury Press, 1969.

—. *God of the Oppressed.* New York: Seabury Press (Crossroad Book), 1978.

Deloria, Vine, Jr. *God is Red.* New York: Grosset & Dunlap, 1973.

Gomez, David F. *Somos Chicanos: Strangers in Our Own Land.* Boston: Beacon Press, 1973.

Hodgson, Peter C. *Children of Freedom: Black Liberation in Christian Perspective.* Philadelphia: Fortress Press, 1974.

Newman, Dorothy K., *et al. Protest, Politics and Prosperity: Black Americans and White Institutions.* New York: Pantheon, 1978.

Schwartz, Barry N., and Robert Disch, eds. *White Racism: Its History, Pathology and Practice.* New York: Dell, 1970.

Wilson, William Julius. *The Declining Significance of Race: Blacks and Changing American Institutions.* Chicago: University of Chicago Press, 1980.

## Chapter 7: The Women's Movement

Daly, Mary. *The Church and the Second Sex* (2nd ed.). New York: Harper & Row, 1975.

Friedan, Betty. *The Second Stage.* New York: Simon & Schuster (Summit Book), 1981.

Gilder, George. *Sexual Suicide.* Chicago: Quadrangle Books, 1973.

Jewett, Paul K. *Man as Male and Female.* Grand Rapids, Mich.: Eerdmans, 1975.

Mount, Eric. *The Feminist Factor.* Richmond, Va.: John Knox Press, 1973.

Ruether, Rosemary Radford, and Eugene Bianchi. *From Machismo to Mutuality.* New York: Paulist Press. 1976.

Ruether, Rosemary Radford, ed. *Religion and Sexism: Images of Women in the Jewish and Christian Traditions.* New York: Simon & Schuster (Touchstone Book), 1974.

Scanzoni, Letha, and Nancy Hardesty. *All We're Meant to Be: A Biblical Approach to Women's Liberation.* Waco, Tex.: Word Books, 1976.

Schlafly, Phyllis. *The Power of the Positive Woman.* Westport, Conn.: Arlington House, 1977.

## Chapter 8: Gay Liberation

Barnhouse, Ruth Tiffany. *Homosexuality: A Symbolic Confusion.* New York: Seabury Press (Crossroad Book), 1977.

Batchelor, Edward, Jr., ed. *Homosexuality and Ethics.* Princeton, N.J.: Pilgrim Press, 1980.

Boswell, John. *Christianity, Social Tolerance, and Homosexuality.* Chicago: University of Chicago Press, 1980.

Jones, Clinton R. *Understanding Gay Relatives and Friends.* New York: Seabury Press, 1978.

Macourt, Malcolm, ed. *Towards a Theology of Gay Liberation.* London: SCM Press, 1977.

McNeill, John J., S.J. *The Church and the Homosexual.* Kansas City, Kans.: Sheed, Andrews and McMeel, 1976.

Scanzoni, Letha, and Virginia Ramey Mollenkott. *Is the Homosexual My Neighbor?* New York: Harper & Row, 1978.

Tripp, C. A. *The Homosexual Matrix.* New York: New American Library, 1976.

# Part Four

# The Christian and the Economic Order

# 9

# Capitalism versus Socialism

What should a Christian look for in evaluating an economic system? One obvious concern would be the success of that system in providing for the economic needs of the population. Any society that enjoys a high level of protection from poverty, living with a sense of confidence in meeting its economic needs, will have reason to be satisfied with its economic system. There are two dimensions to this picture: the *level* of protection from economic want, and the *extent* to which that protection exists throughout the population. In other words, both *production* of wealth and *distribution* of wealth are concerns which we have in evaluating an economic system.

Capitalism, as we understand it today, is a fairly recent phenomenon in world history, dating back to the late eighteenth century. It can be defined as a privately financed competitive market economy that is intent on maintaining a freemarket environment in which the dynamic of supply and demand can fuel production. Its advocates note that its emergence in the Industrial Revolution has correlated with the beginnings of rapid economic growth and consequent upswing in the economic fortunes of the Western world. Capitalism has been credited for the achievement in the United States of a remarkable standard of living, and most Americans would likely defend it against any of its competitors.

While critics do not contest the success of capitalism as a system that facilitates the production of wealth, they are less satisfied with the distribution of wealth in the United States. Here they see more disparity between the rich and the poor than our citizens should be willing to accept. Studies from several sources that compare the United States with other leading industrialized nations reveal significantly more economic inequality in this nation (note the statistics cited in the article by McCulloch, Fenton, and Toland on the percentage of the national income earned by the lowest and highest 20 percent of our population).

212

For many millions of citizens, the comforts and opportunities associated with the middle-class style of life are hopelessly beyond reach.

This disparity between rich and poor, accentuated by the opulence and ostentation of the rich in a society as affluent as our own, has drawn increasing concern and critique from Christian ethicists. From a biblical perspective, Christians are called to place themselves on the side of the poor and the oppressed. Theologian Karl Barth put it succinctly in his *Church Dogmatics:* "God always takes his stand unconditionally and passionately on this side and this side alone: against the lofty and on behalf of the lowly; against those who already enjoy right and privilege and in behalf of those who are denied it and deprived of it." The primary questions for Christians evaluating an economic system thus become: How well does it provide for the poor? How oppressed are those at the bottom of the economic ladder? What kind of opportunity and support is provided for the disadvantaged?

These concerns have led many to conclude that socialism, with its concern for equality, is a system that fits more naturally into a Christian perspective. Capitalism, on the other hand, exalts human freedom as the fundamental good, but its advocates argue that economic freedom is the prerequisite for every other kind of freedom that is precious to us—including the political freedom guaranteed by a democratic form of government. The problem for a capitalistic economy is how to prevent the abuse of freedom in the marketplace when it is united with power. When the acquisitiveness and desire for gain that capitalism would channel into fruitful production becomes greed, power turns into exploitation. The result has been a long history of government attempts to control such excesses without destroying a free-market economy. For the Christian who is convinced of the superiority of capitalism in meeting the economic needs of the people, a primary concern would appear to be the effective collaboration of government and a socially responsible private sector to assure that the concerns of justice are met.

The first article in this chapter, written by McCulloch, Fenton, and Toland—three Roman Catholic priests—levels a strong indictment against capitalism. A major concern is the inequality in the distribution of wealth in the United States, as well as the concentration of political power in the hands of the economic elite. This latter point challenges a thesis in the article by Michael Novak, in which he argues that a democratic state and the notion of an independent individual are not possible apart from a free economy. Perhaps Novak is right, but McCulloch, Fenton, and Toland would regard it as a theoretical argument; they are concerned over the concentration of power in an economic elite whose self-interest does not coincide with that of most Americans. Representatives of business, on the other hand, are likely to maintain that what serves the world of corporate business ultimately serves the economic interest of the people (reminding one of Charles Wilson's comment back in the Eisenhower era: "What's good for General Motors is good for America"). The issue becomes one of responsibility and trust, or the moral use of power.

Michael Novak, a lay theologian and one-time advocate of social protest, is now engaged in a discriminating defense of the business establishment. He addresses the underlying assumptions of "democratic capitalism" and finds them far more acceptable than the assumptions that underlie socialism. While socialism has a more noble vision of the human being, the strength of capitalism is its recognition of our "innate selfishness and corruptibility." This assessment creates a sense of realism, which calls for a system of checks and balances to "transform selfishness and corruptibility into a modicum of creativity, virtue, efficiency, and decency." The argument for capitalism is its success in fulfilling its purpose quite well: to channel our self-interest into the production of the basic goods of life as cheaply and efficiently as possible. The trouble with socialism, says Novak, is that it is built on human goodness and therefore is bound to fail.

A socialist response to this argument would not only deny that human beings are inherently or primarily selfish but also would contend that to assume this is true and to build an economic system on that assumption is to encourage selfishness and to expose millions of people to the exploitation that naturally follows. Michael Manley, a Christian and former Prime Minister of Jamaica, puts it this way:

> To organize an entire society on the basis of an economy which, to function, must operate on the instincts of acquisitiveness, greed, selfishness, and competition is an immoral thing to do. I do not accept the view that man has only one instinct—that of competition and aggression. I believe very profoundly that man is a social being who has an egotistical impulse and a deep social impulse. Obviously in man these two things contend. . . . I am a socialist because to me socialism involves an attempt to create a social and economic system that expresses the social and cooperative nature of man.[1]

Another factor in this discussion that is assuming increased importance is the argument over economic growth. Since the 1960s growing numbers of people have become convinced that we are living in an era now coming to its end, in which unlimited economic growth has been our goal and in which progress has been measured in terms of a more highly developed technology and the multiplication of material goods. It is just these features that mark the success of capitalism as an economic system, and consequently the viability of industrial capitalism for our time is coming under critical reappraisal. The assumption inherent to capitalism is that we can and must maintain economic growth. Two points are being made by those who challenge this assumption: We are confronted with limited resources that cannot be exploited by a capitalist machine in the way they have been in the past; and we live in an environment that is a vast ecological system, which cannot sustain indefinitely the degree of interference imposed by a highly developed industrial economy. This debate, which will become more intense, poses fundamental moral issues involving our care of the earth and the kind of world we will leave to our children and grandchildren.

[1] *The Christian Century,* November 30, 1977, p. 1117.

# The Myths of Capitalism

Lawrence McCulloch, Thomas Fenton,
and Gene Toland

The purpose of this paper is to say that many of the injustices we see all around us cannot be understood and dealt with effectively if we treat them in isolation one from another. It is something like dealing with the weather. If we want to explain why it is cloudy one day and then sunny the next, or why it snows in one place and rains in another, we have to know as much as we can about the weather *system.* The weather at different times and in different places is not simply a collection of isolated events. It is a whole. It is a system.

In the same way, a child dying of malnutrition in one of the slums of Rio, or a black steelworker out of work in Gary, or an important banker riding comfortably in his limousine down Park Avenue—these are not merely isolated events. They are related to and dependent upon one another. They are part of a system.

More specifically this paper contends that the system which creates and sustains much of the hunger, underdevelopment, unemployment and other social ills in the world today is *capitalism.* Capitalism is by its very nature a system which promotes individualism, competition and profit-making with little or no regard for the social services and human needs. As such, it is an unjust system which should be replaced.

In stating this quite strongly and in trying to prove it, it is our intention to raise this issue of capitalism as a legitimate and urgent topic for discussion.

The best way to do this, we feel, is to come to grips with certain myths about capitalism that hide its real nature from us. Again, it is like talking about the weather. As long as we think thunder is caused by Apollo clapping his hands, or lightning is a bolt of Zeus' getting even with one of his arch-rivals, we will never really understand what the weather system is all about. Myths serve a role in poetry and literature but not in trying to understand the vital issues of our day, the issues of world poverty, hunger, underdevelopment, racism, war, etc. For this we need facts, facts that

Reprinted, with deletions, by permission. Written by the authors for the Maryknoll Education Project for Justice and Peace in 1972 and updated by Elaine Fuller in 1979. Lawrence McCulloch, Thomas Fenton, and Eugene Toland are Maryknoll priests.

shed light on the cause of some of these problems and how they can be dealt with.

In this paper we will respond to certain myths about capitalism.... These are myths that are rarely articulated, much less challenged, in many of our church discussions on world justice and peace.

## ORIGINS OF CAPITALISM

MYTH NO. 1: The first capitalist countries (England, France, the Netherlands, etc.) developed by pulling themselves up by their own bootstraps.

FACT: England and other European countries developed largely because they had sea power to dominate the peoples and exploit the resources of newly discovered lands. From the conquest and the pillage of Mexico and Peru by the Spaniards, to the sacking of Indonesia by the Portuguese and the Dutch, to the exploitation of India by the British, the early history of capitalist development is an unbroken record of international exploitation and consequent concentration of wealth in Western Europe.

It is estimated that over 500 million gold *pesos* were exported from Latin American between 1500 and 1600. The total wealth taken out of Indonesia by the Dutch East India Company for the period 1650–1780 amounted to more than 600 million gold *florin*. In 18th Century France, profits from the slave trade amounted to nearly half a billion *livres*. In the British West Indies, the profit from the labor of blacks during the same period amounted to over 300 million pounds. Finally the result of the British plunder of India between 1750 and 1800 is estimated conservatively at 150 million pounds. In other words, the total amount taken by Western Europe from the rest of the world at the beginning stage of its "modern" development comes to over a billion pounds sterling, or more than the capital of all the industrial enterprises which existed in Europe around 1800!

Economists today talk about the necessity of large amounts of capital investment for an industrial economy to reach a point of "take-off," a point of sustained growth. The source of this capital for European industrial expansion came not only from the bitter exploitation of its own working class, e.g. the notorious sweatshops of Lancaster and the coal towns of South Wales, but, to an even greater extent, from the plundering of the human and natural resources of the rest of the world.

Neither, of course, was the development of capitalism in the U.S. free of such plunder. The fortunes of many of our first bankers, merchants, ship builders and plantation owners—i.e., the Pepperells, Cabots, Faneuils, etc. —were directly dependent on the slave trade. Others, such as John Jacob Astor, made millions in the fur trade, plying Native Americans with liquor and even paying others to kill them, to make the new territories of the West safe for trapping and "honest business." And the Robber Barons of the 19th Century not only used cheap Chinese and Filipino labor to build the great railroads that span our continent but matched their European counterparts in exploiting men, women and children in thousands of foundries and company towns throughout America, working people who had come to our shores "yearning to breathe free."

Indeed, while Europe had her colonies spread around the world, we had (even before the Spanish-American War of 1898 gave us Cuba, Puerto Rico and the Philippines) our own "internal colonies," made up of millions of black slaves, Native Americans and poorly paid workers, which generated the capital for our economic growth. . . .

## CAPITALISM AND THE DISTRIBUTION OF WEALTH IN THE U.S.

MYTH NO. 2: Reforms of the capitalist system within the United States have brought about a more equitable distribution of wealth and power among our people than ever before.

FACT: The distribution of wealth in the U.S. is almost identical with the distribution of wealth in India. The only difference is that in the U.S. the economic pie is much bigger and so the results of this maldistribution are not quite as visible. Furthermore, with this wealth goes much of the control over the country's resources, industry, and public services.

In 1941, two-thirds of all manufacturing assests in the nation were controlled by 1,000 large corporations. Thirty years later, through mergers and competition that smaller corporations could not withstand, only 200 giant corporations controlled the same percentage—by then amounting to a cool $350 billion.

Another aspect of this concentration of wealth and control is the growing role of the major banks. Of the 13,000 banks in the United States in 1970, four had over 16 per cent of all bank assets—Bank of America, Chase Manhattan, First National City Bank, and Manufacturers Hanover Trust; the top 50 had 46 per cent. Banks are also increasingly important in terms of corporate stock voting rights. A 1962 study indicated that 80 per cent of all corporate stock was owned by the top 1.6 per cent of the population. There is no evidence that this ratio does not still hold true today.

It is important, however, to know who has voting rights to stock, for that is where the real power lies. Such information is not easy to come by and a great deal remains unknown to the public. The conclusion of a 1978 Congressional study is that "voting rights to stock in large U.S. corporations are concentrated among relatively few bank trust departments (led by Morgan Guaranty Trust Co. of New York), insurance companies, mutual funds and their related investment advisory companies."

The 21 institutions which dominate the ranks of investors include 11 banks, five investment company complexes, four insurance companies and the Kirby Family Group which controls the world's largest investment company complex—Investors Diversified Services, Inc. The rapid growth of pension funds held in stocks is increasing the power of these and other large institutional investors who usually manage the funds. Management powers frequently include voting authority and the discretion to buy and sell. Pension fund stock already amounts to 37 per cent of all stocks held by all categories of institutional investors.

Not only is the wealth of the nation, i.e., the factories, utilities, banks, etc., largely owned by a very small percentage of the population, but the yearly national income is equally maldistributed. According to the Bureau of the Census, in 1978, the lowest fifth of families in the United States receives only 5.2 per cent of the national income while the highest fifth gets 41.5 per cent, or almost eight times as much.

An even more revealing way to look at the economy is through the influence and control which a mere handful of multi-billionaire families and financial groups have exerted for generations. The Rockefeller empire is not a thing of the past. Neither are the Dupont or Mellon trusts relics of another age. Again, precisely because these groups are anxious to keep the extent of their wealth from the public eye, accurate, up-to-date figures are not available. Studies from the 1930s through the 1970s have identified several groups looming on the economic horizon like elephants walking amidst ants. Although these groups regularly have interlocking interests in each other's area of influence, they are nevertheless distinguishable enough:

The Morgan Guaranty Trust Group, which includes in its sphere of influence General Electric, International Nickel, Standard Brands, Campbell Soup, Coca-Cola, Upjohn, Mutual Life Insurance Co. of N.Y., etc.

The Rockefeller Group, which included Chase Manhattan Bank, Equitable Life Assurance Co., Standard Oil of N.J., Eastern Airlines, General Foods, Borden, etc.

The First National City Bank of N.Y. Group, which included Boeing, United Aircraft, Anaconda Copper, National Cash Register, etc.

The Mellon Group, which included Alcoa, Gulf Oil, Westinghouse, etc.

The DuPont Group, which included Dupont Chemical, U.S. Rubber, Bendix Aviation, etc. (The Duponts recently had to sell their controlling interest in General Motors stock due to a court order. But the proceeds were merely reinvested in high growth, frequently defense-related, industries.)

The Chicago Group, which unites many families, such as the McCormicks, the Deerings, the Nemours, and the Fields, included the First

National City Bank of Chicago, Continental Illinois National Bank, International Harvester, Sears Roebuck, Inland Steel, etc. Other families and groups, such as the Harrimans (Philadelphia), the Hannas (Cleveland), the Fords (Detroit), the Crockers (San Francisco), and the Hunts (Dallas) fill out the picture.

Although these families and groups compete with one another in trying to extend their spheres of influence, they also cooperate to run corporations that are too big for any one family or group to control. A good example is A.T.&T. On its board of directors are representatives of Chase Manhattan, First National City of N.Y., the Ford Foundation, the Chicago Group, and Morgan Guaranty Trust. It is truly a "collective possession" of the American upper class.

The effects of this concentration of wealth and power in the hands of a few are evident enough. A.T.&T., for example, is the largest private employer in the country, having over a million people on its payrolls. Forty-five per cent of its employees, however, are paid less than $7,000 per year (before taxes). What is particularly interesting is that only 4 per cent of Bell's white males earn so little whereas 64 per cent of all Spanish-surnamed employees, 79 per cent of all black employees, and 80 per cent of all female employees earn less than $7,000 annually. Indeed, the Equal Employment Opportunity Commission characterized A.T.&T. in 1971 as "without doubt the largest oppressor of woman workers in the U.S."

Does this mean that A.T.&T. is short on cash? Hardly. In 1970 A.T.&T. paid out more than $3 billion to stock and bond holders. In comparison labor costs only amounted to about $7 billion—out of a total annual revenue of $18 billion paid for by phone users all over the country. When we examine who owns the largest shares of A.T.&T. stocks and bonds, we find once again that it is the upper 1.6 per cent of the population. Maintaining this gravy train, then, even at the cost of rising rates and poor service to customers and blatant exploitation of women and minority groups is in the best interest of A.T.&T.'s corporate elite.

Many similar examples could be given, in practically every industry from textiles to steel, from meat packing to grave digging. Ultimately, however, the same simple fact emerges: Money is power. Indeed, the power of the financial oligarchy in the United States rests specifically on the fact that it commands most of the country's money capital. The bank assets controlled by the main financial groups mentioned above are twice as large as the annual budget of the Federal government. With this enormous wealth they dominate the American economy and determine its direction. Armed with the power to make key economic decisions concerning investments and the allocation of resources, they run their affairs and those of the nation according to the one rubric of corporate life: The maximization of profits.

## CAPITALISM AND POLITICAL POWER IN THE U.S.

MYTH NO. 3: Despite the concentration of wealth in our country, we can·
trust in a democratically elected government to work for the welfare of all
the people.

FACT: The small elite that runs our economy also dominates political life,
especially at the Federal level, making radical and far-reaching social reform
almost impossible. Most members of the legislative and executive branches
of the U.S. government are drawn from this financial elite and from the
lawyers and economists who work for it. During the 90th Congress, the House
of Representatives alone had 97 bankers, twelve of whom served on the
House Banking Commission.

One way this group uses its political influence to maintain and even
increase its slice of the national wealth is through its manipulation of the
tax structure. Despite claims of "progressive taxation," the rich and super-
rich have consistently provided themselves with legal gimmicks and loopholes to protect their huge fortunes. The result is that the burden of ever
higher, more unjust taxes increasingly falls onto the backs of lower and
middle income families.

These gimmicks and loopholes are well known: Oil depletion allow-
ances, tax exempt bonds, capital gains, write-offs, executive expense accounts, farm subsidies, stock options, etc. Avoiding taxes and growing fat
at the Federal trough is itself a big business. Here are a few examples:

In 1967, 21 millionaires paid no Federal taxes at all. In 1968, 155 persons
with incomes exceeding $200,000 paid no taxes.

In 1972, 14 corporations paid an effective Federal corporate tax rate
of less than 10 per cent and more than 1 per cent on $3.6 billion in
taxable income. By 1976 the number of companies in this category
had risen to 31 on an aggregate world-wide income of over $29.5
billion.

In 1976, the list of corporations paying *no income tax* included:

U.S. Steel
Bethlehem Steel
Armco Steel
National Steel
Republic Steel
Texas Gulf
American Airlines
Eastern Airlines
Pan Am
Pacific Gas and Electric
Chase Manhattan Corporation

Singer
Phelps Dodge
The Southern Company
Philadelphia Electric Company

These are but a few examples. They should help remind us that what we are dealing with in the United States, as Justice Douglas has said, is a system of socialism for the rich and "free enterprise" for the poor.

Not only do the wealthy use their political influence to manipulate the tax system for their own benefit but, through such groups as the Council on Foreign Relations (presently headed by David Rockefeller) and the Brookings Institute, they have great influence on the shaping of our foreign policy.

Their interest in foreign policy, of course, does not arise from some unique patriotic fervor. It is strictly determined by dollars and cents. By 1970, the book value of U.S. private corporate investment overseas exceeded $65 billion (it was only $11.6 billion in 1945) and was growing rapidly. In stimulating and protecting these lucrative investments the assistance of the government is indispensable. Foreign aid programs, for example, are used to secure concessions from weak foreign governments which fill the coffers of the multinational corporations.

When all else fails, of course, the corporate elite can resort to less subtle, more direct methods of persuasion. The invasion of the Dominican Republic by U.S. marines in 1965 is a classic example. The official reason was to prevent the island from going communist, though Juan Bosch, the popularly elected president deposed by the Marines, was never a communist nor is he one today. The real reason was to protect the interests of U.S. big business, which has for generations made super-profits off the poverty of the Dominican people.

For example, the South Puerto Rico Sugar Co. (5 Hanover Square, N.Y.) whose board of directors intertwines with Rockefeller's Chase Manhattan Bank, gets two-thirds of its sugar from the Dominican Republic. It had 120,000 acres in cane, 110,000 acres of pasture with choice livestock and 45,000 acres held in reserve (and economists wonder why the Dominican Republic has to import food from the U.S. to feed its own people!). It also owns a sugar mill, a furfural plant, a private railroad system, and a dock and bulk sugar loading station.

In addition to this major investment, there was Alcoa Aluminum, owned by the billionaire Mellon family (852,000 tons of bauxite extracted in 1963, profits estimated at 47 per cent), United Fruit, and the First National City Bank of N.Y.

Together, these investments provided huge profits for the American upper class. Because of the "successful" 1965 invasion, they still do today.

The evidence is clear, then, that in the United States we have a financial elite which exercises political influence far out of proportion to its size. This elite uses its power primarily for itself and secondarily, if at all, for the welfare of the majority of Americans.

## CAPITALISM AND PATRIOTISM

MYTH NO. 4: To attack capitalism is unpatriotic; it is to attack the system that has made the United States great.

FACT: To attack capitalism is not unpatriotic for the simple reason that, as we have seen above, most U.S. citizens are not capitalists. The fact that, in a trillion dollar economy, we still have over 30 million people living in poverty and millions more with no real financial security (i.e. mortgages on homes, etc.) is striking proof that our economy is owned by and for a very small elite.

As U.S. citizens we are rightfully proud of our democratic traditions, traditions that uphold the rights of every individual to free speech, freedom of assembly, freedom of religion, etc. We believe in a government of the people, by the people and for the people. We are opposed, as Jefferson said, "to any form of tyranny over the mind of man." As a people, we agree that democracy, while maybe not the neatest and most efficient way to run a country, is still the best.

Because of this pride in democracy, however, when we approach issues of justice and peace we have a difficult time distinguishing democracy from capitalism. Democracy, after all, is a *political* system. It is a system where people vote for candidates who will represent them in government and rule them for a limited period of time. Capitalism, however, is an *economic* system where, for example, one individual owns a factory and hires others to work in it. While few people would deny that democracy is a good thing, capitalism is a horse of a different color. In fact, capitalism is the opposite of democracy, since it is an economic system not owned by the people and run for the people, but a system owned and run by a plutocracy, i.e., the rich and super-rich.

Neither can we say that it is capitalism that has produced such great wealth in the United States. Those who have produced the wealth are the workers, blacks and whites, Greeks, Irish, Polish, and Chicano, generation after generation of hardworking men and women. And it is precisely these people, the working people of all races and creeds and nationalities, who have made this country great, who must constantly struggle even to gain a minimal share in the wealth they have produced, as if it did not belong to them in the first place.

A phrase we hear a lot about today is "community control." In many respects this would represent the best in democracy. Only when the people, both urban and rural, own their own land, their own factories, their own schools, their own banks, their own hospitals, and their own means of protection and law enforcement, will the vision of a truly democratic United States become a reality. In many respects, this is a modern day version of Jeffersonian democracy: A country made up of artisans and family farmers, each person owning a part of the assets of this great land and sharing equally in the fruits of his or her own labor.

But the direction of the economy today is just the opposite. Each year a quarter of a million family farmers leave their land because they can no longer compete with the huge corporate agri-businesses that are gobbling up the countryside and dominating the purchasing and distribution of farm produce. Each year thousands of small business operators close shop because they can no longer compete with the chain stores that undercut and outlast them. Each year hundreds of even medium and large companies are bought out and added to the growing list of subsidiaries of the huge conglomerates.

No, speaking against capitalism is not speaking against what made this country great. The people have made this country great and they deserve full democratic control over the economic as well as political aspects of their life.

## CONCLUSION

We have looked, then, at some of the myths which prevent us from seeing clearly the nature of capitalism and how it really works. It is a myth that capitalism arose more from ingenuity than exploitation; . . . that there is a fair distribution of wealth in the United States; that the interests of the corporate elite in the U.S. are synonymous with the interests of the people; that being against capitalism is unpatriotic. These are myths and they are false.

With these myths gone we can better see the roots of many of the injustices which face us today. Bloated stomachs, chronic unemployment, crowded urban ghettos, rising taxes, the breakdown of social services to the aged, the handicapped, the imprisoned, the lack of money for schools, hospitals, mass transit, and the continuance of imperialistic wars, etc., are all products of a system—a system which reaps excess for the few and scatters crumbs for the many.

As men and women thirsting for justice we are naive if we fail to take a hard, critical look at this system. If we do not do our homework, we might jump to the false conclusion that it is the average worker, the average parishioner, the average white suburbanite who is the culprit. We are more on the mark if we recognize that a common characteristic of the white workers, most women, Chicanos, blacks, farmers, Native Americans, office workers, etc., be they here in the U.S. or in other countries, is that they are exploited by the super-rich in a system designed to be unfair.

Our hope in writing this paper is to provoke discussions about capitalism and to urge U.S. church people to undertake a "radical" analysis of its effects upon the lives of U.S. citizens and people everywhere. In doing this we can learn from the Church in Latin America. For some years it has been grappling with the harsh effects of unjust economic and political systems. In 1968 at Medellin, Colombia, it clearly stated that many of the problems its people face are the results of a *system*—a system of internal colonialism and external neocolonialism.[1] As a result, the Church in Latin America is increasingly rejecting capitalism as a means to economic and human betterment and putting the gospel at the service of building a new kind of society.

We too need to explore the merits of an alternative system based not on competition and the profit motive, but on cooperation and solidarity. Socialism, by its definition, embodies these ideals and has, in a relatively short length of time, proven itself to be a viable alternative to capitalism. Granted, the specific form socialism would take in the United States, the richest country in the world, is an open question. But in light of all the serious problems we have in this country, such a discussion cannot be dismissed outright as naive, unpatriotic or even unchristian. Indeed, the burden of proof lies with those who say that capitalism here or in any country can serve the needs of the poor and the powerless. . . .

# An Underpraised and Undervalued System

## Michael Novak

Socialism, it appears, is like the Volvo: the thinking person's ideology. It is, according to Irving Howe in *World of Our Fathers,* the vital inheritance of Jewish immigrants. It attracts many dissidents of Catholic origin, like Michael Harrington, Garry Will, Rosemary Ruether, and the busy workers at the Center for Concern. According to Henry Ford II, it has

Reprinted by permission from *Worldview* magazine, July–August, 1977. Michael Novak, philosopher, theologian, novelist, and social critic, is currently Resident Scholar in Religion and Public Policy at the American Enterprise Institute in Washington, D.C.

[1]This position was reaffirmed at the Latin American bishops' meeting in Puebla in 1979.

come to dominate in the bosom of the Ford Foundation. On television shows corporate tycoons and small businessmen are invariably corrupt, and on the television news—that lucrative portion of one of the most profitable of all industries—profits in other industries are reported on with faint whiffs of moral disapproval.

The attraction of socialism, there is no doubt, arises from its humanistic vision. "We are united in the affirmation of a positive belief," announced the first issue of *Dissent,* the Democratic Socialist journal edited by Irving Howe and Lewis Coser, in 1954, "... the faith in humanity that for more than one hundred years [has] made men socialists." And a little later in that first issue: "*Socialism is the name of our desire.* And not merely in the sense that it is a vision which, for many people throughout the world, provides some sustenance, but also in the sense that it is a vision which objectifies and gives urgency to the criticism of the human condition in our time." It is a lovely desire, a delicate vision, this socialism. It is an ethic and a vision more fundamental than the economic or political theorems it from time to time enunciates, tries, discards.

How I would like to march in when the Socialist saints come marching in! How noble they are, unswayed by the "tepid liberalism" of the rest of us. So true to brotherhood, sisterhood, compassion, egalitarianism, justice. Even in their reluctant commitment to the flawed Democratic party, made on the grounds of grudging realism, our Socialists trail clouds of moral glory.

Yet each time I look lustfully at the argument for socialism (God knows I do, and forgives me for it) actual people, faces, and experiences leap from memory. I could live in a dream of ideology if hard experience did not awaken me. But economic systems require humble scrutiny. To judge them one must examine plumbing, sanitation, heat, power, light, water, fuel, paper, pen, typewriter, telephone, copier. One must examine things, things, things. Things so humble one may easily use them and never notice, purchase them and never feel the pain of choosing *not* to have some other. Amid abundance one forgets mean scarcity. Freed by affluence, one soars above materialism.

God knows I have tried to soar. Government planning, government spending, government responsibility—and distrust of freedom, distrust of individuals, distrust of free markets, contempt for profits—all these I have favored.

When the government puts buzzers on my seat belts, however, flesh rebels. When I stop to make my ideology concrete—when I ask, "Who *is* this government?"—I squirm. Those who make decisions far away from me constitute no eternal form of truthfulness, decency, and justice. When I have met them—decent folks at HEW, well-meaning missionaries of the Civil Rights Commission, poverty lawyers, publicists for government departments, aides to famous senators and congressmen, organizers from the Peace Corps, and the rest—their uplift leaves me in depression. Ideologues—kindhearted, decent, soft-spoken, sensitive, compassionate propagandists: What else can one say? They have a mission. They wish to make us better.

At first, agreeing with their liberal values, I'm glad *we're* in the government. But then I find *us* a little too missionary, holding out, as it were brassieres to natives, making the world to fit our image. It is so depressing to be told (and to tell others) to be good. I haven't the discipline to be a Socialist. I want to take my chances with the liberties of others and with my own.

When I read learned articles on "planning," my inner eye immediately begins to imagine the faces of the planners. Who will appoint them? Which constituencies will they represent? What types of individuals will find fulfillment in such jobs? It strains credulity to believe that "planners" will be more representative than the Congress is, or than the market is. The class of people most likely to be recruited as planners is not precisely the class to put most trust in. Neither do I see very clearly the checks and balances to be placed against these planners. What standing will they have in our Constitution? Will control surrendered to them in any way come back into possession?

I am not a Platonist about planners. They will be men and women of flesh and blood, like you and me, with interests and positions to protect. They will be insulated from electoral control. They will impose unpopular commands. Planners, one thinks suspiciously: philosopher-kings! No more to be trusted than in Plato's time.

And so the thought has recently become insistent in my doubting mind: If I no longer believe in democratic socialism, is there a form of democratic capitalism I must trust in more? Is there a theory of democratic capitalism not invented yet, beyond the manifestoes of socialism or the classic texts of capitalism?

There are three items in the creed of democratic capitalism I must devoutly believe in: (a) individual freedom and the methods of trial-and-error; (b) the innate selfishness and corruptibility of every human being; and (c) the capacity of a system of checks and balances to transform selfishness and corruptibility into a modicum of creativity, virtue, efficiency, and decency. These, as I uncover them, are the essential inner form of democratic capitalism. Their indispensable core is contained in (b), which may be stated thus: "Do not trust anybody." On this humanistic pessimism is our Constitution founded. For popular consumption, and put in the more optimistic mode of Anglo-Saxon hopefulness, the maxim is more clearly put: "In God we trust." That is, in no one else.

We trust no president, no court, no senator, no congressman, no governor, no sheriff, no public sentiment, no popular mandate—on every source of power that has been the wit of humankind to invent our Constitution commands us to place checks and balances. It so commands us, not from resentment, but from a long-experienced, wise, and irreformable pessimism about the human race. No human being, whether in solitude or in mass assembled, should be entirely trusted. No lesson of experience speaks more clearly, more credibly, to me. It is *unfair* to human beings to place full trust in them; none can bear such weight. Everyone sometimes fails. Inerrancy, infallibility, impeccability—no proper human aspirations, these. *Errare humanum est:* Such wisdom is not new. Even in so intimate a relation as marriage, forgiveness is a necessary grace; no one sustains a total trust. *A fortiori* in the governance of states.

Democratic capitalism is not a system to be trusted; so it announces. This is its intellectual advantage. It does not demand to be acclaimed as the best, most perfect system. In addition to providing the basic goods of life in abundance, cheaply and efficiently, it alone of all the world's known systems generates an entire industry of well-rewarded critics. So eager is it to breed reform and change—and make a buck on it—that no system is in fact more radical. Pell-mell it overturns the habits, traditions, and cultures of the past. Under its tutelage and leadership world process has been accelerated as never before. Conservative? Inertial? Which capitalist of your acquaintance lives in a world like that of a generation ago? Democratic capitalism undermines all historical traditions and institutions (even itself).

To announce support of democratic capitalism it is not necessary to hold that paradise has thereby, or will someday, be reached. It is not necessary to assert that democratic capitalism is a *good* system. It is certainly not a Christian system, nor a highly humanistic one. It is in some ways an evil, corrupt, inefficient, wasteful, and ugly system. One need only assert that it is better than any known alternative.

Socialism, meanwhile, no longer has the status of a dream or an ideal. It has been realized in something like fourscore regimes. Comparing like to like—actualities to actualities, dreams to dreams—it is not clear to me that democratic capitalism is inferior in performance or in dream to socialism. The defense, "Democratic socialism has never yet been fully tried," sounds like a classical apologetic for Christianity. Mind grasps it, doubt remains. Socialism is inherently authoritarian. Its emphasis upon democracy is inconsistent with its impulse to plan and to restrict.

Compared to the democratic capitalist the Socialist is twice born: born first into faith that the individual can be liberated from the present institutions of society; born again into the faith that the individual, so liberated, will be no slave to self but only to the common good. Socialism believes in the saintliness of human individuals under better social forms, democratic capitalism believes in their flawed self-interest under all.

The problem for a person weak in socialistic faith, like myself, is that he finds few allies in present dialogues. I cannot assent to the authoritarianism explicitly in the work of Robert Heilbroner and implicit in the work of John Kenneth Galbraith, Robert Lekachman, Michael Harrington, George Lichtheim, and Irving Howe. Many other defenders of "socialism," of course, are not serious; for them "socialism" functions merely as an expression of resentment about their own role in the scheme of world events. It expresses their hostilities toward themselves and toward the system on which they blame their own deficiencies. They do not truly intend to support the system they would put in its place.

I see few allies either among those who speak for capitalism. Those who publicly defend it often make it worse. Corporate executives and Rotarians use a vocabulary so hoary, so culturally limited, that not even they, one must assume, can believe it, save on ritual occasions. They celebrate themselves, so to speak, in obsolete English—in that classic, dry and dated style of Locke, Smith, Ricardo, and Mill, enlivened by Ayn Rand, stiffened yet again by Milton Friedman. Not very heady stuff. Relics in a cathedral dusted off; rubbings off old tombs.

In ideological warfare democratic capitalism is hopelessly outclassed. Those ads paid for by Mobil Oil on the Op-Ed pages of the *Times* (and other papers) are more deadly in their prose than the editorials surrounding them. I look to them for light, find disappointment. The reason probably is that capitalists have not been trained to think—have, indeed, been tutored *not* to think, *not* to theorize, *not* to dream—rather, to be practical. The radical impulse of capitalism is to set schemes and speculation to one side in order to detect some practical detail that might modify the technology of mouse traps. Socialism's dreams are the soul's response to capitalism's practicality.

Democratic capitalism seems willing to lose any number of ideological battles, provided only that it win the franchise for producing, delivering, and getting paid for goods or services. It will build cars in Kiev, deliver Pepsi to Leningrad, teach computer technology to engineers in Moscow —anything for dollars, no ideology attached. The self-confidence of capitalists is, however, shallow. They believe that what the world wants is goods. They leave the Good beyond their caring—leave it to priests, poets, propagandists. That is why they are losing everywhere. Lenin predicted that capitalists would sell socialism everything necessary for the latter's triumph—socialism could never hope to equal capitalism, but capitalism would destroy itself.

The point is not that democratic capitalism carries no ideology, depends on none. Most certainly it does. Democratic capitalism depends upon a disciplined triumph of the human spirit. Yet it resists reflection upon its own presuppositions. Democratic capitalism can function successfully only in certain types of cultures, in which high values of individual responsibility, social cooperation, and the voluntary spirit have for centuries been nourished. Its severe disinclination toward philosophy allows poisonous effects: (a) the spiritual life of its own citizens is slowly starved; and (b) it cannot compete with socialism on the plain of ideological warfare—it cannot explain itself. It is one of the choicer ironies of history that the economic system most dependent upon, and most supportive of, liberty of spirit should present itself to the world as brute and inarticulate, mute in the language of the spirit.

To be sure, democratic capitalists display an openness and practicality far beyond those of Socialists. They find it easier to borrow shamelessly from Socialist systems—"creeping socialism," the more resistant capitalists call this process—than Socialists from them. Faced with a choice between an elegant theory and successful practicality, democratic capitalists prefer the latter. They prefer what works to what inspires. In the ideological struggle to inspire those millions on this planet who are neither Socialist nor capitalist, this preference, too, is damaging.

Disdainful of their own intellectual task—and disdainful of the intellectuals, symbol-makers, and publicists who might execute it—corporate leaders show no respect for words, images, or critical ideas. Texaco and trust? Paper mills and conservation? Americanism and automobiles? The corporate sector, one comes to believe with despair, is philistine, its leaders not worthy of the system their creativity makes possible.

For generations corporate leaders seemed to think they did not need a theory or an ideology, that all they had to do to prove their case was to produce. They are learning now, perhaps too late, that the realm of ideas has power and attraction of its own. Traditional religion, on which they implicitly relied, has been undercut by Oldsmobiles, expressways, TV sets, suburban barbecues. Whoever says "capital" says dollars; while Socialists seem to feed humanistic, even religious, aspiration. Capitalists seem so materialist. Sensitive souls, repelled, flock elsewhere. "Not by bread alone" is a harsh word for producers.

Here Daniel Bell's much neglected thesis in *The Cultural Contradictions of Capitalism* requires meditation: Democratic capitalism depends upon the life of the spirit, which its practice undercuts. Bell pleads (with some despair) that democratic capitalism must tap again its religious and humanistic sources. It is ironic that capitalism should turn out to be more "godless" than socialism; that its narrow empiricism should undermine the religious spirit more deeply than socialism does. Socialism offers a holistic vision of the self in society, gives history a point, and establishes before the human heart the image of a nonalienated and brotherly way of being. It opposes religion, but on the terrain of religion. Capitalism, indifferent to the spirit, seems acquisitive and shallow.

In a word, democratic capitalism suffers from a lamentable intellectual failure. It does not grasp its own identity. It carries with it, and depends upon, a vision of the responsible individual; moral autonomy; social cooperation and fellow feeling; intellectual and artistic freedom; creativity beyond alienation; religious liberty; many-faceted pluralism; inalienable human rights. In its dreams it is at least the equal of the dreams of socialism. Not by accident do great artists and unfettered intellects, saints and "constituencies of conscience," voluntary associations of many sorts, and initiatives, inventions, and creativities of all kinds multiply in democratic capitalist societies. Why, then, do the proponents of "the free enterprise system" blather about the economic system merely? Why, alarmed by threats to their "free markets," do they invoke an obsolete rhetoric, mainly defensive, narrowly construed, which must repel even those who might in the main agree with them?

For democratic capitalism is not only an economic system; it is also a political system. Indeed, apart from a long institutional history under capitalist tutelage, it is very difficult for a people to be democratic. Without certain economic freedoms, political freedoms lack institutional support. Without a free economy, the idea of the independent individual does not emerge. As Socialist planners acquire political clout, becoming commissars, so inversely, the trial-and-error of the free market inspires citizens to individual initiative, risk, and self-realization. A Ralph Nader opposing General Motors is conceivable under democratic capitalism. Were the auto industry "democratically" controlled by the state, a Ralph Nader would be a "counterrevolutionary," "reactionary" agent, a "traitor against the people." In "popular democracy" totalitarianism lurks.

The religio-humanistic revival pointed to by Daniel Bell requires no return to Jimmy Carter pietism. It calls for an intellectual deepening. In an earlier book, *An End to Ideology,* Professor Bell seemed to praise intense commitment to the practical and the expedient. These, in his latest book, he has diagnosed as a fatal limitation in our system. But there is another sense in that expression, "an end to ideology"—an end to *merely* ideological thinking, to sloganizing, to mindlessly taking sides. Many today hunger for something better than socialism, better than capitalism something we have not yet articulated for ourselves.

For ours is not a system of "free enterprise" merely, nor a "free market system" only, nor a "nonideological" system. Our system is a political system, a democratic system, based upon both a Constitution and practicing institutions that incarnate a "bill of rights." It is, moreover, a philosophical and spiritual system, nourishing and shaping and developing a specific human type, divergent from other human types. It is a moral and cultural system.

There are, indeed, three ways to destroy our system. (1) One can destroy its economic genius. (2) One can destroy its political genius. (3) One can destroy its cultural genius. To attack any one of these is to attack the other two. Too foolishly do some believe that changes at any one of these will leave the others sound.

# 10

# *First World, Third World*

The title of this chapter reflects a jargon that has come into general use in characterizing the economic condition of the world's nations. Though various distinctions have been made (running from three "worlds" to four or more), one common usage is the designation of North America, Europe, Japan, Australia, and white South Africa as First World nations; the Communist countries as Second World; and the countries of Africa, Asia, and Central and South America as Third World—including "developing" nations and those suffering under extreme conditions of economic hardship.

This chapter raises issues involving the relationship of First World, industrial nations to Third World countries. There may be no subject of more crucial import for the peace and stability of the world order. Until now we have been absorbed with the tensions and potential conflict between East and West, or First World and Second World countries. But another potential source of disruption and conflict is between North and South, between the minority of rich and the majority of poor nations of the earth. This potential conflict raises tremendously difficult and complex moral issues. It involves the use of economic and political power in an effort to create a just economic order, an order that would require First World nations to adopt policies and programs that would give Third World countries the opportunity to close the growing economic gap between them.

In 1900 the gap between rich and poor nations in per capita income was 2:1. Today, as the world shrinks to a global village, it is nearly 20:1. One must acknowledge that many factors within the poor nations contribute to this situation, including poor soil and poor climate, exploding populations and an absence of capital and technology, social inequalities which feature a few landowning families of great wealth and the masses of landless peasants, and the absence of effective political leadership. Nonetheless, the impact of First World countries on poor nations has been critical. Colonization of these countries in the nineteenth and twentieth centuries resulted in (1) the transfer of their mineral wealth to the rich countries of the North, and (2) the creation of their continuing economic dependence on the North, since the colonized economies were geared toward providing raw materials for the industrialized nations. This arrangement to this day places a stranglehold on the attempts of Third World nations to develop economic independence and provide for the needs of their own populations.

The article by Roger Shinn focuses on two prominent dimensions of this subject: overpopulation and poverty. He notes that there are significant differences between rich and poor nations both in discerning the causes of overpopulation and poverty and in proposing solutions. It is easy for North Americans to preach birth control to those living in India, for example, but we fail to understand the dependence of Indian parents upon their children and the necessity of having large families—particularly enough sons—to ensure the parents' care in old age. Add to this practical consideration the religious and other cultural factors associated with procreation, and one begins to understand the futility of advocating birth control as *the* solution to overpopulation. The same situation exists in reverse when spokespersons for developing nations point to the need for more equitable distribution of the world's wealth in light of the overconsumption that marks the "American way of life." Obviously, the fact that an average North American uses five times the agricultural resources of an average Indian or African is relevant to the problem of world poverty; but can we expect the individual North American to assume a different life-style any more readily than the individual Indian? On the other hand, ethical implications would demand more of North Americans, for they are not driven by extreme social necessity or religious conviction to follow their life-style. The efforts of a growing number of North Americans to assume a more simple style of life constitute a beginning, but this beginning is challenged by those who insist that we must increase our consumption to keep our economy strong.

The specter of starvation has hovered continuously over many Third World countries. A severe drought in a given year can mean death for millions of people. What is the responsibility of Western countries—and more specifically the United States—in meeting the needs of these people? The magnitude of the problem and the prospect of starvation on a far greater scale in our overpopulated world have led some to advocate an approach used by medics on the battlefield called "triage." It involves dividing the wounded into three groupings: those who will survive without medical help, those who will probably survive with medical help, and those who will probably not survive even with medical help. All resources are then devoted to the middle group, for whom medical aid can make the difference between life and death. The third group is written off as a lost cause. The proposal is that we practice a food triage, limiting our help to stricken nations or regions where there appears to be reason for hope.

A more extreme approach is proposed by Garrett Hardin, called a "lifeboat ethic," in which he refers to rich nations as lifeboats and poor nations as those in the sea who would come aboard. Since space is limited in each lifeboat and overcrowding would result in capsizing and disaster for everyone, Hardin argues that we had best look out for ourselves, for this will be the most humane approach in the long run—at least for our children's children. One might characterize this position as a form of "social Darwinism," or survival of the fittest, where the "fit" are those who happen to have been born in a rich nation. This argument is certainly provocative, and the analogy Hardin uses makes it appear quite convincing. Those who take exception challenge the appropriateness of the lifeboat analogy, noting among other things the presumptuousness of wealthy nations making these kinds of decisions when each of its citizens is in effect holding on to five seats in terms of the excessive energy and food we are consuming.

Barbara Ward has little patience with advocates of triage or lifeboat ethics, for these views to her reflect a morally bankrupt position that does not address the real avenues of change. Instead of withdrawal in an effort to save ourselves, we need the vision and will to work together with Third World countries in a sustained effort to multiply their food production. Instead of creating a worse problem of overpopulation through such efforts, history demonstrates that a higher standard of living would lead to a reduction of the birthrate in these countries.

One of the more eloquent spokesmen for the Third World is the President of Tanzania, Julius K. Nyerere. Educated in the mission schools of his country, he expresses a deep concern for social justice in a world in which the poverty-stricken majority are dominated by a rich minority. The issue is power, and power resides with the wealthy nations in their economic arrangements with poor nations. This division between rich and poor is yet more ominous because it also reflects a division between races. The ultimate issue is not economic development but the development of people, which occurs not through charity but by encouraging responsibility in a spirit of equality and respect. Here the church has an essential role to play, for it provides a basis in religious conviction for the ultimate value of the individual person.

# The Population Crisis: Exploring the Issues

Roger L. Shinn

The population crisis of our time brings together a wide range of issues—technical, cultural, ethical and religious. There are dogmatic answers, usually glib and fallacious. There are more thoughtful answers, but even these are controversial. Helpful policies require research, imagination and careful thinking. Yet delay means increasing suffering and death.

In its most obvious aspects the world population emergency can be stated in terms of arithmetic and common sense. It took all human history until about 1850—perhaps a million years—for the total human population to reach a billion. Now the human race adds a billion in less than 15 years.

Another way to put it is that the world's population now doubles in about 35 years. Continuation of this rate would mean that the earth's 3.6 billion people of 1970 would become 7.2 billion by the year 2005, 14.4 billion by 2040 and so on. Such processes cannot go on forever—even though nobody knows precisely how many people the earth can maintain.

Put beside the exploding population the starvation and malnutrition that haunts the world, and the scope of the crisis becomes obvious. UN data indicate that 400 million people are malnourished to the extent of being incapable of full physical or mental work and seriously susceptible to disease. A far larger two-thirds of the world's population have inadequate diets. A standard estimate is that 10,000 people a day were dying from starvation or consequences of malnutrition in the late 1960s, even before some recent emergencies.

Starvation would be far worse if it were not for the Green Revolution, which has greatly increased food productivity in the hungriest parts of the world. But the new hybrid grains bring their own risks. Their resistance to disease, as compared with old, less productive strains, is not tested. They require chemical fertilizers, now in short supply at the places where they are needed most. Their effectiveness has been shown in a period of excep-

Reprinted by permission from the August 5, 1974 issue of *Christianity and Crisis*. Copyright © 1974 by Christianity and Crisis, Inc. Roger L. Shinn is Reinhold Niebuhr Professor of Social Ethics at Union Theological Seminary, New York and author of numerous works in the field of Christian social ethics.

tionally good climate that cannot be expected to continue permanently. And, even at best, there is little prospect that the Green Revolution will manage to match the next doubling of the world's population, as it did the last.

Add to all this the reduction in the world's fishing catch, probably due to overfishing. And add the expansion of deserts over boundaries of 3500 kilometers at an annual average rate of 30 kilometers. Then consider that the world's food reserves are now [summer 1974] less than a month's supply—the lowest figure in recent times. It is easy to see why demographers project terrifying pictures of the future.

## POLITICAL AND CULTURAL FACTORS

Yet the obvious case for halting the population explosion is not obvious to everybody. Often it is stated in deceptive simplicities. It is no help when so sophisticated an anthropologist as Claude Levi-Strauss says that "the only real problem facing civilization today is the population explosion." People suffering from oppression, war and the malaise that infects so many societies today can only shriek in frustration when the population monomaniacs say their piece. We cannot understand the population problem unless we locate it within its cultural and ethical settings. To do this requires exploration of several issues.

Many people have no direct experience of overpopulation. On the contrary, they see an advantage to themselves or their nations in high rates of reproduction.

For example, last March the Argentine Government restricted the sale of contraceptive pills as part of an effort to double the population by the end of this century. Argentine nationalists relate numbers to power, a familiar style of thought. And when they see overpopulated neighbors eyeing uncultivated lands in Argentina, they decide that they had better fill up their territory.

One of those neighbors, Brazil, with four times the population of Argentina, would like to join the "big powers." Its method includes growth in population and the economy. Compared with these immediate interests, any talk of world population aggregates or of the ecological value of Brazil's uncultivated lands is remote and abstract.

In a different situation, Israel sees itself as a small nation surrounded by far larger, unfriendly neighbors. Although some orthodox Jewish leaders in America have recently called for higher rates of reproduction, American Jews, largely urban and well-educated, tend to have small families. In Israel pronatalist attitudes are more persuasive.

Black people in the U.S. have reasons to distrust white people who worry about high black rates of reproduction. Interestingly, college-educated black people have a slightly lower birthrate than comparable white people, and in general the correlation of birthrates with social position is similar in black and white communities. Such data tell a lot about the relation of population to cultural situation. But black people know enough about their own history to suspect the motives of whites who advise them to limit their numbers.

In all these cases it might be argued that numbers are not power and that population growth may actually interfere with a higher quality of life for the social groups concerned. But that may not be the way they see their experience and political destiny.

The political factors easily merge into a set of wider cultural issues. Arguments for reduced reproduction that are quite persuasive in some cultures may be meaningless in others.

If a society really believes that "the principal work of a woman is to have children," as a Peronist magazine in Argentina has put it, then women will have many children. Particularly if women themselves believe that, demographic information will not compete effectively with their own sense of identity. For this reason an effective response to the population crisis will require a major revision of widespread ideas of female roles and identities.

Similarly, if men demonstrate their *machismo* by proving their fertility, the incentives to reproduction will overcome restraints based on a vague world situation or even on personal poverty. Peer ridicule and wounds to male identity are powerful forces. Cultural habits are not eternal; they can be changed. Demographic necessity may contribute to the change. But the most cogent reasoning, if it ignores the cultural context, is unconvincing.

In some areas a high infant and child mortality rate has been a strong incentive for reproduction. Parents, painfully knowing that infants often die, may crave enough children that some will survive. Such attitudes and habits become deeply imbedded in culture. The introduction of medical means for reducing mortality may, over a period of time, modify behavior.

Roger Revelle of the Harvard Center for Population Studies argues that a reduction of infant mortality is one of the most effective ways of reducing rates of reproduction. His critics, of course, point out that the *immediate* effect of reduced mortality is an increase in population. The relation of immediate and long-range effects is only one of the questions that complicate population policy.

The economic role of children is another important cultural factor. In industrialized societies, where formal education is long and expensive, children are not an obvious economic asset. But societies where even young children are part of the family working team reason differently. Furthermore, in some such societies the economic security of parents in old age depends upon their children.

Consider those societies where the social security "system" assumes the responsibility of male offspring to care for their aged parents. Assume that such a society has long had a high rate of infant and child mortality. Parents then have an overwhelming incentive to produce enough male offspring that one or two will outlive the parents. Fewer children may be economically advantageous to the whole society but not to individual families.

Religious values and tabus often reinforce or modify the other cultural forces that influence procreation. In societies influenced by the Bible certain traditions about sexuality or commands to "fill the earth" have sometimes led to an anticontraceptive mentality. In actual fact the correlation between specific moral-religious teachings and population has been rather small on a worldwide basis, although in specific cases it may be high. But religion as part of the total cultural ethos is a powerful force.

Propagandists who isolate population from its cultural context often wonder why people persist in acting against their best interests, when the threats of the population explosion are so obvious. The answer is that people usually act in accord with their interests, *as they perceive them* in their cultural situations.

## IDEOLOGICAL ISSUES

Debates about population are frequently ideological confrontations in which political and cultural issues become elaborated in opposing pictures of the world and its ailments.

In the characteristic international discussion population is usually a favorite theme of spokesmen from affluent industrialized nations. They point out that highly populated and impoverished countries cannot attain prosperity without limiting population. They buttress their arguments with mountains of data, accurate and relevant.

The usual answer from the developing countries is that their poverty is due to maldistribution of the world's wealth. To them talk of population is the ideology of prosperous nations, who want to preserve their unjust shares of the world's wealth and power. They can produce the statistical data to show that it is the wealthy societies that consume an exorbitant share of the world's resources and threaten the ecosystem.

The two arguments move past each other, each with an invincible logic that does not quite meet the logic it opposes. Take food as an example. The underfed nations point out that there is enough food in the world for everyone, if it is distributed more equally. Furthermore, the world could produce more food than it now produces, if economic incentives and technical skills were put to work. (These claims are literally true. But their execution, even if the will were present, would require transportation systems and economic infrastructures not quickly attainable.)

In terms of strict caloric needs the U.S., to take the most obvious example, is extremely wasteful of food. Meat-producing animals take in five to ten times as many calories as they yield in food. If the people of the U.S. were to give up meat, beer, and whiskey, immense quantities of grain would be released for world consumption. A further step might be the renunciation of coffee and tea, with the release of more land for actual foods. To suggest such ideas is to go so far beyond any present practical possibility as to sound ridiculous. But it does show that the choice of population as the point of attack on starvation is a choice of convenience. Poor nations can reply that the wealthy would consider other points of attack if they really cared.

The logic just rehearsed unveils the ideological bias among many of the enthusiasts for population restraint. But they are not entirely refuted. Suppose, they might answer, the U.S. and other wealthy nations were to make a major effort to feed the starving peoples of the world. Imagine a miracle of generosity in which wealthy people made authentic sacrifices for the poor. Imagine a major restructuring of planetary economics. Unless such efforts were coordinated with a really effective population policy, they would help temporarily at best. Another doubling of the world's population would bring another round of starvation, more extensive than anything experienced now. It is hard to summon a heroic effort with the expectation that it will make things worse in the long run.

The only reasonable conclusion to the ideological argument is to be aware that partisans on both sides can invoke valid facts and reason but can also use facts and reason to shift responsibility from themselves. There is some recent evidence that in settings of mutual trust people can see beyond their ideological biases. For example, a meeting of Asians, gathered by the World Council of Churches (WCC) in Kuala Lumpur, Malaysia in April 1973, made a forceful criticism of international economic injustices and then went on to say: "The problem of poverty and unemployment will defy solution until developing countries severely limit the growth of their populations."

Latin Americans and Africans, for understandable historical reasons, are less likely to make this point than Asians. But all may find some persuasiveness in the example of China, the one developing country that is acting vigorously to limit its population growth.

A recent document of the World Council of Churches, "Population Policy, Social Justice and the Quality of Life" (1973), shows that it is possible in an ecumenical setting to transcend partisan ideological interest and to relate the concern about population to the concern for social justice. Its title wisely links the three issues that are genuinely inseparable.

## THE HUMAN COSTS OF EFFECTIVE CHANGE

There is not the slightest doubt that population growth will slow down. Its continuation is a physical impossibility. The question is what methods and what agonizing costs will bring about the change.

The human race knows many methods of proved effectiveness, but most of them are morally intolerable. For centuries malaria has limited population in some areas. Starvation is another traditional method, now in effect and, by all signs, due for an increase. Infanticide and killing of the aged have worked. And there is no doubt that today mankind knows how to fight wars that could decimate populations.

Such possibilities are worse than the evils they "cure." I mention them because they may come into practice, either by design or by inadvertence.

More often proposed as a deliberate method is abortion, which has been the most common method of birth control on a worldwide basis. (It may be that the IUD is now more prevalent.) The morality of abortion is highly controversial; the least to be said is that it is morally offensive to many people. Contraception is far less controversial, but some persons and societies object to it.

Sexual abstinence or restraint might seem too radical to deserve mention, except that some societies (Ireland and China, for example) have made it effective to some extent. However, few people expect it to stop the population explosion.

If we examine the ideas under serious discussion today, we might divide them into two types. The first can be called the "hardnosed" proposals. Their advocates say that the situation is so desperate as to justify methods that would otherwise be unbearable. They argue that it is more merciful to let some people starve now than to make extraordinary efforts to feed them, with the consequence of multiplying population and starvation in future years. And they argue that the time is approaching, or has come, for compulsory limitation on reproduction.

If such proposals are hardnosed, their advocates insist that they are not hardhearted. As for starvation, it is now going on; and philanthropy that increases it for the next generation is not truly humanitarian. As for compulsion, any social ethic restrains individuals for the sake of the common good. Why should people be allowed to claim an undue share of the world's limited resources for their own offspring when such claims mean misery and death for other people? Enforcement of compulsory limits would admittedly be difficult. It would involve, in the last resort, compulsory sterilization or abortion. But such measures are no more extreme than the compulsory starvation now on the increase.

Opposed to such reasoning are those whom we might call "the humanitarians"—although with the realization that the hardnosed claim to be the true humanitarians. The humanitarian argument is that some kinds of purposeful cruelty are worse than any alternatives they aim to prevent, that some means are so callous that no ends can justify them.

The humanitarians add the practical argument that ruthless methods—and, for that matter, even gentler methods of direct propaganda—do not really work. The more humane and voluntary methods are, in fact, the more effective ones. Philip Hauser of the Population Research Center at the University of Chicago says: "The fact is that decreases in fertility in what are now the economically advanced nations were achieved completely on a voluntary basis." Arthur Dyck, Harvard theologian-demographer, says that the effective forces for reducing reproductive rates have been increased education and increased personal opportunities. He advocates steps toward increased food production and international social justice, involving radical changes in the lifestyles of both affluent and impoverished peoples. Sufficient attention to these issues, he argues, will be more moral and more effective than frontal attacks on the population problem.

Even Dyck grants that "in a situation of last resort, societies might very well decide to ration the number of children per family." But he considers any such compulsion "unjustifiable now and in the indefinite future."

Any ethically sensitive person will hope that Dyck is right. The question that "the hardnosed" ask "the humanitarians" is whether the latter have taken sufficient account of the emergency situation in which the human race now lives. In the first place, the demographic transition in industrialized nations cannot in any sense be a model for the rest of the world. It was "helped" by the Black Death—which reduced the population of Europe by about half and meant that Europe's population in 1600 was about the same as in 1300, despite major economic growth. In the following centuries smallpox, starvation, war, enforced celibacy among the poor and widespread infanticide all worked to limit population. And by the 19th century Europe was exporting people in the greatest migration in human history.

In the second place, the ethically sensitive proposals of Dyck are probably utopian impossibilities. And changes that would require years to accomplish will not save lives now and next year.

## SOME FERVENT BUT TIMID JUDGMENTS

On a topic like this it will not do to stop with the presentation of others' arguments. I must state some personal judgments. They are fervent judgments because the human pain is so great; they are timid judgments because the problem is so overwhelming. The human race has never experienced a population problem on anything like the present scale, and our resources—physical and moral—are inadequate for dealing with it. But try we must. So I urge four actions.

First, affluent America can take major steps to relieve worldwide hunger and to reduce the insufferable gaps between wealthy and poor nations. The Christian churches, in particular, cannot stand by in the face of human wretchedness without denying their own deepest convictions. I would like to believe the same of the American nation. These efforts will not be very effective without an imaginative national leadership, which is not now in evidence. Even so, individuals and groups can act. Churches and voluntary organizations are acting, and they can do more.

Second, such programs require comparable efforts directed at the population problem. These can include research on contraception, as well as designs for social policies that encourage people to exercise their reproductive powers with wisdom and responsibility. They must avoid the offensive paternalism by which presumably wise societies claim to tell foolish societies what to do.

Third, the affluent industrialized world must become more sensitive to its ideological biases. To see the reality of the population crisis is not an ideological bias. But to avoid seeing the ways in which lavish consumption jeopardizes the world is to misperceive the world. And to concentrate on population to the exclusion of equally urgent problems of justice is an ideological corruption so grave as to destroy the capacity for helpful action.

Fourth, affluent societies must quickly begin to envision futures radically different from those that now govern their thinking. What those futures will be, we can rarely guess. But the dream of a consumers' paradise, American style, is not an option for the world. And it is increasingly a dubious option for America.

Each of these proposals, of course, requires elaboration. That work is going on and must continue. When all is said that can now be said, the fact remains that the world must expect immense suffering in the years ahead. The temptation will be great to harden hearts and seek fortresses of security in a threatened and agonized world. Equally great will be the temptation to fatalistic resignation. Those who believe in the freedom of God and his human creatures must find better alternatives than these.

# The Case Against Helping the Poor

## Garrett Hardin

Environmentalists use the metaphor of the earth as a "spaceship" in trying to persuade countries, industries, and people to stop wasting and polluting our natural resources. Since we all share life on this planet, they argue, no single person or institution has the right to destroy, waste, or use more than a fair share of its resources.

But does everyone on earth have an equal right to an equal share of its resources? The spaceship metaphor can be dangerous when used by misguided idealists to justify suicidal policies for sharing our resources through uncontrolled immigration and foreign aid. In their enthusiastic but unrealistic generosity, they confuse the ethics of a spaceship with those of a lifeboat.

A true spaceship would have to be under the control of a captain, since no ship could possibly survive if its course were determined by committee. Spaceship Earth certainly has no captain; the United Nations is merely a toothless tiger, with little power to enforce any policy upon its bickering members.

If we divide the world crudely into rich nations and poor nations, two-thirds of them are desperately poor, and only one-third comparatively rich, with the United States the wealthiest of all. Metaphorically each rich nation can be seen as a lifeboat full of comparatively rich people. In the ocean outside each lifeboat swim the poor of the world, who would like to get in, or at least to share some of the wealth. What should the lifeboat passengers do?

First, we must recognize the limited capacity of any lifeboat. For example, a nation's land has a limited capacity to support a population and as the current energy crisis has shown us, in some ways we have already exceeded the carrying capacity of our land.

**Adrift in a Moral Sea.**   So here we sit, say, 50 people in our lifeboat. To be generous, let us assume it has room for 10 more, making a total capacity of 60. Suppose the 50 of us in the lifeboat see 100 others swimming in the water outside, begging for admission to our boat or for handouts. We have

Reprinted by permission from *Psychology Today Magazine.* Copyright © 1974 Ziff-Davis Publishing Company. Garrett Hardin is Professor of Biology at the University of California, Santa Barbara, and author of *Promethean Ethics* (1980).

several options: we may be tempted to try to live by the Christian ideal of being "our brother's keeper," or by the Marxist ideal of "to each according to his needs." Since the needs of all in the water are the same, and since they can all be seen as "our brothers," we could take them all into our boat, making a total of 150 in a boat designed for 60. The boat swamps, everyone drowns. Complete justice, complete catastrophe.

Since the boat has an unused excess capacity of 10 more passengers, we could admit just 10 more to it. But which 10 do we let in? How do we choose? Do we pick the best 10, the neediest 10, "first come, first served"? And what do we say to the 90 we exclude? If we do let an extra 10 into our lifeboat, we will have lost our "safety factor," an engineering principle of critical importance. For example, if we don't leave room for excess capacity as a safety factor in our country's agriculture, a new plant disease or a bad change in the weather could have disastrous consequences.

Suppose we decide to preserve our small safety factor and admit no more to the lifeboat. Our survival is then possible, although we shall have to be constantly on guard against boarding parties.

While this last solution clearly offers the only means of our survival, it is morally abhorrent to many people. Some say they feel guilty about their good luck. My reply is simple. "Get out and yield your place to others." This may solve the problem of the guilt-ridden person's conscience, but it does not change the ethics of the lifeboat. The needy person to whom the guilt-ridden person yields his place will not himself feel guilty about his good luck. If he did, he would not climb aboard. The net result of conscience-stricken people giving up their unjustly held seats is the elimination of that sort of conscience from the lifeboat.

This is the basic metaphor within which we must work out our solutions. Let us now enrich the image, step by step, with substantive additions from the real world, a world that must solve real and pressing problems of overpopulation and hunger.

The harsh ethics of the lifeboat become even harsher when we consider the reproductive differences between the rich nations and the poor nations. The people inside the lifeboat are doubling in numbers every 87 years; those swimming around outside are doubling, on the average, every 35 years, more than twice as fast as the rich. And since the world's resources are dwindling, the difference in prosperity between the rich and the poor can only increase.

As of 1973, the U.S. had a population of 210 million people, who were increasing by 0.8 percent per year. Outside our lifeboat, let us imagine another 210 million people (say the combined populations of Colombia, Ecuador, Venezuela, Morocco, Pakistan, Thailand and the Philippines), who are increasing at a rate of 3.3 percent per year. Put differently, the doubling time for this aggregate population is 21 years, compared to 87 years for the U.S.

**Multiplying the Rich and the Poor.**   Now suppose the U.S. agreed to pool its resources with those seven countries, with everyone receiving an equal share. Initially the ratio of Americans to non-Americans in this model would be one-to-one. But consider what the ratio would be after 87 years, by which time the Americans would have doubled to a population of 420 million. By then, doubling every 21 years, the other group would have swollen to 354 billion. Each American would have to share the available resources with more than eight people.

But, one could argue, this discussion assumes that current population trends will continue, and they may not. Quite so. Most likely the rate of population increase will decline much faster in the U.S. than it will in the other countries, and there does not seem to be much we can do about it. In sharing with "each according to his needs," we must recognize that needs are determined by population size, which is determined by the rate of reproduction, which at present is regarded as a sovereign right of every nation, poor or not. This being so, the philanthropic load created by the sharing ethic of the spaceship can only increase.

**The Tragedy of the Commons.**   The fundamental error of spaceship ethics, and the sharing it requires, is that it leads to what I call "the tragedy of the commons." Under a system of private property, the men who own property recognize their responsibility to care for it, for if they don't they will eventually suffer. A farmer, for instance, will allow no more cattle in a pasture than its carrying capacity justifies. If he overloads it, erosion sets in, weeds take over, and he loses the use of the pasture.

If a pasture becomes a commons open to all, the right of each to use it may not be matched by a corresponding responsibility to protect it. Asking everyone to use it with discretion will hardly do, for the considerate herdsman who refrains from overloading the commons suffers more than a selfish one who says his needs are greater. If everyone would restrain himself, all would be well; but it takes only one less than everyone to ruin a system of voluntary restraint. In a crowded world of less than perfect human beings, mutual ruin is inevitable if there are no controls. This is the tragedy of the commons.

One of the major tasks of education today should be the creation of such an acute awareness of the dangers of the commons that people will recognize its many varieties. For example, the air and water have become polluted because they are treated as commons. Further growth in the population or per-capita conversion of natural resources into pollutants will only make the problem worse. The same holds true for the fish of the oceans. Fishing fleets have nearly disappeared in many parts of the world, technological improvements in the art of fishing are hastening the day of complete ruin. Only the replacement of the system of the commons with a responsible system of control will save the land, air, water, and oceanic fisheries.

**The World Food Bank.**   In recent years there has been a push to create a new commons called a World Food Bank, an international depository of food reserves to which nations would contribute according to their abilities and from which they would draw according to their needs. This humanitarian proposal has received support from many liberal international groups, and from such prominent citizens as Margaret Mead, U.N. Secretary General Kurt Waldheim, and Senators Edward Kennedy and George McGovern.

A world food bank appeals powerfully to our humanitarian impulses. But before we rush ahead with such a plan, let us recognize where the greatest political push comes from, lest we be disillusioned later. Our experience with the "Food for Peace Program," or Public Law 480, gives us the answer. This program moved billions of dollars worth of U.S. surplus grain to food-short, population-long countries during the past two decades. But when P.L. 480 first became law, a headline in the business magazine *Forbes* revealed the real power behind it. "Feeding the World's Hungry Millions: How It Will Mean Billions for U.S. Business."

And indeed it did. In the years 1960 to 1970, U.S. taxpayers spent a total of $7.9 billion on the Food for Peace program. Between 1948 and 1970, they also paid an additional $50 billion for other economic-aid programs, some of which went for food and food-producing machinery and technology. Though all U.S. taxpayers were forced to contribute to the cost of P.L. 480, certain special interest groups gained handsomely under the program. Farmers did not have to contribute the grain; the government, or rather the taxpayers, bought it from them at full market prices. The increased demand raised prices of farm products generally. The manufacturers of farm machinery, fertilizers and pesticides benefited by the farmers' extra efforts to grow more food. Grain elevators profited from storing the surplus until it could be shipped. Railroads made money hauling it to ports, and shipping lines profited from carrying it overseas. The implementation of P.L. 480 required the creation of a vast government bureaucracy, which then acquired its own vested interest in continuing the program regardless of its merits.

**Extracting Dollars.**   Those who proposed and defended the Food for Peace program in public rarely mentioned its importance to any of these special interests. The public emphasis was always on its humanitarian effects. The combination of silent selfish interests and highly vocal humanitarian apologists made a powerful and successful lobby for extracting money from taxpayers. We can expect the same lobby to push now for the creation of a World Food Bank.

However great the potential benefit to selfish interests, it should not be a decisive argument against a truly humanitarian program. We must ask if such a program would actually do more good than harm, not only momentarily but also in the long run. Those who propose the food bank usually refer to a current "emergency" or "crisis" in terms of world food supply. But what is an emergency? Although they may be infrequent and sudden, everyone knows that emergencies will occur from time to time. A well-run family, company, organization or country prepares for the likelihood of accidents and emergencies. It expects them, it budgets for them, it saves for them.

**Learning the Hard Way.** What happens if some organizations or countries budget for accidents and others do not? If each country is solely responsible for its own well-being, poorly managed ones will suffer. But they can learn from experience. They may mend their ways, and learn to budget for infrequent but certain emergencies. For example, the weather varies from year to year, and periodic crop failures are certain. A wise and competent government saves out of the production of the good years in anticipation of bad years to come. Joseph taught this policy to Pharaoh in Egypt more than 2,000 years ago. Yet the great majority of the governments in the world today do not follow such a policy. They lack either the wisdom or the competence, or both. Should those nations that do manage to put something aside be forced to come to the rescue each time an emergency occurs among the poor nations?

"But it isn't their fault!" Some kindhearted liberals argue. "How can we blame the poor people who are caught in an emergency? Why must they suffer for the sins of their governments?" The concept of blame is simply not relevant here. The real question is, what are the operational consequences of establishing a food bank? If it is open to every country every time a need develops, slovenly rulers will not be motivated to take Joseph's advice. Someone will always come to their aid. Some countries will deposit food in the world food bank, and others will withdraw it. There will be almost no overlap. As a result of such solutions to food shortage emergencies, the poor countries will not learn to mend their ways, and will suffer progressively greater emergencies as their populations grow.

**Population Control the Crude Way.** On the average, poor countries undergo a 2.5 percent increase in population each year; rich countries, about 0.8 percent. Only rich countries have anything in the way of food reserves set aside, and even they do not have as much as they should. Poor countries have none. If poor countries received no food from the outside, the rate of their population growth would be periodically checked by crop failures and famines. But if they can always draw on a world food bank in time of need, their population can continue to grow unchecked, and so will their "need" for aid. In the short run, a world food bank may diminish that need, but in the long run it actually increases the need without limit.

Without some system of worldwide food sharing, the proportion of people in the rich and poor nations might eventually stabilize. The overpopulated poor countries would decrease in numbers, while the rich countries that had room for more people would increase. But with a well-meaning system of sharing, such as a world food bank, the growth differential between the rich and the poor countries will not only persist, it will increase. Because of the higher rate of population growth in the poor countries of the world, 88 percent of today's children are born poor, and only 12 percent rich. Year by year the ratio becomes worse, as the fast-reproducing poor outnumber the slow-reproducing rich.

A world food bank is thus a commons in disguise. People will have more motivation to draw from it than to add to any common store. The less provident and less able will multiply at the expense of the abler and more provident, bringing eventual ruin upon all who share in the commons. Besides, any system of "sharing" that amounts to foreign aid from the rich nations to the poor nations will carry the taint of charity, which will contribute little to the world peace so devoutly desired by those who support the idea of a world food bank.

As past U.S. foreign-aid programs have amply and depressingly demonstrated, international charity frequently inspires mistrust and antagonism rather than gratitude on the part of the recipient nation.

**Chinese Fish and Miracle Rice.**   The modern approach to foreign aid stresses the export of technology and advice, rather than money and food. As an ancient Chinese proverb goes: "Give a man a fish and he will eat for a day; teach him how to fish and he will eat for the rest of his days." Acting on this advice, the Rockefeller and Ford Foundations have financed a number of programs for improving agriculture in the hungry nations. Known as the "Green Revolution," these programs have led to the development of "miracle rice" and "miracle wheat," new strains that offer bigger harvests and greater resistance to crop damage. Norman Borlaug, the Nobel Prize-winning agronomist who, supported by the Rockefeller Foundation, developed "miracle wheat," is one of the most prominent advocates of a world food bank.

Whether or not the Green Revolution can increase food production as much as its champions claim is a debatable but possibly irrelevant point. Those who support this well-intended humanitarian effort should first consider some of the fundamentals of human ecology. Ironically, one man who did was the late Alan Gregg, a vice-president of the Rockefeller Foundation. Two decades ago he expressed strong doubts about the wisdom of such attempts to increase food production. He likened the growth and spread of humanity over the surface of the earth to the spread of cancer in the human body, remarking that "cancerous growths demand food; but, as far as I know, they have never been cured by getting it."

**Overloading the Environment.**   Every human born constitutes a draft on all aspects of the environment: food, air, water, forest, beaches, wildlife, scenery and solitude. Food can, perhaps, be significantly increased to meet a growing demand. But what about clean beaches, unspoiled forests, and solitude? If we satisfy a growing population's need for food, we necessarily decrease its per capita supply of the other resources needed by men.

India, for example, now has a population of 600 million, which increases by 15 million each year. This population already puts a huge load on a relatively impoverished environment. The country's forests are now only a small fraction of what they were three centuries ago, and floods and erosion continually destroy the insufficient farmland that remains. Every one of the 15 million new lives added to India's population puts an additional burden on the environment and increases the economic and social costs of crowding. However humanitarian our intent, every Indian life saved through medical or nutritional assistance from abroad diminishes the quality of life for those who remain, and for subsequent generations. If rich countries make it possible, through foreign aid, for 600 million Indians to swell to 1.2 billion in a mere 28 years, as their current growth rate threatens, will future generations of Indians thank us for hastening the destruction of their environment? Will our good intentions be sufficient excuse for the consequences of our actions?

My final example of a commons in action is one for which the public has the least desire for rational discussion—immigration. Anyone who publicly questions the wisdom of current U.S. immigration policy is promptly charged with bigotry, prejudice, ethnocentrism, chauvinism, isolationism or selfishness. Rather than encounter such accusations, one would rather talk about other matters, leaving immigration policy to wallow in the crosscurrents of special interests that take no account of the good of the whole, or the interests of posterity.

Perhaps we still feel guilty about things we said in the past. Two generations ago the popular press frequently referred to Dagos, Wops, Polacks, Chinks and Krauts, in articles about how America was being "overrun" by foreigners of supposedly inferior genetic stock. But because the implied inferiority of foreigners was used then as justification for keeping them out, people now assume that restrictive policies could only be based on such misguided notions. There are other grounds.

**A Nation of Immigrants.**   Just consider the numbers involved. Our government acknowledges a net inflow of 400,000 immigrants a year. While we have no hard data on the extent of illegal entries educated guesses put the figure at about 600,000 a year. Since the natural increase (excess of births over deaths) of the resident population now runs about 1.7 million per year, the yearly gain from immigration amounts to at least 19 percent of the total annual increase, and may be as much as 37 percent if we include the estimate for illegal immigrants. Considering the growing use of birth control devices, the potential effect of educational campaigns by such organizations as Planned Parenthood Federation of America and Zero Population Growth, and the influence of inflation and the housing shortage, the fertility rate of American women may decline so much that immigration could account for all the yearly increase in population. Should we not at least ask if that is what we want?

For the sake of those who worry about whether the "quality" of the average immigrant compares favorably with the quality of the average resident, let us assume that immigrants and native born citizens are of exactly equal quality, however one defines that term. We will focus here only on quantity; and since our conclusions will depend on nothing else, all charges of bigotry and chauvinism become irrelevant.

**Immigration vs. Food Supply.**   World food banks *move food to the people,* hastening the exhaustion of the environment of the poor countries. Unrestricted immigration, on the other hand, *moves people to the food,* thus speeding up the destruction of the environment of rich countries. We can easily understand why poor people should want to make this latter transfer, but why should rich hosts encourage it?

As in the case of foreign-aid programs immigration receives support from selfish interests and humanitarian impulses. The primary selfish interest in unimpeded immigration is the desire of employers for cheap labor, particularly in industries and trades that offer degrading work. In the past, one wave of foreigners after another was brought into the U.S. to work at wretched jobs for wretched wages. In recent years the Cubans, Puerto Ricans, and Mexicans have had this dubious honor. The interests of the employers of cheap labor mesh well with the guilty silence of the country's liberal intelligentsia. White Anglo-Saxon Protestants are particularly reluctant to call for a closing of the doors to immigration for fear of being called bigots.

But not all countries have such reluctant leadership. Most educated Hawaiians, for example, are keenly aware of the limits of their environment, particularly in terms of population growth. There is only so much room on the islands, and the islanders know it. To Hawaiians, immigrants from the other 49 states present as great a threat as those from other nations. At a recent meeting of Hawaiian government officials in Honolulu, I had the ironic delight of hearing a speaker, who like most of his audience countered: "How can we shut the doors now? We have many friends and relatives in Japan that we'd like to bring here some day so that they can enjoy Hawaii too." The Japanese-American speaker smiled sympathetically and answered: "Yes, but we have children now, and someday we'll have grandchildren too. We can bring more people from Japan only by giving away some of the land that we hope to pass on to our grandchildren some day. What right do we have to do that?"

At this point, I can hear U.S. liberals asking: "How can you justify slamming the door once you're inside? You say that immigrants should be kept out. But aren't we all immigrants, or the descendants of immigrants? If we insist on staying, must we not admit all others?" Our craving for intellectual order leads us to seek and prefer symmetrical rules and morals: a single rule for me and everybody else; the same rule yesterday, today, and tomorrow. Justice, we feel, should not change with time and place.

We Americans of non-Indian ancestry can look upon ourselves as the descendants of thieves who are guilty morally, if not legally, of stealing this land from its Indian owners. Should we then give back the land to the now living American descendants of those Indians? However morally or logically sound this proposal may be, I, for one, am unwilling to live by it and I know no one else who is. Besides, the logical consequence would be absurd. Suppose that, intoxicated with a sense of pure justice, we should decide to turn our land over to the Indians. Since all our other wealth has also been derived from the land, wouldn't we be morally obliged to give that back to the Indians too?

**Pure Justice vs. Reality.**   Clearly, the concept of pure justice produces an infinite regression to absurdity. Centuries ago, wise men invented statutes of limitations to justify the rejection of such pure justice, in the interest of preventing continual disorder. The law zealously defends property right, but only relatively recent property rights. Drawing a line after an arbitrary time has elapsed may be unjust, but the alternatives are worse.

We are all the descendants of thieves, and the world's resources are inequitably distributed. But we must begin the journey to tomorrow from the point where we are today. We cannot remake the past. We cannot safely divide the wealth equitably among all peoples so long as people reproduce at different rates. To do so would guarantee that our grandchildren, and everyone else's grandchildren, would have only a ruined world to inhabit.

To be generous with one's own possessions is quite different from being generous with those of posterity. We should call this point to the attention of those who, from a commendable love of justice and equality, would institute a system of the commons, either in the form of a world food bank, or of unrestricted immigration. We must convince them if we wish to save at least some parts of the world from environmental ruin.

Without a true world government to control reproduction and the use of available resources, the sharing ethic of the spaceship is impossible. For the foreseeable future, our survival demands that we govern our actions by the ethics of a lifeboat, harsh though they may be. Posterity will be satisfied with nothing less.

# Not Triage, But Investment in People, Food, and Water

## Barbara Ward

Now that the House of Representatives has bravely passed its resolution on the "right to food"—the basic human right without which, indeed, all other rights are meaningless—it is perhaps a good moment to try to clear up one or two points of confusion that appear to have been troubling the American mind on the question of food supplies, hunger, and America's moral obligation, particularly to those who are not America's own citizens.

The United States, with Canada and marginal help from Australia, are the only producers of surplus grain. It follows that if any part of the world comes up short or approaches starvation, there is at present only one remedy and it is in Americans' hands. Either they do the emergency feeding or people starve.

It is a heavy moral responsibility. Is it one that has to be accepted?

This is where the moral confusions begin. A strong school of thought argues that it is the flood tide of babies, irresponsibly produced in Asia, Africa and Latin America, that is creating the certainty of malnutrition and risk of famine. If these countries insist on having babies, they must feed them themselves. If hard times set in, food aid from North America —if any—must go strictly to those who can prove they are reducing the baby flood. Otherwise, the responsible suffer. The poor go on increasing.

This is a distinctly Victorian replay of Malthus. He first suggested that population would go on rising to absorb all available supplies and that the poor must be left to starve if they would be incontinent. The British Poor Law was based on this principle. It has now been given a new descriptive analogy in America. The planet is compared to a battlefield. There are not enough medical skills and supplies to go round. So what must the doctors do? Obviously, concentrate on those who can hope to recover. The rest must die. This is the meaning of "triage."

Abandon the unsavable and by so doing concentrate the supplies—in the battlefield, medical skills; in the world at large, surplus food—on those who still have a chance to survive.

Thus the people with stable or stabilizing populations will be able to hold on. The human experiment will continue.

Copyright © 1976 by The New York Times Company. Reprinted by permission from The *New York Times,* November 15, 1976. The late Barbara Ward, British economist and author, was a member of the Pontifical Commission for Justice and Peace and played an important role in formulating Vatican statements on world poverty. Her latest book is *Progress for a Small Planet* (1979).

It is a very simple argument. It has been persuasively supported by noted business leaders, trade-unionists, academics and presumed Presidential advisers. But "triage" is, in fact, so shot through with half truths as to be almost a lie, and so irrelevant to real world issues as to be not much more than an aberration.

Take the half truths first. In the last ten years, at least one-third of the increased world-demand for food has come from North Americans, Europeans and Russians eating steadily more high-protein food. Grain is fed to animals and poultry, and eaten as steak and eggs.

In real energy terms, this is about five times more wasteful than eating grain itself. The result is an average American diet of nearly 2,000 pounds of grain a year—and epidemics of cardiac trouble—and 400 pounds for the average Indian.

It follows that for those worrying about available supplies on the "battlefield," one American equals five Indians in the claims on basic food. And this figure masks the fact that much of the North American eating—and drinking—is pure waste. For instance, the American Medical Association would like to see meat-eating cut by a third to produce a healthier nation.

The second distortion is to suggest that direct food aid is what the world is chiefly seeking from the United States. True, if there were a failed monsoon and the normal Soviet agricultural muddle next year, the need for an actual transfer of grain would have to be faced.

That is why the world food plan, worked out at Secretary of State Henry A. Kissinger's earlier prompting, asks for a modest reserve of grain to be set aside—on the old biblical plan of Joseph's "fat years" being used to prepare for the "lean."

But no conceivable American surplus could deal with the Third World's food needs of the 1980's and 1990's. They can be met only by a sustained advance in food production where productivity is still so low that quadrupling and quintupling of crops is possible, provided investments begin now.

A recent Japanese study has shown that rice responds with copybook reliability to higher irrigation and improved seed. This is why the same world food plan is stressing a steady capital input of $30 billion a year in Third-World farms, with perhaps $5 billion contributed by the old rich and the "oil" rich.

(What irony that this figure is barely a third of what West Germany has to spend each year to offset the health effects of overeating and overdrinking.)

To exclaim and complain about the impossibility of giving away enough American surplus grain (which could not be rice anyway), when the real issue is a sustained effort by all the nations in long-term agricultural investments, simply takes the citizens' minds off the real issue—where they can be of certain assistance—and impresses on them a nonissue that confuses them and helps nobody else.

Happily, the House's food resolution puts long-term international investment in food production firmly back into the center of the picture.

And this investment in the long run is the true answer to the stabilizing of family size. People do not learn restraint from "give-aways." (The arms industry's bribes are proof enough of that.) But the whole experience of the last century is that if parents are given work, responsibility, enough food and safe water, they have the sense to see they do not need endless children as insurance against calamity.

Because of food from the Great Plains and the reform of sanitation, Malthusian fears vanished as an issue in Europe and North America in the 1880's. China is below 2 percent population growth today on the basis of intensive agriculture and popular health measures.

Go to the root of the matter—investment in people, in food, in water —and the Malthus myth will fade in the Third World as it has done already in many parts of it and entirely in the so-called First and Second Worlds.

It may be that this positive strategy of stabilizing population by sustained, skilled and well-directed investment in food production and in clean water suggests less drama than the hair-raising images of inexorably rising tides of children eating like locusts the core out of the whole world's food supplies.

But perhaps we should be wise to prefer relevance to drama. In "triage," there is, after all, a suggestion of the battlefield. If this is how we see the world, are we absolutely certain who deserves to win—the minority of guzzlers who eat 2,000 pounds of grain, or the majority of despairing men of hunger who eat 400 pounds?

History gives uncomfortable answers. No doubt as they left their hot baths and massage parlors for the joys of dining, vomiting and redining, Roman senators must have muttered and complained about the "awkwardness of the barbarians." But the barbarians won. Is this the battlefield we want? And who will "triage" whom?


# On the Division Between Rich and Poor

Julius K. Nyerere


Poverty is not the real problem of the modern world. For we have the knowledge and resources which could enable us to overcome poverty.

From an address to the Ninth General Assembly of the Maryknoll Sisters on October 16, 1970, Maryknoll, New York. Julius K. Nyerere is President of Tanzania.

The real problem—the thing which creates misery, wars and hatred among men—is the division of mankind into rich and poor.

We can see this division at two levels. Within nation states there are a few individuals who have great wealth and whose wealth gives them great power; but the vast majority of people suffer from varying degrees of poverty and deprivation. Even in a country like the United States, this division can be seen. In countries like India, Portugal or Brazil, the contrast between the wealth of a few privileged individuals and the dire poverty of the masses is a crying scandal. And looking at the world as a collection of nation states, we see the same pattern repeated. There are a few wealthy nations which dominate the whole world economically, and therefore politically; and a mass of smaller and poor nations whose destiny, it appears, is to be dominated.

The significance about this division between the rich and the poor is not simply that one man has more food than he can eat, more clothes then he can wear and more houses than he can live in, while others are hungry, unclad and homeless. The significant thing about the division between rich and poor nations is not simply that one has the resources to provide comfort for all its citizens, and the other cannot provide basic services. The reality and depth of the problem arises because the man who is rich has power over the lives of those who are poor, and the rich nation has power over the policies of those which are not rich. Even more important is that our social and economic system, nationally and internationally, supports these divisions and constantly increases them, so that the rich get richer and more powerful, while the poor get relatively ever poorer and less able to control their own future.

This continues despite all the talk of human equality, the fight against poverty, and of development. Still the rich individuals within nations, and the rich nations within the world, go on getting richer very much faster than the poor overcome their poverty. Sometimes this happens through the deliberate decision of the rich, who use their wealth and their power to that end. But often—perhaps more often—it happens "naturally" as a result of the normal workings of the social and economic systems men have constructed for themselves. Just as water from the driest regions of the earth ultimately flows into the oceans where water is already plentiful, so wealth flows from the poorest nations and the poorest individuals into the hands of those nations and those individuals who are already wealthy. A man who can afford to buy only one loaf of bread a day contributes to the profit accruing to the owner of the bakery, despite the fact the owner already has more money than he knows how to use. And the poor nation which sells its primary commodities on the world market in order to buy machines for development finds that the prices it obtains, and the prices it has to pay, are both determined by the "forces of the free market" in which it is a pigmy competing with giants.

For he that hath, to him shall be given; and he that hath not, that also which he hath shall be taken away from him.

Both nationally and internationally this division of mankind into the tiny minority of rich, and the great majority of poor, is rapidly becoming intolerable to the majority—as it should be. The poor nations and the poor peoples of the world are already in rebellion against it; if they do not succeed in securing change which leads towards greater justice, then that rebellion will become an explosion. Injustice and peace are in the long run incompatible; stability in a changing world must mean ordered change towards justice, not mechanical respect for the *status quo.* It is in this context that development has been called another name for peace.

## MAN IS THE PURPOSE

The purpose of development is man. It is the creation of conditions, both material and spiritual, which enable man the individual, and man the species, to become his best. That is easy for Christians to understand because Christianity demands that every man should aspire towards union with God through Christ. But although the Church—as a consequence of its concentration upon man—avoids the error of identifying development with new factories, increased output, or greater national income statistics, experience shows that it all too often makes the opposite error. For the representatives of the Church, and the Church's organizations, frequently act as if man's development is a personal and "internal" matter, which can be divorced from the society and the economy in which he lives and earns his daily bread. They preach resignation; very often they appear to accept as immutable the social, economic, and political framework of the present-day world. They seek to ameliorate intolerable conditions through acts of love and of kindness where the beneficiary of this love and kindness remains an object. But when the victims of poverty and oppression begin to behave like men and try to change those conditions, the representatives of the Church stand aside.

My purpose is to suggest to you that the Church should accept the fact that the development of peoples means rebellion. At a given and decisive point in history men decide to act against those conditions which restrict their freedom as men. I am suggesting that, unless we participate actively in the rebellion against those social structures and economic organizations which condemn men to poverty, humiliation and degradation, then the Church will become irrelevant to man and the Christian religion will degenerate into a set of superstitions accepted by the fearful. Unless the Church, its members and its organizations express God's love for man by involvement and leadership in constructive protest against the present conditions of man, then it will die—and, humanly speaking, deserve to die —because it will then serve no purpose comprehensible to modern man.

For man lives in society. He becomes meaningful to himself and his fellows only as a member of that society. Therefore, to talk of the development of man, and to work for the development of man, must mean the development also of that kind of society which serves man, which enhances his well-being, and preserves his dignity. Thus, the development of peoples involves economic development, social development, and political development. And at this time in man's history, it must imply a divine discontent and a determination for change. For the present condition of men must be unacceptable to all who think of an individual person as a unique creation of a living God. We say man was created in the image of God. I refuse to imagine a God who is poor, ignorant, superstitious, fearful, oppressed, wretched—which is the lot of the majority of those He created in his own image. Men are creators of themselves and their conditions, but under present conditions we are creatures, not of God, but of our fellow men. Surely there can be no dispute among Christians about that. For mankind has never been so united or so disunited; has never had such power for good nor suffered under such evident injustices. Men's capacity has never been so clear, nor so obviously and deliberately denied.

The world is one in technological terms. Men have looked down on the earth from the moon and seen its unity. In jet planes I can travel from Tanzania to New York in a matter of hours. Radio waves enable us to talk to each other—either in love or abuse—without more than a few seconds elapsing between our speech and the hearing of it. Goods are made which include materials and skills from all over the world—and are then put up for sale thousands of miles from their place of manufacture. Yet at the same time as the interdependence of man is increased through the advance of technology, the divisions between men also expand at an ever-increasing rate. The national income per head in the United States is said to be more than $3,200 a year; in Tanzania it is approximately $80—i.e. it would take a Tanzanian 40 years to earn what an American earns in one year, and we are not the poorest nation on earth. Further, it has been estimated that, while the rich countries are adding approximately $60 a year to the per capita income of their citizens, the average increase of per capita income in the poor countries is less than 2 dollars per year. It has been estimated that up to 500 million people on the earth today are suffering from hunger—from never having enough to eat. Further, one out of every two of the world's peoples is suffering from malnutrition— from deficiencies of protein or other essential health-giving foods. And finally, let me remind you that even within the wealthiest countries of the world, the misery and oppression of poverty is experienced by thousands, or even millions, of individuals, families, and groups.

So the world is not one. Its peoples are more divided now, and also more conscious of their divisions, than they have ever been. They are divided between those who are satiated and those who are hungry. They are divided between those with power and those without power. They are divided between those who dominate and those who are dominated, between those who exploit and those who are exploited. And it is the minority which is well fed, and the minority which has secured control over the world's wealth and over their fellow men. Further, in general that minority is distinguished by the color of their skins and by their race. And the nations in which most of that minority of the world's people live have a further distinguishing characteristic—their adoption of the Christian religion. These things cannot continue, and Christians, above all others, must refuse to accept them. For the development of men, and the development of peoples, demands that the world shall become one and that social justice shall replace the present oppressions and inequalities.

## MAN IS A MEMBER OF SOCIETY

In order to achieve this, there must be economic development and equitable distribution of wealth. The poor nations, the poor areas, and the poor peoples must be enabled to increase their output; through fair distribution they must be enabled to expand their consumption of the goods which are necessary for decency and for freedom.

For what is required is not simply an increase in the national income figures of the poor countries, nor a listing of huge increases in the production of this crop or that industry. New factories, roads, farms, and so on, are essential; but they are not enough in themselves. The economic growth must be of such a kind, and so organized, that it benefits the nations and the peoples who are now suffering from poverty. This means that social and political development must go alongside economic development—or even precede it. For unless society is so organized that the people control their own economies and their own economic activity, economic growth will result in increased inequality, both nationally and internationally. Those who control a man's livelihood control a man; his freedom is illusory and his equal humanity is denied when he depends upon others for the right to work and eat. Equally, a nation is not independent if its economic resources are controlled by another nation; political independence is meaningless if a nation does not control the means by which its citizens can earn their living.

In other words, the development of peoples follows from economic development only if this latter is achieved on the basis of the equality and human dignity of all those involved. And human dignity cannot be given to a man by the kindness of others. Indeed, it can be destroyed by kindness which emanates from an action of charity. For human dignity involves equality and freedom, and relations of mutual respect among men. Further it depends on responsibility, and on a conscious participation in the life of the society in which a man moves and works. The whole structure of national societies and of international society is therefore relevant to the development of peoples. And there are few societies which can now be said to serve this purpose; for there are few—if any—which both accept, and are organized to serve, social justice in what has been called the Revolution of Rising Expectations.

Let us be quite clear about this. If the Church is interested in man as an individual, it must express this by its interest in the society of which those individuals are members. For men are shaped by the circumstances in which they live. If they are treated like animals, they will act like animals. If they are denied dignity, they will act without dignity. If they are treated solely as a dispensable means of production, they will become soulless "hands," to whom life is a matter of doing as little work as possible and then escaping into the illusion of happiness and pride through vice.

Therefore, in order to fulfill its own purpose of bringing men to God, the Church must seek to ensure that men can have dignity in their lives and in their work. It must itself become a force of social justice and it must work with other forces of social justice wherever they are, and whatever they are called. Further, the Church must recognize that men can only progress and can only grow in dignity by working for themselves, and working together for their common good. The Church cannot uplift a man; it can only help to provide the conditions and the opportunity for him to cooperate with his fellows to uplift himself.

## COOPERATION WITH NON-CHRISTIANS

It is not necessary to agree with everything a man believes or says, in order to work with him on particular projects or in particular areas of activity. The Church must stand up for what it believes to be right; that is its justification and purpose. But it should welcome all who stand on the same side, and continue regardless of which individuals or groups it is then opposing.

A good does not become evil if a Communist says it is a good; an evil does not become good if a Fascist supports it. Exploiting the poor does not become a right thing to do because Communists call it a wrong thing; production for profit rather than meeting human needs does not become more just because Communists say it leads to injustice. Organizing the society in such a manner that people live together and work together for their common good does not become an evil because it is called socialism. A system based on greed and selfishness does not become good because it is labelled free enterprise. Let the Church choose for itself what is right and what is wrong in accordance with Christian principles, and let it not be affected by what other groups or individuals do or say. But let it welcome cooperation from all those who agree with its judgments.

We know that we are fallible men and that our task is to serve, not to judge. Yet we accept into the Church (provided only that they come to mass every Sunday and pay their dues or contribute to missionary activities) those who create and maintain the present political and economic system. But it is this system which has led to millions being hungry, thirsty, and naked; it is this system which makes men strangers in their own countries because they are poor, powerless, and oppressed; it is this system which condemns millions to preventable sickness, and which makes prisoners of men who have the courage to protest. What right, then, have we to reject those who serve mankind, simply because they refuse to accept the leadership of the Church, or refuse to acknowledge the divinity of Jesus or the existence of God? What right have we to presume that God Almighty takes no notice of those who give dedicated services to those millions of His children who hunger and thirst after justice, just because they do not do it in His Name? If God were to ask the wretched of the earth who are their friends, are we so sure that we know their answer? And is that answer irrelevant to those who seek to serve God?

## THE ROLE OF THE CHURCH

What all this amounts to is a call to the Church to recognize the need for social revolution, and to play a leading role in it. For it is a fact of history that almost all the successful social revolutions which have taken place in the world have been led by people who were themselves beneficiaries under the system they sought to replace. Time and again members of the privileged classes have joined, and often led, the poor or oppressed in their revolts against injustice. The same thing must happen now.

Within the rich countries of the world the beneficiaries of educational opportunity, of good health, and of security must be prepared to stand up and demand justice for those who have up to now been denied these things. Where the poor have already begun to demand a just society, at least some members of the privileged classes must help them and encourage them. Where they have not begun to do so, it is the responsibility of those who have had greater opportunities for development to arouse the poor out of their poverty-induced apathy. And I am saying that Christians should be prominent among those who do this, and that the Church should seek to increase the numbers and the power of those who refuse to acquiesce in established injustices.

Only by its activity in these fields can the Church justify its relevance in the modern world. For the purpose of the Church is Man—his human dignity, and his right to develop himself in freedom. To the service of Man's development, any or all the institutions of any particular society must be sacrificed if this should be necessary. For all human institutions, including the Church, are established in order to serve Man. And it is the institution of the Church, through its members, which should be leading the attack on any organization, or any economic, social, or political structure which oppresses men, and which denies to them the right and power to live as the sons of a loving God.

In the poor countries the Church has this same role to play. It has to be consistently and actively on the side of the poor and unprivileged. It has to lead men towards Godliness by joining with them in the attack against the injustices and deprivation from which they suffer. It must cooperate with all those who are involved in this work; it must reject alliances with those who represent Mammon, and cooperate with all those who are working for Man. Its members must go out as servants of the world, as men and women who wish to share their knowledge and their abilities with those whom they recognize as their brothers and their sisters in Christ. . . .

# SUGGESTIONS FOR FURTHER READING FOR PART FOUR

## Chapter 9: Capitalism versus Socialism

Bell, Daniel. *The Cultural Contradictions of Capitalism.* New York: Basic Books, 1976.

Benne, Robert. *The Ethics of Democratic Capitalism: A Moral Reassessment.* Philadelphia: Fortress Press, 1981.

Berger, Peter L. *Pyramids of Sacrifice: Political Ethics and Social Change.* Garden City, N.Y.: Doubleday, 1976.

Harrington, Michael. *The Twilight of Capitalism.* New York: Simon & Schuster, 1976.

—. *Decade of Decision: The Crisis of the American System.* New York: Simon & Schuster, 1980.

Metz, J. B., and J. P. Jossua. *Christianity and Socialism* (Concilium, 105). New York: Seabury Press, 1978.

Novak, Michael. *The Spirit of Democratic Capitalism.* Washington, D.C.: American Enterprise Institute for Public Policy Research, Simon & Schuster, 1982.

—, ed. *Capitalism and Socialism: A Theological Inquiry.* Washington, D.C.: American Enterprise Institute for Public Policy Research, 1979.

Wogaman, T. Philip. *The Great Economic Debate: An Ethical Analysis.* Philadelphia: Westminster Press, 1976.

## Chapter 10: First World, Third World

Barnet, Richard J. *The Lean Years: Politics in the Age of Scarcity.* New York: Simon & Schuster, 1980.

Brown, Lester. *In the Human Interest: A Strategy to Stabilize World Population.* New York: Norton, 1974.

Brown, Robert McAfee. *Making Peace in the Global Village.* Philadelphia: Westminster Press, 1981.

Goulet, Denis. *The New Moral Order: Development Ethics and Liberation Theology.* Maryknoll, N.Y.: Orbis Books, 1974.

McGinnis, James B. *Bread and Justice: Toward a New International Economic Order.* New York: Paulist Press, 1979.

Presidential Commission on World Hunger. *Overcoming World Hunger: The Challenge Ahead.* Washington, D.C.: U.S. Government Printing Office, 1980.

Servan-Schreiber, Jean-Jacques. *The World Challenge.* New York: Simon & Schuster, 1980.

Simon, Arthur. *Bread for the World.* New York: Paulist Press, 1975.

Stavrianos, L. S. *Global Society: The Third World Comes of Age.* New York: Morrow, 1981.

Ward, Barbara. *Progress for a Small Planet.* New York: Norton, 1979.

# Part Five

# The Christian and Issues of Violence and Justice

# II

# War in the Nuclear Age

One who considers the tragic nature of war, with its wanton destruction of human life and property, may be surprised that Christians have not been able to agree on their moral evaluation of it. To be sure, almost everyone would agree that war is evil, but Christians do not agree on whether participation in war is ever necessary and justifiable. The highest degree of unanimity was undoubtedly found in the first three centuries following the death of Christ, when Christians were often a persecuted minority in the Roman Empire. As a relatively insignificant group of people who had been ostracized by the establishment, and following a Lord who was proclaimed as Prince of Peace, Christians refused to serve in military forces.

The conversion to Christianity of Emperor Constantine in A.D. 312, and the subsequent legitimizing of Christianity as the official religion of the empire, resulted in Christians taking a more open stance on the possibility of their engaging in war. As the theologian Augustine contemplated the ravaging of Roman civilization by the barbarians in the fifth century, it led him to the careful development of certain conditions under which war could be justified—the so-called just war. These conditions, with subsequent development in the Middle Ages, are the following:

1. The cause must be just.
2. The war must be declared and waged by a lawful authority.
3. War must be the only possible means of securing justice.
4. The right means must be employed in the conduct of war (no wanton disregard for life; respect for noncombatants).
5. There must be a reasonable hope of victory.
6. The good probably to be achieved by victory must outweigh the possible evil effects of the war (norm of proportionality).
7. War must be a last resort, only after all peaceful means have been exhausted.

Most Christian churches have espoused the just-war position, their theologians arguing that the presence of evil in the world at times necessitates the use of force in order to ensure a just and humane order. One obvious question is whether criteria for a justifiable war have any relevance for the nuclear age. War

263

during the Middle Ages involved bands of mercenary soldiers who would usually not fight on weekends, and who used weapons that look like peashooters compared to the firepower of nuclear armaments. But advocates argue that just-war criteria assume at least a symbolic value in attempts to keep humane concerns at the forefront in our consideration of war.

A third position Christians have taken is the view that war can be a crusade, in which the faithful aggressively carry out the will of God. The Crusades of the Middle Ages are the primary example of this view, inspired by the Old Testament stories of God's people using the sword against unbelievers. Many Christians in the United States today would regard war directed against Russia or China as a crusade because of their belief that these countries are "godless" and a threat to Christianity.

Many would say that the emergence of the nuclear age has not just changed the nature of war and its destructive potential in terms of quantity or degree, but that war is now *qualitatively* different and must be addressed as such. We can no longer assume that war is inevitable and we must therefore prepare for it. We have now reached the point where war is obsolete, because there will not be a winner and a loser in a nuclear war. Everyone will lose. This view is often called "nuclear pacifism." The military establishment, however, maintains that nuclear warfare can be waged within certain limits in a "meaningful," or purposive, war which could be carried on without massive destruction. This stand poses the question effectively dramatized in the short play by James A. Stegenga, giving flesh-and-blood reality to a subject that may often remain too theoretical. The just war versus pacifism debate also gets a dramatic airing through the reflective observations of one of the characters.

The articles by John C. Bennett and James T. Johnson address further the possibility of waging nuclear war on a limited scale. President Carter's Directive 59 gave political sanction to this possibility. This directive presents a counterforce strategy which provides a rationale for the use of nuclear weapons. Until now, the assumption behind our nuclear weapon strategy was that both the United States and Russia were capable of destroying each other. This fact—called Mutual Assured Destruction, or, appropriately, MAD—provided a strong psychological deterrent to the use of nuclear weapons. With the possibility of counterforce strategy that would avoid massive destruction of population centers, the use of nuclear weapons is encouraged as a workable strategy. The question is no longer whether we should use nuclear weapons, but what are the morally justified parameters for their use? Pentagon officials are clearly planning for war on the assumption that nuclear warfare can be limited to carry out certain well-defined objectives.

Bennett's article is motivated by this possibility. He is extremely dubious about the notion of limited nuclear war, raising the questions whether millions of people would not still be killed and whether the atmosphere would not inevitably be poisoned far beyond our expectation. Furthermore—and this is a growing concern among many people—the very notion of a limited nuclear war encourages military planners to think in terms of first-strike capability, an option not encouraged under the psychological deterrent of MAD. One disturbing factor in this discussion is the crucial "unknowns." Not only is there the question whether limited nuclear warfare is a realistic possibility but there is also the uncertainty concerning the extent of radiation aftereffects from a war thought to be limited.

A different response is provided by James T. Johnson, who is willing to justify a preemptive first strike under certain circumstances. He sees both this and limited nuclear warfare as legitimate possibilities because of the sophisticated new weapons now available in the cruise missile and neutron bomb. The cruise missile's extreme accuracy allows for attacks on "closely delimited target areas" instead of the enemy's large population centers, enabling it to carry out its mission with conventional high-explosive warheads and thus removing the destructive aftereffects of radiation. The neutron bomb's radiation fall-out would also be less, making it preferable, argues Johnson, to other nuclear warheads. This argument concerns Bennett as he contemplates the likelihood of nuclear war. The careful discussion in Johnson's article provides a good example of the kind of moral reasoning ethicists use as they discuss the question of a just war. Johnson assumes that war can and will continue to function as a tragic but likely inevitable way in which nations resolve their differences.

The opposite view is forcefully presented in the statement of the Roman Catholic Church on disarmament. It passionately pleads for a new vision in which the whole dehumanizing course of military and civilian technologies can be counteracted. People will differ on whether the kind of reasoning and conclusion illustrated by Johnson's article is more helpful and meaningful for our present situation, or whether the witness of the church should be concentrated in the direction of this Roman Catholic statement on disarmament. In the former case, moral reasoning is brought to bear on the concrete planning of our military strategists as they seek to carry out the policies of our government. In the latter case, prophetic witness is being made to our people and their government, challenging them with a new vision based on faith, which would give us new priorities and new directions as a nation. What is the appropriate and authentic message of the church in regard to this crucial issue?

# Dunbar's Bremen

James A. Stegenga

*As the lights come up on a large, comfortable, tastefully furnished living room, we hear the television news that General Frank Dunbar is watching intently. He is heavy, rumpled, dressed casually in "civvies"—not the typical starchy general, rather more the GI's general—à la Creighton Abrams—whose common touch and hearty, gruff manner neatly camouflage a sensitive intelligence.*

TV NEWSCASTER: ... and so on this, the 17th day of the war in Europe, the Soviet Union's forces are continuing increasingly effective opposition from NATO defenders, especially in the center of the thousand-mile-long front. ... Here in Amherst, meanwhile, General Frank Dunbar remains secluded under virtual house arrest after being flown back from Europe on Wednesday. General Dunbar was commander of NATO's northern sector until he was relieved by President Vanderveen, after reportedly refusing to obey a direct Presidential order to use tactical nuclear weapons in the European war. ... Finally, the Wall Street plunge seems to have bottomed out, with analysts predicting. ...

*Dunbar uses a remote control gadget to switch off the set. Margaret Broughman-Dunbar has quietly entered to stand behind her husband's chair. She is a handsome 50, daughter of a prominent British scientist, and in her own right an important essayist and Amherst College professor of classics.*

MARGARET: Any *good* news from over there?

FRANK: Very little. Damned little. We're getting the shit kicked out of us for the most part, though there are some bright spots. Eddie—Eddie Hobbs, you remember him (*she nods "yes"*)—is doing OK in Austria. The Air Force boys are proving that our pilots and our gadgets are even better than we'd ever hoped they'd be. And the British—they may not be rulers of the sea, but they're doing a damn good job of chasing subs away from our convoys. But overall—we sure as hell haven't started *winning.*

Reprinted by permission from the January 19, 1981 issue of *Christianity and Crisis.* Copyright © 1981 by Christianity and Crisis, Inc. James A. Stegenga is Professor of Political Science at Purdue University and author of *The Global Community* (1981).

M:   And you? How are you today? Still feeling a bit punk?

F:   Better. I'm a survivor, you know that. Just going to be a tad grumpy for the next few days, OK? Will you forgive me?

M:   Of course. *(Pauses.)* Frank, will they court-martial you?

F:   Oh, I doubt it. When this madness is over, one way or the other, "they" will all have better things to do than hassle an old, has-been soldier.

M:   Then why is Charlie Pierce sneaking up here today? *(Frank looks up.)* He called while you were out jogging. Said to look for him a little after noon. Said he'd park a few blocks away and walk in through the ravine. All very mysterious for old, fat, stodgy, rich-folks-lawyer Charlie Pierce, no?

F:   I wanted him to avoid the vultures of the fourth estate camped out front. And I wanted some advice and counsel before *I* have to go out front and talk to them, to congressmen, and maybe even to his excellency, folksy Bob Vanderveen if he should summon me.

M:   Mmmmmmm.

F:   And Charlie may be fat. But "old"? Remember, toots, he was my classmate at the Point. Anyway, he's damned smart—left the Army, didn't he, before he got too old to do anything else? And is out there in the real world, making the kind of loot that a guy with a British princess for a wife ought to be making, eh?

M:   Oh, twaddle. *(Doorbell rings.)* Probably Charlie. I'll let him in, but then I've got to sneak out myself to quarrel a bit with the dean. Life must go on and all that, right? *(She turns to go.)*

F:   Margaret. *(She stops.)* Thanks, toots. For everything. For putting up with me.

M:   Noblesse oblige. *(Smiles warmly and goes. Frank pokes through a foot locker until he finds a large rolled-up map of Europe, thumbtacks it to the front of a bookcase, and steps back just as Charles V. Pierce, who is everything Margaret said he was, enters unnoticed.)*

CHARLIE:   You always were a map nut, even way back at the Point, Frank!

F:   Charlie! *(Embrace.)* *Good* to see you. Say, gonna have to get you to stay a few days and take up jogging. You've had too many four-martini lunches. But I should talk, eh? How the hell are you anyway?

C:   Oh, about as good as could be expected. Living under the shadow of the mushroom cloud, watching the bottom fall out of the market, reposing my hopes for mankind's survival in—for Pete's sake—ol' Bob Vanderveen, the fighting Dutch prosecutor from—Christ, of all places, Kalamazoo. Other than that, who's complaining? Seriously, though, how are *you?*

F:   Okay. Oh, a little bruised around the edges. Scared. Irritated. Sorry to see my illustrious career fold up quite like this. But that's why I asked you to come up. To find out how I'm doing. How am I doing, counselor?

C:   Did you get me here for legal advice? Precedent to some kind of court-martial proceedings you're expecting?

F:   Partly. But mostly to help me in a broader sense, Charlie. As an old, trusted, admired friend and wordsmith. To help me put my thoughts together before I have to start telling my story to those people out there on my front lawn, to Corky and the rest of the gang at the Pentagon, to Congressman Rogers and *his* gang, to ol' Bob Vanderveen. *(Stops. Pauses.)* How *am* I doing out there, Charlie?

C:   Not so good, pal. Catching it already from several quarters. Probably gonna catch it soon from the others. *(Opens his case, rummages around in it.)* I spent Thursday evening reading that collection of reports and reprints you had delivered. I now know more than I ever wanted to know about tactical nukes, Lance missiles, atomic demolition munitions, et cetera. Give me the old M-1 Army. Glad I bailed out in time. And these legal pieces *(still removing things from his briefcase)* and odds and ends from philosophy quarterlies took me back to my law school days. But I read it all. Most of yesterday I spent at the Pentagon chatting informally with some of our old buddies. Those guys are mostly pretty happy that ol' Bob wants to flex his prosecutorial muscles and hang you out to dry. "Flat refusal to obey a direct Presidential order in time of war." Et cetera. Not good, pal.

F:   But you're here anyway.

C:   Oh, sure. Beats chasing ambulances. Famous client, interesting case. You can probably even afford my fee ... if the whole balloon doesn't go up before I get my bill into the mails.

F:   So, what's next?

C:   I want to hear from you what your reasons for refusal were. Let's start with that. I want to take some notes, ask pesky questions that won't compare with the nasty ones you'll get later from others.

F:   Okay. *(Starts to pace, recollecting.)* On D plus 13, Tuesday the 19th, Al Sorley, commanding the 47th, responsible for this piece of my territory, roughly from Münster up through the Netherlands to the Channel *(pointing this out on the map he's hung)* ... Al called, a little frantic. Things were very rough up there. The Russians had swept pretty easily across most of that open plains area, grabbing some cities and bypassing others, and overrunning and decimating our troops by the tens of thousands.

C:    So what did he want?

F:    He wanted me—demanded of me would almost be a better way to put it—to ask the President for authority to use tactical nukes to knock out the Bremen airfield. You'll remember, the Russians had seized it on day two. Well, they were using it very effectively to launch devastating airstrikes and close air support for their ground operations. I checked around, talked to intelligence and the weather guys. Called Al back and said I just couldn't do it.

C:    And your reasons? *(Picks yellow legal pad from his case, starts to take notes.)*

F:    Too many of our troops and West German troops were still being held there as POWs. And the city of Bremen—a big city, Charlie—is very close to the airfield and, that day, downwind of it.

Al told me he "only" wanted six or eight five-kiloton bursts—to pock up the runways, knock out the tower and shops, and catch a couple dozen planes on the ground. But that would just have caused too damned much collateral damage. Most of those American and German soldiers would die. And who knows how many tens of thousands of Bremen civilians would have gotten burned or hit with lethal radiation. As important as it was as a military target, the damage would have been way out of proportion and much less discriminating than I thought—think—we ought to at least try damned hard to be. *(Pauses, thoughtfully.)*

C:    Then?

F:    Then Al hung up on me, went over my head, called SACEUR [Supreme Allied Commander, Europe], General Butch Thornton, who contacted the President with the request. Next thing I know, Vanderveen himself is calling me direct in person on an open line, all full of wartime vim and vigor. That flaming asshole is having The Big Adventure, the time of his life, playing Churchill in the bunker, saving the Western world with all those colored telephones. Orders me to launch the strike Al requested.

I tried talking him out of it, reasoning and arguing with him . . . you know, like two grown-ups might do. Then he reaches down deep and gets out his Patton line, just like George C. Scott did it: "General, if you haven't got the stomach for modern warfare or the sense of duty to obey your President, I'll have to find me another general who does." Canned me, stuck poor Al into my slot and flew me home Wednesday.

C:    And the Bremen airfield?

F *(Quietly.)*:    Hit, very hard, Thursday the 21st. *(Awkward pause.)*

C:   Our old buddies at the Pentagon seem mostly to be convinced by the argument of "military necessity" in the matter. They think you should have swallowed your qualms and launched the strike.

F:   Well, Charlie, I suppose we've all been wrestling with these things for years. How to arrange the various principles and rules. What takes precedence. How to decide, if and when they conflict. Where to draw the lines. You'll remember, we used to argue this stuff in Mendelski's class at the Point.

C:   I'll have to admit I didn't take it all that seriously.

F:   Some did, some didn't. But after Viet Nam, even some of the cynics did some rethinking. There were all those seminars and anthologies about war and morality. We were all trying to answer "What would we do IF . . .?"

C:   And where did you come down?

F:   I made up my mind a long time ago. I wanted to save some little bit of honor for my dubious profession if I could. Even in the midst of Raymond Aron's century of total war, even surrounded by the amazing gadgets and the incredible firepower that science and technology have "blessed" us with, blessed even a company commander with. The only way—it seemed to this poor, slow mind—was to hang on for all I was worth to the old, tried, true principles of proportionality and discrimination. I just couldn't accept the idea that when things get really tough we can cite "military necessity" and just forget all the other principles and rules of engagement, all the supposedly inferior rules worked out over the millennia by soldiers and thinkers to regulate combat in some rudimentary ways at least.

I made up my mind to try as best I could, even under the chaotic conditions of combat, to remain as thoughtful and careful as it was so much easier to be in the Command and General Staff College classrooms. I hoped the day would never come when I'd have to refuse a superior order to do something that my reason, education, training and conscience would tell me was improper, even if effective and superficially "necessary." But I hoped, too, that I'd have the courage to do what I did Tuesday.

C:   But couldn't you have used the nukes against the Bremen field, Frank, and then taken refuge in what some of these writers (pointing to the pile of reprints) call the principle of double effect, sanctioning some evil, or collateral damage in this case, as incidental and secondary to the accomplishment of the intended good? As unintended and regrettable, but as a tolerable price to pay for the accomplishment of the primary objective, and excusable? (A little apologetically.) I have to ask these pesky questions, Frank. Believe me, others will put them a lot more harshly.

F: Let me answer you a little crudely, Charlie. The principle of double effect doesn't mean that if I see a fly on your forehead, I'm allowed to swing at it with a two-by-four. It doesn't let me "destroy the village in order to save it." If you take it seriously, it isn't a loophole. It isn't there to give me a moral license to do whatever I want. It calls for a moral *judgment.* And it says that the supposedly incidental damage of an action has to be substantially less of an evil than the supposedly primary damage is of a good. In this case, the "unintended" damage would have included a lot of dead American prisoners of war and even more dead Germans— innocent, civilian, noncombatants. So, yes, I could have used double effect as a "refuge." But not as an answer.

C: Okay. Let me try another argument out on you. Some at the shop were puzzled that you refused to use the nukes at Bremen even though you had already authorized the use of quite a few nukes in other situations during the first 12 miserable days. How do you answer that, Frank?

F: Very different situations, Charlie, carefully evaluated separately. In each of these other cases I decided that the nukes could be used consistently with the principles I just mentioned: proportionality, discrimination, military need—in its place, double effect—carefully weighed.

C: So you don't have anything against tactical nuclear weapons, per se?

F: If I had my 'druthers, Charlie, they'd never have been invented. Give me the World War II or Korea arsenal any day. Or maybe the elegant forms and gadgets of the Middle Ages, even. But, no, I don't have anything against nukes per se. I think they *can* be used very occasionally, selectively, carefully ... well within my understanding of what you lawyers would call *ius in bello* restrictions. Mainly, that is, consistent with the principles of proportionality and discrimination.

C: Maybe you could run down through those instances of the use of tactical nukes during the first 12 days for me?

F: Fine, I've even made some notes. *(Finds them.)* On day one, I authorized the detonation of 12 or 13 atomic demolition munition devices, ADMs we call them, in the passes and narrow defiles just east of Fulda *(pointing out the spot on the map).* ADMs are clearly defensive weapons, no offensive potentiality whatsoever. We'd very quietly prechambered and prepositioned—"seeded," if you will—these atomic mines there during the late 70's. Planted those near villages in deeper holes so that when they went off they'd cause rock slides to block roads but the bursts wouldn't break the surface to release any radiation. Planted some nearer the surface under bridges in remote areas. That entire area is pretty remote, rugged. Planted several very small ones—tenth of a kiloton and even less in yield—just under the surface of some roads in densely wooded areas to crater the roads and blow down the surrounding trees to inhibit traffic off the roads and through the forests. It worked, you know. We caught over 400 tanks and associated equipment and military personnel during the first few days.

C:   Collateral damage?

F:   Minimal. Almost no civilian casualties. Most of the few people living in that rugged area had left when the crisis really heated up a month ago because they knew Soviet armor would be coming through their neighborbood. And I suppose they knew, too, or at least suspected, that we'd have some pretty dramatic welcoming activities laid on. *(Rising.)* But, say, some host I am. It's past noon. Can I get you a drink?

C:   Sounds good. Especially after my hike through your own mountain passes out back. Scotch, if you have it.

F *(While making drinks.):* On day three, I agreed to use nukes about 15 miles out to sea in the Channel. The Soviets were moving up an amphibious landing group to help with their sweep into the Lowlands. And a couple of the boats in the groups were doing a lot of electronic intelligence and fire control work to support the sweep. Small nukes, but better for such sizable moving targets than anything conventional I had. Delivered by very accurate air-to-surface missiles. Precision guided munitions. What the media call "smart bombs." No civilians in the way, of course, nothing but bona fide combatants. Radiation dissipated long before it reached shore.

C:   Tactically and ethically kosher, then?

F:   I thought so. A clearly and purely military target, collection of them, really. And, of course, Thornton, the Pentagon and Vanderveen were also pleased to have been able to make a second demonstration to the Soviets —in addition to the ADMs three days earlier—that we meant business, were determined, were willing to use nuclear weapons to defend Europe. Symbols of intent, you might say, designed to persuade the Soviets to halt their attack. But very carefully and selectively executed signals.

C:   Intrawar deterrence?

F:   I suppose you could put it that way. Let's see. *(Going back to his notes.)* On day five I agreed to Freddie Wolowitz's request that several eight-inch howitzer shells, each carrying mini-nuke warheads set at less than a tenth of a kiloton yield—some of these things have selectable yields, just turn the dial!—that several howitzer shells be used to take out a big heavy-duty railroad bridge across the Weser. About here *(pointing to the map)*. It was crucial to deny the Soviets that bridge as we fell back.

And again, hardly any, if any, civilians got caught. Nobody lives near the east end of the bridge—big swampy marshland—and Freddie's intelligence people had ascertained that the people in the village at the west end had joined the hundreds of thousands of West German refugees that have been clogging the roads all the way to France. Besides that, we had a convenient opportunity to demonstrate that we were prepared to use nukes on land above ground . . . so as to encourage the Russian commanders to keep their troops dispersed, spread out along the front. They had already started to bunch up for some concentrated assaults along the line, but the bridge strike encouraged them to spread back out again into troop formations better designed to survive battlefield nukes . . . and not quite so good at assaulting weak points in our lines.

C:   Understood. I assume the commanders in the other sectors along the front were making similar demonstrations and tactical strikes?

F:   Very selectively. Keeping to the game plan. Well within the rules. On day eight I approved a strike with Lance missiles armed with somewhat larger nukes against 17 supply dumps and staging areas to the enemy's rear in East Germany. All 17 had been carefully selected a couple of years ago. None was within ten miles of a town. All were important military targets. Fourteen were put out of business, three others were damaged badly, that's how accurate these delivery systems have become.

C:   Could have used some of those gadgets in Korea, in my war. But go on.

F:   On day 11 we used tactical nuclear weapons delivered by airplane-carried precision guided munitions . . .

C:   Smart bombs, again?

F:   Right. To hit a train rolling across Poland from Russia full of chemical agents, nerve gas canisters. The Polish resistance tipped us. Suggested a dandy remote location. Got the few nearby natives out of the way. And helped us time the strike. It was appropriate to use nukes on that target, too, rather than conventional weapons because we wanted that particular cargo incinerated rather than just derailed or blown up. Again, minimal collateral damage.

C:   That's it?

F:   That's all the nukes I authorized. One unauthorized use in my command. A jumpy young lieutenant colonel who'd just taken over a badly mauled artillery unit. Let loose a few six-inch shells at some tanks advancing through a pretty heavily populated area. Killed about 90 tanks, which made it possible for him to extricate what was left of his unit. But killed a hell of a lot of natives, too. Not acceptable. Not intended. We started an investigation right away and got the colonel a desk job.

C:  I thought nukes were under tighter command control than that.

F:  Most are. For all practical purposes the bombs and missiles remain under SACEUR and Presidential control. But once nuclear warhead artillery shells for the six- and eight-inch guns have been distributed, the local commanders do have access to them. In the fog, chaos and pressures of battle, it's damned hard to control these released shells in the hands of commanders who've been encircled or are about to be overrun. In the old cliché, accidents will happen. I'm not sure, though, that even that kid— 34, I think—can fairly be held responsible for violating the code. Not exactly the My Lai of the 1980's, I shouldn't think. And I'd argue that responsibility certainly wouldn't go any farther up the chain.

C:  Well, it's something to look into. I may want to get more details from you later. Guess I'm willing, for the moment anyway, to buy your arguments that you felt you had sufficient reason to refuse Vanderveen's Bremen order even though you had already used lots of nukes in what do seem to me to be ways that paid proper attention to the legal and ethical norms that you've set for yourself.

F:  But?

C:  Well, I guess I'm a bit surprised at the precision that makes it possible to use even tactical nuclears in the discriminating ways you've described. Guess I'd thought that once battlefield nukes were used, the European landscape—especially West Germany—would be devastated. One of these pieces *(searching through them, finds it)*—here, it's this one by Cohen and Van Cleave. They mention Operation Carte Blanche, a war game in which, let's see, 335 nukes were hypothetically exploded and nearly four million people got "killed," including lots of civilians. Quite a mess, I'd say.

F:  That exercise took place in 1955, Charlie. The nukes were bigger then because no one was contemplating their use except in connection with all-out strategic war between the superpowers. Most were Hiroshima-type 15-plus kiloton bombs. Now we've got mini-nukes down to a tenth of a kiloton in yield, some even smaller—down to a twentieth of a kiloton. And our delivery is much more accurate and precise today, mostly because of electronics and computers.

It gets pretty complicated mathematically, Charlie, but the staff guys can demonstrate that the use of a few nukes is apt to do *less* collateral damage—knocking out those staging areas and dumps I mentioned, say— than using the many more conventional bombs that would have to be used to have the same chance of completely knocking out the same target. There are some examples of the calculations in that piece by whatshisname, Cane, in that assortment I gave you. Hell, there were studies done back in the mid-70's at RAND, Stanford Research Institute and Lockheed that showed that both sides in a European war could use *hundreds* of nukes without doing the damage done in Europe's cities and towns during World War II.

C:   *If* the Russians cooperated in developing mini-nukes, smart bombs and a selective targeting doctrine as fastidious as yours?

F:   And they seem to have, too. There were signs they would, too, back in the mid-70's. I sent over that piece by Galen, didn't I? He reports on the studies there that suggested that the Soviets had long had a selective targeting plan for the European theater.

C:   But I seem to remember that the Soviets usually talked as if they actually believed in what they used to call, as I recollect, the "indivisibility of nuclear war," that nuclear war was nuclear war and that they had no plans to use battlefield nukes in the discriminating way you say you've tried to use them.

F:   Rhetoric designed to enhance the credibility of their deterrent, Charlie. Scare the Germans with big talk about how Europe would be devastated if war started. Make us all believe they were so clumsy and bull-headed, dogmatic and unable to develop accurate systems for delivering small nukes, that we would somehow be more frightened of them, give up ourselves on the potentialities of tactical nukes if they wouldn't parallel our doctrines and equipment, and be cowed into concessions in Western Europe. An almost classic case of the usual gulf between declaratory policy and action policy, if you like.

C:   Well, that gets us to one other line of questions I wanted to explore, Frank, if you don't mind. First, though, could I hit you for a refill?

F:   Sure. What other line? *(Goes to mix refills, returns while Charlie continues.)*

C:   Well, I'd like to explore one final ethical angle. Not because it's gonna come up in court, if we ever go to court, because it's not. More to prod you to get your thoughts together for the broader purposes you mentioned at the outset.

F:   Fine with me. Shoot.

C:   I told you that you were catching it already from several quarters. Most of what you've said might, just *might,* satisfy some of our fraternity brothers. But your flank or rear, if you'll pardon me, might also be exposed. See the *Times'* editorial this morning?

F:   Nope.

C:   I'll read you some of it. *(Gets the* Times *from his case, reads.)*

It's laudable that General Dunbar, citing grounds of conscience and his understanding of the ethical norms supposed to govern an officer in combat, refused President Vanderveen's immoderate—some would say outrageous—order to destroy Bremen in order to destroy the Bremen airfield.

Et cetera. But ... *(Looks up.)* Here's their main point. *(Reading again.)*

... General Dunbar, together with the other highest ranking officers and their civilian superiors, must take his share of the blame for the fact that it was the United States and not the Soviet Union that first used nuclear weapons in this war, crossing the nuclear threshold for the first time since 1945, violating the well-established firebreak, and setting us all off on a course that may well result in escalation to the level of strategic exchange and wholesale global catastrophe. If we go that far, and many analysts suggest it is now virtually inevitable that we will, General Dunbar's admirable battlefield restraint and moral fussiness will not rescue him from damnation by whatever survivors are around to write the post-mortems.

Endquote, pal. Heavy stuff. *(Frank is pacing, collecting his thoughts.)* Is there a great moral issue there, Frank? What might be called the "first use" issue?

F *(Softly, slowly at first):* I—we—thought the Soviets *had* already used them first. Their doctrine, their field exercises, all indicated that they would use battlefield nukes from the moment they jumped off. Intelligence was ambiguous. Our so-called theatre was a madhouse, Charlie. The intensity of the battle, the noise, the confusion, the pace of everything was just simply incredible. *(Shakes his head.)*
People—all of us—are just way out of their league with this hardware. Talk about the fog of war has got the wrong meteorological metaphor, believe me. More like the monsoon or cyclone of war.
A thousand-mile-long front. A contact "line" a hundred miles deep. Ten thousand tanks. Seventy percent casualties in a 15,000-man division in four days, four *days,* Charlie, not four months. Lots of young captains forced into the command of battalions and even regiments. Using fuel and ammunition at such a rate that some of the other sector and division commanders were almost *forced* to use nukes because they'd run so low on conventional stuff. *(Pauses.)*
Anyway, intelligence was ambiguous. Couldn't get any straight answers from anyone. Navy intelligence said they didn't think the Russians had used them but couldn't be sure. Air Force satellite intelligence swore they'd detected bursts against not only our reconnaissance and communications satellites in orbit on day one but also against some of our shipping in the North Atlantic. German intelligence swore that the Soviets had not used nukes yet. But we wondered if they could be trusted since they had

good reasons for hoping that we would hold off on using our nukes on their pretty landscape.

C:   I always thought the monitoring gadgetry would be able to detect the radioactivity.

F:   Imperfectly, pal, imperfectly. These people are wizards at demonstrating Murphy's law. And the Peter Principle was working overtime, too. Thornton asked the President point blank—when he called on day one to get Presidential release of the nukes—if Vanderveen himself knew whether the Soviets had used nukes yet at that point and Vanderveen just dithered and waffled as usual.

C:   But now we know that the Russians had not yet used them. That we used them first.

F:   So what? *(Charlie looks up, eyebrows raised.)* No, I'm serious. I've given it a lot of thought, Charlie. I'd rather we'd not have used them first. But, really, what difference does it make, ethically, who uses the damned things first? For starters, they attacked us, they lose a couple moral points right there, okay? Secondly, if my own use of small nukes is consistent with the tried, true, tested, refined, honorable principles of proportionality and discrimination—if they're so small and used so carefully as to do zero, or minimal, collateral damage to civilians, property and the landscape—then that so-called threshold or firebreak that everyone's so worried about doesn't mean a thing.

C:   Are you so sure?

F:   The nukes I used were no different—in their moral significance—from the so-called "conventional" weapons I was using, some of which are in some ways more damaging and destructive. In either case you've got some chemical activity going on that results in explosive power. What difference does it make—morally here again, okay?—what difference does it make if the chemicals are combining rapidly in combustion or fragmenting even more rapidly in fission?

C:   Well, some would say, some in fact are already saying, that you and the prez, we all, I guess—let me see, how does today's *Post* editorial put it? They're all ganging up on you, the eastern establishment press, maybe Spiro Agnew was right? *(Finds his Post, reads from the editorial.)* Quote . . . moved the conflict into another arena, escalating what might well have remained a conventional war into a nuclear war that will now almost certainly escalate to engulf us all. Endquote.

F:   Bullshit. My—our—use of small nukes didn't escalate anything. One. The level of destructiveness is not escalated, or not escalated very damned much, when two small tactical nukes are used to take out a bridge or blow up a mountain pass instead of the 15 or 20 old-fashioned blockbusters that might have been used instead. Two. The *geographical* scope of the war isn't escalated by tactical nukes. For the most part the conflict has been confined to the European space. And since Moscow achieved a second strike capability in the 60's, everyone has accepted, deep down anyway, the decoupling of European events from the Moscow/Washington mutual threat game. So the conflict will very probably remain confined to Europe even if one or the other side starts to lose badly.

C:  I hope you're right. You've got more faith than I have in cool heads prevailing, my friend.

F:  Anyway, to the limited extent that it's spilled beyond the European space, it's spilled over lots more because of airplanes, missiles, ocean-going ships, satellites and electronics than because of the nuclear nature of some of the weaponry. And three. The political stakes, it seems to me, are clearly limited and limiting. I'd argue that these variables—scale, geography, politics—define the important firebreaks, not technology in the abstract. Not technology at all, except insofar as technology along with important other factors determines scale.

C:  Well . . .

F:  In fact, I *could* argue, I think, that I set a good model. That it was positively good for me to be the first to use nukes because I used them properly. Better for me to have set some precedents for others to notice than to have some ham-handed Igor or latter-day LeMay be the first user.

C:  In summary, then, you don't agree that using battlefield nukes will automatically result in escalation to the strategic level?

F:  Not at all. That's the old dogma of the indivisibility of nuclear war again that we fault the Russians for holding, though if they ever held it for a while to bolster their deterrence bluffs and threats in the 60's when they were a paranoid second-best, they almost certainly dropped it quietly years ago in their serious planning sessions. Interestingly enough, German General Graf von Kielmansegg—you've got his article there—says this is an American dogma, too, and calls for what he calls the demythologizing of nuclear weapons and the development of different policies and procedures for different kinds of nukes instead of treating them all the same, whether they're mini-nukes of below a tenth of a kiloton or megaton strategic weapons.

C:  But, Frank, wouldn't it really be very difficult to wage a limited nuclear war for very long without the psychological and political pressures to escalate becoming just unbearable?

F: The so-called limited *strategic* nuclear war, involving counterforce strikes against Soviet and American military targets and thence maybe on up the ladder to the controlled exchange of cities—city for city, tit for tat, Minsk for Detroit—would probably be uncontrollable because of the inevitable heavy collateral damage, fallout, and the psychological and political pressures to escalate. But I really don't believe that war in Europe, or in the Middle East, or wherever on the periphery, calls into play the same factors and pressures, at least not on the decision-makers in Moscow and Washington. If this war escalates so that the Americans and Russians start using strategic nuclear weaponry against each others' homelands, with less and less concern for adherence to the dual principles of proportionality and discrimination . . .

C *(Simultaneously with Frank's last line.):*—proportionality and discrimination, I know.

F *(Giving Charlie a quizzical look, continues.):* . . . it won't be because we crossed some imaginary nuclear threshold two weeks ago very reluctantly, defensively, carefully and, in my view, properly. It'll be because the leaders on both sides consciously expanded the stakes, took the next steps, decided to enlarge the geographical arena of the conflict and cranked up the big guns.

C: No responsibility to the guy who casts the first blow? The first nuclear blow, that is?

F: Not in my judgment. Look, Charlie, I—the President, Thornton, the other generals, *we*—are not like some guy on the top of the hill who pushes the first boulder and has to take responsibility for the avalanche that follows. Nobody who starts an avalanche can turn it off once it's started. After that it's all just physics, gravity, momentum, motion out of control of human agency.

But, Charlie, diplomacy—still going on, I notice, even in the midst of this fracas—and warfare are not like an avalanche. You hear loose talk that war has its own escalatory dynamic. That's what it is, loose talk, and it obscures the fact that each notch up the ladder requires human action. Based on perceptions, cognitions, emotions, choices, practical military considerations, and, dammit, moral values *(nearly shouting)*.

C: Easy, easy.

F: Sorry. *(Calming a bit.)* But, Charlie, if our prez and his new northern sector general . . . or the gangsters in the Kremlin . . . crank this one up to the level of strategic exchanges of megaton-yield weaponry, they can't get off the moral hook by pointing the accusing finger at me for crossing their damned nuclear threshold. I'm happy to bear the responsibility for my own actions. I'm probably not responsible for actions taken later by others that were almost inevitable or almost unavoidable because of the context that my earlier actions only helped to shape. I'm sure as hell not responsible for actions taken later by others that were clearly avoidable choices or at least not at all inevitable. There's no reason obvious to me why the people in charge can't remain in control and keep to the limits—political, geographic, et cetera—they've settled upon. Warfare, even warfare involving nuclear weapons, though it's untidy and unpredictable and filled with awful pressures, God knows, is not usually completely uncontrolled or in some fundamental way uncontrollable. Tactical nuclear warfare doesn't inexorably and automatically have to escalate to all-out strategic nuclear war. If we keep saying that it does, we'll make it happen.

C:   Well, Frank, I gotta say you make some good points. A little surprising, even distressing. But, uh, persuasive. *(Sound of front door closing. Margaret reenters.)*

F:   Did you get your way with the dean, as usual?

M:   Partly. Small thing. And he's distracted, not much inclined to refuse just now. How about you two? Have you old soldiers been getting your ducks in a row?

C:   Pretty well. Frank's been . . .

M:   Don't tell me, Charlie. Let me guess. By now Frank has almost convinced you that he was right to refuse Vanderveen's order. But also that using nukes *can* be squared with just war doctrine—proportionality, discrimination, all that. Right?

C:   *(Puzzled.)* Well. . . .

M:   Oh, don't look so perplexed, Charlie. Lawyers shouldn't; not good for their image. Frank and I have been having the same discussion that you two have just had for, must be, 30 years. War and Ethics. Mostly calmly, like two civilized debaters. Did you know that we first met in debate at Oxford during Frank's Rhodes year there?

C:   But you were never convinced?

M:   I married a Yank soldier. I love him dearly, still. And I respect him, too. Partly because of his attachment to that old Catholic code of his. It's important. It's *something*, at least.

C:   But . . .?

M:   Oh, I don't want to do this. Please.

F:   No. Go ahead, toots. Charlie ought to hear it, your reservations. Might even do your old Yank warrior some good to have his mouthpiece properly briefed.

M:   I don't know if I'm up to it. The time's just so wrong.

F:   It's not going to get any better, Margaret.

M:   *(Pause.)* All right, then. *(Longer pause. While gathering her thoughts, she makes herself a drink. Finally speaks, to both Frank and Charlie.)* Your just war code is better than nothing: *Some* rules, *sometimes* respected, by *some* soldiers. The most conscientious ones. Like you, Frank.

F:   Thanks for that, anyway.

M:   But it's. . . . There are too many things wrong with it. It's too ambiguous, for starters, too susceptible to diverse idiosyncratic interpretation for it to serve as a dependable operating code of conduct. And it's too loose, the tests are too permissive. The code makes it too easy for you to find an excuse, a license to do almost whatever you really want to do.

F:   To use tactical nukes, say?

M:   Yes.

C:   Oh, I dunno. It didn't seem that easy for Frank to satisfy himself. And I think I pressed him pretty hard too. . . .

M *(Stops him with her hand.):*   Please, Charlie. I really don't want to *argue* all this. Just let me sort of "recite" it, okay?

C:   Okay. Sorry. I'll just take notes. *(Does.)*

M *(Again, to both Frank and Charlie.):* Your code also helps to perpetuate the militarization of public policy. Just war theory—at least the part of it Frank uses—simply isn't *political* enough.

C:   But Frank's a soldier, not a politician. He's never even been a very good Pentagon politician.

M *(Laughs, while Frank grins uneasily.):*   Wonderful, Charlie. That's *exactly* what Frank always says. And I always remind him of what Clausewitz said, that war is the ultimate extension of politics.

C:   I still don't get your point.

M:   All right. First, the parts of just-war theory that Frank has been expounding to you are really just a battlefield code. If I may be strident for a moment, they provide us with an etiquette of mass slaughter. As I've said, I'm glad it exists . . . even though sometimes I think too many people take false comfort in the knowledge that at least some of the military do have a code of ethics, so *our* side won't do the dastardly things the *other* side will.

C:   But you're concerned with the bigger picture?

M:   Yes. The other part of the code. The part that tells us when we can go to war with a good conscience, when, if ever, war is justified. and I've come to believe that this part of just-war theory helps make our politics topsy turvy. It encourages us to put primary things second, secondary things first.

C:   What's primary, Margaret? What's secondary?

M:   What are the basic, the ultimate goals of politics? I'd say they're life, liberty, justice, happiness, dignity, well-being. *Human* rights, *human* interests. Truly fundamental goals that modern warfare, even following your battlefield code, sacrifices or at least endangers at the outset. And all for the sake of secondary, penultimate values.

C:   Such as?

M:   Sovereignty. Territorial boundaries. The existing political and economic order. Defense of the state. National credibility. National "honor."

F *(Can't help breaking in.):*   But look, toots, some of those values you call "primary" can't survive except by protecting the values you make secondary. It's just elementary that without some kind of order you can't have liberty, maybe not even life. You can't really have justice without some kind of state . . . *(Frowns at himself.)* Sorry, Margaret, I know I shouldn't butt in.

C:   But if you hadn't said it, I would have. And then I'd follow up with some examples. What about Hitler? Or our Civil War? I know it was a mixed bag, but it did have something to do with freeing the slaves. For that matter, what about *this* war? If the Soviets take over Europe, a whole lot of very basic values are going right down the drain.

M:   Those are good questions. As Frank knows, I once thought they were unanswerable. Not any more.

C:   Anyway, I don't see how just-war theory has anything to do with your "topsy turviness."

M:   Okay. Let me ask you a rhetorical question. What threatens our national interest more, Castro's Cuba or the erosion of our topsoil—in Iowa, say?

C:   Well . . .

M:   I think you know *my* answer. Once that topsoil is gone—and it's going at an astonishing rate—it's gone, there's no way to replenish it. Now that's a *serious* problem, a whole lot more serious than anything Fidel Castro could conceivably do to this country. But which problem gets more attention from politicians, the media, the people? Obviously, it's Cuba, that "Communist spearhead 90 miles off our shores." Now, why is this?

C:   I want to hear *your* answer, Margaret.

M:   Thanks, Charlie. Just what the form called for. Frank, could you freshen my drink? *(He does.)* Charlie, I think it's because not only our policies but our minds have been militarized. Maybe even our souls. *(Pauses reflectively and nods thanks to Frank for the drink he returns to her.)* Just by surviving in "our" space, as we think of it, Castro tweaks our noses, so he gets more attention than he deserves. Besides, Cuba can be defined as a military problem. It can be "war gamed." By making us think of Cuba as a dangerous enemy, politicians can press the patriotism button and get us to rally behind them. Erosion, in contrast, isn't a military problem and it isn't an external problem. It can only be solved by changing *ourselves,* our whole way of doing agriculture. That would be hard. It would be divisive. It would take real political and technical genius to solve the problem. So we turn away from it. We refuse to define it as a serious challenge to the national interest.

C:   I'm not sure I see how just-war theory has much of anything to do with all this.

M:   Because it has such a powerful hold on our thinking, our definitions, our policies. And it's so statist, so nationalistic, so preoccupied with things military. It's less interested in human rights and human interests than it pretends to be, than it should be. Military defense of the nation against military attack is always and automatically primary. Other values, other challenges, other tasks are subordinated or neglected. Your code would have us go to war to prevent Russian soldiers from moving our border back a foot; but the code doesn't see erosion as a national interest problem because erosion doesn't involve military assault by foreign forces invading across a territorial border. And erosion is just one example. Think of energy conservation. The black underclass. The condition of our schools. Armed to the teeth, we look the other way.

C:   I think you exaggerate, Margaret. But I guess I follow you, at least.

M:   Your just-war code also strikes me as badly dated, passed by. Maybe, just maybe, despite its militaristic and nationalistic flavors, it wasn't so seriously flawed 200 years ago, even 50 years ago. *(Pauses.)* Even back then, though, the rule that violence must discriminate between combatants and noncombatants was probably unfair to combatants—making them fair game—since most of them were unwilling conscripts who were innocent civilians and thus immune, protected, the day before their luck ran out and they were drafted, usually because they'd been too careless in their choice of parents and had been born into the wrong social stratum. All those nice young boys. . . . *(Stops, sort of lost, distracted.)*

C: *(Bringing her back to the point.)* But these days . . .?

M: Today—at least since World War II, I'd say—the code's anachronistic. With modern weaponry and large armies, war is so vast, so complex, so messy. The cyclone metaphor you always use, Frank. Well, it's just unrealistic to expect that warriors can obey the restraints in the midst of the cyclone. And aren't impossible-to-obey commands generally recognized as devoid of moral force?

C: Well, I suppose strictly speaking, technically. . . .

M: Atrocities are inevitable. Let me remind you, Charlie, of what actually happened to Bremen this week. We all saw the aerial photographs on television. *(Both Charlie and Frank shift uneasily.)* If you know in advance that atrocities are going to occur, don't you have an obligation to refrain from participating? If it's impossible for the conduct *of* war to be ethical, then resort *to* war can't ever be ethical either, can it? So isn't the code, the entirety of just-war doctrine, a dead letter, morally?

C: And you would replace it with . . .?

M: Oh, I'm not sure. *(To Frank.)* This is where we always get stuck, isn't it, dear? This is where I usually insist that war is a cultural artifact, something that didn't have to be, that need not have dominated human history the way it has. Then I insist that, in any case, technology has rendered it too dangerous an activity today, an obsolete game. It follows that if war is obsolete, then Frank is improperly helping to prop it up, delaying the development of progressive alternatives, unethically squandering his considerable gifts by withholding them from the pitiful little efforts you see here and there to create a replacement for war as a final arbiter. Et cetera. At which point in the argument—sorry, debate—Frank gets either defensive or sullen, maybe because by this time I'm getting a bit shrill. Our general debate tends to degenerate.

C: That's a bit lofty, Margaret. Let me bring you down to earth: Suppose the nation is attacked. What would you have the leaders *do?*

M: Keep the *ultimate,* human, goals in mind. Resist nonviolently, perhaps. Maybe even surrender, followed by pleading, coping with the occupation of it comes, patiently pressing for change.

C: *(Startled.)* Surrender?

M: Isn't that what the Danes did when the Nazis arrived? It was so obviously more sensible, more protective of real human values than to order the citizenry to fight under the code. And die to the last man, woman and child. Wasn't it?

F:   But, Margaret, Denmark had no choice!

M:   You mean because it was too little to fight. Yes. And I would argue that today—confronted with the dimensions of the threat posed by nuclear weapons and the rest of the gadgetry—*all* countries, even the most powerful, are "little countries." If we truly care about ethics, about all those ultimate values, if we care about our own lives, our children, the planet, we have to find—to create, really—some kind of policy analogous to what Denmark did.

F:   So you've finally moved all the way to pacifism, Margaret.

M:   Maybe. I guess so. I'm less impressed with Christian just-war theory and more impressed than I was before with the *other* Christian argument, Christian pacifism, the Sermon on the Mount, turn the other cheek and all. But I could put it in terms of an ethical humanist view that I'm also finding more and more congenial: That warfare *per se* is an improper activity, like slavery or the ritual sacrifice of maidens, say. Never justified. And that no matter how honorably the very finest soldiers—like you, Frank—try to behave, they'll still be acting immorally. You've been an honorable soldier, darling. The most honorable, I really think, in all the world. But . . . and this is hard for me to say . . . I can't believe any longer that soldiering itself can be honorable.

C:   Oh, Margaret. That's going a bit far, isn't it?

M: Is it, Charlie? I don't think so any more. I think the pacifist is right in preaching that love, trust, hope and confidence—what Christians call "faith"—hold more promise than violence and war do. Love, hope, the rest . . . they ennoble, they respect the sanctity of life. Maybe they simply must be the stance of those who want consistency, self-respect, serenity —for the Christian, salvation. And peace.

C:   That's a lot to take in. A little romantic, a little unrealistic, though, no?

M:   I know it can sound goopy, Charlie. Or "womanish." But do you think Martin Luther King was goopy? Or Gandhi? Or that French pastor in World War II who made his whole village into a refuge for Jews? I know that neither King nor Gandhi did all they hoped to do. I know they were both shot to death. But they weren't *defeated.* It was the British Empire that lost, it was Bull Connor and all his buddies. And they were not defeated by violence . . . unless it was their own.

  To me, now, it seems these people—Gandhi, King, their followers— were less "visionary" and "romantic" than the so-called "realists"—those think-tank gurus who thought deterrence would work forever, that sensible Russians and Americans would always remain in control of nuclear weapons that they'd never use, that global business could go on as usual, indefinitely. As of today, Charlie, how would you measure the goopiness index in *that* kind of thinking?

C: Well, I don't know. As between. . . .

F: Needless to say, Charlie, I've never been able to buy into that position. Not in today's global jungle. Much as I'd like to see warfare go the way of slavery into history's dustbin, the world is just not there yet. Those who followed your advice, toots, and laid down their arms would be quickly swallowed up.

M: But your own code grew out of Judaeo-Christian teachings. Most of your comrades in arms profess to be Christians. Why do you all assume that evil would definitely triumph? Why do you have so little confidence that right would prevail? Why do you have so little faith in your own God's benevolence? How can you quite so casually, sometimes almost cynically, just brush aside that whole collection of pacifist imperatives that your own Christ set down?

F: That's not fair. We don't "casually" brush them aside. But we do pay a lot of attention to history, Margaret, and it does have sobering lessons. Maybe war *didn't* have to dominate history. Maybe it's *not* in our genes. Maybe we did invent it, tragically, a few thousand years ago. Maybe we can get rid of it someday. But calling for its abolition now, especially now, is asking for the moon. We're *at war*, Margaret. What you're suggesting is. . . .

   *(As Frank is saying this last, a door slams off-stage; an attractive, thirty-ish woman bursts excitedly into the room. She is Karen Monroe, who lives next door.)*

KAREN:   Peg! Frank! What do you suppose it means? *(Sees Charlie.)* Oh, sorry. Didn't know you had company.

M:   Charlie Pierce, Karen Monroe, our next-door neighbor. What do we suppose *what* means, Karen?

K:   You haven't heard? Quick, turn on your TV.

   *(Frank does so, and the group turns to the set.)*

TV NEWSCASTER:   . . . surprise appearance in the White House newsroom by President Derek Evans, who assumed office just hours ago, following what we have been told was a debilitating stroke suffered by President Vanderveen. Vice-Pres . . . uh, President Evans also reminded us of the earlier angry Soviet denunciations of United States use of nuclear weapons in Europe. Now, he said, scattered intelligence reports indicate that the leaders in the Kremlin *may* be following up these verbal attacks by preparing a limited nuclear reprisal attack, possibly including some United States targets. Finally, President Evans—who is known to have differences with former President Vanderveen's policies on nuclear weapons—announced that he will address the nation over all major networks at 8 o'clock this evening to inform us of the decisions that he and his advisers have made for dealing with what he called "this unparalleled crisis." Now, back to our regular programming. . . .

*(Frank uses his remote control gadget to switch off the television. There is a long pause.)*

C *(Quietly.):* So. Back from the brink? Or further into the cyclone?

*(Action on stage freezes. Slowly, the curtain falls.)*

# Countering the Theory of Limited Nuclear War

## John C. Bennett

A new situation in regard to the possession and possible use of nuclear weapons has crept up on the American people. The axiom that formerly prevailed—that we possess nuclear weapons only to prevent their use— is gradually losing force, and now many persons close to the centers of decision-making have the idea that we should be prepared actually to use our nuclear weapons in the hope of coming out ahead of any adversary.

## TWO SCHOOLS OF THOUGHT

I was first made aware of this gradual shift when I read an article by Leon Sigal in *Foreign Policy* (spring 1979) in which he describes two schools of thought in the Pentagon—the "stable balancers," who still believe in possessing nuclear weapons to prevent their use, and the "war-fighting" school. At that time he thought that the first group was in the majority, but since then an increasing acceptance of the second position seems to

Copyright 1981 Christian Century Foundation. Reprinted by permission from the January 7–14, 1981 issue of *The Christian Century*.

have developed in the context of belief in the possibility of limited nuclear wars. This idea was given special emphasis in the general discussion of the new presidential directive for nuclear strategy (Directive 59) limiting use of these weapons to targeting the nuclear forces and installations of the adversary.

This change of mind in the Pentagon about the use of nuclear weapons gives the American churches a chance to come to a much clearer and more forceful position on nuclear weapons and nuclear war than has generally been the case. Many initiatives in the churches have called attention to the need to control the arms race, and both Roman Catholic teaching and ecumenical teaching in the context of the World Council of Churches have been clear in seeing nuclear war, or any other form of total war, to be in absolute conflict with Christian faith. But in U.S. churches one conflict has not been well articulated—that of absolute pacifists and nuclear pacifists on the one hand (those who cannot justify the possession of nuclear weapons and who by implication favor unilateral nuclear disarmament), and those on the other hand who have reluctantly accepted the view that the possession of nuclear weapons in a structure of mutual nuclear deterrence is the surest way under present conditions to prevent nuclear war. Today, in view of the recent changes in government thinking, it should be possible for both groups in the churches to work together in opposition to the limited-nuclear-war theorists.

A new factor affecting decision-making is the development of a community of nuclear experts who live in a world of their own that others do not understand. The distinction between the nuclear specialists and those outside the field differs from the more familiar contrast between the role of the military and that of civilians. These experts spend their lives designing nuclear weapons, projecting nuclear strategies, and dreaming about the scenarios of nuclear war. They may as civilians occupy "think tanks," and they may either as civilians or as members of the military work in the Pentagon.

In a recent article Lord Solly Zuckerman, former chief scientific adviser to the British government, writes about the situation with which he was familiar in his country:

> The men in the nuclear weapons laboratories on both sides have succeeded in creating a world with an irrational foundation, on which a new set of political realities has in turn been built. They have become the alchemists of our times, working in secret ways which cannot be divulged, casting spells which embrace us all [Weekly *Manchester Guardian*, October 19, 1980].

He adds that "the more destructive power there is, so, one must assume they imagine, the greater chance of military success." Political leaders are likely to take many more facts and values into account, and this has often been true of military leaders as well, but there is a danger that such leaders may listen to these nuclear experts with their specialized vision, and perhaps in making desperate decisions trust the specialists' judgment about limited nuclear war. Fortunately there is a large and independent scientific community which can warn us all against arcane judgments.

Quite apart from Directive 59, the idea of limited nuclear war has been considered by those who think in terms of using tactical nuclear weapons in situations far from our shores where we might be at a disadvantage because of a lack of conventional weapons capability. It seems to be taken for granted that, if we were losing in a confrontation with the Soviet Union in any part of the world, we would use tactical nuclear weapons, perhaps initiating their use to save us from defeat. Such an instance seems to pose the greatest danger of our getting involved in nuclear war—a situation where we would be "backing into it."

But doesn't the Soviet Union also have tactical nuclear weapons? If their use were stepped up on both sides, what chance would there be of keeping the war limited, since the important barrier to escalation—the nuclear threshold—would have been crossed? Also, one side or the other might then attack in another part of the world where its strength was greater and by this route lead to a great enlargement of the war with unforeseen consequences.

The strategy of Directive 59 would be less limited in its effects than is usually recognized. Nuclear experts admit that there would be millions of casualties, between 10 million and 20 million in the country first targeted, and since it is doubtful that the target country's retaliatory force could be fully destroyed, there would probably be millions of casualties on the other side. What is almost never said is that thousands of nuclear explosions, *whatever their targets*, would have a damaging effect on the atmosphere of the whole northern hemisphere. Does anyone know—or even try to take account of—the extent to which radioactive materials would spread over a continent even when the targets are limited?

A prior consideration is that the very policy of preparation to strike the nuclear forces of the other side involves a first-strike capability that becomes a temptation for the other side to strike first, perhaps against cities, thus making nuclear war more likely than it is now.

There is no way of stretching Christian ethics, or any other humane ethics, to justify such preparations or to justify the initiation of nuclear war, even if the intention is to keep it limited. There are only two ways to think of war in Christian terms. One is the way of the pacifist minority, which has some influence on the sensitivities of others. The other way is to recognize that some uses of military force are justified, but always on the condition that they be limited—limited in their effect on noncombatants, limited by the possibility of perceiving strong chances that the war would make possible a better peace.

The Second Vatican Council spoke for the ecumenical Christian conscience when it said: "Any act of war aimed indiscriminately at the destruction of entire cities or extensive areas along with their population is a crime against God and man himself." Catholic teaching about the criteria for justified war allows for a "double effect" and recognizes that even when the main target is military, many noncombatants are likely to be in the neighborhood and to be victims. Hence there must be some sense of proportionality in justifying the military action by relating the number of "side-effect" victims to the purpose of the action. But when the side effect consists of 10 million to 20 million casualties, many of them noncombatants, there is no possibility of justifying the action. Nuclear war would produce in addition many indirect or delayed side effects which have never entered into the traditional discussion of the "just" and "unjust" war.

## CONSIDERING THE SIDE EFFECTS

The side effects to which I shall now turn should be lifted up for emphasis in the churches partly because they are generally neglected and partly because they clearly mark the difference between nuclear war and previous forms of war. The latter consideration is important because one aspect of the current changes in military philosophy is a tendency to say that nuclear weapons are just an extension of other means of fighting. It would be well to reflect on the fact that, horrible as World War II was in its destructiveness, the nations most devastated have in large measure been restored. The prosperity and political health of both Germany and Japan illustrate this regeneration.

As for the indirect and delayed effects of nuclear war, there would first be the struggle of the survivors to bury the dead and to find their way across radioactive soil to find food and medical care. How many doctors and nurses would have survived? How many survivors would even in the early stages become victims of hopeless illnesses?

If there were thousands of nuclear explosions in two countries, the effect on the atmosphere would be serious regardless of the targets. A report of the United States Arms Control and Disarmament Agency titled "Worldwide Effects of Nuclear War," as quoted by Francis X. Winters (in *Ethics and Nuclear Strategy*, by Harold P. Ford and Francis X. Winters [Orbis, 1977], p. 147), gives the following estimates of the effect on the atmosphere of an all-out nuclear war:

> Such a war would destroy 30 to 70 per cent of the ozone layer in the entire northern hemisphere and between 20 and 40 per cent of it in the southern hemisphere as well. The destruction of the ozone layer would have truly apocalyptic consequences, such as a two- to three-year destruction of agricul-

ture (because of a change of even one degree in the average temperature), disabling sunburn or snow blindness, and disruption of communications.

A counterforce war that did not target the cities might have a somewhat reduced effect, but how much less destructive it would be we do not know; and in any case there is no good reason to be optimistic that a limited war could be kept limited in a time of desperation.

How great would be the increase of hunger in this country and on other continents as a side effect of nuclear war? How much of the radioactive land would be uninhabitable and for how long? I recall that when there was talk of a possible meltdown at Three Mile Island, it was assumed that after such an accident, a large area of Pennsylvania would be uninhabitable for some time. How would thousands of intended nuclear explosions compare in their effect with one such accident?

How many of the survivors could expect to have cancer in ten or 20 years? What would be the genetic effects of so many explosions on the children and later descendants of the survivors? How far have military or political planners gone in trying to get answers to such questions? What right have the decision-makers of this generation to deprive future generations of so much of the material and cultural capital that they should be able to inherit?

## EFFECT ON THE MORALE OF THE WORLD

Another side effect of nuclear war would be the impact on the morale of the world, especially that part of the world most visited by destruction, as well as the morale of onlookers, perhaps in the southern hemisphere, who could well despair of the reason and conscience of the human race and fear for their own future.

Two political realists have stressed the importance for our nation to be ready to use power, including military power in some situations: theologian Reinhold Niebuhr and Hans Morgenthau, the most renowned of American political scientists who emphasized international relations. Niebuhr wrote of nuclear war: "Could a civilization loaded with this monstrous guilt have enough moral health to survive?" (*Christianity and Crisis*, November 13, 1961).

Morgenthau declared that only a person "who is possessed not only by extreme optimism but by an almost unthinking faith" can believe "that civilization, any civilization, Western or other, could survive such an unprecedented catastrophe" (*Commentary*, October 1961). He even went so far as to say that such a war would destroy for the secularist without a transcendent faith the meaning of life. He added that it would destroy even the meaning of death, as it would rob death of all individuality. Said Morgenthau: "The possibility of nuclear death, by destroying the meaning of life and death, has reduced to absurd clichés the noble words of yesterday. To defend freedom and civilization is absurd when to defend them amounts to destroying them" ("Death in the Nuclear Age," *Commentary*, September 1961).

One might try to reduce the impact of these words by saying that Morgenthau had in mind an all-out nuclear war and that they might not apply fully to the more limited counterforce war in the minds of some of our military planners. Quite apart from the fact that a limited nuclear war would not be as limited as is usually suggested, there is the great risk that it would lead to an all-out war. Shortly before his death, Morgenthau wrote: "The use of nuclear weapons, even if at first on a limited scale, would unleash unmitigated disaster, which could lead to the destruction of both belligerents" (*New Republic,* October 20, 1979).

I think that this political scientist is a better guide than the nuclear experts and military planners. We should add to what he said that many nonbelligerent neighbors would be caught in the cross fire; they too would suffer from any damage done to the atmosphere. In our American discussion this fact is seldom mentioned, and it should receive special attention in the churches.

In defense of what interests and values would all this destruction be wrought? At present we can easily imagine that we might become involved in nuclear war for the sake of oil or for the sake of freedom. In either case, it would be self-defeating. Such a war would probably destroy the oil wells and installations so that they would be unusable for a long time, and it would destroy the industrial civilization that needs so much oil.

Moreover, the institution of freedom would probably be among the casualties. Survivors trying to put their world together again would require authoritarian government, and there would be a serious break in the continuity of institutions and traditions. One can imagine how difficult it would be to restore the precious and precarious traditions of freedom.

Herbert Butterfield, British diplomatic historian and lay theologian, put the matter very well: "With modern weapons we could easily put civilization back a thousand years, while the course of a single century can produce a colossal transition from despotic regimes to a system of liberty" (*International Conflict in the Twentieth Century—A Christian View,* by Herbert Butterfield [Harper, 1960]).

## THE RESPONSIBILITY OF THE CHURCHES

If the churches are loyal to the purposes of God as known through Christ for humanity and for this earth, they will give major—and that means much-increased—attention to the prevention of nuclear war. This task will involve exerting pressure on both public opinion and government when either is tempted to become carelessly confrontational or belligerent; it will also involve continuous pressure for control of the arms race, leading to radical reduction of armaments. Today there is more talk about linkage between arms control and other issues related to the Soviet Union. I hope that the new administration will not push this concept too far, because arms control is in the interest of the security of both superpowers, quite apart from other considerations. Also, since it would reduce the danger of nuclear war, it is in the interests of everyone.

As a nonpacifist (though no hawk!) who assumes that we cannot dispense with the use of power, sometimes military power, in international relations, I would raise the question whether the concerns expressed in this article might inhibit all use of military force regardless of the provocation and regardless of what values might be at stake in particular situations. My answer is No, but these concerns do mean that there would be a heavier burden of proof on the use of military power than formerly.

The clearest imperative is that we should avoid initiating a nuclear stage in what is supposed to be a limited war. I doubt that we would ever be tempted to use such weapons to initiate a nuclear war, though we cannot put that beyond possibility if military and political planners became convinced that they could, by a "limited" first strike, destroy the capacity of the other side to retaliate. That would be a terrible wrong in itself because of the inevitable side effects and the number of innocent people who would be immediately killed and wounded. It would be an appalling case of political recklessness.

There will be need of more cool-headedness and political skill among policymakers than ever before, and among both policymakers and public there will be a need for commitments, for sensitivity and prudence, and for a willingness to take account of the fears and insecurities of the other side. The overarching fact in this context is that nuclear war itself is the greatest threat to the superpowers, to their neighbors, and to all people.

# The Cruise Missile and the Neutron Bomb: Some Moral Reflections

James T. Johnson

The cruise missile and the neutron bomb, two weapons recently developed in this country, have sharpened both military and moral questions.

Reprinted, with deletions, by permission from *Worldview* magazine, December, 1977. James T. Johnson teaches in the Department of Religion at Douglass College, Rutgers University, and is the author of *Ideology, Reason and the Limitation of War* (1975) and *Just War Tradition and the Restraint of War* (1981).

Neither weapon is radically new: the German V-1 "buzz bomb" of World War II was a primitive cruise missile, and the neutron bomb is a further development in the line of fission and fusion warheads dating from World War II. Nevertheless, on the basis of information made public about the new weapons, they appear to differ fundamentally from their antecedents. It is necessary to ask about the moral relevance of these differences.

## THE CRUISE MISSILE

The new cruise missiles are unlike the "buzz bombs" of World War II in two morally significant ways: their accuracy and the variety of types of warheads available for them.

**Accuracy.**   The German missile killed indiscriminately where it fell, and the place of impact could be controlled only by the vector heading on which it was launched and the amount of fuel it carried. Thus it could hit only very large targets—those the size of a metropolitan area. British cities, principally London, and their environs were the chosen targets of the V-1. The development of this weapon must be understood in the immediate context of counterpopulation aerial bombing by both Axis and Allies during World War II. The "buzz bomb" campaign against Britain was simultaneously a measure of psychological warfare against the British population to undermine support for the war effort and a measure of retaliation for the Allied bombing of German cities. The V-1 was a counterpopulation weapon both in intention and in actual use; its inaccuracy kept it from being anything else.

The cruise missiles now being developed for United States use, however, are claimed to be extremely accurate. These new weapons could be used against enemy population centers in event of war, but because they are so accurate they could be limited to attacks on enemy missile-launching areas, military installations, concentrations of troops, and other targets directly related to the capability of an enemy to prosecute the war. Herein lies the moral difference with the earlier weapon. Such use would be morally discriminate in avoiding direct, intentional harm to noncombatants, their property, and the civilization of the enemy understood generally, as opposed to the moral indiscriminacy of the V-1, whose chief aim was to kill noncombatants, destroy noncombatant property, and disrupt civilian life as much as possible, with military damage only an incidental possibility.

In the same way, the cruise missile can be distinguished from current strategic nuclear warhead delivery systems, whose limitations remain a powerful argument for counterpopulation strategies such as mutual assured destruction (MAD). Together with the expected ability of the new cruise missile to avoid detection in flight and so reach its intended target, its accuracy could make possible for the first time since the thermonuclear arms race began a defense strategy oriented principally or entirely around the concept of counterforce or counterforces warfare (the former referring to attacks directed against only the enemy's strategic thermonuclear capability, the latter directed as well to destroying conventional and tactical nuclear fighting ability). From the moral standpoint this would be a step of the utmost importance. The "balance of terror" concept retained in MAD strategy requires either that counterpopulation warfare be intended and, in event of war, actually waged, or that it be intended but never really meant to be carried through, or that it never really even be intended but exist as only a massive bluff. However understood, an important component of strategy for the superpowers remains the counterpopulation threat. Such a threat is extremely hard to justify in moral terms.

Let me examine some of the principal arguments. About the most positive thing that can be said about a strategy oriented toward the intentional destruction of noncombatants is that fear of a counterpopulation thermonuclear war may have helped to prevent any use of nuclear weapons at all in warfare since 1945. Correspondingly, one of the most negative things one might say about counterforce or counterforces strategy is that by removing the fear that war would mean massive harm to whole populations such strategy would make war between the superpowers more possible. Again, it could be argued that the former kind of strategy is the more moral, since it depends on the *retaliatory* capacity of our own thermonuclear weapons and thus is truly defensive: A counterpopulation attack against an enemy would come only after his own *aggressive* first strike. Counterforce or counterforces stategy on the other hand—this argument continues—is inherently aggressive, since a pre-emptive first strike would be required to destroy an enemy's capacity to attack our own cities and noncombatant population.

Debate over these points is hardly new; yet they do rise again in the context of the cruise missile. Let me make a brief response to the arguments *against* counterforce or counterforces strategy and *for* counterpopulation "balance of terror" or MAD strategy.

First, the claim that the balance of terror has prevented thermonuclear war is extremely difficult to assess. The central question here is whether a counterforce/counterforces strategy would be as successful a deterrent. It is hard to see why not, since the destruction of an enemy's military power would, after all, open his population to direct attacks against which he would have no power to defend, leaving counterpopulation war still a distinct possibility in the absence of surrender. Thus the deterrent effect of fear of counterpopulation war would remain, but the possibility of resort to such war would be removed to second place.

A related question is whether and to what degree strategic policy is determined by consideration of possible harm to noncombatants as op-

posed to possible destruction of one's own war-making capacity relative
to that of the enemy. Clausewitz argued in *On War*, Book I, that the
enemy's military "should first be destroyed, then the country subdued,"
and there is no reason to think that contemporary strategic planning has
strayed far from such a priority. The aim of counterpopulation strategy is
to destroy military power by undermining resolve to use it through the
threat to population centers; counterforce or counterforces strategy aims
directly at the military power. In short, there is little or no reason to think
that counterforce or counterforces strategy based on the high accuracy
and relative invulnerability of the cruise missile would be a less effective
deterrent to thermonuclear war between the superpowers than the counterpopulation strategies of the past.

As to the matter of the supposed moral superiority of a retaliatory strike
as opposed to a first strike, the difference between first and second use of
force is not the same as the distinction between defense and aggression.
Admittedly, recent international law places an onus on first use of force,
while condoning, tacitly or explicitly, second use. But the moral tradition
of the just war is not so simplistic, admitting that it is sometimes justified
for a state to make first use of force in defense against an enemy who
clearly intends an unjust, aggressive military action against it. By putting
the emphasis on priority of use of force, international law obscures or
ignores the question of justice, which has moral priority. Even if counter-
force/counterforces strategy, developed around the cruise missile, envi-
sioned a first strike, this is certainly an insufficient moral argument against
it; the decision whether to launch a pre-emptive first strike against an
enemy may be a justified one, or it may not, depending on circumstances.
By contrast, the decision to launch a counterpopulation attack, whether
by means of a first or a second or later strike, *always* stands under a moral
shadow because of its very nature as a violation of noncombatant life.

If noncombatant immunity (or, in other words, the moral principle of
discrimination) is to be taken seriously in thinking about war, the cruise
missile represents a definite positive movement in weapons development.
After nearly a generation of strategic thought that never strayed far from
the idea of direct attack to enemy population centers, the cruise missile's
claimed capability to penetrate defenses and strike with extreme accuracy
closely delimited target areas opens up seriously the possibility of a strategy based on attacks not aimed at destroying large numbers of citizens of
an enemy country but, instead, at the enemy military power—the legitimate aim of war according not only to Clausewitz but the moral tradition
of just war as well.

**Warheads.**   The V-1 of World War II was armed only with conventional
high explosives—though had the German program to develop the atomic
bomb succeeded, it might also have been the first nuclear missile. But in
either case the nature of this weapon would have remained the same: a

counterpopulation device whose technical limitations fitted its mission of direct destruction of noncombatant persons and property. The new cruise missile, as already argued, is a different sort of weapon entirely, one whose capabilities allow it to be targeted directly against enemy military power. Indeed, the nature of the warheads that can be used for arming it underscores this difference. A few brief comments on the available options must suffice for the moment, since the matter of warheads will be raised again in more detail.

1.  High-yield strategic nuclear warheads. In this case the cruise missile differs morally from current nuclear warhead delivery systems only in its accuracy and ability to penetrate defenses. The same moral problem exists for the cruise missile as for current delivery systems, mitigated only by these two factors. The fact remains that when the target is close to a population center, the very power of strategic warheads implies heavy destruction in the noncombatant areas. But the mitigating factors are important, since they suggest that fewer strategic warheads may be necessary to destroy a given military target, such as a hardened underground missile silo. As a result, the total destruction would be lowered in the area surrounding the intended target. Morally as well as militarily this represents no mean advantage.

2.  Low-yield tactical nuclear warheads. Current delivery systems of such warheads are already both precise and difficult to defend against; such weapons are, furthermore, meant to be employed against enemy military forces, not against noncombatants. So the advantages proffered by the cruise missile seem already to have been reached in the tactical nuclear realm. Indeed, from one perspective the cruise missile appears to offer a definite disadvantage as regards the limitation of war. If deployed for tactical use, it could extend the theatre of operations (if such a term remains relevant) so far beyond the area of actual fighting by troops as to raise substantially the level of destruction to combatant and noncombatant alike. Yet the ability of cruise missiles armed with warheads of the "tactical" type to reach staging areas, arsenals, strategic bases, and so on might also reduce the need for directing large warheads of the strategic variety at such military targets, with the possibility of lowering total intended and collateral destruction.

3.  Conventional high-explosive warheads. If the cruise missile is capable in fact of the accuracy claimed for it, this ability to discriminate between targets at long range appears to enhance the possibility of using conventional high-explosive instead of nuclear warheads for tactical and even some strategic use. The V-1, militarily speaking, was a poor retaliatory answer to obliteration bombing of German cities because of the limited destructive power of its warhead. But morally this limited radius of harm was an advantage; it remains so.

After war is done everybody is a noncombatant, and nuclear war because of its long-term effects represents an inherent violation of noncombatancy. If cruise missiles, because of their cheapness, their accuracy, their ability to penetrate defenses, and their ease of utilization in combat can credibly be armed with conventional high-explosive instead of nuclear warheads, this would be a desirable step back, back onto the path that leads to one of the most ancient principles in the Western tradition on limiting war: the need to avoid wartime destruction that persists in its effects long after the end of the war.

## THE NEUTRON BOMB

The idea of a "death ray" for use in combat is a fantasy of long standing among science fiction writers and fans, as well as among some military people and weapons developers. As it turns out, it is the neutron bomb, or enhanced radiation warhead, and not some laser-like device, that appears to bring that fantasy to reality.

Even in conventional weapons, of course, there is radiation, heat radiation, that can kill or incapacitate, and nuclear devices add the more lethal forms of radiation that result from fission and fusion. But with conventional explosives the effect of the blast is more deadly than that of the heat, and in atomic fission and fusion weapons of the types currently deployed the component of destructiveness related to the blast still balances or outweighs that related to radiation emitted. The neutron bomb alters this balance: Blast effect is intentionally kept small, so as to minimize property damage in the area of detonation, while neutron radiation effect is enhanced, so as to multiply the effect of the warhead on life in the area. Neutron radiation is, moreover, not a long-enduring type, so that the lingering effect of radioactivity would be proportionate to the size of the blast, not the number of people killed or incapacitated by radiation sickness.

This new weapon raises a moral question of utmost importance: What sort of restraints on harm to persons and property in war should be sought? The past gives us, broadly speaking, two different kinds of answers. One, which Paul Ramsey has identified as central to the Christian just-war tradition, begins with the *principle of charity.* The other, which can be called the *principle of civilization,* can be identified in contemporary international law and recent military doctrine but is best understood by means of the theory and practice of limited war in the eighteenth century, when the idea of civilization first appeared as a conscious principle of restraint in war.

**The Principle of Charity.**   This principle, as Ramsey defines it, expresses itself via two intermediate concepts, an absolute principle of discrimination and a relative principle of proportion. The Christian just-war idea associated with these concepts both permits violence in the service of Christian love and limits that violence in direction and extent.

Simplifying greatly: In war the principle of discrimination prohibits all direct, intended harm to those not actively participating in the waging of war. This is noncombatant immunity defined in terms of *function,* excluding, as Ramsey puts it in *The Just War* (1968), "persons in command positions . . . even though they wear tweed suits" and all civilians who are in close material cooperation. It is also an *absolute* definition of noncombatant immunity: noncombatants may never be proceeded against in order to reach combatants through them. The only harm they may receive, according to this charity-based principle of discrimination, is that which is indirect and unintentional. Accordingly, counterpopulation warfare is not a moral possibility.

Ramsey identifies the principle of proportion as secondary to that of discrimination; it defines the level and extent of the harm that can morally be done where any harm at all is permitted. This principle thus bears heavily on matters such as weapons limitation and specific tactical use of given weapons. It is a relative principle, defining allowable destruction in war in terms of response to what has been done or what is intended.

The result of understanding these two principles in this way can be put through a simple example. One justification offered at the time of the atomic bombing of Hiroshima and Nagasaki was that the total number of deaths caused by the bombs was less than the number that would have been caused by continuing the war to a finish by conventional means. This judgment depends on a version of the principle of proportion; it must be rejected, on the terms defined by Ramsey, since the atomic attacks were counterpopulation attacks, whose intent and purpose was the destruction of noncombatants. The absolute immunity of noncombatants from direct, intentional attack takes moral priority over calculations of relative damage. Thus it is conceivable that charity might require, in some cases, more deaths than a moral system that put prior weight on proportion, since human death as such is not what charity seeks to avoid. Its focus is rather upon distinguishing allowable harm, including death as the extreme possibility, from that which is not allowable; thus the directly intended death of any and all combatants is, in the extreme, permitted, but that of any one noncombatant is to be avoided.

What does this perspective imply in the case of the neutron bomb? The purpose of this weapon is to kill or incapacitate persons in the target area within a short time after detonation while leaving minimal residual radiation and causing limited property damage. In practice, people would be incapacitated by radiation sickness within minutes or hours, followed by the death of most persons affected within a day. *All* persons in the target area who are not protected against neutron radiation will suffer these effects; the weapon is indiscriminate over its area of effectiveness.

But charity requires that combatants be distinguished from noncombatants in war. According to Ramsey the permission to harm the former follows from the desire to protect the latter, and the permission that is granted is strictly limited: Not only must the noncombatant never be harmed directly and intentionally, even the combatant may be harmed only in proportion to the evil attempted and only so much as necessary to prevent his succeeding in his aim. Not only would the effect of the neutron warhead be felt by all people within the target area; this effect, serious radiation sickness and/or death to all unprotected people in that area, would be of the most serious kind. This suggests that this weapon is not only indiscriminate but disproportionate.

Yet discrimination, in Ramsey's terms, means the absence of *direct, intentional* attack on noncombatants. It can be granted that some weapons are more capable of being used discriminately than others; at the lower end of the scale of destructiveness, for example, a rifle can be used with more discrimination than a shotgun or machine gun. While discrimination remains a *moral* term defining the *choice* made in a particular instance to use a given weapon or not, or to use it one way as opposed to another, the adaptability of the weapon to discriminating use is also morally relevant. In this regard the enhanced radiation warhead may have an advantage not possessed by the tactical nuclear and high-explosive warheads it presumably would displace. But to explore this we must leave behind the idea that direct, intentional attack means also *immediate effect:* we must consider the long-term effects on noncombatants that can be foreseen and calculated, and which can therefore be weighed in the scales of directness and intentionality.

What distinguishes the neutron warhead from the other types it would replace is the relatively smaller long-term effect it is asserted to have. Let us consider a situation in which the target is a certain military force, located in an area from which the noncombatants have fled. Here the possibility of immediate, direct, intentional harm to noncombatants is lacking and the principle of discrimination is therefore satisfied. But the blast damage caused by conventional high explosives and tactical nuclear warheads of sufficient number to perform the military mission, plus the residual radiation left behind by the latter weapons, would substantially outweigh that caused by neutron warheads in sufficient numbers. I suggest that blast damage and/or residual radiation of dangerous levels must be considered also in determining whether any nondiscriminating harm to noncombatants has occurred. After the wave of war has passed and the noncombatant inhabitants return to their homes and work, the destruction and radiation danger they will encounter, which will undoubtedly affect them in their attempts to pick up their lives once again, become significant factors in answering the question whether the attack was one in which direct damage to noncombatants was part of the intention that led to it. From the perspective of discrimination the long-term effects of particular weapons are thus important, as the amount and types of such effects help to determine whether the intention was in fact to damage noncombatants, either immediately or through the lasting impact of the weapon on their lives, or whether the damage caused to noncombatants was, by the moral rule of double effect, a secondary and indirect result of a permitted action against combatants. In cases such as the one sketched here there does seem to exist the possibility that the neutron warhead can be used with moral discrimination, as opposed to current tactical nuclear warheads and even conventional high explosives.

Shifting perspective to the question of proportionality, the same considerations can be employed to argue that the total level of damage is likely to be less with the neutron warhead than with the other two types it would displace. The effect upon military personnel is, of course, expected to be as great with the new weapon as with other types; its advantage over conventional high-explosive and current tactical nuclear warheads is lowered damage to property, while compared to the latter weapons it also promises less long-term danger to life from radiation left behind after the blast. If the total effect on the belligerent populations and those people in particular whose homes and livelihoods are found in the combat area is taken into account, the new weapon emerges as possibly a more proportionate means of waging modern war.

Still, from the perspective of the principle of charity, the question of discrimination remains prior. With the principle of civilization, as we shall see, the priorities are considerably altered, with the result the principal stress on proportionality. Since the argument from proportion is the same in either case, it is better taken up in fuller detail below.

**The Principle of Civilization.** This terms is borrowed from Georg Schwarzenberger, who employs it in his *A Manual of International Law* (1967) to identify the principle of restraint in international law on war that opposes the principle of military necessity. . . .

[T]he best way to understand [the principle of civilization] is to approach it through the past. Conscious realization of the need to protect the values of a common civilization appears to have dawned upon Europeans in the eighteenth century. Emmerich de Vattel, writing in the late 1730's, decried (without recalling biblical precedent) the uprooting of vines and the cutting down of fruit trees, acts that leave a country desolate for many years after a war and that cannot be dictated by prudence or necessity but only by "hatred and fury" (*The Law of Nations,* Book III, Section 166). In the next breath he denounced the bombardment, spoliation, burning, or other defacement of "fine edifices" that "do honour to human society, and do not contribute to the enemy's power." Justifying this, he added: "He who [destroys such edifices] thus declares himself an enemy to mankind" (Section 168). Here it is the interests and values of society that must be maintained, not those of some poorly understood abstraction: "mankind" for Vattel was not the "humanity" of contemporary international law but the "human society" that he personally knew and inhabited.

Such a concept was not merely to be found in a theoretical writer on international law like Vattel; it was expressed in the eighteenth-century pattern of limited warfare, in which the maintenance of cultural stability was a higher goal than any justifying *cause de guerre* of an eighteenth-century sovereign. This idea of the proper scope of warfare disappeared from fashion with the wars of the French Revolution and Napoleon. Two developments aided the process: the rise of large national armies fired with patriotic zeal, who replace relatively small bodies of paid professionals motivated by love for the color of the sovereign's gold, and the conceptualization of "absolute war" by Clausewitz early in the nineteenth century. Recent wars have paralleled the national wars of the Napoleonic period, with high levels of ideological fervor justifying extreme measures in combat. The strategies of massive counterpopulation warfare that have predominated since World War II reflect this conception of war, and the enormous destructive capabilities of thermonuclear weapons are the best tools yet devised to implement the desire to destroy the enemy totally in the service of the high cause of one's own nation.

It is only in a context of limited warfare that the neutron warhead makes any sense. . . .

[But] there are serous questions as to whether such limited warfare is realistically conceivable under present conditions. To make it so would require the disappearance of the ideological rivalry that has in the past fueled the notion that any war between the superpowers must be a total struggle to the death of one or both. And it would require that reliance upon weapons and strategies of massive counterpopulation destruction give way to others appropriate to lower and more discriminating levels of combat. In connection with this latter requisite, some effective restraint would have to be found to prevent a limited conflict from escalating into a total one. The question of the level of ideological hatred or the question of an effective firebreak aside, the enhanced-radiation warhead appears to be a weapon that would fit well into a contemporary version of the limited war idea outlined above.

This is especially pertinent in reference to possible warfare between NATO and Warsaw Pact forces on the European continent. As compared to currently deployed tactical atomic warheads, the neutron warhead holds the promise of an encounter between the two armies that, though still killing large numbers of people, would maintain the physical infrastructures of life relatively undamaged.

What this might mean in reality must not, of course, be conceived in utopian terms: The neutron warhead remains, fundamentally, a tactical atomic weapon, and NATO use of such warheads in combat would almost certainly bring Warsaw Pact use of its own nonenhanced radiation tactical atomic weapons. Thus the advantages claimed for the neutron device (less property damage and lower amounts of residual radiation) would in significant degree be lost; further, even a European war with only contemporary conventional (i.e., nonnuclear) weaponry could be enormously destructive, as World War II testifies; and finally, the loss of life such war would bring has to be taken with great seriousness.

Ideally, perhaps, the weapons of war would only temporarily incapacitate and not leave any lasting harm to persons, property, and the artifacts of past civilization; such "clean" war is not the prospect held out by the neutron bomb. Rather, it offers the possibility of a war in which life might be totally annihilated, while the shells of cities and towns, with transportation arteries, factories, household appliances intact, would remain. The enormous loss of life in World War I brought upheaval in European society; it is difficult to foresee what human society would become in the aftermath of a land war fought with neutron warheads. Only compared to the alternative of an all-out strategic nuclear exchange would such a war be a limited one.

**Restraints on Harm to Persons and Property: Some Final Reflections.**
It is tempting but inaccurate to identify the principle of discrimination based in Christian charity with prior concern for protection of persons while associating the principle of proportion that is determined by the value of civilization with protection of property. But in fact, as argued above, protection of property is also an aim included in discrimination; and proportion, in the sense this term acquires in the context of limited war theory and practice, may include the total destruction of not only people but property in the theatre of war. The real distinction is to be found in the difference between discrimination and proportion themselves: The former, when based in charity, requires an absolute distinction between combatant and noncombatant, and no direct, intended harm to the latter; and proportion, when based in the principle of civilization, requires an assessment of the costs before any military operation is undertaken, any new weapon deployed, or any existing weapon used. This is a difference of profound nature, signifying the difference of intent between the just-war idea, as Ramsey presents it, and the idea of limited war whose classic definition is provided by eighteenth-century theory and practice. Though it is possible to conceive of a situation in which the neutron warhead could be used in accord with the charitable principle of discrimination, it is nevertheless true that the limited-war principle of proportion would allow neutron bomb warfare in a wider variety of circumstances, still according to the overall moral value of preserving civilization. What is one to say about this difference?

In the first place, the binding force of Christian morality is felt only by Christians. While reflection on the requirements of charity should be part of the process by which a Christian statesman or military officer reaches a decision, it is difficult to argue that the policy choices of a morally pluralistic nation should be guided by Christian morality. Where the judgment of the majority of citizens is influenced by such considerations, though, and this judgment is made known in the public forum, we have another matter entirely. For this reason it is incumbent on every individual to consider, from his own moral perspective, the implications of weapons systems and strategies, new and old.

But it is also true that through most of its history the implications of Christian teaching on war have not been understood as Ramsey presents them, utilizing an analysis of Augustine and Thomas Aquinas. Historically, the just-war tradition developed not only alongside of but intermingled with the limited-war tradition, and the restraints imposed by the Church at times were less restrictive than those resting on secular bases. There is some reason, then, for even a Christian to reflect seriously on the implications of the concept of limited war, in spite of the concept's prior emphasis on proportionality and its relegation of the principle of discrimination to an idea based in geography. The reason follows from the historical nature of moral traditions, which preserve the experience of a community of people professing common moral values in its ongoing existence through time. This means understanding Ramsey's interpretation of the just-war idea as but one expression within the overall tradition, and it also means taking seriously those periods in which just-war thinking imposed weaker restrictions on permissible violence than were imposed by other sources. Further, it means not forgetting that out-and-out syncretism between secular and religious thought on war made modern international law possible by creating, by the dawn of the modern period, a unified doctrine expressing cultural consensus on limiting war. Because of this last consideration it is wrong, in the final analysis, to think of the principle of civilization found in the limited war concept and in international law as something entirely separate from Christian moral tradition. Their intermingled history makes such a sharp distinction impossible, even for the eighteenth-century Age of Enlightenment. How far it is appropriate in our own time depends on the weight given traditional concepts and principles of war.

Though as a weapon it is far from ideal for keeping at a minimum the damage of war to civilization, the enhanced radiation warhead represents movement toward such a goal when we make the comparison with the other weapons of contemporary warfare it is designed to replace. The neutron bomb is also clearly within the limited-war tradition that allows noncombatant destruction within zones while attempting to preserve noncombatants from harm elsewhere. In these respects it is preferable to the weapons it would replace, especially when the factor of long-term damage is considered.

It is this moralist's judgment that the neutron warhead, like the cruise missile, represents a morally significant alternative for planning and actually fighting war, should war become inevitable.

# Statement on Disarmament

## The Roman Catholic Church

The armaments race is to be condemned unreservedly. By virtue of the nature of modern weapons and the situation prevailing on our planet, even when motivated by a concern for legitimate defense, the armaments race is in fact:

**A Danger.**   In terms of the possible total or partial use of these weapons or the threat thereof, with deterrence, carried to the point of blackmail, accepted as the norm in relations with other nations.

**An Injustice.**   For it constitutes a violation of law by asserting the primacy of force and a form of theft. The massive budgets allocated to the manufacture and stockpiling of weapons is tantamount to misappropriation of funds by the "managers" of the large nations or favored blocs.

The obvious contradiction between the waste involved in the overproduction of military devices and the extent of unsatisfied vital needs is in itself an act of aggression against those who are the victims of it (in both developing countries and in the marginal and poor elements in rich societies). It is an act of aggression which amounts to a crime, for even when they are not used, by their cost alone, armaments kill the poor by causing them to starve.

The condemnation by the Council, reiterated by the 1974 Synod, is understandable: "The armaments race is an extremely grave affliction for humanity and does intolerable harm to the poor."

**A Mistake.**   One of the chief arguments ordinarily invoked in favor of the armaments race is the economic crisis and unemployment which would result from the closure of military factories and arsenals. That would be true if there were to be constant redeployments. The conversion of military manufacturing plants and military markets for civilian purposes is equally possible, if trouble is taken to plan ahead. It is all the more feasible in that it would create jobs by making it possible to undertake the large-scale projects which prove necessary for the protection of the environment and the satisfaction of other human needs.

This statement of the Holy See on disarmament was a response to the United Nations document of May 7, 1976 entitled "Strengthening of the Role of the United Nations in the Field of Disarmament." References to "the Council" are to Vatican II. Quotations without a noted source are from earlier church documents.

**A Wrong.**   Refusal to undertake this conversion "is completely incompatible with the spirit of humanity and still more with the spirit of Christianity" because "it is unthinkable that no other work can be found for hundreds of thousands of workers than the production of instruments of death" (Paul VI, speech to the Diplomatic Corps, February 10, 1972).

**Folly.**   This system of international relations, based on fear, danger and injustice, is a kind of collective hysteria, a folly that will be judged by history. It is meaningless because it is a means which does not achieve its end. The armaments race does not ensure security.

In the case of nuclear weapons, it does not afford any additional security because there is already a surplus of such instruments (overkill); it creates additional risks by introducing elements of instability which could upset the "balance of terror."

As to traditional weapons, their proliferation (especially in the Third World countries with trade in arms) creates regional imbalances and can thus generate conflicts or fuel those in progress.

In any case, whether it is a matter of nuclear weapons or traditional weapons, of great or small powers, the armaments race has become a cumulative process, which has its own dynamics, independent of any aggressive feelings, and which escapes the control of states. It is a machine gone mad.

It is often said of disarmament that it is a "worn out" or "tired cause" because of its many failures. It is said, for example, that there has been too much talk about it, for too long a time, without any visible results.

But is it not rather the cause of armament that is worn out? Is it not the premise underlying the armaments race that gives further proof that it is antiquated and anachronistic? If one gauges the success or effectiveness of armaments by the peace they achieve, would it not be more appropriate to speak of failure?

The Council is categorical. It absolutely condemns the use of weapons of mass destruction. It is, in fact, the only "excommunication" to be found in the Council documents.

"Endorsing the condemnations of total war already expressed by recent Popes, this Holy Synod declares: Any act of war aimed indiscriminately at the destruction of entire cities . . . and their inhabitants, is a crime against God and against humanity itself, which must be condemned firmly and without hesitation."

As to deterrence, "If it has served, paradoxically, to deter possible adversaries" this can be seen at the very most as "a delay granted us from on high," in short, a respite which we must "use to advantage" and very quickly, because time is not on our side. "By accumulating weapons, far from eliminating the causes of war we are in danger of gradually increasing them. . . . Instead of actually defusing conflicts between nations, we are spreading the contagion to other parts of the world."

This armed competition can therefore only be viewed as a means of transition from "the ancient servitude of war" to a new system, a new solution, new "methods which will enable us to settle our differences in a manner worthier of humanity."

Otherwise this mad armaments race will maintain a false peace, a false security. It will become an end rather than the means it had the illusion of being. It will perpetuate the established disorder. It will be a perversion of peace.

Whether or not the time seems right, Christians, following the Vicar of Christ, must denounce humanity's scientific preparations for its own demise. They must also alert public opinion to the growing perils resulting from nuclear excesses (explosions) and from the transport, stockpiling and proliferation of atomic weapons. "Humankind, already in great peril, runs the risk, despite its admirable scientific knowledge, of reaching the fatal point at which it will no longer be able to experience any peace but the formidable peace of death."

The severity of the diagnosis is thus clear. In the eyes of the Church, the present situation of would-be security is to be condemned in the name of peace, which it does not ensure. Particularly on account of atomic weapons: "Let these shameful weapons be banned" and "let this terrible art, which consists in manufacturing, multiplying and storing bombs to terrorize the people . . . be outlawed. . . . Let us pray that this murderous device does not kill peace while seeking it" (Paul VI, Message on the Twentieth Anniversary of Hiroshima, August 8, 1965).

It must also be condemned in the name of natural morality and the ideal of the Gospels: The armaments race is against humanity and against God. This mad race must therefore be outlawed from the standpoint of ethics, for two main reasons:

1.  When the damage caused is disproportionate to the values we are seeking to safeguard, "it is better to suffer injustice than to defend ourselves" (Pius XII). We still have the right and the duty of active, albeit nonviolent, resistance to unjust oppression, in the name of human rights and human dignity.

It is no longer merely a matter of cold war, but of an offensive action, of an inadmissible aggression and oppression: "The power of arms does not legitimize any use of this force for political and military ends."

2.  It constitutes a provocation which explains—psychologically, economically, and politically—the emergence and growth of another kind of competition: the small armaments race. Terrorism, in fact, often appears to be the last means of defense against this abuse of power by the large nations and a violent protest against the injustice created or perpetuated by the use of threat thereof on the part of better-armed states.

This use of big weapons by the industrialized states has also had the effect of involving the developing countries in a similar armaments race. An increasing portion of the military budgets of certain less-favored countries further retards their economic growth. The rise of authoritarian political regimes in the Third World is both the cause and the effect of increased purchases (and hence, sales) of weapons by the industrial powers.

This use of financial resources for military purposes means, on the other hand, a slowing down or reduction of aid. It renders more difficult the transfer of resources so often desired and requested by Paul VI.

This would not be the case if the nations which had the greatest resources in the field of armaments finally agreed to slow down and then stop pursuing the armaments race as a means of achieving hegemony, and not simply as a means of protecting the property and lives of their nationals.

Paul VI's solemn entreaty to the representatives of all the world's peoples, in his address to the United Nations on October 4, 1965, is more timely and valid than ever: "Let the weapons fall from your hands."

Thus the duty is just as clear as the diagnosis: The armaments race must be stopped.

Can the Church, for its part, go no further in its recommendations and teaching?

Can no other solutions be found to break out of this vicious circle and cast off the spell of mistrust?

In the quarter century following the last world war, have not a certain number of reconciliations called in question the premise that security rests solely on military strength? Have not historians and politicians been surprised to see that the reasons behind these catastrophic historic clashes amounted to very little, and to see how little was also needed to turn hostility into collaboration? If war is the meeting point of two fears, is not peace the outcome of two confidences restored, or to be restored as soon as possible, before setting in motion the process of military escalation?

Are not the times we are living in conducive to this kind of outlook?

Will not the peoples engaged in the insane quantitative and qualitative armaments race eventually stop from exhaustion like athletes in a running race? Has not the time come to make use of opposites and to transform the excess of war or threats into the conquest and preservation of peace?

Disarmament is not a separate reality, a separate "thing in itself." It is part of a whole. It must, of course, be envisaged for its own sake and with its own methods, out of a concern for scientific, legal, political and spiritual clarity. It calls for and requires appropriate techniques, disciplines and people. It must, however, at all times, be viewed and achieved in close connection with the two other great realities of the day: the development and organization of international society. Disarm, develop, institutionalize: one and the same problem, one and the same solution.

Only the pressure and common sense of public opinion can avert the emergence of two parallel and often contradictory histories: the history of civilizations and the history of dehumanizing military or civilian technologies.

The role of political groups (parties in power or in opposition, press representing political opinion, etc.) should be decisive in guiding the foreign policy of their governments in a peaceful direction.

In this "general assent of nations whereby all war can be completely prohibited," scientists have a very special role to play. Pope Paul VI makes an urgent appeal to them: "Humankind must collect itself, and try to find within itself, in its leaders and in its teachers, the strength and wisdom to reject the maleficent uses of destructive science. . . . Rather, it should ask science the secret of doing good to itself" (Address to the Pontifical Academy of Science, April 27, 1968).

Disarmament is not simply a matter of good will. It cannot be improvised. It will be costly, as in the case of tearing down an old building in order to replace it by a new one. The conversion of the armaments industries, and the armaments trade in particular, is a matter for technologists. It requires "extensive and bold study."

A "disarmament strategy" cannot be confined to criteria of efficiency or profitability. It must be based on ethical, cultural and spiritual considerations. It will call, in future years, for profound reflection on the part of philosophers and theologians, particularly concerning the concepts of "self-defense," "nation," and of national sovereignty, which is all too often viewed in terms of absolute autarky.

It will also need "prophets," provided they are genuine: people who speak out—"heralds," catalysts and "mystics," in both the broad and the narrow sense of the word—to enlist and mobilize energies and their potential for unity, dialogue and cooperation.

In short, the basis and motive force of disarmament is "mutual confidence." Recourse to war can be replaced only by "dynamics of peace."

Disarmament requires, as a first condition, not the suppression, but the sublimation of warlike instincts of people (as hunter, plunderer, dominator) by engaging all in the service "of the civil construction of peace."

We must find substitutes for war, by providing alternative wars to be won. Disarmament is inseparable from the other goals of unity, justice, harmony and development of the whole human family.

The victory of disarmament is none other than the victory of peace. Its only chance lies in being incorporated into the grand design, the "new history" of humankind.

# 12

# Capital Punishment

One of the greatest concerns of the public in recent years has been the growing incidence of crime. Many residents of cities in the United States have become so fearful that they have turned their homes into armed camps, and many more dare not walk the streets at night. This situation has increased the demand for stronger laws as well as for more stringent police enforcement. But the public seems to have relatively little concern for, and understanding of, the effectiveness of our criminal justice system and its impact on attempts to maintain civil order and peace. Of the many problems and disputed issues in this area, one that has been perennially debated is capital punishment.

Does the state have the right to take life in an act of retributive justice? People appealing to the Bible have responded both Yes and No to this question. Those who find support for the death penalty cite Genesis 9:6 ("Whoever sheds the blood of man, by man shall his blood be shed . . .") as the Old Testament sanction. Others view this verse on the background of Genesis 4–6, which deals with corruption and taking vengeance, and see the verse as stating a fact and a limitation, rather than advocating vengeance. The law of talion (legal retaliation) is seen as a concession, rather than the divine will that life be taken. In the New Testament, a verse used in support of capital punishment has been Saint Paul's statement that the government "does not bear the sword in vain" (Romans 13:4). Whether this verse actually refers to the death penalty has been debated. Paul is speaking of the state's right to govern, and some argue that his use of the word "sword" refers to judicial authority, not to the sword used by Roman authorities in executing criminals (which is a different Greek term than the one Paul used).

Those arguing against the death penalty on biblical grounds note that the one direct reference to this subject is found in John 8, where Jesus addresses the woman guilty of a capital offense. He does not deny that the Mosaic law condemns her, but he questions the moral authority of those who would judge and execute her ("Let him who is without sin among you be the first to throw a stone at her") and introduces his authority to forgive sin. Such an incident illustrates the difficulty in attempting to find in particular passages a direct answer to a social issue. If one were to take the primary message of the New Testament as the forgiving, reconciling love of God in Christ Jesus, how would one relate this message to the issue of capital punishment?

The problem becomes one of relating the legitimate concern of the state to dispense justice to a higher vision of human relationships marked by love and reconciliation. In a criminal justice system, these ideals would presumably express themselves in the development of a system of rehabilitation that would reclaim the lives of offenders, not simply incarcerate or execute them. Many argue on utilitarian grounds for this rehabilitative approach, claiming that any added expense would be more than repaid in the long run when offenders are regained as productive members of society. The present system, in other words, does not really serve the best interests of society. Proponents of capital punishment, on the other hand, argue that those who take life have in effect forfeited the right to have their "ultimate welfare" taken seriously by the state. The state should take no risk in preserving the welfare of society by removing the offender "for good."

In recent years the death penalty has caused growing discontent in churches that have historically maintained its legitimacy. In the Roman Catholic Church, for example, moral theologians have questioned the appropriateness of the death penalty in light of their church's position on abortion. Does not a "pro-life" position challenge other forms of life taking, as in war or capital punishment? This is an argument on grounds of principle, affirming the sanctity of life and its inviolable character. Others have raised questions on utilitarian grounds, looking at the effects of capital punishment in maintaining a society relatively free of violent crime. Here the lack of evidence demonstrating the effectiveness of capital punishment as a deterrent to crime has raised further questions about its appropriateness. Another factor that has led to much disenchantment with the death penalty is the apparent injustice of our whole system of criminal justice, which consigns to death row an inordinately large proportion of the poor and members of racial minorities. Evidence of this fact was established in an investigation of death row in North Carolina, the state with the greatest number of persons sentenced to die (roughly one-third of the national total). Of those condemned, 65 percent were black and, by the court's own definition, 62 percent were poor.

As Hugo A. Bedau notes in the first selection of this chapter, the legal setting for the current discussion was established in the 1970s with two Supreme Court decisions. The first one in 1972 (*Furman v. Georgia*) ruled that the death penalty as it was imposed and carried out constituted "cruel and unusual punishment." In the second of two decisions in 1976 (*Gregg v. Georgia*), the Supreme Court ruled that the sentence of death "does not invariably violate the Constitution." Many thought that the court's decision in 1972 was a first step toward the abolition of the death penalty, but the 1976 decision repudiated that assumption. It made clear that the issue was not the inherent cruelty of the death sentence, but the need for "objective standards to guide, regularize, and make rationally reviewable" the manner in which the death sentence is imposed. Since these decisions the states have been busy establishing standards that would legitimize the death penalty.

Bedau's article, written on behalf of the American Civil Liberties Union and distributed by it, is a vigorous attack on the death penalty based on "two facts": its failure to deter crime and its inherent unfairness. Others have joined these arguments with the question whether our history in recent years has not been marked by a civilizing influence that has placed capital punishment increasingly under moral judgment. Is a growing sensitivity to the inviolable character of life denied in this act? Bedau notes a developing trend in the decisions of other countries to abolish the death penalty, but apprehension over a growing crime rate has fueled support for capital punishment in the United States.

Diametrically opposed to Bedau on this issue is Ernest van den Haag. The differences in their judgments of what is morally acceptable are sufficiently great to make one wonder whether the two of them could communicate on this subject. For example, Bedau finds the possibility of putting an innocent person to death so abhorrent that he challenges the fundamental notion of capital punishment; van den Haag is willing to take in stride a certain measure of unavoidable capriciousness or accident which might result in injustice and even the death of an innocent person. He accuses the opponents of capital punishment of engaging in a sham argument when they point out inequalities in the administration of this penalty, for that is not the essential moral question. Bedau, on the other hand, sees these inequalities as reinforcing reasons of principle as he seeks to utilize every argument that may speak to those uncertain about this issue. The ultimate difference between these two arguments, as van den Haag perceives it, involves the value put on life. He asks, "Does a social value system in which life itself, however it is lived, becomes the highest of goods enhance the value of human life or cheapen it?" To van den Haag, vengeance in the form of taking the life of one who has taken life is not barbaric, but a means of affirming the value of human life.

# The Case Against the Death Penalty

Hugo A. Bedau

## INTRODUCTION

On January 17, 1977, Gary Mark Gilmore was killed by a firing squad in Utah and thereby became the first person to be legally executed anywhere in the nation in nearly ten years. That executions would resume was all but guaranteed when, six months earlier, the Supreme Court upheld the constitutionality of capital punishment. Thus, the national experiment with abolition of capital punishment is, at least temporarily, at an end.

In 1967, all executions were suspended by the federal courts pending the resolution of various constitutional objections to capital punishment. In 1972, with more than 600 persons under death sentence in 32 states, the Supreme Court declared that under the existing laws "the imposition and carrying out of the death penalty . . . constitutes cruel and unusual punishment in violation of the Eighth and Fourteenth Amendments." (*Furman v. Georgia*, 408 U.S. 238) To make the nationwide impact of its decision unmistakable, the Court also summarily reversed death sentences in the many cases then before it, involving a tremendous range of statutes, crimes, and fact situations.

In the immediate aftermath of the *Furman* decision, many commentators made much of the narrowness of the victory and the lack of firm consensus among the five-man majority on the Court. The ACLU [American Civil Liberties Union] and other groups opposed to capital punishment were encouraged by the agreement among the majority Justices on several major points:

1. The majority agreed that the death penalty is cruel and unusual punishment because it is imposed infrequently and under no clear standards;
2. The majority agreed that the purpose of the death penalty, whether it be retribution or deterrence, cannot be achieved when it is so rarely and unpredictably used;
3. The majority agreed that one purpose of the Eighth and Fourteenth Amendments is to bar legislatures from imposing punishments that, because of the way they are administered, serve no valid social purpose;

Reprinted by courtesy of Professor Hugo Adam Bedau and the American Civil Liberties Union. Hugo A. Bedau is Austin B. Fletcher Professor of Philosophy at Tufts University. He is the author of several books on political philosophy and on capital punishment, including *The Courts, the Constitution, and Capital Punishment* (1977).

4. All the Court, with the exception of Justice William Rehnquist, expressed personal opposition to capital punishment;
5. All the Court, again excepting Justice Rehnquist, expressed the belief that capital sentencing is arbitrary and disbelief that it is uniquely effective in deterring crime.

Only two Justices, Thurgood Marshall and William Brennan, were willing to find the death penalty *per se* unconstitutional. The other three Justices in the majority concentrated their objections on the way death penalty laws were applied, finding the result so "harsh, freakish, and arbitrary" as to be constitutionally unacceptable.

In the four years after *Furman,* however, public opinion, legislative backlash, and trial court sentencing all combined to undermine the *Furman* ruling. The seeds for these developments were evident in *Furman* itself, because the Court did not strike down all possible forms of capital punishment legislation.

After the *Furman* decision, more than 600 persons were convicted and sentenced to death under new capital punishment statutes enacted by legislatures in thirty states and designed to meet the Court's objections. These laws took two basic forms. About half the legislatures enacted statutes that made the death penalty mandatory for certain specified crimes. In other states, a bifurcated or two-stage trial procedure was established, in which the jury was first to determine guilt or innocence, and then to choose imprisonment or death in the light of certain aggravating or mitigating circumstances.

In July 1976, the Supreme Court ruled again on the death penalty, attempting to alleviate some of the confusion that had resulted from the *Furman* decision. In *Woodson v. North Carolina,* the Court declared that the mandatory death penalty for first degree murder was unconstitutional under the Eighth and Fourteenth Amendments. In a plurality opinion for the Court, Justice Potter Stewart argued that mandatory death statutes treat all persons convicted of a given offence "not as uniquely individual human beings, but as members of a faceless, undifferentiated mass to be subjected to the blind infliction of the penalty of death." Prisoners who had been sentenced to death under such statutes are being resentenced to life imprisonment.

At the same time, in *Gregg v. Georgia,* the Court moved in the opposite direction, holding that "the punishment of death does not invariably violate the Constitution." The Court upheld the "guided-discretion" type of statute, requiring "objective standards to guide, regularize, and make rationally reviewable the process for imposing the sentence of death."

The chief effect of these rulings was a clarification of the *Furman* holding favorable to those who believe the death penalty is constitutionally

permissible. Of the two obvious statutory possibilities left open by *Furman*
—mandatory and guided-discretion death sentencing—the latter has been
affirmed by the Court as an acceptable alternative. Thus the states as well
as Congress have before them authoritative statutory models for death
penalty legislation, and one must expect to see several legislatures enact
death penalties patterned after those the Court upheld in Georgia,
Florida, and Texas. At the same time, the Court's decisions have brought
prisoners sentenced to death under such statutes to the very threshold of
execution.

Despite the Supreme Court's 1976 ruling in *Gregg v. Georgia*, a severe
setback to efforts to declare the death penalty unconstitutional, the ACLU
continues to oppose capital punishment on moral and practical, as well as
on constitutional, grounds:

1. Capital punishment is cruel and unusual. It is a relic of the earliest days
   of penology, when slavery, branding, and other corporal punishments
   were commonplace. Like those other barbaric practices, it has no place
   in a civilized society.
2. Capital punishment denies due process of law. Its imposition is arbitrary
   and irrevocable. It forever deprives an individual of the benefits of new
   law or new evidence that might affect a conviction.
3. The worst and most dangerous criminals are rarely the ones executed.
   The death penalty is applied randomly at best and discriminatorily at
   worst. It violates the constitutional guarantee of the equal protection of
   the laws because it is imposed almost exclusively against members of
   racial minorities, the poor, the uneducated—persons who are victims of
   overt discrimination in the sentencing process or who are unable to afford
   the expert and dedicated legal counsel that is available to those with
   means.
4. The moral and constitutional defects in death penalty laws are not appreciably altered by shifting from mandatory to discretionary sentencing, or
   from unfettered discretion to guided discretion. These changes are
   largely cosmetic. They only mask the underlying arbitrariness of a criminal procedure where death is a possible penalty.
5. Executions in prison give society the unmistakable message that life
   ceases to be sacred when it is thought useful to take it and that violence
   is legitimate when it is thought justified by pragmatic concerns that appeal to those having the legal power to kill.
6. Reliance on the death penalty obscures the true causes of crime and
   distracts attention from the effective resources of society to control it.
7. Capital punishment is wasteful of resources, demanding a disproportionate expenditure of time and energy by courts, prosecuting attorneys,
   defense attorneys, juries, courtroom and correctional personnel; it burdens unduly the system of criminal justice, and it is therefore counterproductive as an instrument for society's control of violent crime. It
   epitomizes the tragic inefficacy and brutality of the resort to violence
   rather than reason for the solution of difficult social problems.

Two facts—plainly recognized by the majority opinions of the Supreme Court in *Furman* and *Woodson,* and not refuted in *Gregg*—buttress our entire case: *capital punishment does not deter crime, and the death penalty in theory and in practice is unfair and inequitable.*

## DETERRENCE

The argument most often cited in support of capital punishment is that it deters capital crimes more effectively than terms of imprisonment. This theory is founded on wish, not fact. The argument against the deterrent efficacy of the death penalty takes three mutually supportive forms.

1.   Any punishment can be an effective deterrent only if it is consistently and promptly employed. Capital punishment does not meet those conditions. Only a small proportion of first-degree murderers is sentenced to death, and even fewer are executed.

Between 1930 and 1960 there was one execution for every 70 homicides. During the decade 1951–1960, nine out of ten persons convicted of first-degree murder were not executed, and in the decade of the 1960s executions became still rarer. In the 1970s, with an annual average of nearly 20,000 homicides, death sentences averaged about 100 per year.

The delay in carrying out the death sentence has become notorious. Between 1961 and 1970, the average time spent in prison under sentence of death rose from 14.4 months to 32.6 months.[1]

The sobering lesson is that we must either abolish the death penalty or try to enhance its deterrent value by abandoning the procedural safeguards and constitutional rights of suspects, defendants, and convicts in order to reduce delay, with the attendant high risk of executing innocent persons. The former alternative is surely the only tolerable one: repeal the death penalty entirely in favor of a more efficiently administrable mode of punishment.

2.   Persons who commit murder and other crimes of personal violence either premeditate them or they do not. If they do not, then it is impossible to imagine how any punishment could deter. The vast majority of capital crimes is committed during a moment of great emotional stress, in fear, or under the influence of drugs or alcohol, when logical thinking has been suspended. Impulsive or expressive violence is inflicted by persons heedless of the consequence to themselves as well as to others. In cases where the crime is premeditated, the criminal ordinarily expects to escape detection, arrest, and conviction. It is impossible to see how the threat of a severe punishment can deter an individual who does not expect to get caught.

[1]See *National Prisoner Statistics.*

Gangland killings, air piracy, and kidnapping for ransom are among the more obvious categories of capitally punishable crimes that continue to be committed because some individuals think they are too clever to get caught. Political terrorism is usually committed in the name of an ideology that honors its martyrs. Trying to cope with terrorism by threatening death for terrorists leaves untouched the underlying causes and ignores the many political and diplomatic sanctions (such as treaties against asylum for international terrorists) that could appreciably lower its incidence.

3. If, however, there is the possibility that severe punishment does deter crime, then long-term imprisonment is severe enough to cause any rational person not to commit violence. The vast preponderance of the evidence shows that the death penalty is no more effective than imprisonment in deterring crime and that it may even be an incitement to criminal violence:

(A) When the death penalty is used in a given state, there is no decrease in the subsequent rate of criminal homicide in that state. In the 1940s in Philadelphia, for instance, there were as many murders after well-publicized executions as before.[2]

(B) Use of the death penalty in a given state may increase the subsequent rate of criminal homicide in that state. In the years from 1946 through 1955 in California, for example, homicide tended to increase in the days immediately prior to an execution.[3]

(C) Death-penalty states as a group do not have lower rates of criminal homicide than non-death penalty states. Between 1928 and 1949, average homicide rates in death-penalty states were between two and three times higher than in abolition states.[4]

(D) States that abolish the death penalty do not show an increased rate of criminal homicide after abolition. In Oregon, for instance, which had no death penalty between 1915 and 1920, the homicide rate was 4.0 persons per 100,000 population in 1918, 4.9 in 1919, 4.1 in 1920—and rose to 7.7 in 1921, the first year after the death penalty was restored, and then subsided so that by 1925–1926 it was where it had been in 1919–1920.[5]

(E) States that have reinstated the death penalty after abolishing it have not shown a decreased rate of criminal homicide. In Delaware, for example, where the death penalty was abolished between 1958 and 1961, the

[2]Dann, *The Deterrent Effect of Capital Punishment* (1935); Savitz, in *J. Criminal Law, Criminology & Police Science* (1958).
[3]Graves, in Bedau, ed., *The Death Penalty in America* (1967).
[4]Schuessler, in *The Annals* (1952); Reckless, in *Crime & Delinquency* (1969).
[5]Sellin, *The Death Penalty* (1959); Wolfgang, in "Capital Punishment," *H.R. Hearings* (1972).

annual average homicide rate increased after restoration by 3.7 persons per 100,000 population.[6]

(F) In two neighboring states—one with the death penalty and the other without it—the one with the death penalty does not show a consistently lower rate of criminal homicide. For example, in Michigan, which has no death penalty, the homicide rate per 100,000 population averaged 3.49 between 1940 and 1955; in the neighboring state of Indiana, which executed nine persons during that period, the homicide rate was 3.5.[7]

(G) Police officers on duty do not suffer a higher rate of criminal assault and homicide in states that have abolished the death penalty than they do in death penalty states. Between 1928 and 1948, for instance, the rates of homicide and of assault on police in Chicago were half again greater than in Detroit; yet 55 executions were carried out in Cook County (Illinois) during these same years, and none in Michigan.[8]

(H) Prisoners and prison personnel do not suffer a higher rate of criminal assault and homicide from lifeterm prisoners in abolition states than they do in death penalty states. In 1965, for example, ten abolition states reported a total of eight prison homicides in four states and none in the other six, whereas 37 death penalty states reported a total of 53 prison homicides in 20 states and none in the other 17.[9]

Actual experience establishes these conclusions beyond reasonable doubt. No comparable body of evidence contradicts these conclusions.[10]

One recent investigation, using methods pioneered by economists, has reported findings in the opposite direction. This research purports to show that for the years from 1933 through 1967, each additional execution in the United States might have saved eight lives.[11] Subsequently, several qualified investigators have independently examined this claim, and all have rejected it.[12] The controversy is a highly technical one in econometrics, but the gist of the criticism is conveyed in these brief remarks by Justice Thurgood Marshall: " . . . the study is defective because it compares execution and homicide rates on a nationwide, rather than a State-by-State, basis. The aggregation of data from all States—including those that

[6]Sellin, *The Death Penalty* (1959); Samuelson, in *J. Criminal Law, Criminology & Police Science* (1969).

[7]Sellin, *The Death Penalty* (1959); Wolfgang, in "Capital Punishment," *H.R. Hearings* (1972); Zimring and Hawkins, *Deterrence* (1973).

[8]Sellin and Campion, in Bedau, ed., *The Death Penalty in America* (1967); Carderelli, in *J. Criminal Law, Criminology & Police Science* (1968).

[9]Sellin, ed., *Capital Punishment* (1967); Buffum, in *Prison J.* (1973).

[10]Baldus and Cole, in *Yale Law J.* (1975).

[11]Ehrlich, in *American Economic Review* (1974).

[12]Bowers and Pierce, in *Yale Law J.* (1975); Passell, in *Stanford Law Review* (1975); Passell and Taylor, in Bedau and Pierce, eds., *Capital Punishment in the United States* (1976).

have abolished the death penalty—obscures the relationship between murder and execution rates . . . [A] decrease in the execution risk in one State combined with an increase in the murder rate in another State would, all other things being equal, suggest a deterrent effect that quite obviously would not exist. . . . The most compelling criticism . . . is that . . . [the] conclusions are extremely sensitive to the choice of time period included in the regression analysis. Analysis . . . reveals that all empirical support for the deterrent effect of capital punishment disappears when the five most recent years [i.e., 1963–67] are removed from [the] time series—that is to say, whether a decrease in the execution risk corresponds to an increase or a decrease in the murder rate depends on the ending point of the sample period. This finding has cast severe doubts on the reliability of [the] . . . conclusions.[13] Even the majority of the Court in *Gregg* conceded that this alleged new evidence of a deterrent effect in the death penalty was "inconclusive."

In addition, cases have been clinically documented where the death penalty actually incited the capital crimes that it was supposed to deter. These include instances of the so-called suicide-murder syndrome—persons who wanted but feared to take their own lives, and committed murder so that society would kill them.

Other cases are examples of the so-called executioner syndrome—persons who became the self-appointed ministers of death and used killing—the ultimate weapon legitimated by society's acceptance of capital punishment—to avenge real or fancied wrongs.[14] Indeed, the more that is known about the mind of the murderer, the more obvious it becomes that the picture of a rational and calculated decision to kill, upon which the supposed deterrent effect of capital punishment depends, is almost never encountered in real life.

It must, of course, be conceded that inflicting the death penalty guarantees that the condemned person will commit no further crimes. This is a preventive, not a deterrent, function of executions. Furthermore, it is too high a price to pay when studies show that very few convicted murderers ever commit another crime of violence.[15] Recidivism among murderers does occasionally happen; it can be prevented only by executing all persons convicted of criminal homicide. Such a policy is too inhumane and brutal to be taken seriously. Society would never tolerate dozens of executions daily, yet nothing less would suffice.

---

[13]Gregg v. Georgia, 44 *U.S.L.J.*, 5230 (1976), Justices Brennan and Marshall, dissenting opinion.

[14]West, Solomon, and Diamond, in *American J. of Orthopsychiatry* (1975).

[15]Auerback, in *Georgia J. of Corrections* (1974).

## UNFAIRNESS

Constitutional due process as well as elementary justice require that the judicial functions of trial and sentencing, especially where the irreversible sanction of the death penalty is involved, be conducted with fundamental fairness. In both rape and murder cases (since 1930, 99 per cent of all executions have been for these crimes), there has been substantial evidence to show that courts have been arbitrary, racially biased, and unfair in the way in which they have tried and sentenced some persons to prison and others to death.

More than thirty years ago, Gunnar Myrdal, in his classic *An American Dilemma* (1944), reported that "the South makes the widest application of the death penalty, and Negro criminals come in for much more than their share of the executions." Statistics confirm this discrimination, only it is not confined to the South. Since 1930, 3,859 persons have been executed in the United States. Of these, 2,066, or 54 per cent, were black. For the crime of murder, 3,334 have been executed; 1,630, or 49 per cent, were black. During these years blacks were about 9 per cent of population. For rape, punishable by death in 1972 in only sixteen states and by the federal government, 455 have been executed, all but two in the South; 405, or 90 per cent, were black.[16] Racial discrimination was one of the grounds on which the Supreme Court relied in *Furman* in ruling the death penalty unconstitutional.

More exact statistical studies show that the higher rate of executions of blacks for rape and homicide cannot be explained by any factor except the race of the defendant. In Pennsylvania, for example, it has been shown that only the defendant's race explains the fact that among individuals convicted of felony murder and sentenced to death a lower percentage of blacks than whites eventually has their sentences commuted to imprisonment.[17]

In New Jersey, it was shown that juries tended to bring in death sentences for blacks convicted of felony murder more readily than they did for whites convicted of the same offense.[18] In Massachusetts, it has been shown that where black offenders are involved in rape-murder, the courts are less lenient than with white offenders.[19] Despite a whole new set of capital statutes enacted since 1972, bias in death sentencing has not abated. An examination of 800 condemned prisoners in 28 states before and after *Furman* showed that the new post-*Furman* death statutes did

---

[16]See *National Prisoner Statistics* (1969).
[17]Wolfgang, Kelly, and Nolde, in *J. Criminal Law, Criminology & Police Science* (1962).
[18]Wolf, in *Rutgers Law Review* (1964).
[19]Bedau, in *Suffolk U. Law Review* (1976).

little or nothing to reduce the preponderance of blacks on death row. The evidence shows that "nationwide and especially in the West, the proportion of non-whites who received the death penalty is significantly higher than it was before the 1972 decision."[20]

The race of the victim, as well as the offender, is a significant factor. Crimes against whites are disproportionately more likely to receive a death sentence. Though blacks constitute 54 per cent of murder victims, only 13 per cent of the people on death row had black victims, while 87 per cent had white victims.[21]

No doubt the most thorough statistical proof of racial bias in capital punishment has been provided in connection with rape. In 1965, 3,000 rape convictions in 250 counties in 11 Southern states were carefully studied. The results consistently pointed to the race of defendant (and of the victim) as the decisive factor(s) in how the courts would dispose of the case.

One analyst noted: "Negroes convicted of rape are disproportionately frequently sentenced to death." Moreover, "of over two dozen possible aggravating non-racial variables that could account for the higher proportion of Negroes sentenced to death upon conviction of rape, not one of these non-racial factors has withstood the tests of statistical significance. . . . We are now prepared to assert that a significantly higher proportion of blacks are sentenced to death upon conviction of rape . . . because they are black . . . and the victims were white."[22]

Such evidence of racial discrimination at both the trial and commutation phases of death penalty proceedings has not been shown in every state. In some states, e.g., California, studies have revealed no evidence of race discrimination.[23] The California study did, however, show discrimination against the poor; and in our society racial minorities are, of course, disproportionately poor. A defendant's poverty, lack of firm social roots in the community, inadequate legal representation at trial or on appeal—all these have in the past been common factors among death row populations.

A study of post-*Furman* death row inmates confirms the trend: 62 per cent were unskilled, service, or domestic workers, while only 3 per cent were professional or technical workers. Fully 60 per cent of those on death row were unemployed at the time of their crimes.[24] In North Carolina, the

---

[20]*The New York Times,* April 4, 1976, p. 42; see also Riedel, in *Temple Law Quarterly* (1976).

[21]Riedel, in *Temple Law Quarterly* (1976).

[22]Wolfgang, in "Capital Punishment," *H. R. Hearings* (1972), pp. 178, 179; Wolfgang and Riedel, in *The Annals* (1973).

[23]*Stanford Law Review* (1969).

[24]Riedel, in *Temple Law Quarterly* (1976).

vast majority was represented by appointed counsel; most of these lawyers had less than five years experience.[25]

Clinton Duffy, former warden of San Quentin Prison in California and witness to over 150 executions, has testified that in his experience capital punishment is "a privilege of the poor."[26] Michael DiSalle, former governor of Ohio, agrees: "During my experience as Governor of Ohio, I found that the men in death row had one thing in common: they were penniless ... the fact that they had no money was a principal factor in their being condemned to death."[27]

Justice, it is often insisted, requires the death penalty as the only suitable retribution for heinous crimes. This claim will not bear scrutiny. All punishment by its nature is retributive, not only the death penalty. Whatever legitimacy, therefore, is to be found in punishment as just retribution can in principle be satisfied without recourse to executions.

It is also obvious that the death penalty could be defended on retributive grounds only for the crime of murder, and not for any of the many other crimes so frequently made subject to this mode of punishment (rape, kidnapping, espionage, treason). Few defenders of the death penalty are willing to confine themselves consistently to the narrow scope afforded by retribution. Execution is more than a punishment exacted in retribution for the taking of a life. As Camus wrote, "For there to be equivalence, the death penalty would have to punish a criminal who had warned his victim of the date at which he would inflict a horrible death on him and who, from that moment onward, had confined him at his mercy for months. Such a monster is not encountered in private life."[28]

Furthermore, fairness and equity in punishment have claims upon us in the name of justice no less strong than retribution. The demonstrated inequities in the actual administration of capital punishment should tip the balance against it in the judgment of fair-minded and impartial observers. Indeed, nothing would be so likely to turn the public against the death penalty, once and for all, as would fair and equitable use of executions, without regard to race, sex, age, or social class. As former Supreme Court Justice Arthur Goldberg has written, "The deliberate, institutionalized taking of human life by the state is the greatest conceivable degradation to the dignity of the human personality."[29] The public demand for justice in the administration of criminal law can best be met by the total abolition of the death penalty.

[25]*The Charlotte Observer,* April 1, 1974, p. 1.
[26]Duffy, in "To Abolish the Death Penalty," *Senate Hearings* (1968).
[27]DiSalle, in "To Abolish the Death Penalty," *Senate Hearings* (1968), p. 11.
[28]Camus, "Reflections on the Guillotine," in *Resistance, Rebellion and Death* (1960).
[29]*The Boston Globe,* August 16, 1976, p. 17.

In this light the recent decisions of the Supreme Court upholding the constitutionality of guided discretion capital statutes appear quite unpersuasive. The issues were examined in some detail by the Supreme Court in 1971. Justice John Marshall Harlan, writing for the Court, noted: " . . . the history of capital punishment for homicides . . . reveals continual efforts, uniformly unsuccessful, to identify before the fact those homicides for which the slayer should die. . . . Those who have come to grips with the hard task of actually attempting to draft means of channeling capital sentencing discretion have confirmed the lesson taught by history. . . . To identify before the fact those characteristics of criminal homicides and their perpetrators which call for the death penalty, and to express these characteristics in language which can be fairly understood and applied by the sentencing authority, appear to be tasks which are beyond present human ability." (*McGautha v. California*, 402 U.S. 183)

Chief Justice Warren Burger, in his dissent from the majority in the *Furman* case, singled out these very words of Justice Harlan to express his own skepticism at the possibility of drawing up suitable standards to guide juries or of drafting sufficiently narrow capital statutes.

Yet, five years later, in the *Gregg* decision, the majority of the Supreme Court abandoned the wisdom of Justice Harlan and ruled as though the new guided-discretion statutes could accomplish the impossible. The truth is that death statutes such as Georgia's "do not effectively restrict the discretion of juries by any real standards. They never will. No society is going to kill everybody who meets certain preset verbal requirements, put on the statute books without awareness or coverage of the infinity of special factors the real world can produce."[30]

Even if these statutes were to succeed in guiding the jury's choice of sentence, a vast reservoir of discretion remains: the prosecutor's decision concerning whether to prosecute for a capital or lesser crime, the court's willingness to accept a plea of guilty, the jury's decision about which degree of murder to convict, the decision on insanity, the eventual decision by the governor on clemency—these are choices about which the public remains uninformed and for most of which there are no identifiable standards.

Discretion in the criminal justice system is unavoidable. Society clearly wishes to mitigate the harshness of capital punishment by allowing mercy for some persons. But when discretion is used, as it always has been, to mark for death the poor, the friendless, the uneducated, the members of racial minorities, the despised, then discretion becomes injustice.

Thoughtful citizens, who in contemplating capital punishment in the abstract might support it, must condemn it in actual practice.

[30]Black, *Capital Punishment: The Inevitability of Caprice and Mistake* (1974).

## IRREVERSIBILITY

Unlike all other criminal punishments, the death penalty is uniquely irrevocable. Two hundred years ago, Lafayette said, "I shall ask for the abolition of the punishment of death until I have the infallibility of human judgment demonstrated to me." Few proponents of capital punishment would argue that this institution is worth the execution of innocent people, but rather that there is no real possibility of innocent people being executed. Yet a large body of evidence shows that innocent people are often convicted of crimes, including capital crimes, and that some of them have been executed.

In recent decades, it is true that there are no undisputed cases of persons who were executed and then exonerated after it was too late. Nevertheless, the possibility of such error remains to haunt any society that insists on using the death penalty. Moreover, the record is full of cases where execution of the innocent has been narrowly averted. Since 1900 in this country, there has been on the average one case per year in which an entirely innocent person was convicted of murder, and many of these persons were sentenced to death.[31]

In 1975, only a year before the Supreme Court affirmed the constitutionality of capital punishment, two cases came to light in which six persons had been wrongly condemned. In Florida, two black men, Freddie Pitts and Wilbert Lee, were released from prison after twelve years awaiting execution for a murder they never committed. Though a white man confessed, it took a nine-year legal battle before the Governor would grant them a pardon.[32] Had the execution of Pitts and Lee not been stayed while the constitutionality of the death penalty was argued in the courts, these two innocent men probably would not be alive today. Just months after Pitts and Lee were released, authorities in New Mexico had to release four men who had spent eighteen months on death row for murder when the real killer confessed.[33]

Overzealous prosecution, mistaken eye-witness testimony, faulty police work, a defendant's previous criminal record, inept defense counsel, community pressure for a conviction—these factors help explain why the judicial system cannot guarantee that justice will never miscarry. To retain the death penalty in the face of the demonstrable failures of the

---

[31]See Bedau, ed., *The Death Penalty in America* (1967); MacNamara, in *Crime and Delinquency* (1969).

[32]Miller, *Invitation to a Lynching* (1975); also *The New York Times,* September 20, 1975, p. 1.

[33]*The Detroit News,* December 16, 1975.

system is unreasonable, especially since there are no strong counter-balancing factors in favor of the death penalty.


## BARBAROUSNESS

The classic form of execution, still in use in several states, is hanging. Ideally, the neck will be broken, but if the drop is too short there will be a slow and agonizing death by strangulation. If the drop is too long the head will be torn off.

The first major substitute for hanging was electrocution, the most widely used form of execution in this country. The condemned prisoner is led—or dragged—into the death chamber, strapped into the chair, and electrodes fastened to head and legs. When the switch is thrown the body strains, jolting as the voltage is raised and lowered. Often smoke rises from the head. There is the awful odor of burning flesh. No one knows how long electrocuted individuals retain consciousness.

An attempt to improve on electrocution was the gas chamber. The prisoner is strapped into a chair, a container of sulphuric acid underneath. The chamber is sealed and cyanide is dropped into the acid to form lethal gas. As the gas fills the chamber, the prisoner turns purple and drools. The eyes pop. Unconsciousness may not come for several minutes, but even then the body continues to struggle for air.

Only one state still legalizes the firing squad. Utah gives its condemned the choice between hanging and shooting. Most have chosen the latter. The prisoner is strapped to a chair, and hooded. A target is pinned to the chest. Five marksmen, one with blanks, take aim.

In the last moments before being put to death, human beings may simply disintegrate. From the chaplain of San Quentin we have this account of the execution of Leanderess Riley:

"At nine-fifty, Associate Warden Rigg and the doctors came in. I told Leanderess to say a prayer to himself, if he did not care to have me pray, and to relax into God's care. He did not seem to hear me. When the doctors started to approach his cell, he made a throaty, gutteral growling sound. Frantically, at random, he picked up some of the old legal papers on his table and began passing them through the bars to the associate warden, as if they were appeals or writs. A guard unlocked his cell. He gripped the bars with both hands and began a long, shrieking cry. It was a bone-chilling, wordless cry. The guards grabbed him, wrested him violently away from the bars. The old shirt and trousers were stripped off. His flailing arms and legs were forced into the new white shirt and fresh blue denims. The guards needed all their strength to hold him while the doctor taped the end of the stethoscope in place.

"The deep-throated cry, alternately moaning and shrieking, continued. Leanderess had to be carried to the gas chamber, fighting, writhing all the way. As the witnesses watched in horror, the guards stuffed him into the chair. One guard threw his weight against the struggling little Negro while the other jerked the straps tight. They backed out, slammed the door on him.

"Leanderess didn't stop screaming or struggling. Associate Warden Rigg was about to signal for the dropping of the gas pellets when we all saw Riley's small hands break free from the straps. He pulled at the other buckles, was about to free himself.

"The Associate Warden withheld his signal. San Quentin had never executed a man raging wildly around the gas chamber. He ordered the guards to go in again and restrap the frenzied man. One of the guards said later he had to cinch the straps down so tightly the second time that he was ashamed of himself.

"Again the door was closed. Again Leanderess managed to free his small, thin-wristed right hand from the straps. Riggs gave the order to drop the pellets. Working furiously, Leanderess freed his left hand. The chest strap came off next. Still shrieking and moaning, he was working on the waist strap when the gas hit him. He put both hands over his face to hold it away. Then his hands fell, his head arched back. His eyes remained open. His heart beat continued to register for two minutes, but his shrieking stopped and his head slowly dropped."[34]

Most people observing an execution are horrified and disgusted. Revulsion at the duty to supervise and witness executions is one reason why so many prison wardens, people unsentimental about crime and criminals, are opponents of capital punishment.

In some people, however, executions seem to appeal to strange aberrant impulses and give an outlet to sadistic urges. Warden Lewis Lawes wrote of the many requests he received to watch electrocutions, and told that when the job of executioner became vacant, "I received more than seven hundred applications for the position, many of them offering cut-rate prices."[35]

Public executions were common in this country during the 19th century; the last one was as recent as 1938 in Kentucky, when 20,000 people gathered to watch a man hang. Delight in brutality, pain, violence and death may always be with us. But surely we must conclude that it is best for the law not to encourage these impulses. When the government sanctions, commands, and ceremoniously carries out the execution of a prisoner, it lends support to this dark side of human nature.

[34]Eshelman and Riley, *Death Row Chaplain* (1962).
[35]Lawes, *Life and Death at Sing Sing* (1928).

# FINANCIAL COSTS

It is sometimes suggested that abolishing capital punishment is unfair to the taxpayer, as though life imprisonment were a great financial burden and obviously more expensive than a hanging, electrocution, or gassing. And so it is, if one does not take into account all the relevant costs. A capital trial generally takes longer than one in which the death penalty is not involved, and lengthy appeals almost invariable follow. Trial and appeal costs, including the time of judges, prosecutors, public defenders, and court reporters, and the high costs of briefs are all borne by the taxpayer. *Time* magazine reported that the commutation of death sentences of 15 Arkansas prisoners saved the state an estimated $1.5 million, considering the many appeals that would have been argued.[36]

Richard McGee, administrator of the California correctional system, has written: "The actual costs of execution, the cost of operating the super-maximum security condemned unit, the years spent by some inmates in condemned status, and a pro-rata share of top-level prison officials' time spent in administering the units, add up to a cost substantially greater than the cost to retain them in prison the rest of their lives."[37] An economically valid and comprehensive cost-accounting of capital punishment versus life imprisonment has never been conducted. What information we do have suggests that the economic cost of execution does not make it a "better buy" then life imprisonment.

# ABOLITION TRENDS

Abolition of the death penalty in the United States also needs to be put into international perspective. In 1962, it was reported to the Council of Europe that "the facts clearly show that the death penalty is regarded in Europe as something of an anachronism. . . ."[38] None of the countries of western Europe except France and Spain has used the death penalty in the past decade. In many, it is unconstitutional. In Great Britain, it was abolished (except for treason) in 1971. Canada abolished it in July 1976. The United Nation's Economic and Social Council continues to affirm its formal resolution that, throughout the world, it is desirable to "progressively restrict the number of offenses for which the death penalty might be imposed, with a view to the desirability of abolishing this punishment."[39]

[36] *Time*, January 11, 1971, p. 50.
[37] McGee, in *Federal Probation* (1964).
[38] Ancel, *The Death Penalty in European Countries* (1962).
[39] UN, Ecosoc, Official Records 58th Sess., Suppl. 1, p.36.

Once in use everywhere and for a great variety of crimes, the death penalty today is generally forbidden by law and even more widely abandoned in practice. The unmistakable trend is toward the complete abolition of capital punishment.

# The Collapse of the Case Against Capital Punishment

Ernest van den Haag

Three questions about the death penalty so overlap that they must each be answered. I shall ask seriatim: Is the death penalty constitutional? Is it useful? Is it morally justifiable?

## THE CONSTITUTIONAL QUESTION

The Fifth Amendment states that no one shall be "deprived of life, liberty, or property without due process of law," implying a "due process of law" to deprive persons of life. The Eighth Amendment prohibits "cruel and unusual punishment." It is unlikely that this prohibition was meant to supersede the Fifth Amendment, since the amendments were simultaneously enacted in 1791.[1]

The Fourteenth Amendment, enacted in 1868, reasserted and explicitly extended to the states the implied authority to "deprive of life, liberty, or property" by "due process of law." Thus, to regard the death penalty as an unconstitutional one must believe that the standards which determine

---

Reprinted, with deletions, by permission of the author. From *National Review*, March 31, 1978. Ernest van den Haag has taught criminal justice at several universities and is author of *Punishing Criminals* (1975).

[1]Apparently the punishment must be both—else cruel *or* unusual would have done. Historically it appears that punishments were prohibited if unusual in 1791 *and* cruel: the Framers did want to prohibit punishments, even cruel ones, only if already unusual in 1791; they did prohibit new (unusual) punishments if cruel. The Eighth Amendment was not meant to apply to the death penalty in 1791 since it was not unusual then; nor was the Eighth Amendment intended to be used against capital punishment in the future, regardless of whether it may have come to be considered cruel: it is neither a new penalty nor one unusual in 1791.

what is "cruel and unusual" have so evolved since 1868 as to prohibit now what was authorized then, and that the Constitution authorizes the courts to overrule laws in the light of *new* moral standards. What might these standards be? And what shape must their evolution take to be constitutionally decisive?

**Consensus.** A moral consensus, intellectual or popular, could have evolved to find execution "cruel and unusual." It did not. Intellectual opinion is divided. Polls suggest that most people would vote for the death penalty. Congress recently has legislated the death penalty for skyjacking under certain conditions. The representative assemblies of two-thirds of the states did re-enact capital punishment when previous laws were found constitutionally defective.[2]

If, however, there were a consensus against the death penalty, the Constitution expects the political process, rather than judicial decisions, to reflect it. Courts are meant to interpret the laws made by the political process and to set constitutional limits to it—not to replace it by responding to a presumed moral consensus. Surely the "cruel and unusual" phrase was not meant to authorize the courts to become legislatures.[3] Thus, neither a consensus of moral opinion nor a moral discovery by judges is meant to be disguised as a constitutional interpretation. Even when revealed by a burning bush, new moral norms were not meant to become constitutional norms by means of court decisions.[4] To be sure, the courts in the past have occasionally done away with obsolete kinds of punishment—but never in the face of legislative and popular opposition and re-enactment. Abolitionists constantly press the courts now to create rather than to confirm obsolescence. That courts are urged to do what so clearly is for voters and lawmakers to decide suggests that the absence of consensus for abolition is recognized by the opponents of capital punishment. What then can the phrase "cruel and unusual punishment" mean today?

**"Cruel"** may be understood to mean excessive—punitive without, or beyond, a rational-utilitarian purpose. Since capital punishment excludes rehabilitation and is not needed for incapacitation, the remaining rational-

[2]There may be a consensus against the death penalty among the college educated. If so, it demonstrates a) the power of indoctrination wielded by sociologists; b) the fact that those who are least threatened by violence are most inclined to do without the death penalty. College graduates are less often threatened by murder than the uneducated.

[3]See Chief Justice Burger dissenting in *Furman:* "In a democratic society legislatures not courts are constituted to respond to the will and consequently the moral values of the people."

[4]The First Amendment might be invoked against such sources of revelation. When specific laws do not suffice to decide a case, courts, to be sure, make decisions based on general legal principles. But the death penalty (as distinguished from applications) raises no serious legal problem.

utilitarian purpose would be deterrence, the reduction of the rate at which the crime punished is committed by others. I shall consider this reduction below. Here I wish to note that, if the criterion for the constitutionality of any punishment were an actual demonstration of its rational-utilitarian effectiveness, all legal punishments would be in as much constitutional jeopardy as the death penalty. Are fines for corporations deterrent? rehabilitative? incapacitative? Is a jail term for marijuana possession? Has it ever been established that ten years in prison are doubly as deterrent as five, or at least sufficiently more deterrent? (I don't pretend to know what "sufficiently" might mean: whether 10 per cent or 80 per cent added deterrence would warrant 100 per cent added severity.)

The Constitution certainly does not require a demonstration of rational-utilitarian effects for any punishment. Such a demonstration so far has not been available. To demand it for one penalty—however grave—and not for others, when it is known that no such demonstration is available, or has been required hitherto for any punishment, seems unjustified. Penalties have always been regarded as constitutional if they can be plausibly intended (rather than demonstrated) to be effective (useful), and if they are not grossly excessive, i.e., unjust.

Justice, a rational but non-utilitarian purpose of punishment, requires that it be proportioned to the felt gravity of the crime. Thus, constitutional justice authorizes, even calls for, a higher penalty the graver the crime. One cannot demand that this constitutionally required escalation stop short of the death penalty unless one furnishes positive proof of its irrationality by showing injustice, i.e., disproportionality (to the felt gravity of the crime punished or to other punishments of similar crimes), as well as ineffectiveness, i.e., uselessness in reducing the crime rate. There is no proof of cruelty here in either sense.

**"Unusual"** is generally interpreted to mean either randomly capricious and therefore unconstitutional, or capricious in a biased, discriminatory way, so as particularly to burden specifiable groups, and therefore unconstitutional. (Random arbitrariness might violate the Eighth, biased arbitrariness the Fourteenth Amendment, which promises "the equal protection of the laws.") Apart from the historical interpretation noted above (footnote 1), "unusual" seems to mean "unequal" then. The dictionary equivalent—"rare"—seems to be regarded as relevant only inasmuch as it implies "unequal." Indeed it is hard to see why rarity should be objectionable otherwise.

For the sake of argument, let me grant that either or both forms of capriciousness prevail[5] and that they are less tolerable with respect to the

---

[5]Attention should be drawn to John Hagan's "Extralegal Attributes and Criminal Sentencing" (*Law and Society Review*, Spring 1974), which throws doubt on much of the discrimination which sociologists have found.

death penalty than with respect to milder penalties—which certainly are not meted out less capriciously. However prevalent, neither form of capriciousness would argue for abolishing the death penalty. Capriciousness is not inherent in that penalty, or in any penalty, but occurs in its distribution. Therefore, the remedy lies in changing the laws and procedures which distribute the penalty. It is the process of distribution which is capable of discriminating, not that which it distributes.

**Unavoidable Capriciousness.** If capricious distribution places some convicts, or groups of convicts, at an unwarranted disadvantage,[6] can it be remedied enough to satisfy the Eighth and Fourteenth Amendments? Some capriciousness is unavoidable because decisions of the criminal justice system necessarily rest on accidental factors at many points, such as the presence or absence of witnesses to an act; or the cleverness or clumsiness of police officers who exercise their discretion in arresting suspects and seizing evidence. All court decisions must rest on the available and admissible evidence for, rather than actuality of, guilt. Availability of evidence is necessarily accidental to the actuality of whatever it is that the evidence is needed for. Accident is the capriciousness of fate.

Now, if possible without loss of other desiderata, accident and human capriciousness should be minimized. But, obviously, discretionary judgments cannot be avoided altogether. The Framers of the Constitution were certainly aware of the unavoidable elements of discretion which affect all human decisions, including those of police officers, of prosecutors, and of the courts. Because it always was unavoidable, discretion no more speaks against the constitutionality of the criminal justice system or of any of its penalties now than it did when the Constitution was written—unless something has evolved since, to make unavoidable discretion, tolerable before, intolerable now, at least for the death penalty. I know of no such evolution; and I would think it was up to the legislative branch of government to register it had it occurred.

The Constitution, though it enjoins us to minimize capriciousness, does not enjoin a standard of unattainable perfection or exclude penalties because that standard has not been attained.[7] Actually, modern legislative trends hitherto have favored enlargement of discretion in the judicial process. I have always thought that enlargement to be excessive, immoral, irrational, and possibly unconstitutional—even when not abused for pur-

[6]I am referring throughout to discrimination among those already convicted of capital crimes. That discrimination can be tested. However, the fact that a higher proportion of blacks, or poor people, than of whites, or rich people, are found guilty of capital crimes does not *ipso facto* indicate discrimination, any more than does the fact that a comparatively high proportion of blacks or poor people become professional baseball players or boxers.

[7]Although this is the burden of Charles Black's *Capital Punishment: The Inevitability of Caprice and Mistake* (Norton, 1974)....

poses of discrimination. Yet, though we should not enlarge it *praeter neces-sitatem,* some discretion is unavoidable and even desirable, and no reason for giving up any punishment.

**Avoidable Capriciousness.** Capriciousness should be prevented by abolishing penalties capriciously distributed only in one case: when it is so unavoidable and so excessive that penalties are randomly distributed between the guilty and the innocent. When that is not the case, the abuses of discretion which lead to discrimination against particular groups of defendants or convicts certainly require correction, but not abolition of the penalty abused by maldistribution.

## PRELIMINARY MORAL ISSUES

**Justice and Equality.** Regardless of constitutional interpretation, the morality and legitimacy of the abolitionist argument from capriciousness, or discretion, or discrimination, would be more persuasive if it were alleged that those selectively executed are not guilty. But the argument merely maintains that some other guilty but more favored persons, or groups, escape the death penalty. This is hardly sufficient for letting anyone else found guilty escape the penalty. On the contrary, that some guilty persons or groups elude it argues for extending the death penalty to them. Surely "due process of law" is meant to do justice; and "the equal protection of the law" is meant to extend justice equally to all. Nor do I read the Constitution to command us to prefer equality to justice. When we clamor for "equal justice for all" it is justice which is to be equalized and extended, and which therefore is the prior desideratum, not to be forsaken and replaced by equality but rather to be extended.

Justice requires punishing the guilty—as many of the guilty as possible, even if only some can be punished—and sparing the innocent—as many of the innocent as possible, even if not all are spared. Morally, justice must always be preferred to equality. It would surely be wrong to treat everybody with equal injustice in preference to meting out justice at least to some. Justice then cannot ever permit sparing some guilty persons, or punishing some innocent ones, for the sake of equality—because others have been unjustly spared or punished. In practice, penalties never could be applied if we insisted that they cannot be inflicted on any guilty person unless we can make sure that they are equally applied to all other guilty persons. Anyone familiar with law enforcement knows that punishments can be inflicted only on an unavoidably capricious, at best a random, selection of the guilty. I see no more merit in the attempt to persuade the courts to let all capital-crime defendants go free of capital punishment because some have wrongly escaped it than I see in an attempt to persuade the courts to let all burglars go because some have wrongly escaped imprisonment.

Although it hardly warrants serious discussion, the argument from capriciousness looms large in briefs and decisions because for the last seventy years courts have tried—unproductively—to prevent errors of procedure, or of evidence collection, or of decision-making, by the paradoxical method of letting defendants go free as a punishment, or warning, or deterrent, to errant law enforcers. The strategy admittedly never has prevented the errors it was designed to prevent—although it has released countless guilty persons. But however ineffective it be, the strategy had a rational purpose. The rationality, on the other hand, of arguing that a penalty must be abolished because of allegations that some guilty persons escape it, is hard to fathom—even though the argument was accepted by some Justices of the Supreme Court.

**The Essential Moral Question.**   Is the death penalty morally just and/or useful? This is the essential moral, as distinguished from constitutional, question. Discrimination is irrelevant to this moral question. If the death penalty were distributed quite equally and uncapriciously and with superhuman perfection to all the guilty, but was morally unjust, it would remain unjust in each case. Contrariwise, if the death penalty is morally just, however discriminatorily applied to only some of the guilty, it does remain just in each case in which it is applied. Thus, if it were applied exclusively to guilty males, and never to guilty females, the death penalty, though unequally applied, would remain just. For justice consists in punishing the guilty and sparing the innocent, and its equal extension, though desirable, is not part of it. It is part of equality, not of justice (or injustice), which is what equality equalizes. The same consideration would apply if some benefit were distributed only to males but not equally to deserving females. The inequality would not argue against the benefit, or against distribution to deserving males, but rather for distribution to equally deserving females. Analogously, the nondistribution of the death penalty to guilty females would argue for applying it to them as well, and not against applying it to guilty males.

The utilitarian (political) effects of unequal justice may well be detrimental to the social fabric because they outrage our passion for equality, particularly for equality before the law. Unequal justice is also morally repellent. Nonetheless unequal justice is justice still. What is repellent is the incompleteness, the inequality, not the justice. The guilty do not become innocent or less deserving of punishment because others escaped it. Nor does any innocent deserve punishment because others suffer it. Justice remains just, however unequal, while injustice remains unjust, however equal. However much each is desired, justice and equality are not identical. Equality before the law should be extended and enforced, then—but not at the expense of justice.

**Maldistribution among the Guilty: A Sham Argument.**   Capriciousness, at any rate, is used as a sham argument against capital punishment by all abolitionists I have ever known. They would oppose the death penalty if it could be meted out without any discretion whatsoever. They would oppose the death penalty in a homogeneous country without racial discrimination. And they would oppose the death penalty if the incomes of those executed and of those spared were the same. Abolitionists oppose the death penalty, not its possible maldistribution. They should have the courage of their convictions.

**Maldistribution between the Guilty and the Innocent: Another Sham Argument.**   What about persons executed in error? The objection here is not that some of the guilty get away, but that some of the innocent do not —a matter far more serious than discrimination among the guilty. Yet, when urged by abolitionists, this too is a sham argument, as are all distributional arguments. For abolitionists are opposed to the death penalty for the guilty as much as for the innocent. Hence, the question of guilt, if at all relevant to their position, cannot be decisive for them. Guilt is decisive only to those who urge the death penalty for the guilty. They must worry about distribution—part of the justice they seek.

**Miscarriages of Justice.**   The execution of innocents believed guilty is a miscarriage of justice which must be opposed whenever detected. But such miscarriages of justice do not warrant abolition of the death penalty. Unless the moral drawbacks of an activity or practice, which include the possible death of innocent bystanders, outweigh the moral advantages, which include the innocent lives that might be saved by it, the activity is warranted. Most human activities—construction, manufacturing, automobile and air traffic, sports, not to speak of wars and revolutions—cause the death of some innocent bystanders. Nevertheless, if the advantages sufficiently outweigh the disadvantages, human activities, including those of the penal system with all its punishments, are morally justified. Consider now the advantages in question.

# DETERRENCE

**New Evidence.**   Is there evidence for the usefulness of the death penalty in securing the life of the citizens? Researchers in the past found no statistical evidence for the effects sought: i.e., marginal deterrent effects, deterrent effects over and above those of alternative sanctions. However, in the last few years new and more sophisticated research has led, for instance, Professor Isaac Ehrlich to conclude that over the period 1933–1969, "An additional execution per year ... may have resulted on the average in seven or eight fewer murders."[8] Other investigators have

---

[8]"The Deterrent Effect of Capital Punishment: A Question of Life and Death," *American Economic Review,* June 1975. In the period studied capital punishment was already infrequent and uncertain. Its deterrent effect might be greater when more frequently imposed for capital crimes, so that a prospective offender would feel more certain of it.

confirmed Ehrlich's tentative results. Not surprisingly, refutations have been attempted, and Professor Ehrlich has answered them. He has also published a new cross-sectional analysis of the data which confirms the conclusions of his original (time-series) study.[9] The matter will remain controversial for some time.[10] but two tentative conclusions can be drawn with some confidence by now. First, Ehrlich has shown that previous investigations, which did not find deterrent effects of the death penalty, suffer from fatal defects. Second, there is now some likelihood—much more than hitherto—of demonstrating marginal deterrent effects statistically.

**The Choice.**    Thus, with respect to deterrence, we must choose 1) to trade the certain shortening of the life of a convicted murderer for the survival of between seven and eight innocent victims whose future murder by others may be less likely if the convicted murderer is executed. Or 2) to trade the certain lengthening of the life of a convicted murderer for the possible loss of the lives of between seven and eight innocent victims, who may be more likely to be murdered by others because of our failure to execute the convicted murderer.[11]

If we were certain that executions have a zero marginal effect, they could not be justified in deterrent terms. But even the pre-Ehrlich investigations never did demonstrate this. They merely found that an above-zero effect cannot be demonstrated statistically. While we do not know at present the degree of confidence with which we can assign an above-zero marginal deterrent effect to executions, we can be more confident than in the past. It seems morally indefensible to let convicted murderers survive at the probable—even at the merely possible—expense of the lives of innocent victims who might have been spared had the murderers been executed.

**Non-deterrence as a Sham Argument.**    Most of the studies purporting to show that capital punishment produces no added deterrence, or that

[9] See *Journal of Legal Studies,* January 1977; *Journal of Political Economy,* June 1977; and (this is the cross-sectional analysis) *American Economic Review,* June 1977.

[10] *Per contra* see Brian Forst in *Minnesota Law Review,* May 1977, and *Deterrence and Incapacitation* (National Academy of Sciences, Washington, D.C., 1978). By now statistical analyses of the effects of the death penalty have become a veritable cottage industry. This has happened since Ehrlich found deterrent effects. No one much bothered when Thorsten Sellin found none. Still, it is too early for more than tentative conclusions. The two papers mentioned above are replied to, more than adequately in my view, in Isaac Ehrlich's "Fear of Deterrence," *Journal of Legal Studies,* June 1977.

[11] I thought that prudence as well as morality commanded us to choose the first alternative even when I believed that the degree of probability and the extent of deterrent effects might remain unknown. (See my "On Deterrence and the Death Penalty," *Journal of Criminal Law, Criminology, and Police Science,* June 1969.) The probability is more likely to become known now and to be greater than was apparent a few years ago.

it cannot be shown to do so, were made by abolitionists, such as Professor Thorsten Sellin. They were used to show the futility of the death penalty. Relying on their intuition as well as on these studies, many abolitionists still are convinced that the death penalty is no more deterrent than life imprisonment. And they sincerely believe that the failure of capital punishment to produce additional deterrence argues for abolishing it. However, the more passionate and committed abolitionists use the asserted ineffectiveness of the death penalty as a deterrent as a sham argument—just as they use alleged capriciousness and maldistribution in application. They use the argument for debating purposes—but actually would abolish the death penalty even if it were an effective deterrent, just as they would abolish the death penalty if it were neither discriminatorily nor otherwise maldistributed.

Professors Charles Black (Yale Law School) and Hugo Adam Bedau (Tufts, Philosophy) are both well known for their public commitment to abolition of the death penalty, attested to by numerous writings. At a symposium held on October 15, 1977 at the Arizona State University at Tempe, Arizona, they were asked to entertain the hypothesis—whether or not contrary to fact—that the death penalty is strongly deterrent over and above alternative penalties: Would they favor abolition in the face of conclusive proof of a strong deterrent effect over and above that of alternative penalties? Both gentlemen answered affirmatively. They were asked whether they would still abolish the death penalty if they knew that abolition (and replacement by life imprisonment) would increase the homicide rate by 10 per cent, 20 per cent, 50 per cent, 100 per cent, or 1,000 per cent. Both gentlemen continued to answer affirmatively.

I am forced to conclude that Professors Black and Bedau think the lives of convicted murderers (however small their number) are more worth preserving than the lives of an indefinite number of innocent victims (however great their number). Or, the principle of abolition is more important to them than the lives of any number of innocent murder victims who would be spared if convicted murderers were executed.

I have had occasion subsequently to ask former Attorney General Ramsey Clark the same questions; he answered as Professors Black and Bedau did, stressing that nothing could persuade him to favor the penalty—however deterrent it might be. (Mr. Clark has kindly permitted me to quote his view here.)

Now, Professors Black and Bedau and Mr. Clark do *not* believe that the death penalty adds deterrence. They do not believe therefore—regardless of the evidence—that abolition would cause an increase in the homicide rate. But the question they were asked, and which—after some dodging —they answered forthrightly, had nothing to do with the acceptance or rejection of the deterrent effect of the death penalty. It was a hypothetical question: If it were deterrent, would you still abolish the death penalty? Would you still abolish it if it were very deterrent, so that abolition would lead to a quantum jump in the murder rate? They answered affirmatively.

These totally committed abolitionists, then, are not interested in deterrence. They claim that the death penalty does not add to deterrence only as a sham argument. Actually, whether or not the death penalty deters is, to them, irrelevant. The intransigence of these committed humanitarians is puzzling as well as inhumane. Passionate ideological commitments have been known to have such effects. These otherwise kind and occasionally reasonable persons do not want to see murderers executed ever—however many innocent lives can be saved thereby. *Fiat injustitia, pereat humanitas.*

**Experiments?** In principle one could experiment to test the deterrent effect of capital punishment. The most direct way would be to legislate the death penalty for certain kinds of murder if committed on weekdays, but never on Sunday. Or, on Monday, Wednesday, and Friday, and not on other days; on other days, life imprisonment would be the maximum sentence. (The days could be changed around every few years to avoid possible bias.) I am convinced there will be fewer murders on death-penalty than on life-imprisonment days. Unfortunately the experiment faces formidable obstacles.[12]

**The Burden of Proof of Usefulness.** Let me add a common-sense remark. Our penal system rests on the proposition that more severe penalties are more deterrent than less severe penalties. We assume, rightly, I believe, that a $5 fine deters rape less than a $500 fine, and that the threat of five years in prison will deter more than either fine.[13] This assumption of the penal system rests on the common experience that, once aware of them, people learn to avoid natural dangers the more likely these are to be injurious and the more severe the likely injuries. Else the survival of the human race would be hard to explain. People endowed with ordinary

---

[12]Though it would isolate deterrent effects of the punishment from incapacitating effects, and also from the effect of Durkheimian "normative validation" when it does not depend on threats. Still, it is not acceptable to our sense of justice that people guilty of the same crime would deliberately get different punishments and that the difference would be made to depend deliberately on a factor irrelevant to the nature of the crime or of the criminal.

[13]As indicated before, demonstrations are not available for the exact addition to deterrence of each added degree of severity in various circumstances, and with respect to various acts. We have coasted so far on a sea of plausible assumptions. (It is not contended, of course, that the degree of severity alone determines deterrent effects. Other factors may reinforce or offset the effect of severity be it on the motivational [incentive] side, or as added costs and risks.)

common sense (a class that includes a modest but significant number of sociologists) have found no reason why behavior with respect to legal dangers should differ from behavior with respect to natural dangers. Indeed, it doesn't. Hence, all legal systems proportion threatened penalties to the gravity of crimes, both to do justice and to achieve deterrence in proportion to that gravity.

But if, *ceteris paribus*, the more severe the penalty the greater the deterrent effect, then the most severe available penalty—the death penalty—would have the greatest deterrent effect. Arguments to the contrary assume either that capital crimes never are deterrable (sometimes merely because not all capital crimes have been deterred), or that, beyond life imprisonment, the deterrent effect of added severity is necessarily zero. Perhaps. But the burden of proof must be borne by those who presume to have located the point of zero marginal returns before the death penalty.

**The Threat of Death Needed in Special Circumstances.** Another common-sense observation. Without the death penalty, we necessarily confer immunity on just those persons most likely to be in need of deterrent threats: thus, prisoners serving life sentences can kill fellow prisoners or guards with impunity. Prison wardens are unlikely to be able to prevent violence in prisons as long as they give humane treatment to inmates and have no serious threats of additional punishment available for the murderers among them who are already serving life sentences. I cannot see the moral or utilitarian reasons for giving permanent immunity to homicidal life prisoners, thereby endangering the other prisoners and the guards, in effect preferring the life prisoners to their victims who *could* be punished if they murdered.

Outside prison an offender who expects a life sentence for his offense may murder his victim, or witnesses, or the arresting officer, to improve his chances of escaping. He could not be threatened with an additional penalty for his additional crime—an open invitation. Only the death penalty could deter in such cases.[14] If there is but a possibility that it will, we should retain it. But I believe there is a *probability* that the threat of the death penalty will deter.

**Reserved for the Worst Crimes.** However, effective deterrence requires that the threat of the ultimate penalty be reserved for the worst crime from which the offender may be deterred by that threat. Hence, the extreme punishment should not be prescribed when the offender, because already threatened by it, might feel he can add further crimes with impunity. Thus, rape, or kidnapping, should not incur the death penalty, while

---

[14]Particularly since he, unlike the person already in custody, may have much to gain from his additional crime (see footnote 18).

killing the victim of either crime should.[15] (The death penalty for rape may actually function as an incentive to murder the victim/witness.) This may not stop an Eichmann after his first murder; but it will stop most people before. To be sure, an offender not deterred from murdering one victim by the threat of execution is unlikely to be deterred from additional murders by further threats. The range of effective punishments is not infinite; on the contrary, it is necessarily more restricted than the range of possible crimes. Some offenders cannot be deterred by any threat. But most people can be; and most people respond to the size of the threat addressed to them. Since death is the ultimate penalty—the greatest threat available—it must be reserved for the ultimate crime even though it cannot always prevent it.

## SOME POPULAR ARGUMENTS

Consider now some popular arguments against capital punishment.

**Barbarization.**   According to Beccaria, with the death penalty the "laws which punish homicide . . . themselves commit it," thus giving "an example of barbarity." Those who speak of "legalized murder" use an oxymoronic phrase to echo this allegation. However, punishments—fines, incarcerations, or executions—although often physically identical to the crimes punished, are neither crimes, nor their moral equivalent. The difference between crimes and lawful acts, including punishments, is not physical, but legal: crimes differ from other acts by being unlawful. Driving a stolen car is a crime, though not physically distinguishable from driving a car lawfully owned. Unlawful imprisonment and kidnapping need not differ physically from the lawful arrest and incarceration used to punish unlawful imprisonment and kidnapping. Finally, whether a lawful punishment gives an "example of barbarity" depends on how the moral difference between crime and punishment is perceived. To suggest that

[15]The Supreme Court has decided that capital punishment for rape (at least of adults) is "cruel and unusual" (*Coker v. Georgia,* 1977). For the reasons stated in the text, I welcome the decision—but not the justification given by the Supreme Court. The penalty may indeed be as excessive as the court feels it is, but not in the constitutional sense of being irrationally or extravagantly so, and thus contrary to the Eighth Amendment. The seriousness of the crime of rape and the appropriateness of the death penalty for it are matters for political rather than judicial institutions to decide. I should vote against the death penalty for rape —and not only for the reasons stated in the text above; but the Court should have left the matter to the vote of the citizens.

The charge of racially discriminatory application was most often justified when the penalty was inflicted for rape. Yet I doubt that the charge will be dropped, or that the agitation against the death penalty will stop, once it is no longer inflicted for rape. Discrimination never was more than a pretext used by abolitionists.

its physical quality, *ipso facto,* morally disqualifies the punishment is to assume what is to be shown.

It is quite possible that all displays of violence, criminal or punitive, influence people to engage in unlawful imitations. This seems one good reason not to have public executions. But it does not argue against executions. Objections to displaying on TV the process of violently subduing a resistant offender do not argue against actually subduing him.[16] Arguments against the public display of vivisections, or of the effects of painful medications, do not argue against either. Arguments against public executions, then, do not argue against executions.[17] The deterrent effect of punishments depends on their being known. But it does not depend on punishments being carried out publicly. The threat of imprisonment deters, but incarcerated persons are not on public display.

**Crimes of Passion.** Abolitionists often maintain that most capital crimes are "acts of passion" which a) could not be restrained by the threat of the death penalty, and b) do not deserve it morally even if other crimes might. It is not clear to me why a crime motivated by, say, sexual passion is morally less deserving of punishment than one motivated by passion for money. Is the sexual passion morally more respectable than others? or more gripping? or just more popular? Generally, is violence in personal conflicts morally more excusable than violence among people who do not know each other? A precarious case might be made for such a view, but I shall not attempt to make it.

Perhaps it is true, however, that many murders are irrational "acts of passion" which cannot be deterred by the threat of the death penalty. Either for this reason or because "crimes of passion" are thought less blameworthy than other homicides, most "crimes of passion" are not punishable by death now.[18]

But if most murders are irrational acts, it would therefore seem that the traditional threat of the death penalty has succeeded in deterring most rational people, or most people when rational, from committing murder, and the fear of the penalty continues to deter all but those who are so irrational that they cannot be deterred by any threat. Hardly a reason for abolishing the death penalty. Indeed, that capital crimes are committed

---

[16]There is a good argument here against unnecessary public displays of violence. (See my "What to Do about TV Violence," *The Alternative,* August/September 1976.)

[17]It may be noted that in Beccaria's time executions were regarded as public entertainments....

[18]I have reservations on both these counts, being convinced that many crimes among relatives, friends, and associates are as blameworthy and as deterrable as crimes among strangers. Thus, major heroin dealers in New York are threatened with life imprisonment. In the absence of the death penalty they find it advantageous to have witnesses killed. Such murders surely are not acts of passion in the classical sense, though they occur among associates. They are, in practice, encouraged by the present penal law in New York.

mostly by irrational persons and only by some rational ones would suggest that more rational persons might commit these crimes if the penalty were lower. This hardly argues against capital punishment. Else we would have to abolish penalties whenever they succeed in deterring people. Yet abolitionists urge that capital punishment be abolished because capital crimes are most often committed by the irrational—as though deterring the rational is not quite enough. . . .

## FINAL MORAL CONSIDERATIONS

**The Motive of Revenge.**   One objection to capital punishment is that it gratifies the desire for revenge, regarded as morally unworthy. The Bible has the Lord declare: "Vengeance is mine" (Romans 12:19). He thus legitimized vengeance and reserved it to Himself, probably because it would otherwise be disruptive. But He did not deprecate the desire for vengeance.

Indeed Romans 12:19 barely precedes Romans 13:4, which tells us that the ruler "beareth not the sword in vain: for he is the minister of God, a revenger to execute wrath upon him that doeth evil." It is not unreasonable to interpret Romans 12:19 to suggest that revenge is to be delegated by the injured to the ruler, "the minister of God" who is "to execute wrath." The Bible also enjoins, "The murderer shall surely be put to death" (Numbers 35:16–18), recognizing that the death penalty can be warranted—whatever the motive. Religious tradition certainly suggests no less. However, since religion expects justice and vengeance in the world to come, the faithful may dispense with either in this world, and with any particular penalties—though they seldom have. But a secular state must do justice here and now—it cannot assume that another power, elsewhere, will do justice where its courts did not.

The motives for the death penalty may indeed include vengeance. Vengeance is a compensatory and psychologically reparatory satisfaction for an injured party, group, or society. I do not see wherein it is morally blameworthy. When regulated and controlled by law, vengeance is also socially useful: legal vengeance solidifies social solidarity against lawbreakers and probably is the only alternative to the disruptive private revenge of those who feel harmed. Abolitionists want to promise murderers that what they did to their victims will never be done to them. That promise strikes most people as psychologically incongruous. It is.

At any rate, vengeance is irrelevant to the function of the death penalty. It must be justified independently, by its purpose, whatever the motive. An action, a rule, or a penalty cannot be justified or discredited by the motive for it. No rule should be discarded or regarded as morally wrong (or right) because of the motive of those who support it. Actions, rules, or penalties are justified not by the motives of supporters but by their purpose and by their effectiveness in achieving it without excessively impairing other objectives.[19] Capital punishment is warranted if it achieves its purpose—doing justice and deterring crime—regardless of whether or not it is motivated by vengeful feelings.

**Characteristics.** Before turning to its purely moral aspects, we must examine some specific characteristics of capital punishment. It is feared above all punishments because 1) it is not merely irreversible, as most other penalties are, but also irrevocable; 2) it hastens an event which, unlike pain, deprivation, or injury, is unique in every life and never has been reported on by anyone. Death is an experience that cannot actually be experienced and that ends all experience. Actually, being dead is no different from not being born—a (non)experience we all had before being born. But death is not so perceived. The process of dying, a quite different matter, is confused with it. In turn, dying is feared mainly because death is anticipated—even though death is feared because confused with dying. At any rate, the fear of death is universal and is often attached to the penalty that hastens it—as though without that penalty death would not come. 3) However, the penalty is feared for another reason as well. When death is imposed as a deliberate punishment by one's fellow men, it signifies a complete severing of human solidarity. The convict is explicitly and dramatically rejected by his fellow humans, found unworthy of their society, of sharing life with them. The rejection exacerbates the natural separation anxiety of those who expect imminent death, the fear of final annihilation. Inchoate as these characteristics are in most minds, the specific deterrent effect of executions depends on them and the moral justification of the death penalty, and above and beyond the deterrent effect, does no less.

**Methodological Aside.** Hitherto I have relied on logic and fact. Without relinquishing either, I must appeal to plausibility as well, as I turn to questions of morality unalloyed by other issues. For, whatever ancillary service facts and logic can render, what one is persuaded to accept as morally right or wrong depends on what appears to be plausible in the end. Outside the realm of morals one relies on plausibility only in the beginning.

**The Value of Life.** If there is nothing for the sake of which one may be put to death, can there ever be anything worth risking one's life for? If there is nothing worth dying for, is there any moral value worth living for? Is a life that cannot be transcended by—and given up, or taken, for—anything beyond itself more valuable than one that can be transcended? Can it be that existence, life itself, is the highest moral value, never to be

---

[19]Different motives (the reason why something is done) may generate the same action (what is done), purpose, or intent, just as the same motive may lead to different actions.

given up, or taken, for the sake of anything? And, psychologically, does a social value system in which life itself, however it is lived, becomes the highest of goods enhance the value of human life or cheapen it? I shall content myself here with raising these questions.[20]

*Homo Homini Res Sacra.* "The life of each man should be sacred to each other man," the ancients tell us. They unflinchingly executed murderers.[21] They realized it is not enough to proclaim the sacredness and inviolability of human life. It must be secured as well, by threatening with the loss of their own life those who violate what has been proclaimed as inviolable—the right of innocents to live. Else the inviolability of human life is neither credibly proclaimed nor actually protected. No society can profess that the lives of its members are secure if those who did not allow innocent others to continue living are themselves allowed to continue living—at the expense of the community. To punish a murderer by incarcerating him as one does a pickpocket cannot but cheapen human life. Murder differs in quality from other crimes and deserves, therefore, a punishment that differs in quality from other punishments. There is a discontinuity. It should be underlined, not blurred.

If it were shown that no punishment is more deterrent than a trivial fine, capital punishment for murder would remain just, even if not useful. For murder is not a trifling offense. Punishment must be proportioned to the gravity of the crime, if only to denounce it and to vindicate the importance of the norm violated. Wherefore all penal systems proportion punishments to crimes. The worse the crime the higher the penalty deserved. Why not then the highest penalty—death—for the worst crime—wanton murder? Those rejecting the death penalty have the burden of showing that no crime ever deserves capital punishment[22] —a burden which they have not so far been willing to bear.

Abolitionists insist that we all have an imprescriptible right to live to our natural term: if the innocent victim had a right to live, so does the murderer. That takes egalitarianism too far for my taste. The crime sets victim and murderer apart; if the victim did, the murderer does not deserve to

[20]Insofar as these questions are psychological, empirical evidence would not be irrelevant. But it is likely to be evaluated in terms depending on moral views.

[21]Not always. On the disastrous consequences of periodic failure to do so, Sir Henry Maine waxes eloquent with sorrow in his *Ancient Law* (pp. 408–9).

[22]One may argue that some crimes deserve more than execution and that the above reasoning would justify punitive torture as well. Perhaps. But torture, unlike death, is generally rejected. Therefore penalties have been reduced to a few kinds—fines, confinement, and execution. The issue is academic because, unlike the death penalty, torture has become repulsive to us. (Some reasons for this public revulsion are listed in Chapter 17 of my *Punishing Criminals,* Basic Books, 1975.) As was noted above the range of punishments is bound to be more limited than the range of crimes. We do not accept some punishments, however much deserved they may be.

live. If innocents are to be secure in their lives murderers cannot be. The thought that murderers are to be given as much right to live as their victims oppresses me. So does the thought that a Stalin, a Hitler, an Idi Amin should have as much right to live as their victims did.

**Failure of Nerve.**   Never to execute a wrongdoer, regardless of how depraved his acts, is to proclaim that no act can be so irredeemably vicious as to deserve death—that no human being can be wicked enough to be deprived of life. Who actually can believe that? I find it easier to believe that those who affect such a view suffer from a failure of nerve. They do not think themselves—and therefore anyone else—competent to decide questions of life and death. Aware of human frailty, they shudder at the gravity of the decision and refuse to make it. The irrevocability of a verdict of death is contrary to the modern spirit that likes to pretend that nothing ever is definitive, that everything is open-ended, that doubts must always be entertained and revisions must always remain possible. Such an attitude may be helpful to the reflections of inquiring philosophers and scientists; but it is not proper for courts. They must make final judgments beyond a reasonable doubt. They must decide. They can evade decisions on life and death only by giving up their paramount duties: to do justice, to secure the lives of the citizens, and to vindicate the norms society holds inviolable.

One may object that the death penalty either cannot actually achieve the vindication of violated norms, or is not needed for it. If so, failure to inflict death on the criminal does not belittle the crime, or imply that the life of the criminal is of greater importance than the moral value he violated or the harm he did to his victim. But it is not so. In all societies the degree of social disapproval of wicked acts is expressed in the degree of punishment threatened.[23] Thus, punishments both proclaim and enforce social values according to the importance given to them. There is no other way for society to affirm its values. There is no other effective way of denouncing socially disapproved acts. To refuse to punish any crime with death is to suggest that the negative value of a crime can never exceed the positive value of the life of the person who committed. it. I find that proposition quite implausible.

[23]Social approval is usually not unanimous, and the system of rewards reflects it less.

# SUGGESTIONS FOR FURTHER READING FOR PART FIVE

## Chapter 11: War in the Nuclear Age

Aukerman, Dale. *Darkening Valley*. New York: Seabury Press, 1981.

Bainton, Roland H. *Christian Attitudes toward War and Peace*. Nashville, Tenn.: Abingdon, 1960.

Barnet, Richard J. *Real Security: Restoring American Power in a Dangerous Decade*. New York: Simon & Schuster, 1981.

Clouse, Robert G. *War: Four Christian Views*. Downers Grove, Ill.: Inter Varsity Press, 1981.

Dumbaugh, Donald, ed. *On Earth Peace*. Elgin, Ill.: Brethren Press, 1978.

Fallows, James. *National Defense*. New York: Random House, 1981.

Hackett, John, *et al. The Third World War: August, 1985*. New York: Macmillan, 1979.

Johnson, James. T. *Just War Tradition and the Restraint of War: A Moral and Historical Inquiry*. Princeton, N.J.: Princeton University Press, 1981.

Lens, Sidney. *The Day before Doomsday: An Anatomy of the Nuclear Arms Race*. Boston: Beacon Press, 1978.

Myrdal, Alva. *The Game of Disarmament: How the United States and Russia Run the Arms Race*. New York: Pantheon, 1978.

Shannon, Thomas, ed. *War or Peace? The Search for New Answers*. Maryknoll, N.Y.: Orbis Books, 1980.

Walzer, Michael. *Just and Unjust Wars*. New York: Basic Books, 1977.

## Chapter 12: Capital Punishment

Bedau, Hugo. *The Courts, the Constitution, and Capital Punishment*. Lexington, Mass.: Lexington Books, 1977.

—, ed. *The Death Penalty in America* (third ed.). Chicago: Aldine, 1982.

Black, Charles. *Capital Punishment: The Inevitability of Caprice and Mistake*. New York: Norton, 1974.

DeWolf, L. Harold. *Crime and Justice in America*. New York: Harper & Row, 1975.

Downie, Leonard, Jr. *Justice Denied: The Case for Reform of the Courts*. Baltimore: Penguin Books, 1972.

McCafferty, James A., ed. *Capital Punishment*. New York: Liber-Atherton, 1972.

McHugh, Gerald A. *Christian Faith and Criminal Justice: Toward a Christian Response to Crime and Punishment*. New York: Paulist Press, 1978.

Mitford, Jessica. *Kind and Usual Punishment: The Prison Business*. New York: Random House, 1974.

van den Haag, Ernest. *Punishing Criminals*. New York: Basic Books, 1975.

Wilson, James Q. *Thinking about Crime*. New York: Basic Books, 1975.

# Part Six

## The Christian
## and Bioethical Issues

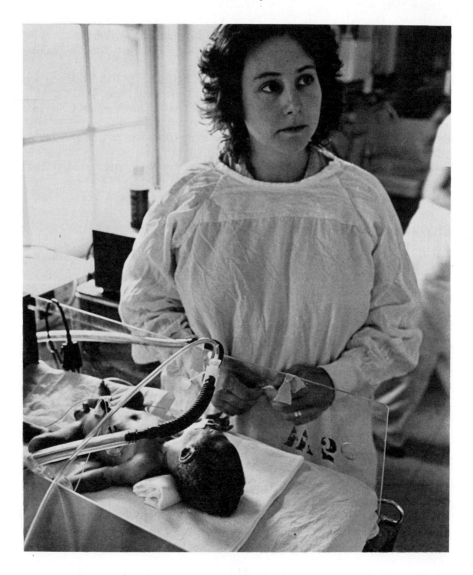

# 13

# The Future
# of Humanity

The impact of technology on the biological and medical sciences during the last few decades has been dramatic, and what it promises for the future both stretches the imagination and sobers the mind. Some of the most exciting and beneficial developments in behalf of humankind appear to be taking place in biomedicine, but there is growing uneasiness over the double-edged character of these advances: Our capacity to help people is accompanied by the possibility of misuse. Thus, scientists who look into the crystal ball have expressed both optimism and pessimism.

Developments in fetology illustrate some of the problems foreseen. With recent technological advances, we can identify and diagnose genetic defects (for example, Down's syndrome, Tay-Sachs disease) while the fetus is *in utero.* When we are able to treat such a fetus effectively it will be a tremendous advance, but at present, diagnosis is often followed by elective abortion. In the future not only will the diseased fetus be diagnosed but also the healthy one who is a carrier of certain genetic diseases. Should our concern to cure disease be accompanied with a concern to prevent the continuation of particular diseases by aborting all unborn carriers? The suggestion sounds morally repulsive, but concern over the deterioration of the human genetic pool has made some scientists think in such terms. It has been suggested that the rather common disease of cystic fibrosis could be eliminated within 40 years by screening all pregnancies and aborting possibly millions of fetuses who, though unaffected by the disease, are diagnosed as carriers.

The possibilities of genetic "engineering" make it apparent that the fundamental question is: What does it mean to be human? There has been a growing effort to arrive at, and apply, certain normative values that will affirm the uniqueness

347

and "givenness" of the individual person in the face of possible assaults by scientists absorbed in the fascinating possibilities of genetic technology. Do we have the autonomy today, or at any time, to decide what human beings will be in the future? Are there limits to what changes and alterations should be made through genetic manipulation, or are we such "open-ended" creatures that we should be allowed in our autonomy to create the "ideal" human specimen and multiply the virtues that we believe will enhance the future of human life? On the one hand, our capacity to design our future is hailed as a natural result of our being the one species that understands its origins; on the other hand, we are cautioned by the words of Nobel laureate George Beadle: "Man knows enough but is not yet wise enough to make man." Reservations against genetic experimentation rest either on principle or on the pragmatic argument that we are still unprepared to administer a world in which we exercise this kind of sovereignty over the development of our race.

The article by Fay Angus dramatizes some of the dilemmas involved in the advances of biotechnology. *In vitro* fertilization, for example, appears to be a marvelous answer to a couple unable to have its own children. But when procreation is removed from the "natural" way in which babies come into being, there is the possibility of producing children for individuals who are not married. What are the parameters for responsible action here? How do we balance the rights of the individual and the long-range welfare of society in such cases? The realm of "biolaw" is obviously going to be marked by intense activity in the coming years; the question is whether we have the moral consensus needed to provide a wise and consistent direction in these developments.

Those who argue for eugenics programs to improve the race do so on moral grounds: If we have a sense of responsibility to the future of our race, we will take the measures necessary to ensure its survival. The obvious question is factual: Are the biological engineers correct in their prediction that our race can survive only through genetic and surgical improvement, or does this view betray the bias of those trained in the natural sciences? Can the challenges of the future be met through enhancing our environment in ways that do not involve such an assault on individual autonomy? Also warranted is the question whether any elite should be given the awesome power involved in making these decisions.

John Fletcher registers a vote of confidence in the direction our society will take in dealing with the developments in human genetics. Turning from the more spectacular but remote possibilities discussed in eugenics programs, he addresses the immediate problems raised by genetic disease. He provides us with an important guideline for the proper utilization of genetic technology in the concept of consent. Any grandiose scheme of genetic improvement of our race would constitute an assault on future generations as a result of irreversible experimentation performed without their consent. Some would question the meaningfulness of "consent" when applied to those not yet conceived or born; and perhaps inherent in Fletcher's position is a moral concern over the uncertainty of the total impact of such experimentation. His contention that human genetics should focus on therapy in regard to specific genetic disease, rather than "improving" the race, also follows from this guideline.

Improving the race could become the overriding goal of our society. It is argued that values of personal freedom and individual autonomy would become obsolete in light of the more cherished values of an improved progeny and an improved race. A vigorous government policy could conceivably hasten this development. We are already becoming accustomed to the idea that we are "articles of manufacture"—today plastic surgery, drug therapy, and other forms of biological and behavioral therapy change us, both physically and mentally, and enhance our appearance and ability to function. We learned long ago to be passive objects at the hands of beauty and health entrepreneurs, who promise to keep us perpetually young and attractive. Perhaps we are already well on the way to acceptance of eugenics programs that will involve extensive genetic and prenatal improvement.

A final observation should be made on the values pertinent to this discussion. We have noted already that the Christian's ethical viewpoint on a given issue may be indistinguishable from, say, that of the humanist. Even though they use different arguments (the Christian's involve theological convictions), they may arrive at the same ethical conclusion. In regard to the ethics of genetic technology, the fundamental value at stake appears to be one on which both humanist and Christian can agree in their common affirmation of the uniqueness and ultimate value of the individual person. The importance of such an affirmation is probably difficult to overemphasize as we face the issues that the future will bring.

# The Promise and Perils of Genetic Meddling

Fay Angus

Carrying with it both risk and benefit, the genetic age is upon us, and one thing is sure—"the future ain't what it used to be!"

Arthur Kornberg, professor of biochemistry at Stanford University, says of recent advances, "We are on the verge of a revolution in the chemical basis of medicine that is as profound as the revolutionary developments in physics and chemistry early in this century that gave us quantum mechanics and a new understanding of the atom and its arrangements.

"We have already learned how to take apart and rearrange DNA—deoxyribonucleic acid—in which the chemistry of heredity is spelled out. As a result it's now very simple to create new genetic arrangements, to make new chromosomes and new species.

"In many respects, these discoveries will change the basis of modern medicine, much as antibiotics did several decades ago." Perhaps, for instance, within the next two decades a chemical analysis of the brain will provide the first clear explanation of the broad scope of human emotions —a launching pad to the core of consciousness and thought, and their relation to brain structure and function.

We have reached an intersection in human destiny that rattles our complacency and asks, "Where are we going and do we really want to get there?"

Robert Sinsheimer of the University of California, Santa Cruz, notes that today is a time of "intense self-doubt, corroding confidence, and a crippling resolve; a time of troubled present and ominous future. . . . Hence, it is not surprising that so great a triumph as man's discovery of the molecular basis of inheritance should provoke fear instead of joy, breed suspicion instead of zest, and spawn the troubled anguish of indecision instead of the proud relief of understanding."

Science bristles at any interference with its right to freedom of inquiry. It is a camp divided; some say, "It's our job to do the research, and society's job to cope with what we do." But others admit the wake of hazard left

Reprinted by permission from *Christianity Today,* issue of May 8, 1981. Copyright © 1981 *Christianity Today.* Fay Angus is a freelance writer residing in California.

by the course of nuclear fission, and, like Alvin Toffler, caution, "If we do not learn from history, we shall be compelled to relive it. True. But if we do not change the future we shall be compelled to endure it. And that could be worse."

We are developing ways to manipulate the genetic programming of the very structure of life. These methods hold promise for what geneticists call "an escape from the tyranny of inheritance." This is good news for eliminating genetically based diseases. But, we ask, At what price? A society parented in a laboratory, controlled by scientists, robbed of humanity?

In our society, we develop our ethics by gathering information, discussing it publicly, deciding and acting individually, and, in time, by arriving at a consensus of what appears to be good for mankind. Our personal and social ethical codes are authorized by common consent, then implemented through legislation.

As push comes to shove, self-interest groups are jockeying for position to influence the age. It is imperative that we examine the issues and respond from a biblical understanding of the sanctity of God's gift of life.

## CREATING TO SPECIFICATION

The issue of manipulating reproduction triggered public concern with the birth in 1978 in Oldham, England, of Louise Brown, the first baby conceived *in vitro* (in a test tube). Since that time, Dr. Mukherjec of Calcutta, India, has safely delivered a child fertilized from a frozen embryo, a technique that ushers in the potential of selective breeding from life placed "on hold." Commercial exploitation of what is now being called the ultimate consumer trip has already been established through corporations such as IDANT in New York. It pays $20 for each "acceptable" ejaculate from some 60 carefully selected regular depositors to its sperm bank. The frozen sperm units are then sold for $35 to subscribing doctors.

Gemetrics in Chicago offers gender selection through technologies capable of separating X chromosome- and Y chromosome-carrying sperm (male sperm swim faster, making separation easier) and has successfully engineered 10 full-term births, 7 boys and 3 girls.

The surrogate mother (advertised as womb for rent) receives a fee of between $10,000 and $20,000 per term. Dr. Richard Levine, a Louisville, Kentucky, physician, has 25 women under contract as surrogates. Five pregnancies are under way and he anticipates 100 or more babies delivered through his service by the end of 1981. The program hit a snag in January, however, when Attorney General Steven L. Beshear filed for a declaratory judgment on the ground that this violates the Kentucky adoption statutes. In *Doe* v. *Kelley*, the Michigan lower court has said surrogate mothering is illegal because a mother may not be paid money for giving up her right to her own natural child. Children may not be sold in Michigan.

Contracts covering parents and surrogate mothers have brought a new dimension into biolaw. Most states prohibit an exchange of money as payment for adopting children. Lawyers and jurists are now considering whether surrogate services violate statutes prohibiting prostitution. Possible arguments charging discrimination may be sounded if a man is permitted to sell his sperm, but a woman is not permitted to rent her womb!

The good news that parents desperate for a child of their own may get one by reproductive manipulation, must be balanced against the potential bad news.

Applications are now being sent to single men and women for these reproductive consumer services—launching yet another assault on the already shaky traditional family. Will *in vitro* fertilization, embryo transfer, and surrogate wombs for rent be available to single people? Will they be extended to the homosexual? Will laboratory-controlled bioparenting produce a quasi-orphaned society?

Science will reach the ultimate in reproductive manipulation when *in vitro* fertilization extends to incubation in an artificial womb for full-term laboratory delivery. Scientists have anticipated this technology for the very near future and have already achieved it in part by sustaining premature babies with increasing success—at Children's Hospital, San Diego, one has been delivered 23 weeks from conception weighing only one pound one ounce.

There is enormous appeal in the right of every child to be born free of genetic defects, and bioengineered to be the most productive human possible. But what are we to do with the substandard embryo, and who is qualified to decide the acceptable standards? Screening through amniocentesis, ultrasound scanning, and fetoscopy provides options that further complicate the already explosive issue of abortion.

Controversial theologian Joseph Fletcher even claims, "To deliberately and knowingly bring a diseased or defective child into the world injures society, very probably injures the family, and certainly injures the individual who is born in that condition."

In 1979, a New Jersey court ruled that even though impaired (in this case, with Down's syndrome), life was more valuable than no life at all. It observed that the ability to "love and be loved and to experience happiness and pleasure—emotions which are truly the essence of life," was more important than the suffering endured.

But on the opposite side, in a June 1980 decision involving Tay-Sachs disease, Judge Bernard Jefferson of the California Court of Appeals affirmed the "*un*birth-right" of a child when he ruled that not only parents, but possibly even a physician and laboratory, could be sued for negligently not having aborted the fetus.

Dr. Jokichi Takamine, president of the Alcoholism Council of Southern California, says research shows that genetics plays a classic role in predisposition toward alcoholism (10 to 20 percent on the mother's side; 25 to 55 percent on the father's side). Since alcoholism is a major sociological problem, this poses the serious question of whether genetic abortion will be called for on such frivolous grounds as predisposition toward alcoholism. Abortion for reasons of depression or gender might be next.

Does the fetus have the right, independent of society or even of its own parents, to be born? Such a question will generate strands in a tangled web that will keep courtrooms tied up in legal debate over many years.

Statistics on longevity show that the number of people living to reach 100 years or over has increased 43 percent in the last five years.

Biomedicine has given us artificial corneas and lenses, artificial intestines, and synthetic joints and limbs. At the University of Southern California, research continues toward developing an artificial pancreas—a device that will monitor the level of blood sugar in the body and, when necessary, automatically dispense corrective doses of insulin.

A nuclear-powered heart that will run continuously and automatically for longer than the average human lifespan is being tested in animals. Scientists at the University of Utah have produced an artificial kidney to be carried in a backpack. Miniaturization will make it possible to implant surgically an electrodialysis unit. Synthetic blood is being studied, not to substitute completely for blood, but to augment massive transfusions in open-heart surgery and total blood recirculation.

Biochemists at George Washington University think that one day we will be able to regenerate arms and legs; they are encouraged in this by the chemical combination present in children (but lacking in adults) that permits spontaneous regrowth of fingertips. Studies in Philadelphia bring the possibility of regrowing damaged organs through cloning. One scientist at the Wistar Institute introduced hydrocortisone into the culture of "old" human cells, giving them the thrust to continue "reproducing." Scientists may refine and expand this technology to induce the regeneration of organs.

Studies at Cal Tech and laboratories around the country are pushing hard toward a method of shutting off the body's aging process. Once the genetic time clock is found, researchers can regulate it.

With the millions of possibilities from recombinant DNA and genetic surgery, scientists anticipate the eventual control of genetically based diseases. This alone might extend life to a length reminiscent of the patriarchs! Some futurists are even convinced that we are approaching what they call an "Impending Society of Immortals."

## BEHAVIOR MODIFICATION

Neurobiologists are discovering that memory, concentration, fear, aggression, joy, love, peace, and a long list of other human functions and emotions are directly linked to chemical and electrical transmitters in the brain. A few whiffs of vasopressin can stimulate memory in cases of amnesia and senility. Lithium is aiding the successful treatment of mental disorders. At Stanford, researchers have found that naloxone, a chemical known to block the action of endorphins in the brain, has brought relief to severely impaired schizophrenics who have auditory hallucinations.

Others, in test runs, are successfully stimulating the brain electronically to ease chronic pain, give back the use of paralyzed limbs, and, in some cases, to modify behavior.

All this is good news, but we may be given pause on learning that over one million school children in the United States are now on some type of drug that modifies behavior for the purpose of improving their function, both in and out of the classroom. Ritalin and Dexedrine are those drugs most commonly used.

Research at the Tulane University School of Medicine shows that students injected with ACTH (adrenocorticotrophic hormone) and MSH (melanocyte-stimulating hormone) were better able to spend longer and more effective periods in concentrating on their studies and also to remember geometrical figures that were flashed before them.

Since calculators, computers, videotapes, and an increasing number of "external" aids are an acceptable part of the educational process, proponents of gene therapy ask why we should not program "internal" biochemical and biogenetic change for future generations. To a school system plagued with violence and deteriorating academic achievement, control through behavior modification and gene therapy is tempting. The great leap forward in scientific discovery has awakened public response. That we may eliminate the problems of retarded children and schizophrenics, empty our mental hospitals through genetic and chemical processes, and wipe out sickle cell anemia, Tay-Sachs, Gauche's, and other genetic diseases to free our children from "the chromosomal lottery," is all good news. But again, we ask ourselves, At what price?

## BIOHAZARD

How does scientific freedom intersect with social responsibility? A decade ago, international experts gathered together at a symposium in New York to consider "Ethical Issues in Human Genetics."

At that time, Robert Sinsheimer of Cal Tech (he is now chancellor of the University of California, Santa Cruz) was a powerful voice of caution with his penetrating statements. "For what purpose," he asked, "should we alter our genes? To whom should we give this power? To those who have already perverted physics into atomic weapons, chemistry into poison gas, or electronics into guided missiles? If we make men gods, are they to be gods of war?"

He further declared, "One of the greatest threats to the rational development of genetic modification will appear if it should become captive to irrational nationalist purposes. For this reason I think it is imperative that we begin now to establish international cooperation in, and regulation of, this entire enterprise."

In June 1980, by a slim 5-to-4 margin, the U.S. Supreme Court applied the patent law written by Thomas Jefferson in 1793 to new forms of life created in the laboratory—living organisms. (The generally accepted definition of "living" is that a substance be capable of reproducing, a process such as occurs in cell division.)

The Supreme Court deliberately chose not to address what one might regard as the deeper issues, either of philosophy, or ethics, or biological hazard. In their opinion, that was not their job (but rather, the responsibility of Congress). Their job was simply to decide whether or not, under the terms of the patent laws of 1793 and subsequent modifications, living organisms were or were not included. They decided by a margin of one vote that they were included and could be patented.

In an interview with Dr. Sinsheimer, I asked, "Is this going to head us into a commercial exploitation of certain genetic consumer items?" He replied, "Sure—no question about it!" Such commercial development of biotechnology could well limit free exchange of information at the level of laboratory research.

On the critical subject of risk, or "biohazard," Sinsheimer warned of advertently or inadvertently creating something we do not want: "Dangerous organisms already exist, but that doesn't mean one couldn't add new ones, or one that had particularly noxious qualities. I don't think it's likely, but it is possible."

By its guidelines, the National Institutes of Health still forbids many experiments as too dangerous. This raises an old paradox: "If the research is safe, why will science agree to restrictions?" and, "If science agrees to restrictions, how can it claim the research is safe?"

In August 1980, the news broke that Ian Kennedy, a virologist at the University of California, San Diego, studying the sindbis virus, had cloned a rare African forest virus, semliki, which had a higher risk classification and was not approved for cloning under NIH safety guidelines. This was believed to be the first such violation of the federal government's regulations on cloning and recombinant DNA. The university's biosafety committee put the cloned material in a special "containment" freezer and launched an investigation. Kennedy has vacated his position.

Sinsheimer commented, "This illustrates one of the concerns people have had—that scientists do make mistakes, and accidents do happen. You don't always accomplish what you set out to accomplish. That's why some of us felt that's a reason for maintaining more stringent guidelines. This is an illustration that all procedures are fallible."

In waving the flag of caution, Sinsheimer is joined by many other internationally respected scientists. In a letter to *Science* magazine titled "The Dangers of Genetic Meddling," Erwin Chargaff of Columbia University says, "You can stop splitting the atom; you may even decide not to kill entire populations by the use of a few bombs, but *you cannot recall a new form of life!* Once you have constructed a viable E. coli cell carrying a plasmid DNA into which a piece of eukaryotic DNA has been spliced, it will survive you, and your children, and your children's children. . . . The world is given to us on loan. We come and we go; and after a time we leave earth and air and water to others who come after us. My generation, or perhaps the one preceding mine, has been the first to engage, under the leadership of the exact sciences, in a destructive colonial war against nature. The future will curse us for it."

On the other hand, Arthur Kornberg calls for a balanced response: "Any knowledge can be misapplied. Whether scientists engage in improper activity will ultimately depend on the ethics and morality of the community. But if you operate in a climate of fear in which you see only the unfortunate and evil developments, then you simply can't make any progress."

## CHRISTIAN PERSPECTIVE

Some knowledge accumulates faster than the wisdom to manage it. Some have defined this as "dangerous knowledge." Looking at some recent discoveries, we are tempted to exclaim, "We ain't wise enough to be this smart!"

A Christian response to the good news/bad news on the biogenetic manipulation of life comes from Lewis Smedes, professor of ethics at Fuller Theological Seminary in Pasadena, California:

"Christians are given two ingredients that exist in tension. One of them is our belief in the supremacy of a sovereign God. He is a God who superintends life. But he superintends it in a way that is collaborative with human agencies. He even does this to the point of working out his divine providence through such radically new technologies as genetic tampering or genetic manipulation—or to use much nicer words, genetic surgery or genetic counseling.

"The second ingredient in the tension is the human propensity for evil. The potential for evil in this new technology is great. Are we going to live in a society where some people have the prerogative of basically altering the humanity of other people, whether it is still in the embryo stage of growth, or fully developed? The arrogance of that is enough to give us pause. Plain and simple common sense says, 'Please go slowly, with all careful deliberation. We have at stake the future of the human race!'"

As those who survived the experiments at Auschwitz will attest, political control of scientific technology has etched its horror across history. It is a legacy we must remember.

The expanding dimensions of knowledge present the Pandora dilemma —promise in counterpoint with peril. We too may become the victims of our own unleashed curiosity. Will the decisions we make as a generation change not only the course of human destiny but the very structure of human life? To quote Chargaff, will "the future curse us for it"? We pray not.

As never before, it is crucial that the Christian community raise responsibly to defend a root of its biblical foundation—the sanctity of human life.

"In the beginning God created. . . . God created man in his own image, . . . male and female created he them."

If man is to play God, then Genesis will need to be redefined.

# Applied Genetics: No Ultimate Threat

John Fletcher

Ethics, like any human enterprise, has frontiers. The frontiers of ethics are along areas of human action in which social change has outstripped the guidance and experience available to us as we seek to use our freedom and understand ourselves. One such area is certainly what is happening and what is proposed to happen in the application of knowledge of human genetics to disease, procreation, and family-planning. Some call this whole area "genetic engineering"; this is an unfortunate term leading to the belief that there are only mechanical solutions to genetic problems. Actually, applied human genetics is now, and promises to continue to be, an arena of intense ethical conflict.

Reprinted by permission from *Engage/Social Action*, October, 1973. Published by the United Methodist Board of Church and Society and the United Church of Christ Center for Social Action, 100 Maryland Avenue N.E., Washington, D.C. John Fletcher, Episcopal minister and educator, has written extensively in the area of medical ethics.

## GENETIC DECISIONS INVOLVE DEBATE ON MORALITY

In the noisy heat of making decisions in genetic counselling, genetic screening, in the laboratory, in a planning or policy group, what we most often debate is "morality." Should we or should we not approve a specific proposal: i.e. to do research in genetics on newly dead or dying fetuses following abortion? Concern for morality appeals for guidelines to inform *what* we should do or avoid in specific situations. Morality is always concrete. When we get at some distance from decisions and pressure, as in articles or at conferences, we can develop the *whys* and *wherefores* which uphold or deny certain courses of action. Seeking and giving guidance in the light of what we believe about the meaning of life and death, good and evil, is ethics. Presumably, there should be a coherence between the reasons for decisions and the actual shape of decisions, but on close examination we find a gap, a moral fissure, between what we intend and what we do.

Because applied human genetics involves power at least equal to, if not greater in human destiny, than atomic energy, there has been intense interdisciplinary study of the ethical, social, and legal issues involved not only in the *whats* of genetics, but in the *whys*. In the past four years theological and philosophical discussions between scientists and their colleagues from other disciplines including theology have occurred. This is important since the stakes in applied human genetics are very high, indeed, the highest. The continuation of the human story may depend, in part, on how great a moral fissure appears between what we intend and what we do, genetically.

## PROBLEMS EMERGE FROM PREVENTING
## GENETIC DISEASE

What are the crucial activities in present applied genetics? What is being proposed? And what are the ethical and theological implications of these advances?

In the interest of space, I shall not discuss any proposed "eugenics" program, such as sperm-bank programs for selection of "outstanding" genotypes, or the suggestion that we should prenatally adopt our children by selecting sperm and ova from outstanding persons, fertilize them in laboratory conditions, and when all is "normal," the fertilized egg would be implanted in the womb of a woman who will grow the fetus and adopt it for her own. Such proposals seem exotic and far-fetched in the political and ethical senses.

Of far more immediate interest are problems emerging from a range of strategies and proposals for treatment of prevention of the effects and causes of genetic disease. The concept of genetic disease is complex, since genetic disease must not be compared to any of the infectious diseases (malaria, typhoid, etc.) which have been so much reduced in developed societies. A large number of diseases are caused by interplay between genetic (hereditary) and environmental forces. For example, those people whose ancestry originated in regions highly plagued by malaria developed a genetic protection, the "sickling gene." Sickle cell anemia occurs today in children whose parents are carriers of the gene, and, because malaria has been essentially overcome in developed societies, the sickling gene has no positive function.

A concept of "genetic health" is as complex as that of genetic disease. What does it mean to be genetically "healthy" when each person is estimated to carry a small number of lethal genes? There is no way to be "clean" genetically. We are all genetically in trouble, yet some are in deeper trouble than others depending on what natural selection and their parents have dealt them. A simple breakdown of the types of genetic disease by Arno Motulsky, a geneticist, will reveal that these conditions are too widespread to quarantine the offenders as in a typhoid epidemic:

Diseases caused by problematic number of structure of chromosomes; e.g. Down's syndrome 1/600 births.
Diseases caused by mutations affecting a single gene; e.g. hemophilia, sickle cell anemia, cystic fibrosis.
Diseases caused by interaction of several genes; e.g. hypertension, diabetes.
Diseases caused by mother/child incompatibility; e.g. Rh disease of the newborn.

These examples of the four types of genetic diseases have large numbers of affected persons and carriers. The political and ethical problems posed by starting a crusade to "eradicate" any of these diseases would mean an intervention into the real life chances of real people our society presently supports. We must re-educate ourselves as to genetic disease. As the history of the screening for sickle cell disease and its carrier state already shows, it is no simple matter to speak of "control" of that disease or its carriers. The first spate of laws, state and municipal, referring to sickle cell screening, tend to be riddled with medical and racial mythology. For example, in an effort to screen premaritally for sickle hemoglobin, the legislature of New York stated:

". . . . such test as may be necessary shall be given to each applicant for a marriage license who is not of the Caucasian, Indian or Oriental race for the purposes of discovering the existence of sickle cell anemia" (N.Y. State, Chap. 994, Sect. 13, Session Law 1972).

This extraordinary statement obscures two crucial facts: others than blacks may carry the trait, and the test discloses carrier status, not the disease. Clearing up the mythology about disease and race go hand-in-hand with re-educating ourselves.


## ACTIVE AND PROPOSED METHODS OF TREATMENT

Treatment of the expressions of genetic disease, sometimes called "euphenics," encompasses a vast range of medical techniques. Diet-regulated treatments can control a genetic disease (PKU) leading to mental retardation. Hemophilia can be treated by injection of the needed protein substance. When an excess of substance is the problem, such as excess copper in liver and brain (Wilson's disease), the copper can be removed by drugs. Transplanting genetically abnormal kidneys with donor kidneys has been increasingly performed. These techniques raise essentially no questions which have not already been considered in medical ethics.

When we move beyond these treatments to ideas for engineering human development, such as Joshua Lederberg's suggestion that we regulate the size of the human brain by prenatal or early postnatal intervention, new ethical conflicts definitely arise. Whose babies would be the first chosen for this socio-medical experiment, and who would decide how large a brain they should have? How would physicians ever morally get to know that the experiment is really safe? Brain engineering of this type would still be "euphenics," since it would involve changing what is biologically given. When one moves from the goal of treatment of a known disease to socially planned change in human development, the ethical problems escalate.

Unique to genetic disease, and lying somewhere between treatment and prevention, are techniques of genetic counselling, prenatal diagnosis, and genetic screening. Every couple who knows that they are at risk because an ill child has already been born should have genetic counselling. This type of counselling usually involves no complex ethical problems, since the goal is to inform parents on risk of recurrence.

If a new pregnancy occurs, the parents can have the option of prenatal diagnosis. Withdrawal of amniotic fluid from a pregnant woman permits cells of the fetus to be cultured and pictures taken for the inspection of physicians. Diagnosis of several dozen genetic diseases is now possible. If the diagnosis is negative, the parents are relieved from the terror of not knowing, and barring technological error, they can look forward to the birth of a healthy child. If the diagnosis is positive, the parents have a choice of abortion (with or without hysterotomy),[1] or allowing another ill child to be born.

## DECISIONS CAUSE GREAT MORAL SUFFERING

For parents who desperately want children, deciding to abort their own child is a terrible prospect. In a study with twenty-five couples who sought tests in pregnancy, I found them willing to accept abortion of a seriously ill child, although these decisions were made with great moral suffering. My own view is that abortion is acceptable when it can be shown that the defect is sufficiently serious to threaten a meaningful life, and that the presence of a defective child would be a serious threat to the family involved.

It is not inevitable that disaster follows the birth of defective children. Through new techniques called "amnioscopy," it will be possible to inspect the fetus in the first and second month of development. If it were discovered that a fetus with only one arm was developing, is that a sufficient reason for abortion? I believe not. As applied genetics increases, however, there will be many more types of border-line cases.

Parents of children who were diagnosed as free from genetic disease found that they were not out of the woods ethically, even though they were free from the fear of the unknown. Entering the test means that they contemplate the abortion of the child. If the child is healthy, they then begin to imagine what it will be like to tell the child *why* they had him or her tested, since children will find out. "What would you have done if I had been like sister?" they imagined the child asking. As one parent said to me, there is "no good way to explain to your own child that you might have had a part in deciding the end of his life."

Sidney Callahan, an author, has worried that such children might think that their parents would do away with them if they became very ill. My own position is that parents must not rationalize away the threat to the bond with their children posed by the test by saying something like: "You would have preferred not to be alive if you had been like your sister." Since when is it ethical for a stronger group to argue that a weaker group would be better off dead! A more directly honest, and responsible, answer is: "We decided to do it because we could not bear up under the strain of having another sick child." So we can see how applied human genetics has already begun to affect the way parents and children relate, as well as the way parents learn their roles.

It is more responsible for parents to seek knowledge from prenatal diagnosis so that they can act upon facts, than it is for them to refuse to

[1][Late abortion by a small Caesarean section—Eds.]

know. Once in possession of the facts, the parents should not be coerced in any way, towards either abortion or allowing the child to be born. They should be informed about the real nature of the illness prior to testing. Some geneticists promote a social policy which approves a long-range strategy of abortion of genetically defective fetuses following diagnosis. I disagree with this concept, because the healing and not the elimination of handicapped human life should be our goal. We must not become accustomed to abortion of illness or confuse abortion with therapy.

## GENETIC SCREENING PROGRAMS INCREASING

Genetic screening programs are springing up rapidly in this country, especially around Tay-Sachs disease, carried almost always by Jews of Eastern European descent, and sickle cell anemia, carried largely by those of African ancestry. Various degrees of coercion can be built into screening programs. Some states require each black child to be tested before entering first grade. In my estimation, this type of coercion is repressive. It singles out black children, while others than blacks can carry the disease. A more voluntary and educational approach to recruiting screenees, such as is done in New Jersey, is definitely advisable.

The advantages to screening are that early knowledge about one's genetic make-up can enter into marriage and procreation decisions, and in screening newborns for a disease like PKU, treatment can be introduced which reverses the ill effects of the disease. The moral problems of screening revolve around issues of privacy, possible stigmatization, and the anxiety which can be caused when an uninformed person mistakenly assumes he is a carrier, or confuses the carrier state with the disease itself. Because screening usually takes place in large groups, it is difficult to practice "informed consent," but such should be the rule.

## METHODS TO REPLACE DEFICIENT ENZYMES AT HAND

Two methods actually close to reproduction in the treatment of genetic disease involve attempts to replace deficient enzymes or to add chemicals to unstable enzymes to correct them. These methods will be considered experimental until proven safe, and the rules of human experimentation should apply. Through advances in techniques of laparoscopy, human eggs can be obtained from a female donor and fertilized *in vitro* by a donor. Suppose that in the case of a couple who both carried the gene for a disease, the egg of the mother was fertilized by a sperm derived from a non-husband donor, grown for a space *in vitro* and then reintroduced for final gestation in her womb. Would this differ in any respect from present practices of a sperm donation by other than one's husband? If it could be shown that the *in vitro* growth period and re-entry were safe for the developing child, and if this knowledge can be obtained without excessive risk to any presently living fetuses, I see no moral reason to object to this type of prevention of genetic disease, assuming the parents' full consent.

It is also conceivable that the technique called "cloning" will be advanced as a way of preventing genetic disease. Cloning builds upon the proof in experiments with frogs that whole copies of an existing individual can be replicated out of cells taken from germ plasm, and projects the possibility onto humans. The result would be a child who was the identical twin of the father or mother, assuming that only in the case of couple-carriers cloning would be recommended. Cloning has such great technical and ethical problems related even to testing its feasibility in humans as to rule it out as a practical choice.

## GENETIC THERAPY PROPOSALS

Finally, there have been several major proposals for "genetic therapy," based largely on the possibility that healthy genetic material could be carried by a virus to replace unhealthy material. Many geneticists who have reviewed the feasibility of gene therapy by this method emphasize the technical difficulties and foresee a long period of development.

My own preference is to help to steer applied human genetics in the direction of therapeutic goals rather than toward questionable social goals, such as the alleviation of aggression or the prenatal stimulation of brain size. My reason for this revolves around the concept of consent, which is not only a cornerstone of medical ethics, but of political ethics. Since genetic experimentation is irreversible, the more grandiose plans for positive eugenics would not be ethical. If our generation decided to experiment on another generation without its consent (and how could they consent?), this would constitute an act of aggression. Yet we must not be frightened into putting a freeze on the application of genetic knowledge to disease.

Task forces of scientists, public figures, and their colleagues in ethics need now to be selecting the genetic diseases against which we will direct research and ultimately, therapy. The guidelines for which diseases will be chosen are not easy to compose, but they should include the frequency of the disease, its severity, and the feasibility of developing a therapy. We must restrain our power to change the next generation, but we must not restrain our need to be merciful or to heal.

I do not believe that a technological society is gradually dehumanizing us. Humans make culture. We are co-creators, with God, of the total fabric in which we live. Man has the initiative in the culture-making process. The roots of dehumanization lie deeper in us than the effects of technology upon us. There is no ultimate threat to the concept of the sanctity of life or the individual from genetic knowledge. What we must speak out against is the hasty and often biased way genetic experimentation may be used, or the too hasty translation of genetic knowledge into laws which further depress and debase minority groups.

Some will be afraid of applied genetics on the grounds that we should not "play God" and that we are not wise enough to use the knowledge. Since none of us can provide the basic possibility of life, we cannot play God. We shall always be secondary creators and never primary. We will not be wise enough to use knowledge perfectly, but we should not restrain actions directed toward relieving the obvious suffering caused by an unfeeling genetic fate.

# 14

# Abortion

What constitutes human life? This is a question that may not appear to be overly difficult to answer in the abstract—we could likely agree on a textbook definition of human life. But this question locates the fundamental issue that has been intensely debated in recent decades as it relates to the very beginning and the very end of life. At these two opposite extremes things can become fuzzy in our attempt to answer this question. The two topics of abortion and euthanasia express the moral issues at stake in this debate, and we address them now in these two concluding chapters. Abortion and euthanasia have long been debated by Christians and society at large, but the debate has been intensified because of the advances in medical technology and the new situations created by these advances in the treatment of both nascent life (fetology) and the terminally ill.

The subject of abortion has been particularly divisive in our society. At one extreme in this debate are those who maintain that the fetus is essentially tissue belonging to the woman, having no independent humanity of its own. On the opposite side are those who argue that the fetus is a human being, innocent and totally dependent upon us, whose rights to life must be protected against the so-called rights of the woman. The first view absolutizes the rights of the woman, the second view does the same for the fetus. Each of these positions denies that there is a moral issue in terms of competing values; there is simply a clear-cut answer to the question of abortion (either for or against) without any need to consider the circumstances in each particular case. Between the advocates of these two positions stand those who are compelled to find a more nuanced point of view. They believe that one cannot give an absolute answer covering every case of contemplated abortion. On the contrary, each case must be considered in light of its own circumstances.

In order to gain a picture of the present situation in the abortion debate, a brief review of the legal setting is necessary. Abortion had been governed by state laws in this country, which uniformly prohibited it. In 1959 the American Law

Institute proposed that abortion be legalized in cases where, upon certification of two physicians, an interruption of the pregnancy was required for the "physical or mental health" of the mother. In 1962 the American Bar Association suggested the liberalizing of abortion laws, allowing abortion in cases of incest, rape, and in those instances where the physical and mental well-being of the woman was at stake (just what constitutes a meaningful threat to mental health or well-being was clearly destined to become an issue). With Colorado taking the lead in 1967, a number of states liberalized their abortion laws according to the model suggested by the American Bar Association. Some statutes were changed to the point that women could receive an abortion with no questions asked—"abortion on demand."

The legal struggle that ensued soon reached the Supreme Court. The cases of *Roe v. Wade* and *Doe v. Bolton* (January 22, 1973) marked an important turning point in the abortion debate. In these decisions the court struck down both the older, more restrictive legislation operative in 30 states and the more lenient legislation of 16 other states. By a 7:2 vote the court affirmed the right of a woman to have an abortion in the first trimester of her pregnancy; it also declared that the state's interest in the health of the mother and in the potentiality of human life may lead it to regulate abortion procedures in the second trimester and to regulate and possibly proscribe abortion after viability of the fetus. Even after viability, however, abortion must be permitted if there would be danger to the life or health of the mother.

Justice Blackmun's majority opinion tried to skirt the complicated moral questions concerning abortion. "We need not resolve the difficult question of when life begins," he wrote, stating that the court could not resolve an issue on which those who work in the disciplines of medicine, theology, and philosophy do not agree. Instead, the court based its decision on four supports: (1) It noted that historically there has been no consistent opposition to abortion because of differing judgments concerning the time when the fetus developed into a person; (2) it observed that the late nineteenth-century laws establishing a clear pattern of opposition to abortion were frequently motivated by the danger of abortion to the health of the mother, a factor that has been altered by modern technology; (3) it determined that the rights of privacy guaranteed by the Fourteenth Amendment protect a woman's decision to have an abortion in the first stage of pregnancy, but do not eliminate state interest in later stages out of concern for the woman's health and for the "potentiality of life"; and (4) it declared that the word "person" in the Fourteenth Amendment cannot be used to include the unborn. By its legal discussion and its preference for the phrase "potentiality of life," the court took a clear position on the question of when life begins, the issue it wanted to avoid!

Anti-abortionists, having lost the judicial battle, turned to Congress in an effort to create legislation that would make abortion illegal. Senator James Buckley of New York introduced the "Human Life Amendment," which would constitutionally outlaw abortion, but so far it has not gotten past the Senate. More recently, bills have been introduced in Congress that would define life as beginning at conception. Another approach has been taken by the "Hatch Amendment," which would allow the states to pass restrictive abortion laws. The legal issue is clearly far from settled; the intensity of this debate has spawned groups —particularly on the "pro-life" side—which have practiced an avid "one-issue" politics in an effort to secure a President and Congress favoring their side.

People's deep feelings on the subject of abortion have resulted in emotion-laden argument that does not hesitate to misrepresent an opposing position or verbally abuse those who disagree. Richard A. McCormick's article addresses this problem by recommending some rules to raise the level of discussion. What moral claim does "a person in the process of becoming" make upon us? He allows that the way in which one defines "nascent life" or "person" will betray one's position in this debate, and he does not pretend to be above the debate in stipulating rules for it. One can see his concern for fetal life in his statement that the substance of the church's conviction is that "abortion is tolerable only when it is a life-saving, therefore also life-serving, intervention." But he is not pressing his viewpoint here; he is making an effective case for a more careful, measured presentation of one's viewpoint.

Rachel Conrad Wahlberg explores this issue through its existential, experiential reality, the perspective of the pregnant woman, for which there is no comparable male experience. While emphasizing the woman's control over the fetus, she also describes the conflicting sense of the woman living under threat, not in control, in a society whose laws and mores favor men. To illustrate this discrimination, she asks why the married woman is not able to offer an infant for adoption as well as the unmarried woman. It appears that a woman's only defense is to claim autonomy over her own body. To Wahlberg the issue of the beginning of life is clear: Because of the dependency of the fetus, its parasitical relationship to its mother, it is at best "potentially human," "nearly human." Still, Wahlberg notes that most women would not seek an abortion after feeling the fetus move and declares that, ideally, abortion should be limited to the first trimester (a narrower view than the Supreme Court eventually adopted).

Beyond the question of the nature of human life—the critical issue in this debate—is the secondary question, When does human life begin? Albert C. Outler addresses the latter question at some length, concluding that every attempt to determine what he labels the "magic moment" is doomed to failure. Since there is such a variety of conclusions in which the "moment" is moved from conception to well beyond birth, and no proof for any particular view, Outler invites us to live "as if" human life begins at conception, believing that this option has stronger moral implications for the preservation of the value of life than does the opposite possibility. While not opposing therapeutic abortion, Outler suggests that the practice of general abortion will so numb our moral sensitivities that the principle of the sanctity of human life (as expressed in social revulsion against infanticide and euthanasia) will be severely qualified.

# Abortion: Rules for Debate

Richard A. McCormick

There are a million legal abortions done annually in the United States. If this is what many people think it is (unjustified killing of human beings, in most cases), then it certainly constitutes the major moral tragedy of our country. In contrast, over many years 50,000 Americans were lost in Vietnam. About the problem of abortion and its regulation, however, Americans are profoundly polarized, and there seems little hope of unlocking deeply protected positions to reach any kind of national consensus. Yet surely that is desirable on an issue so grave.

I have been professionally involved in this problem for well over 20 years, on podium and in print, and above all in many hundreds of hours of conversation. Such experiences do not necessarily increase wisdom. But they do generate some rather clear impressions about the quality of discourse on the problem of abortion. I have to conclude, regrettably, that the level of conversation is deplorably low. On both sides, slogans are used as if they were arguments; the sound level rises as verbal bludgeoning and interruptions multiply; the dialogue of the deaf continues. Some of our most prestigious new media (e.g., *The New York Times, The Washington Post*) support policies that stem from moral positions whose premises and assumptions they have not sufficiently examined, let alone argued. The same can be said of some anti-abortionists in the policies they propose. An executive assistant in the Senate told me recently that the two most obnoxious lobbies on the hill are the anti-abortionists and the pro-abortionists. Briefly, civil conversation on this subject has all but disappeared. Perhaps now is the time for camping in abortion clinics. . . . But I think not, at least in the sense that such tactics should not replace disciplined argument.

Many of us have become bone weary of this discussion. But to yield to such fatigue would be to run from a problem, not wrestle with it. If stay we ought and must, then it may be of help to propose a set of "rules for conversation," the observance of which could nudge us toward more communicative conversation. That is surely a modest achievement, but

Reprinted with permission of America Press, Inc., 106 West 56th Street, New York, N.Y. 10019. Copyright © 1978 All rights reserved. From *America*, July 22, 1978. Richard A. McCormick, S.J., is Rose F. Kennedy Professor of Christian Ethics at the Center for Bioethics, The Kennedy Institute at Georgetown University, and author of numerous articles and books in the area of social ethics.

where the level of discourse is as chaotic and sclerotic as it is, modesty recommends itself, especially when so many begged questions and non sequiturs are traceable to violations of some of the fundamental points raised below. I do not believe these guidelines call for compromise or abandonment of anyone's moral conviction. At least they are not deliberately calculated to do this. Basic moral convictions have roots, after all, in some rather nonrational (which is not to say irrational) layers of our being. Rather, these suggestions are but attempts to vent and circumvent the frustrations that cling to bad arguments. In qualifying certain arguments as "bad," one unavoidably gives his position away at some point. But that is neither here nor there if the points made have independent validity. Perhaps the following can be helpful.

**Attempt to Identify Areas of Agreement.**    Where issues are urgent and disputants have enormous personal stakes and investments, there is a tendency to draw sharp lines very quickly and begin the shootout. Anything else strikes the frank, let-it-hang-out American mind as hypocrisy. We have, it is argued, seen too many instances where a spade is called a shovel. Serious moral issues only get postponed by such politesse. Well and good. But this misses an important point: There are broad areas of agreement in this matter, and explicitly speaking of them at times will at least soften the din of conversation and soundproof the atmosphere. Some of those areas are the following.

Both those who find abortion morally repugnant and those who do not would agree that abortion is, in most cases, a tragic thing, an undesirable thing. It is not a tooth extraction though some heavy doses of wishful thinking and sanitized language ("the procedure") sometimes present it this way. Therefore, all discussants should be clear-headedly and whole-heartedly behind policies that attempt to frustrate the personal and social causes of abortion. One thinks immediately of better sex education (which is not equivalent to so-called plumbing instructions), better prenatal and perinatal care, reduced poverty, various forms of family support, more adequate institutional care of developmentally disabled children, etc. Furthermore, anyone who sees abortion as a sometimes tragic necessity should in consistency be practically supportive of alternatives to this procedure. While these two areas of agreement will not eliminate differences, they will—especially in combination with an overall concern for the quality of life at all stages—inspire the stirrings of mutual respect that improve the climate of discussion. That is no little achievement in this area.

**Avoid the Use of Slogans.**    Slogans are the weapon of the crusader, one who sees his role as warfare, generally against those sharply defined as "the enemy." Fighting for good causes dearly has its place, as do slogans. The political rally or the protest demonstration are good examples. But slogans are not very enlightening conversational tools, simply because they bypass and effectively subvert the process of communication.

I have in mind two current examples. The first is the use of the term "murder" to describe abortion. "Murder" is a composite value term that means (morally) unjustified killing of another person. There are also legal qualifiers to what is to count as murder. To use that term does not clarify an argument if the very issue at stake is justifiability. Rather it brands a position and, incidentally, those who hold it. It is a conversation stopper. Moreover, the term "murder" is absolutely unnecessary in the defense of the traditional Christian position on abortion.

On the other hand, "a woman has a right to her own body" is not an argument. It is the conclusion of an often unexamined argument and therefore a slogan with some highly questionable assumptions. For instance: that the fetus is, for these purposes, a part of the woman's body; that rights over one's body are absolute; that abortion has nothing to do with a husband, etc. To rattle some of these assumptions, it is sufficient to point out that few would grant that a woman's rights over her own body include the right to take thalidomide during pregnancy. The Supreme Court of our nation has gone pretty far in endorsing some of these assumptions. But even justices not above the use of a little "raw judicial power" would choke, I think, on the above slogan as an apt way to summarize the issue.

**Represent the Opposing Position Accurately and Fairly.** Even to mention this seems something of an insult. It contains an implied accusation. Unfortunately, the accusation is too often on target. For instance, those opposed to abortion sometimes argue that the woman who has an abortion is "anti-life" or has no concern for her fetus. This may be the case sometimes, but I believe it does not take sufficient account of the sense of desperate conflict experienced by many women who seek abortions. A sense of tragedy would not exist if women had no concern for their intrauterine offspring.

On the other hand, those who disagree with a highly restrictive moral position on abortion sometimes describe this position as "absolutist" and say that it involves "total preoccupation with the status of the unborn." This is the wording of the unfortunate "Call to Concern" (*Christianity and Crisis,* Oct. 3, 1977), which was aimed explicitly at the American Catholic hierarchy. The track record of the hierarchy on social concerns over a broad range of issues is enough to reveal the calumnious character of such protests. As Notre Dame's James Burtchaell wrote apropos of this manifesto: "Ethicians are expected to restrain themselves from misrepresenting positions with which they disagree" (*Christianity and Crisis,* Nov. 14, 1977).

**Distinguish the Pairs Right-Wrong, Good-Bad.** Repeatedly I have heard discussants say of a woman who has had an abortion: "She thought at the time and afterward that it was not morally wrong." Or: "She is convinced she made the right decision." It is then immediately added that the moral character of an action depends above all on the perceptions of the person performing it.

Indeed it does. But the term "moral character" needs a further distinction. One who desires to do and intends to do what is supportive and promotive of others (beneficence), performs a *good* act. That person may actually and mistakenly do what is unfortunately harmful, and then the action is morally *wrong*, but it is morally good. On the contrary, one who acts from motives of selfishness, hatred, envy, performs an evil, or *bad,* act. Thus, a surgeon may act out of the most selfish and despicable motives as he performs brilliant lifesaving surgery. His action is morally *bad* but morally *right.* One's action can, therefore, be morally good, but still morally wrong. It can be morally right, but morally bad.

The discussion about abortion concerns moral rightness and wrongness. This argument is not settled or even much enlightened by appealing to what a person thought of it at the time, or thinks of it afterward. Nor is it settled by the good and upright intentions of the woman or the physician. Those who destroyed villages in Vietnam to liberate them often undoubtedly acted from the best of intentions, but were morally wrong.

Not only is this distinction important in itself; beyond its own importance, it allows one to disagree agreeably—that is, without implying, suggesting or predicating moral evil of the person one believes to be morally wrong. This would be a precious gain in a discussion that often witnesses this particular and serious collapse of courtesy.

**Try to Identify the Core Issue at Stake.** There are, of course, many issues that cluster around the subject of abortion. There are issues of health (fetal, maternal), family stability, justice (e.g., rape), illegitimacy, etc. They are all genuine concerns and can represent sources or real hardship and suffering. Those who believe that abortion is sometimes justifiable have made a judgment that the hardships of the woman or family take precedence over nascent life in moral calculation. Those who take an opposing view weight the scales differently.

The core issue is, therefore, the evaluation of nascent life. By this I do not refer to the question about the beginning of personhood. That is a legitimate and important discussion. But the definition of "person" is often elaborated with a purpose in mind. That is, one defines and then grants or does not grant personhood in terms of what one wants to do and thinks it appropriate to do with nonpersons. That this can be a dog-chasing-tail definition is quite clear. As Princeton's Paul Ramsey is fond of saying: Does one really need a Ph.D. from Harvard to be a person, or is a functioning cerebral cortex quite sufficient?

The core issue, then, concerns the moral claims the nascent human being (what Pope Paul VI, in a brilliant finesse, referred to as *personne en devenir,* a person in the process of becoming) makes on us. Do these frequently or only very rarely yield to what appear to be extremely difficult alternatives? And above all, why or why not? That is, in my judgment, the heart of the abortion debate. It must be met head on. It is illumined neither by flat statements about the inviolable rights of fetuses nor by assertions about a woman's freedom of choice. These promulgate a conclusion. They do not share with us how one arrived at it.

**Admit Doubts, Difficulties, and Weaknesses in One's Own Position.**
When people are passionately concerned with a subject, as they should be in this case, they tend to overlook or even closet their own doubts and problems. Understandable as this is—Who will cast the first stone?—it is not a service to the truth or to good moral argument.

For instance, those with permissive views on abortion (who often favor Medicaid funding) sometimes argue that denial of Medicaid funding means a return to the back-alley butchers for many thousands of poor. This is deceptively appealing to a sensitive social conscience. But it fails to deal with the fact that in some, perhaps very many places, there is precious little price differential between the butchers and the clinics that now offer abortion services. So why go to the butchers? Furthermore, it conveniently overlooks the fact, noted by Daniel Callahan (*Christianity and Crisis,* Jan. 8, 1973), that the woman most commonly seeking an abortion is not the poor, overburdened mother of many children, but "an unmarried, very young woman of modest, or relatively affluent means whose main 'indication' for abortion will be her expressed wish not to have a [this] child [now]." Or, again, it is occasionally argued that in a pluralistic society we should refrain from imposing our moral views on others. This was the solution of *The New York Times* (Jan. 23, 1973) when it welcomed the Wade-Bolton decisions of the Supreme Court. It stated: "Nothing in the Court's approach ought to give affront to persons who oppose all abortion for reasons of religion or individual conviction. They can stand as firmly as ever for those principles, provided they do not seek to impede the freedom of those with an opposite view."

I agree with Union Theological's Roger Shinn when he says that this view is simplistic and disguises its own weaknesses. He wrote: "If a person or group honestly believes that abortion is the killing of persons, there is no moral comfort in being told, 'Nobody requires you to kill. We are only giving permission to others to do what you consider killing.' " The protester ought surely to reply that one key function of law is to protect minorities of all types: political, racial, religious and, as here, unborn.

On the other hand, the traditional Christian view on abortion (until recently, universally proposed by the Christian churches) was that the fetus was inviolable from the moment of conception. There are, I believe, certain phenomena in the preimplantation period that raise doubts and questions about evaluation—and that is all, namely, they do not yield certainties. I have in mind the twinning process, the estimated number of spontaneous abortions (thought to be huge), and, above all, the rare process of recombination to two fertilized ova into one. To admit that such phenomena raise serious evaluative problems is quite in place, if as a matter of fact they do. Indeed, I would argue that it is a disservice to the overall health and viability of the traditional Christian evaluation to extend its clarity and certainty into areas where there are grounds for residual and nagging doubts.

**Distinguish the Formulation and Substance of a Moral Conviction.**    This may seem a refined, even supertechnical and sophisticated, guideline better left in the footnotes of the ethical elite. Actually, I believe it is enormously important for bringing conversationalists out of their trenches. And it applies to both sides of this national debate.

For instance, not a few anti-abortionists appeal to the formulations of recent official Catholic leaders in stating their moral convictions. Specifically, Pius XI and Pius XII both state (and, with them, traditional Catholic ethical treatises on abortion) that direct abortion was never permissible, even to save the life of the mother. As this was understood, it meant simply and drastically: Better two deaths than one murder. Concretely, if the only alternatives facing a woman and physician were either abort or lose both mother and child, the conclusion was drawn that even then the direct disposing of the fetus was morally wrong.

That is a formulation—and almost no one, whether liberal or conservative, endorses the conclusion as an adequate and accurate way of communicating the basic value judgment (substance) of the matter. Some moral theologians would say, in contrast to the popes, that in this instance the abortion is indirect and permissible. Others would say, again in contrast to the popes, that it is direct but still permissible. For instance, the Catholic Bishop of Augsburg, Josef Stimpfle, recently stated: "He who performs an abortion, except to save the life of the mother, sins gravely and burdens his conscience with the killing of human life." A similar statement was made by the entire Belgian hierarchy in its 1973 declaration on abortion. Of those very rare and desperate conflict instances, the Belgian bishops stated: "The moral principle which ought to govern the intervention can be formulated as follows: Since two lives are at stake, one will, while doing everything possible to save both, attempt to save one rather than to allow two to perish." What is clear is that all would arrive at a conclusion different from the official one, even though the language might differ in each case.

The point here is, of course, that ethical formulations, being the product of human language, philosophy and imperfection, are only more or less adequate to the substance of our moral convictions at a given time. They will always show the imprint of human handling. This was explicitly acknowledged by Pope John XXIII in his speech (Oct. 11, 1962) opening the

Second Vatican Council. It was echoed by Vatican II in "*Gaudium et Spes*": "Furthermore, while adhering to the methods and requirements proper to theology, theologians are invited to seek continually for more suitable ways of communicating doctrine to the men of their times. For the deposit of faith or revealed truths are one thing; the manner in which they are formulated without violence to their meaning and significance is another" (n. 62).

This statement must be properly understood. Otherwise theology could easily be reduced to word shuffling. If there is a distinction between substance and formulation, there is also an extremely close, indeed inseparable, connection. One might say they are related as are body and soul. The connection is so intimate that it is difficult to know just what the substance is amidst variation of formulation. The formulation can easily betray the substance. Furthermore, because of this close connection, it is frequently difficult to know just what is changeable, what permanent. Where abortion is concerned, one could argue that the church's *substantial* conviction is that abortion is tolerable only when it is a life-saving, therefore also life-serving, intervention. Be that as it may, to conduct discussion as if substance and formulation were identical is to get enslaved to formulations. Such captivity forecloses conversations.

On the other hand, something similar must be said of the 1973 abortion decisions of the U.S. Supreme Court. The Court was "evolutionary" in interpreting the notion of liberty enacted in 1868 as the 14th Amendment to the Constitution. There is no evidence that the Congress and states understood that amendment to include the liberty to abort. Yet the Court asserts that "liberty" there must be read in a way consistent with the demands of the present day. Therefore, it concluded that the right to terminate pregnancy is "implicit in the concept of ordered liberty."

That is but a formulation of the notion of constitutionally assured liberty, and to treat it as more than that, as an ironclad edict, is to preempt legal development. Indeed, the Court itself gives this away when it treats the term "person" in the Constitution in a very static and nondevelopmental way, as John Noonan has repeatedly pointed out. It looks at the meaning of the term at the time of the adoption of the Constitution and freezes it there—just the opposite of what it does with the term "liberty." Such vagaries reveal that the Court's decisions and dicta are hardly identical with the substance of the Constitution. To argue as if they were is to confuse legal substance and legal formulations, and to choke off conversation. In brief, we must know and treasure our traditions without being enslaved by them.

**Distinguish Morality and Public Policy.**   It is the temptation of the Anglo-American tradition to identify these two. We are a pragmatic and litigious people for whom law is the answer to all problems, the only answer and a fully adequate answer. Thus, many people confuse morality and public policy. If something is removed from the penal code, it is viewed as morally right and permissible. And if an act is seen as morally wrong, many want it made illegal. Behold the "there ought to be a law" syndrome.

This is not only conceptually wrong; it is conversationally mischievous. It gets people with strong moral convictions locked into debates about public policy, as if only one public policy were possible given a certain moral position. That is simplistic. While morality and law are intimately related, they are obviously not identical. The closer we get to basic human rights, however, the closer the relationship ought to be in a well-ordered society. It is quite possible for those with permissive moral convictions on abortion to believe that more regulation is required than is presently provided in the Wade and Bolton decisions. Contrarily, it is possible for those with more stringent moral persuasions to argue that there are several ways in which these might be mirrored in public policy.

I am not arguing here for this or that public policy (though I am personally deeply dissatisfied with the present one on nearly all grounds). The point, rather, is that public discourse would be immeasurably purified if care were taken by disputants to relate morality and public policy in a more nuanced way than now prevails.

**Distinguish Morality and Pastoral Care or Practice.** A moral statement is one that attempts to summarize the moral right or wrong, and then invites to its realization in our conduct. As the well-known Redemptorist theologian Bernard Häring words it: Moral theology operates on a level "where questions are raised about general rules or considerations that would justify a particular moral judgment" (*Medical Ethics,* p. 89). A moral statement is thus an abstract statement, not in the sense that it has nothing to do with real life, or with particular decisions, but in the sense that it abstracts or prescinds from the ability of this or that person to understand it and live it.

Pastoral care (and pastoral statements), by contrast, looks to the art of the possible. It deals with an individual where that person is in terms of his or her strengths, perceptions, biography, circumstances (financial, medical, educational, familial, psychological). Although pastoral care attempts to expand perspectives and maximize strengths, it recognizes at times the limits of these attempts.

Concretely, one with strong convictions about the moral wrongfulness of abortion could and should be one who realizes that there are many who by education, familial and religious background, economic circumstances, are, or appear to be, simply incapable in those circumstances of assimilating such convictions and living them out, at least here and now. This means that compassion and understanding extended to the woman who is contemplating an abortion or has had one need by no means require abandonment of one's moral convictions. Similarly, it means that a strong and unswerving adherence to a moral position need not connote the absence of pastoral compassion and deafness to the resonances of tragic circumstances. I believe that if more people understood this, the abortion discussion would occur in an atmosphere of greater tranquility, sensitivity, and humaneness—and therefore contain more genuine communication.

**Incorporate the Woman's Perspective, or Women's Perspectives.** I include this because, well, frankly, I have been told to. And I am sure that there are many who will complain: "Yes, and you put it last." To which a single response is appropriate: "Yes, for emphasis." In the many discussions I have had on abortion where women have been involved in the discussion, one thing is clear: Women feel they have been left out of the discussion. This seems true of both so-called pro-choice women and so-called pro-life adherents.

But being told to is hardly a decisive reason for urging this point. And it is not my chief reason. Women rightly, if at times one-sidedly and abrasively, insist that they are the ones who carry pregnancies and sometimes feel all but compelled to have abortions. Thus, they argue two things: 1) They ought to have an influential voice in this discussion; 2) up to and including the present, they feel they have not had such a voice.

There are all kinds of shouts that will be heard when this suggestion is raised. We are familiar with most of them. For instance, some will argue paternal rights against the Supreme Court's 1976 *Planned Parenthood v. Danforth* decision. Others will ask: Which women are you talking about, pro-life or pro-choice? And then, of course, they will begin issuing passes to the discussion on the basis of predetermined positions. Still others will wonder why the fetus does not have a proxy with at least equal say. And so on. One can see and admit the point in all these ripostes. There is nothing in femaleness as such that makes women more or less vulnerable to error or bias in moral discourse than men, yet when all is shrieked and done, the basic point remains valid: The abortion discussion proceeds at its own peril if it ignores women's perspectives. As Martin I. Silvermann remarked in a recent issue of *Sh'ma:* "The arguments change when you must face the women" (Jan, 20, 1978).

One need not make premature peace with radical feminists or knee-jerk pro-abortionists to say this. Quite the contrary. One need only be familiar with the growing body of literature on abortion by women (e.g. Linda Bird Francke's *The Ambivalence of Abortion,* Random House, or Sidney Callahan's essays on abortion) to believe that the woman's perspective is an important ingredient in this discussion. To those who believe that this is tantamount to conferring infallibility on Gloria Steinem, it must be pointed out that in nearly every national poll, women test out more conservatively than men on the morality of abortion.

These are but a few guidelines for discussion. I am sure that there are many more, perhaps some of even greater importance than the ones mentioned. Be that as it may, I am convinced that attention to these points cannot hurt the national debate. It may even help. Specifically, it may prevent good people from making bad arguments—chief of which, of course, is that it is only bad people who make bad ones.

# The Woman and the Fetus: "One Flesh"?

## Rachel Conrad Wahlberg

... and those who make decisions of common concern must expect the decisions to be examined by those who are concerned. [John L. McKenzie in the *National Catholic Reporter,* March 26, 1971, book report supplement, page 1-A]

In discussions of abortion, the person most concerned is rarely mentioned: the pregnant woman. How does it feel to a woman to experience pregnancy and its dilemmas? What is the existential, experiential reality of carrying a fetus? Is the fetus "your own" in the sense that your hair is your own? Why or why not?

Consider the decisions you can make about your body. You can drink to excess, you can smoke three packs a day, you can take drugs—in spite of the dangers of these actions. You can practice birth control, or choose not to. You can starve yourself or gorge yourself on food to the hazard of your health. You can have your body tattooed, your ears pierced, your nose reshaped. You can decide to have or not to have an operation. Your appendix is your own and you can have it removed. Your kidneys are yours and you can decide to give one of them to another family member in an emergency. You can even commit suicide. You are free to control your body in these and a hundred more ways. But if you are a woman?

Copyright 1971 Christian Century Foundation. Reprinted by permission for the September 8, 1971 issue of *The Christian Century.* Rachel Conrad Wahlberg is a freelance writer and author of *Jesus and the Freed Woman* (1978).

**I**

If you are a woman, a human female, then, beginning at age 10 to 12, an egg is sent every month from the ovaries through the fallopian tubes into the uterus. The egg, you might say, is your own, whether you want it or not. This is the way you are created, this is the system established by nature for populating the earth. So the child-woman accepts her reproductive system as her own, though not without exasperation, impatience, resentment. She may take some pride in the fact that she can have children. Just the same, she finds menstruation a nauseous bother all her adolescent and most of her adult life. There is no choice but to get used to it.

But consider what is involved. Over a period of 36 years in a woman's life, 400 or more eggs or ova make the monthly fallopian trip. If the ovum is not fertilized, it is expelled at some time between menstrual periods—even though it has potential life in it. And the uterus lining, unused for fetal nourishment that month, is expelled through menstruation. Many women are ignorant of this so-called ovulation process, are aware only of menstruation. But for every woman, it is one of her own eggs that travels through the fallopian tubes each month, the lining of her own uterus that is expelled each month in menstruation.

Now, there is a tendency in our society—perhaps in all societies—simply to view the female reproductive system as "a part of nature," along with the male system. But in fact the latter is in no way similar in inconvenience or potential hazard. For a boy, nocturnal emissions are bothersome but not dangerous. For an adult male, when millions of sperm are deposited in the marriage (or nonmarriage) partner, the danger of pregnancy is once removed. He may feel concerned, but it is the woman's problem. It happens to her, to her body. The decision-making falls to her.

In fact from puberty on a woman makes decisions during her monthly cycle. If she has cramps, she decides to take medication. She may decide to avoid certain activities during the period. If she is involved in a sexual relationship, she makes a decision about birth control—when, what type—and seeks medical advice. It cannot be overemphasized that the woman's reproductive system is already within the orbit of her decision-making.

Thus, since the egg is the woman's, if the man's sperm meets it the question arises: Whose is the fertilized egg, the zygote? It does not appear to belong to the man. If it did, if he had control over it, we would know that a brave new world had arrived. We would adopt the horse-breeders' phrase and speak of a child as "by Tom out of Sue"—Sue being a vessel for Tom's sperm, not a person who contributes her half of the child's genes. That is, the woman would be a mere incubator for the male's child.

(Theologically, has not Mary been presented in this fashion—as if Mary's ovum really made no contribution to Jesus, as if the Holy Spirit and a nameless humanity mysteriously combined to form the human-divine Jesus? Of course, when this dogma was formulated the genetic contribution of male and female was not yet understood and the greater concern was with paternity.)

However, to the woman who experiences the monthly cycle, the fertilized egg is still *her* monthly egg. True, as it attaches to the uterus and cell division begins, its human potential becomes real, both theoretically and biologically. But existentially the case is quite different. Uterine attachment and cell division happen silently. No bugle blows, no one knows—not even the woman. There is only, a week or so after the sexual act at ovulation time, a missed period. There is only an awareness of possibilities.

## II

How does a woman feel when she suspects the presence in her womb of the zygote? First she considers the delay in menstruation. Almost every woman will run late occasionally in a 28–30 day cycle. Even missing a month or several months may not mean that she is pregnant. So at first she worries about the date. Did she count incorrectly? (Few women mark a calendar unless they are intent on becoming pregnant or are counting for birth control.) After years of counting, the date of her last period becomes a blur. Also, perhaps she desires or rejects childbearing. She wants the period or she doesn't—or, paradoxically, it can be both/and. She wants a child but hadn't planned it now. A woman never "wants" a period except to assure her that she is not pregnant.

But note: as yet she has no feeling of a-person-within-me. There is nothing to see, nothing to feel. Only the missed period (a minority of women experience other symptoms, but in many cases these must be attributed to causes other than pregnancy). The situation can be tantalizing—hopeful or frightening. If she goes to a doctor he may perform a test to confirm a possible pregnancy. However, if she is married he will probably recommend her waiting until the second missed period to determine her situation. Thus for weeks she may exist in a limbo of not knowing, a state of mental-emotional concern and anguish.

If she tells no one, neither her husband nor lover, doctor nor friend, she can put off facing her dilemma and bolster her sense of being in control. She is a whole person, with a certain question, a certain puzzle in her mind. Since she has missed a period, she knows that she may be "with child" (that biblical term has more meaning for the last months of pregnancy when she feels bulk and movement); but just now she may refuse to accept the possibility, so that she can still feel that she is in control.

If the woman does not confide in anyone she can live in this limbo for quite a while. She may have a feeling of: If I don't let on, it will go away. (A friend of mine convinced herself for four months that her fifth pregnancy was a tumor.) On the other hand she may be delighted over the prospect of having a baby but hold off telling in order to surprise family and friends. All her time in "limbo" she feels she is one individual, one person—a woman with an interior condition, an interior knowledge, that no one can see or share.

But once aware that there is a knot, a mass within her, she must come out of limbo. She knows now that the egg was fertilized, that she missed her period because the uterus lining is nourishing a fetus. She realizes now that a parasite is living in her and feeding on her, is enclosed by her, a being entirely subhuman, entirely dependent on her.

Most discussions of abortion ignore this personal angle—the experiential, existential reality of a parasite within. Impersonally—medically, morally, legally—there may seem to be two entities, the woman and the fetus. But for the woman there is one entity, her body—me. *To her, the fetus seems to be a part of her own body.*

In a very real sense, the female body is an incubator growing a parasite. But while commercial incubators are external to that which is incubated, the human or animal female incubator is itself fed upon, is itself a part of the live-giving, life-consuming process. The parasitical aspect is reflected in the fact that a mother's health can be dragged down during pregnancy if she is not getting the proper nourishment. Mysteriously, the fetus feeds on the nourishment of her body without her knowledge or consent.

Has mankind in any period of history truly given thought to the fact that the fetus feeds on the mother's body without any consideration for her needs? Who is the victim here? In poverty-stricken areas, in countries where people are starving, the pregnant mother's food is converted to the needs of the fetus, and the nursing mother becomes emaciated as the breast gives up the nourishment of her body. There is a cannibalistic aspect here: the fetus actually feeds on the mother's body. True, this is nature, and is in one sense a beautiful process. Nevertheless the fetus can drain the mother of protein and bone nutritives like calcium, causing loss of weight and health.

Is it any wonder that a woman wants to have the right to decide whether her body is to be used in this fashion? Helpless, the fetus feeds on the mother. Helplessly, she is fed on. Because of this interaction, she feels that the fetus *is* her own body.

## III

There is nothing similar in the experience of the male. He can observe the woman, be sympathetic, defensive, judgmental, apprehensive. But he cannot ever feel the personal bodily involvement of having a fetus growing enormously within him, using, draining his body. That is why many men seem curiously callous and indifferent to the woman's involvement (though I must admit that even William Buckley agreed when Betty Friedan said to him on a recent television interview: "If you had a uterus in your body, wouldn't you feel you were more important than what was in the uterus?").

The woman feels both that the fetus is *she* and that it is *hers*. It is her *possession* since it is submerged in her. Thus the self-fetus relationship is unique; "it" seems a part of and uses her. Enclosed by her body, it can grow nowhere else. No one can see it or touch it. After a few months, it moves, evidencing life—but within her, the autonomous person. For nine months it is a part of her body. It never feels alien. According to current science, the body rejects foreign tissue. *If the fetus were alien tissue, the body would reject it.* This, it seems to me, is the most convincing argument that the fetus is a part of the mother's body until birth.

The enclosed organism—strictly a potential human, a subhuman, a nearly human—is not autonomous. It has no use of its potential senses. It cannot speak, smell, breathe, touch, respond to light. It cannot eat, drink, walk. Not until the last months can it move, kick, jerk, shift, respond to loud noise, all within limits in the incubator body. The fetus is not viable; it cannot live alone until the last two or three months of intrauterine existence, and then only under the most favorable, medically assisted conditions. By all these standards it is not a full human being.

## IV

Thus it seems absurd to women that Grisez and others argue that "the embryo from conception until birth is a living, human individual" (*National Catholic Reporter,* March 26, 1971, page 5-A). True, it begins to take on person-characteristics, growth and movement, during the last half of pregnancy, but still only within me, within my body-world, my sphere. It cannot become a real person until it separates from my body during birth. Thus, the fetus-mother relationship is unique, is indeed "one flesh." Again, is it any wonder that the woman feels that the fetus belongs to her, is a part of her?

The fact is that the woman already has some right of decision over pregnancy. She may deliberately take vitamins and calcium, she may deliberately eat more and better food and avoid smoking or drugs, if she thinks this course will benefit the fetus. Or, she may neglect the needs of the fetus through ignorance—through eating poorly or not seeking medical care. She may diet to keep the baby small, or—trusting old wives' tales—she may "eat for two" to ensure a big healthy baby. Or, knowing that it may harm the fetus, she may smoke or consume drugs or alcohol excessively. Finally, she could, deliberately or inadvertently, take action to induce a miscarriage. Such action can be as deliberate as a planned abortion—and has never been regarded as shocking or as meriting religious or social opprobrium. (To my knowledge there is no law against willfully inducing miscarriage.)

Yes, the woman already exercises some control over the fetus. Thus, to the woman who does not meekly accept the situation, the question becomes: Can I decide to do something with this part of my own body, flesh of my flesh, blood of my blood, ovum from my ovaries—if I do not want to be a mother or do not want to have another child? Am I free or am I bound? Shall I bring on a miscarriage if I can, or get an abortion? Or, if I am unmarried, shall I have the baby and offer it for adoption?

Note the power implicit in this last question: she can offer it for adoption. She has the right to give this to-be-born life to another person or family or to an agency which can place it with appropriate parents. In our society this is the unquestioned right of the *unmarried girl.* The married mother is not conceded this right. It is extremely rare for a married woman to negotiate with anyone to accept her child after she delivers it. Why does such action seem unnatural for a married woman, but natural, or socially desirable, for an unmarried woman? Partly, perhaps, because the married woman is expected to take her husband's wishes into consideration.

The crucial point for the woman is: she feels that if she does not have power of decision over the contents of her uterus, then the fetus has a certain power over her. It can take over her life—impose new duties on her, force her to quit a job and to give her time and energy to child care —a task she may not be ready for or may already have had enough of. In this sense if the woman is not in control the pregnancy takes control. She becomes a housing-incubator for a potential being who can change her life for 20 years. If she has no power of decision, she is undoubtedly being used against her will—whether through carelessness or ineffective methods of birth control—for procreation. Obviously, her will may cooperate, may coincide with her condition. But if it does not, she is in an oppressed position, the position most women have been in for centuries. She is at the mercy of her reproductive system.

# V

It seems clear the the dice are loaded against the woman. In her lifetime her system readies several hundred ova for fertilization. Hence she lives for year with the overriding question: *How shall I avoid becoming pregnant except for the few times that I choose to have a child?* The male expels a few million sperm during every sexual act, but he doesn't suffer the consequences save insofar as he may have to support a child. The woman is trapped into dealing constantly with her procreative powers—and not just once a month, since she is never sure just when the egg is vulnerable. A woman lives defensively.

Obviously, for the average woman a safe birth control method is the answer to her 36-year dilemma. Unfortunately, many methods are inneffective or dangerous for some reason. Yet because the mature, sexually relating woman is always under threat, always battling fear, she is forced to consider almost every means of avoiding pregnancy: abstinence or "chastity"; constant attention to her chosen method of birth control; abortion; or having a hysterectomy or her tubes tied if she can persuade a doctor to perform the operation—which he is unlikely to do until after she has had several children. A man can have a vasectomy whenever he wants, but a woman cannot have a hysterectomy or tube-tying on request.

Most women do not want to reject the fetus once it has begun to move. Ideally, abortion should be limited to the premovement period, the first 12 to 14 weeks. Incidentally, it ought to be possible for a married as well as an unmarried woman to give her baby for adoption, but this would require a reorienting of social understanding.

As a consequence of her feeling that the fetus is part of her body until gestation is complete, a woman faces two questions: (1) As an autonomous individual, do I have a right to make decisions not only about menstruation, birth control, sex relations, but also about what is in and of my body and seems to be me? (2) Since pregnancy is a traumatic condition which can change my whole life, how can I safely avoid pregnancy except for the few children I desire? Although in most marriages husband and wife will agree about pregnancy, I hold that women should have the primary power of decision because of three pertinent factors: the woman has the pregnancy—the man can't share it; the woman gives birth—the man can't experience it; and the woman is in general responsible for child care, not the man. Since women are ludicrously oversupplied with ova, the sexually active must have protection from unwanted pregnancies. To be free and not slaves, women must have power of decision over their reproductive systems.

# The Beginnings of Personhood: Theological Considerations

## Albert C. Outler

There are two fairly obvious constants in the abortion debate thus far.[1] The first is a general agreement, by all but the hard-line abortionists, that abortion is a genuine *moral* dilemma—not least because all its crucial terms are actually question begging. This might suggest the prudence of a suspended judgment, but we have no such option. Abortion is a stark dilemma confronting us now—with far-reaching decisions that have already been made about it on presumptions about human existence that run far past verified knowledge. The resulting crisis has generated more heat than light and many of us are more eager to defend our prejudices than to reach for a new consensus. Hence, our adversary proceedings in a problem-area that is as baffling as life itself, since it clearly *may*—as some of us believe it clearly *does*—involve just that; life, death, and destiny.

A second constant in the debate is its reflection of the mercurial shifts in popular opinion in recent years—shifts that are functions of the cataclysmic collapse of the moral-demand systems that have guided Western society (more or less!) for two millennia.[2] Twenty years ago, there were not two sides in the debate, really. Ten years ago, our findings would have

Reprinted by permission from *Perkins School of Theology Journal,* Fall 1973, pp. 28–34. This article was first presented at the Symposium on Abortion at Perkins School of Theology in 1973. Albert C. Outler has taught at Yale Divinity School and Perkins School of Theology at Southern Methodist University, and is the author of a number of books, including *John Wesley* (1964).

[1]Cf., e.g., Robert E. Cooke, ed., *The Terrible Choice: The Abortion Dilemma* (New York, 1968)—the proceedings of "An International Conference on Abortion," sponsored by Harvard Divinity School; or Kenneth Vaux, ed., *Who Shall Live?*, "The Houston Conference on Ethics in Medicine and Technology" (Philadelphia, 1970); or the even more recent *Symposium on the Beginnings of Personhood* at The Institute of Religion and Human Development (Houston, 1975) under the chairmanship of Dr. Albert Moracewski, O.P. See also *The Hastings Center Report, Vol. 2, No. 5* (November, 1972).

[2]Cf. Philip Rieff, *The Triumph of the Therapeutic* (London, 1966), p. xi and ch. I.

been practically foreclosed by the then-prevailing sentiments.[3] Now, there is a *real* debate in which many pro-abortionists, flushed with victory, are confident that the future is theirs.

In all such upheavals of customary morality, familiar terms become newly ambiguous and value judgments, long distilled into ordinary language, require new analyses and transvaluations. In the abortion debate, such transvaluations confront us at every turn, all of them buttressed by self-assured rationalizations. Is fetal life already human or still subhuman, personal or nonpersonal? The answer here, obviously, depends on the biases of one's notions about "human" and "personal." Then there is that poignant phrase, "unwanted life"—which naturally prompts such questions as "Unwanted by *whom?*" and "Why?" Again, there is the notion of "privacy," whose connotation has been so dramatically extended by the Supreme Court. But just how private an affair is pregnancy, after all—since, from time immemorial, it has been the primal *social* event in most human communities? If feticide is innocuous, why then should medical research on aborted fetuses be disallowed?[4] Every answer to all such questions (and many others like them) is rooted in our intuitions as to what human fetal life amounts to and these intuitions rest, in turn, on our prior convictions as to what makes human life human, in the first place.

This, then, is the focal question of all our common concerns: What is the truly *human,* what are its real origins and grounds, what are its valid ends? If the human person is understood as a divine intention, with a transcendental ground and context, this will surely guide our analysis of its origins. If abortion is a matter of life and death—*human* life and *human* death—then all decisions about it should reflect this awe-full supposition. If, on the other hand, a fetus is mere tissue—and never more than subhuman till birth—then abortion is an elective, minor surgery and we may cast aside

[3]Cf. the Report of the decennial of the Lambeth Conference of Anglican Bishops (1960), and the special statement of the National Council of Churches (1961): "All Christians are agreed in condemning abortions [on demand].... The destruction of life already begun cannot be condoned as a method of family limitation." Karl Barth (*Church Dogmatics* III-IV, 1961, pp. 415–16) called abortion "a monstrous thing"; Dietrich Bonhoeffer (*Ethics,* 1955, pp. 175–76) denounced it as "nothing but murder." Helmut Thielicke (*The Ethics of Sex,* 1964, p. 227) says that "in abortion, the order of creation is infringed upon...." Cf. Robert F. Drinan, "Contemporary Protestant Thinking on Abortion" in *America,* #117 (December 9, 1967), pp. 713ff. By this time, though, Joseph Fletcher had joined the pro-abortionist ranks; cf. *Situation Ethics* (Westminster, 1966). Since then, the switch to official church support for abortion on demand has almost been pell-mell. Cf. *The Book of Discipline of the United Methodist Church,* Part III, 572-D.

[4]Cf. *The New York Times,* April 11, 1973, for a report on the action to this effect by the *National Institutes of Health.*

our scruples and disregard all outcries against this kind of "slaughter of the innocents."[5] But this either/or (*either* human life *or* mere tissue) is just precisely the issue that still remains undecided—except on arbitrary grounds—and cannot finally be resolved by any of the arguments that I have yet heard, or have been able to conceive.

The deepest confusion in the debate stems from the confusion generated by the tradition of body-soul dualism which has lasted so long, from its origins in Persia and Greece, through Western philosophy and theology, down to our own times.[6] And it is confusing, since all its versions involve *some* kind of invidious comparison between "lower" and "higher" levels in the *humanum,* and it commits one to *some* sort of "magic moment theory" as to when and how animal tissue becomes "ensouled" or "animated"—and hence to some "magic moment" along the human lifeline when the defenseless finally deserves to be defended. Now the difficulty here is that every decision about such a moment is arbitrary, despite all the arguments for or against it.[7] For instance, in a recent (very interesting!) lecture at Rice University, Dr. Engelhardt concluded that, "though the fetus is obviously an example of *human life,* it is in *no way* suggestive of *personal* life."[8] It's a wry comfort for a theologian to catch a scientist in such a hyperbole, since we, too, have the same bad habit of saying "none at all" when we mean "not much." Thus, at the very least, it would seem to be simply a fact that some fetuses do, in *some* ways, suggest "personal life" to *some* people! But the real point at issue here is the thesis that something (a fetus) which is *totally* devoid of *any* sign of "personal life" should then regularly develop into "personal life" and to nothing else except a "personal life"—unless accidentally thwarted in its normal development. This is at once a commonplace and a profound ambiguity.

The same "magic moment theory" has been carried further, with less sophistication, by the Supreme Court. Mr. Justice Blackmun began with

---

[5]Cf. the almost startling shift from his former position by an eminent black theologian, in C. Eric Lincoln's "Why I Reversed My Stand on Laissez-Faire Abortion," *The Christian Century,* Vol. XC, No. 17 (April 25, 1973), pp. 477–79.

[6]Cf. D. R. G. Owen, *Body and Soul: A Study on the Christian View of Man* (Westminster, 1956).

[7]From a one-sided interpretation of Descartes' dualism—the passivity of "body" (*res extensa*)—has come the mechanistic tradition of "Man, the Machine" that runs unbroken from Holbach and La Mettrie down to B. F. Skinner's *Beyond Freedom and Dignity* (Knopf, 1971).

[8]"The Ontology of Abortion," February 16, 1973, p. 27. Cf. the lecture we have just heard, "The Beginnings of Personhood," May 15, 1973, p. 21: "There is *nothing* 'personal' about the fetus."

what, apparently, is a *fait accompli* in constitutional law: viz. that "the term 'person' does not include the unborn."[9] But then he found it possible (arbitrarily, of course) to divide pregnancy into progressive trimesters, with disparate values arbitrarily assigned to each successive trimester—from none, to some, to a good deal.

This is less helpful than it was meant to be, for *birth* is not *the* "magic moment," either. Even "normal" neonates (as well as the premature ones) are not yet decisively human, in their neurological or social maturations. And a discouragingly large fraction of the population never attain to Dr. Engelhardt's norm of "rationality" as the sign of "personhood."[10] Most neurologists agree, or so I am told, that an infant is not yet distinctively "human" until its frontal granular cortex is integrated into the rest of the brain—about the third month *after* birth.[11] Pediatricians and sociologists largely agree that social differentations take longer than that![12] Professor Lederberg specifies "the acquisition of language" as the *transitus* when an infant "enters the cultural tradition which has been the special attribute of man."[13] Dr. Engelhardt disjoins "the human-biological process" (devoid of "intrinsic value") from "the human-personal process" which climaxes (if it ever does) in "rationality, consciousness, and self-consciousness."[14] As a distinction, this is illuminating. As a radical disjunction, it excludes a very large number of human beings (the very young, the subnormal, the senescent) from "personhood"—from whence it would follow that they are devoid of intrinsic personal value, or any morally assured human status!

It would follow, further, that human status may validly be decided by dominant codes of social evaluation. When human life is "socially appreciated" its value is thereby assured. By the same token, "unwanted life" would have no such value and no such assurance. This principle might then, with equal consistency, cover not only unappreciated fetuses but also defectives in variety, and the unwanted old as well. I know that such extensions of this principle of social validation are often denied, and I do not propose to belabor all its consequences. What I am suggesting, however, is that the "magic moment" approach entails unmanageable ambiguities and that all conceptions of "personhood" that presume to resolve the dilemma of abortion—as innocuous on the one hand, or absolutely proscribed, on the other—are too crude to correspond to the

[9]*Roe v. Wade*, in *Supreme Court Reporter*, February 15, 1973.

[10]Cf. Engelhardt, *supra*, p. 20.

[11]Cf. James Skinner, M.D., "Neurological Considerations Relevant to the Beginnings of Personhood," in the transcript of The Houston Symposium (1973), *op. cit.*, pp. 11–12; 76–78.

[12]Cf. Robert Zeller, M.D., in The Houston Symposium, *op. cit.*, pp. 12–13.

[13]Joshua Lederberg, "A Geneticist Looks at Contraception and Abortion," in *Annals of Internal Medicine*, Vol. 67, No. 3, Part 2 (September 1967), pp. 26–27.

[14]Engelhardt, *supra*, p. 20.

nuances of personal existence, as we know it in ourselves, and intuit it in others.

Thus, it would seem that the strength of the pro-abortion cause lies in its sentimental appeal: positively, to current approved social values (e.g., population control); negatively, to the personal values of the anguished mother of her rights. These are certainly not negligible considerations, either, for an overpopulated planet, with underdeveloped technologies of contraception, and a newly promiscuous society, there is bound to be a plethora of unwanted pregnancies and anguished mothers. What is more, the world is already overburdened with lives that might very well be adjudged "unwanted" on any calculus of *social utility*.

But here the ways part again. When the case for contraception is linked too closely with the case for or against abortion, nothing but confusion follows, since most of the analogies are misleading. The prevention of conception, or nidification—at one end of the spectrum—and adoption, on the other, represent a common view of human life and personhood that is very different from the notion that the human life process, once stabilized, may be terminated without moral scruple. For in the decision for or against abortion, what is being weighed is the *life* of the fetus against the *anguish* of the mother, and these incommensurables create a profound moral dilemma.

This may serve to bring the issue between utilitarians and theological views of life into focus (and to give the phrase in my title, "theological considerations," some specificity). If with the utilitarians and secularists, you are confident that human life is autonomous, in this world, and that human values are created and validated by social consensus, then, obviously, there are no "theological considerations" pertinent to this question (or any other)—and the rest of what I shall be saying is bound to sound a mite uncouth. For I am prepared to affirm, openly and without much embarrassment—except for my awareness of how unfashionable it may appear to some of you—that the primal origins, the continuing ground and final ends of human life are truly transcendental. In the Christian tradition, at least, to be human and personal is to be God's own special creation. Our lives and potentials are ours on trust from God. They are, therefore, never at our own selfish disposal. All our truly human experiences (identity, freedom, insight, hope, love) are also self-transcending—despite their being bracketed in space and time. The *humanum* is a genuine oddity, differing from its animal congeners not only in kind but in degree as well.[15] And, in the Christian tradition, this self-transcendence has been

[15]This is the central issue in Mortimer Adler, *The Difference of Man and the Difference It Makes* (New York: Holt, Rinehart and Winston, 1967), and this is Adler's "conclusion," although he is very much aware of its problematic character. What is clear is that if men are to act and be treated as moral agents, a difference in kind is presupposed thereby (pp. 292–94).

valued as a sign of life's *sacredness*—a way of pointing to God's involvement in, and concern for, the human enterprise. Thus, the notion of life's sacral quality places it over against all merely utilitarian codes.

Terms like "person," "personality," "personhood," "self" are all codewords for a trans-empirical reality. Whatever it is that they denote, it does not "exist" in space and time or in the causal nexus; all our efforts at introspection are infinitely regressive.[16] "Personhood" is not a *part* of the human organism, nor is it inserted into a process of organic development at some magic moment. It *is* the human organism oriented toward its transcendental matrix, in which it lives and moves and has its human being.[17] The self is "there" long before self-consciousness or any self-conscious acceptance or rejection of the primal intention which it represents. Thus, its lifeline stretches from an aboriginal God-knows-when to an eschatological God-knows-whenever—and all our efforts to draw precise lines between subhuman and truly human are dangerously parallel to our other efforts to distinguish between "inferior" and "superior" human beings.

In this theological perspective, therefore, "personhood" is a divine intention operating in a life-long process that runs from nidification till death.[18] It is never perfectly achieved and it is all too often thwarted in ways too tragic for glib rationalizations or even bitter tears. Our personhood is our identity, and this is always experienced as prevenient. *Homo est et qui est in futurus* (as Tertullian put it): "He who is ever going to be a man already is one."[19] Dr. Engelhardt has rightly observed that "stepping on a pile of acorns is not the same as destroying a forest of oaks."[20] But abortion is rather more like clipping off a sprouted sapling, and that's a categorically different business.

There is a human-biological continuum that is life-long, and there is also a human-personal continuum equally life-long—always in the making and always reaching out beyond. Both processes, unsurprisingly, have somatic substrates that are also life-long and concurrent. Our DNA codings are primal and perduring. The "hard-wired receptors" that make possible our earliest experiences are correlated with "the soft-wired receptors" that are malleable to culture—and they are active from birth to death.[21] Hu-

---

[16]Cf. a similar comment about "intelligence" in Carl Eisdorfer, M.D., "Intellectual and Cognitive Changes in the Aged," in Busse and Pfeiffer (eds.), *Behavior and Adaptation in Later Life* (Boston, 1969), p. 238.

[17]Cf. St. Paul's reported allocution on Mars' Hill in Acts 17:24–28.

[18]Cf. Karl Rahner, *Hominisation; The Evolutionary Origin of Man as a Theological Problem* (Herder & Herder, 1965).

[19]Tertullian, *Apology*, IX: . . . *etiam fructus omnis iam in semine est* ("because the fruit is already in the seed").

[20]Engelhardt, *supra*, p. 21.

[21]An hypothesis of Dr. Skinner's, *op. cit.*, pp. 9–10.

man thought and feeling are functions of cranial and blood-chemical processes and yet the brain does not secrete thought and blood-chemical explanations of consciousness are significantly inadequate. Instead of searching for magic moments when the subpersonal becomes personal, we would do better to envisage each individual human process as a unique slice of being, in which "personhood" is its "longitudinal axis"—each with its own divine intention and destiny.

One of Christianity's oldest traditions is the sacredness of human life, as implications of the Christian convictions about God and the good life. If all persons are equally the creatures of the one God, then none of these creatures is authorized to play god toward any other. And if all persons are cherished by God, regardless of merit, we ought also to cherish each other in the same spirit. This was the ground on which the early Christians rejected the prevalent Graeco-Roman codes of sexuality in which abortion and infanticide were commonplace.[22] It was not that these codes were not socially useful—as population controls, etc.—and they help cut down the welfare rolls! But the Christian moralists found them profoundly irreligious and proposed instead an ethic of compassion (adopted from their Jewish matrix) that proscribed abortion and encouraged "adoption."[23]

The theological ground for such an ethic was God's hallowing of life through sex and pregnancy, in the familial matrix. The value of this human life or that is not, in the first instance, "intrinsic." It comes, instead, from God's special and costing love. This impulse of compassion for the defenseless has always been the glory of the Christian ethic at its best. And despite our shameful record in practice (or malpractice!) its influence has been strong enough through the centuries to call down Nietzsche's scorn upon it as an ethic of weakness—unfit for any race of Supermen.

The essence of the tradition is that no human life has a right to its own self-enhancement at the cost of other human life. And it is all of human life that is sacred, from its mysterious origins to its equally mysterious ends. In the sex-procreation-fetus-infant-family syndrome we see a paradigm of human obligation at every level: freedom of choice issuing in consequences that are then accepted as personal and collective responsibilities.

[22]Cf. W. E. H. Lecky, *History of European Morals, From Augustus to Charlemagne* (London, 1894), I, 45, 92, and II, 20–24. For example, "The general opinion among the ancients seems to have been that the foetus was but a part of the mother and that she had the same right to destroy it as to cauterise a tumour upon her body" (I, 92).

[23]Cf. Lecky, *Ibid.,* II, 20–24 on abortion; and then pp. 24–39 for a summary of Christianity's crusade against infanticide. See also David M. Feldman, *Birth Control in Jewish Law* (New York, 1968), Part 5, pp. 251–96, and Immanual Jakobovitz, *Jewish Medical Ethics* (New York, 1959), especially pp. 190–91. Typical Christian condemnations of abortion and infanticide may be seen in Tertullian, *Apology,* IX, in Minucius Felix, *Octavius,* 30, and *The Epistle to Diognetus,* 5 ("Like everyone else, Christians marry and have children but they do not 'expose' their infants").

Care for the unborn is a mutuality between weaker and stronger. It is the essence of every relationship of unselfish love.

Always, therefore, we are driven back to this bedrock perplexity about the human status of the fetus and the neonate—and any warrants we may allege for their disposability. Obviously, the right to life is in no way absolute—death itself is sufficient evidence of *this!* There is, therefore, an undeniable case for some kinds of "therapeutic" abortions, and I would be greatly interested in the exploration of this category with a view to its possible enlargement—if such explorations could start from some higher view of fetal life than mere tissue.

My own conviction is that we not only lack *proof* that a fetus is mere tissue but that all the probabilities look the other way. And if it is only *probable* that a fetus is a human being—and thus personal, in the sense of being a divine intention—then we would do better to recognize abortion as a moral evil in every case and thus, even when chosen, a tragic option of what has been judged to be the lesser of two real evils. And if it is this serious, then every decision, for or against it, is a momentous crisis demanding the solemn involvement of *all* the parties concerned—and with all feasible alternatives conscientiously canvassed.[24]

The issue comes down to this: whether or not human-personal life is a real continuum[25] and whether or not it is truly sacred. For if it is, then fetal life, infant life, senescent life—even when "unwanted"—deserve humane care and compassion, even when pitted against the personal values of youthful or adult lives. And I believe that our continuing scruples against infanticide and euthanasia are the residues of an older conscience that where human *life* is at stake, life outweighs *utility.* Once *that* conscience goes, the only barriers between us and Auschwitz will be societal moods that, on their record, can give us very little real security.

Abortion is now *legal* (up to "viability")—and this leaves us with the agonizing *moral* issue as to whether, or whenever, it is "right" (still, I would insist, in the sense of the lesser of two evils). This shift from legal to moral grounds might very well be an advance—*if* the value-shaping agencies in our society were agreed that abortion is a life-and-death choice; *if* there were legal and social supports for conscientious doctors in their newly appointed role as killers as well as healers; *if* we had a

[24]It is worth noting how casually, in a pro-abortion article in the April *Reader's Digest* (1973), p. 280, Dr. William Sweeney speaks of "killing the baby."

[25]Cf. Louis Dupré, "A New Approach to the Abortion Problem," in The Houston Symposium (1973), p. 6. "If personhood is irreducible to its functions alone, its origins cannot be an acquired reality. This leaves us no choice but to place that origin at the beginning of human life. All human life then is personal at least in a minimal way, though by no means to an equal degree."

general will in our society to extend our collective commitments to the unborn and the newly born; and *if,* above all, there were any prospects in our time for higher standards of responsible sexuality. What has actually happened, however, is that in our liberation from abortion as a "crime," many of us have also rejected any assessment of it as a *moral evil*—and this will further hasten the disintegration of our communal morality.

It has occasionally been explained to me somewhat impatiently, that an aging, WASP, male, theologian cannot possibly understand human realities and the human damage of unacceptable pregancies—and, therefore, that all my notions about abortion are "academic." My response to this is also *ad hominem,* and it comes in two parts: the one frankly sentimental; the other grimly prophetic. My personal sentiments in this matter root in the fact that we are adoptive parents and that none of our adopted children would have seen the light of day in these new times. To tell me *now* that the social values that might have accrued to their three anguished mothers (had they aborted) would have out-weighed the human and personal worth of these three persons is, I'm afraid, moral nonsense.

And as for my prophetic forebodings, it seems certain that in America alone, over the next few years, millions of fetal lives will be snuffed out—*with little moral outcry!* There are ways of arguing that this is not comparable to the Nazi holocaust, or to the tragedy in Indo-China, or the widening stains of child abuse here at home. But it will be comparable statistically—and morally it will be even more ominous, for it will be sponsored by many whose professional ordinations are to healing and compassion. Moreover, it will have, for its rationalization, theories of fetal life that define it as a chattel to a mother's private value-judgments. Who then will be surprised if our human sensitivities are still further calloused, if sex becomes yet more promiscuous—with our scruples against euthanasia crumbling and the moral cements of our society dissolving?

I began by stressing how little we really can ever *know* about the mystery of human origins and, therefore, about the final grounds for human compassion.[26] And I'm still unable to *prove* the thesis that I have been urging: that human life is sacred and, therefore, precious at every point along the entire human lifeline. But, obviously, the alternative theories—which fix a point before which a fetus has no human standing—are equally *unproved* and unproveable. This leaves us at a dialogical impasse.

---

[26]Cf. B. A. Brody, "Abortion and the Law" in *The Journal of Philosophy,* Vol. 68 (June, 1971), pp. 357–69 and especially p. 357: "The status of the fetus and of whether destroying the fetus constitutes the taking of a human life . . . seem difficult, if not impossible, to resolve on rational grounds [alone]." Brody concludes against abortion on demand because of the *possibility* of its involving the destruction of human life.

Our best recourse, in such a situation, is to look to the *practical* consequences of the two contrary perspectives, each taken in turn *as if* it were
true. If fetal life is regarded *as if* it were human and sacred and potentially
personal in some truly important sense—*as if* its values were rooted in its
transcendental origins and ends—then it must not readily be violated by
others on grounds of disparate self-interests. If, on the contrary, fetal life
is viewed *as if* it were subhuman, *as if* its values were conferred on it, or
denied it, by other human beings, in terms of self-interest or social sentiment, then abortion is a legitimate failsafe against defective births and
beyond that, euthanasia an acceptable failsafe against lives no longer useful. By then, of course, abortion would have ceased to be the central issue,
but rather human life itself. But that, precisely, is what this debate has
been all about, all along!

# 15

# Euthanasia: Elective Death

In recent years our country has witnessed a growing campaign on behalf of the right of each individual to a "death with dignity." One of the factors most often cited for the need to legalize the right to choose death is the vast strides in medical technology which have resulted in prolonging the course of dying. Today patients who would otherwise die can be kept "alive" through machinery which maintains their vital functions. Proponents of euthanasia argue that the medical profession's attempt to do all in its power to maintain life imposes life upon the dying when it is no longer meaningful and even constitutes an indignity. In such a case "letting a person die" is usually called "passive," or "negative," euthanasia, and doctors and ethicists generally agree that there comes a time when "pulling the plug" is the only appropriate action.

But the argument for elective death goes beyond this situation, and then the ethical issue becomes acute. For example, should an elderly person who is afflicted with a terminal illness and who wants to die be given a pain-killing drug, which would be increased until the dosage reaches the lethal stage? Such an act is called "active," or "positive," euthanasia and at the present time would be legally judged as murder. But many state legislatures are considering bills that would legalize such a practice. The argument on behalf of active euthanasia is related to the argument of pro-abortionists: We who are living have the autonomy—the human right—to decide whether a given life should be continued or terminated. In the case of abortion the decision concerns fetal life, but in the case of euthanasia, since it involves a mature human being, the decision must be made by the individual person.

But, of course, euthanasia can also involve the infant, so that the argument becomes a more obvious extension of the pro-abortion position. Should laws be passed that give parents the right to terminate the life of the newborn if their child is severely deformed or mentally retarded? In supporting efforts to pass such laws, euthanasia advocates argue that "meaningful life" has a moral weight and importance that supersedes the concept of "biological life." Considerable attention is being given today to defining what constitutes a "human" life, with the implication that we should be able to terminate life that is not truly human. An incident that occurred several years ago at Johns Hopkins University hospital dramatically illustrates a consequence of this argument: A newborn baby with Down's syndrome was discovered to have a blocked intestine. Because the child was retarded, the parents refused to permit the necessary operation; the infant remained in the hospital and lingered on for two weeks before dying of starvation and dehydration.

The selection by Andrew Varga places this subject within the larger context of humane care for the dying person. Varga rejects euthanasia as an overt act committed in order to bring immediate death (positive, or active, euthanasia), but sees a crucial moral difference between that act and the decision to refuse treatments that would prolong the course of dying for a patient who is terminally ill (negative, or passive, euthanasia). Many who agree with Varga's distinction argue that for the sake of clarity we need to find a different term to designate what is called negative euthanasia (one writer proposes "benemortasia," a word with the same literal meaning as "euthanasia," but taken from the Latin instead of the Greek).

Joseph Fletcher argues that there is no moral difference between putting to death by an overt act and putting to death by refusing to maintain life. In his comment on the torturous experience of Bernard Bard's family, Fletcher maintains that our society is guilty of an idolatrous attitude toward life when it denies such a family the right to terminate the life of their unfortunate child. He attributes positive ethical value to such a decision, rather than to let a child linger on until death mercifully strikes. Fletcher is a situationist, for whom the end result of one's decision—which is determined by the situation—constitutes its ethical value. On the basis of that position, one could also argue—as many parents whose children are afflicted with Down's syndrome have—that the care and nurture of a seriously handicapped child can deepen the sense of humanity in parents and the other children. Fletcher's attempt to define the human quality of life, on the other hand ("To be human is to be self-aware, consciously related to others, capable of rationality"), would appear to affirm an absolute by which one could make a judgment for every case, quite apart from the consequences.

Traditionally Christians have resisted any argument for actively terminating the life of a person, whatever the circumstances, because they believe that life is a gift of God and not something to be taken away by human decision. Many are concerned that if our society lifted this prohibition—even in limited circumstances in the hospital wards of terminally ill patients—the door would be open to a growing sense of human autonomy over life and a consequent cheapening of life. The notion of life as a gift is also tied to the notion of life as a mystery not wholly capable of our comprehension. This sense of mystery is allied with our sense of the sanctity of life, which Christians have seen as an important bulwark in maintaining a humane social order. Some religious thinkers such as Albert Schweitzer have related this sense of reverence to all forms of life.

Most people would likely agree that it is not humane to work heroically to prolong the life of an elderly patient who is lying in a coma with no hope of recovery. But the threat of lawsuits has often caused doctors and hospitals to connect such patients with intensive-care, life-preserving equipment. Once this has been done, medical personnel are understandably cautious about removing this equipment, even in cases that give no hope for recovery. Because of the increase in such cases, various groups have been promoting the "living will," a document signed by the patient and witnesses which releases doctors from any obligation to maintain life in the patient when there are no honest grounds for hope. Such a document is now legally recognized in 11 states; in a number of cases it has protected the hospital and staff from legal action when life-saving equipment has been removed. Largely because of the efforts of "pro-life" groups, however, most states have not been willing to give legal sanction to the living will. In one state a judge recently overruled a mother's objections to further blood transfusions for her son, who was terminally ill with cancer. The man was retarded, with a mental age of about 18 months, and the judge decided that "it is unrealistic to attempt to determine whether he would want to continue potentially life-prolonging treatment if he were competent."

There are further ramifications to this issue. Members of the medical profession have raised serious questions about their image in the mind of the public if their sole purpose is not furthering life at all costs. They argue that the preferred course might be not to legalize passive euthanasia, even if it is generally practiced, but to leave it within the realm of medical ethics and trust in the good judgment of the attending physician. Even when legal suits have been brought against doctors for active euthanasia, juries have tended to make the decisive issue the doctors' intent—was it carelessness, malice, or compassion—and to decide in their favor if their motives were acceptable. Another aspect of the issue which is likely to receive more public attention in the coming years is suicide. If one argues for euthanasia on grounds of human autonomy and the concept of a "life worth living," then to legitimate suicide would appear to be the next logical step. This possibility dramatically raises the issue involved in the ongoing debate over "right to life" in our society: Are we facing a moral crisis (judgment) as a society that has lost its sense of reverence for life, or are we struggling toward a more humane ethic in claiming that the individual should have autonomy over life itself? If the latter is the case, where do we draw the lines to ensure that this autonomy is exercised on compassionate grounds, rather than on grounds of convenience or other questionable motives?

# Ethical Issues of Aging and Dying

Andrew Varga

Human beings are the only living beings who know that they are going to die. There is nothing more certain in a person's life than death. Yet death is a fact of life that we do not like to think or speak about. We may have conversations about business, sports, fashion, even sex, at a party, but death is a topic one must avoid in order not to upset the pleasant mood of a gathering. What we don't like to speak about we don't like to see either. In advanced societies, the critically ill and the dying are taken to hospitals, separated from the healthy, even from the family. Excepting the cases of sudden death, most people die in hospitals, in a strange environment. Machines are attached to them until the last moment; they become a case, a number for the doctor and hospital personnel. Relatives are allowed only short visits and they have to wait outside the hospital room to get information about their loved ones from a nurse. There seems to be a conspiracy not to tell the dying person that the end is approaching. The patient is fed false hope that everything will be all right. Most dying persons, however, know and feel that the end is at hand. They cannot talk to anybody about it, however, because nobody wants to speak about death. It is really cruel to abandon our loved ones this way just when they need us most.

Centuries ago, in more simple times, death was not banished to a separated and closely guarded territory where only a few persons were allowed to see it. People died at home surrounded by the family, relatives and neighbors. Children saw their grandparents and parents die. As they were growing up, they became more and more familiar with the reality of death, their own death included. When their time came, they knew what to expect and what to do to get ready for the "big journey." Since most of the serious diseases were fatal, people were warned in time of their imminent death. It was the duty of the physician or of a friend to act as *nuntius mortis*, the messenger of death, to tell the patient that his earthly pilgrimage was coming to an end. With the advent of modern medicine when people began to die in hospitals, physicians and relatives abandoned their role of telling the terminally ill that death was approach-

Reprinted from *The Main Issues in Bioethics* by Andrew C. Varga. Copyright © 1980 by Andrew C. Varga. Andrew Varga, S.J., teaches philosophy at Fordham University.

ing. Instead of being frank with the dying, physicians and family members began to play a game of concealing the truth from their patients and loved ones. The insensitivity of the artificial and impersonal atmosphere surrounding the dying has grown to such a degree that a natural reaction to change the situation had to set in. Two decades ago, slowly but perceptibly, more and more persons began to speak and write about death and dying, first in Europe, then in America. Workshops on the problems of death and dying were organized and various movements and associations began to transform the impersonal, businesslike atmosphere surrounding the dying.

A young British physician and former nurse, Dr. Cicely Saunders, pioneered an idea in the early 1960s to respond to the great need of caring for the terminally ill in a human, loving manner. She reached back to the Middle Ages for the idea of a *hospice. Hospes* is Latin for "host, guest." Hence *hospitium,* a hospice, was a place where travelers were received as guests. The hospice was maintained by a community of people, usually a religious order, who cared for travelers and the sick. Dr. Saunders opened her modern hospice in 1966 in London and named it after Saint Christopher, the patron saint of travelers. Here, she and her hospice community look after people whose earthly pilgrimage is nearing its end. It is not a hospital for curing people, but a homelike place where the terminally ill are cared for. Relatives, including children, are encouraged to come and stay with their loved ones as long as they can. Patients may walk around, chat with each other, eat their meals in the cafeteria if they prefer to and are able. The whole atmosphere is as homelike as possible. Even garden parties are held when the weather is suitable. Although staffed mostly by Catholic nuns and physicians, St. Christopher's Hospice is nonsectarian. It has become a model for the modern way of caring for the dying.

At the same time, the practical aspects of understanding and assisting the dying have been systematically explored. Dr. Elisabeth Kubler-Ross, a Swiss-born psychiatrist . . . has done universally acclaimed pioneering work in this field. In her book, *On Death and Dying,* she identified five typical stages in the attitudes of the dying. They start with denial and isolation ("No, not me. It cannot be true."), passing to anger ("Why me?"), bargaining ("God may be more favorable if I ask nicely.") and depression, then leading finally and often to acceptance. Understanding these typical phases, some or all of which the dying person may go through, helps us better to assist the dying.

Modern hygiene and medicine have succeeded in prolonging man's life span, but finally all human beings must die. For many the length of the last illness may be stretched out. The dying process can even be expanded by the artificial sustaining of some of the vital functions. How long a terminal illness and the dying process should be drawn out or shortened by medical intervention is the subject of heated controversy in hospitals, the media, and even the courts. The term *euthanasia* (Greek for "good death") is used in connection with this problem. Unfortunately, this term is often applied in a confusing way that only clouds the issue. It is important, then, that we clearly identify and evaluate the problems in this area.

Euthanasia, in general, means the causing of an easy or painless death to a patient who is dying of a terminal illness. Death can be induced by the patient himself without the knowledge and cooperation of any other persons. Or it can be effected by others at the request or with the consent of the patient. In all these cases it is called *voluntary euthanasia.* If death is induced against the will or without the knowledge of the patient, we speak of *involuntary euthanasia.*

The means by which death is brought about can be a positive intervention, for instance, an overdose of sleeping pills or other medication, or an injection of potassium chloride, that quickly causes death. Sometimes the term *mercy killing* is used for this kind of action. Usually, however, it is called *positive,* or *active,* or *direct euthanasia.*

The omission of useless treatment, that is, not prolonging the dying process by life-sustaining machines, such as a respirator, is called *negative* or *passive* or *indirect euthanasia.*

Definitions may be helpful but they do not in themselves solve the moral problems involved. The question remains whether or not there is any difference, from the moral point of view, between the omission and the performance of an act. Can the omission of a treatment be equivalent to the killing of a patient? Does "pulling the plug" of the respirator directly kill the patient? Is the failure to put a patient on the machine, and letting him die, morally different from taking him off the machine? What is the moral difference here between omission and action, omission and commission? Is the patient or the doctor morally obliged to forestall death as long as possible? And by what means? All these questions must be examined.

**Involuntary Positive or Active Euthanasia** is the direct killing of a patient without his consent. May this ever be justified? An example of involuntary positive euthanasia was Hitler's eugenic euthanasia order that was issued in October, 1939. (It was deceptively antedated September 1, 1939 as if it had been connected with the beginning of the military campaign against Poland.) More than 80,000 German and Austrian mental patients, epileptics, feebleminded and deformed persons were killed in gas chambers in 1940 and 1941. The law originally dealt only with small children but the age was raised later. The moral question is whether an individual or any public authority is allowed forcibly to take the life of an innocent person whether that person is a baby, a crippled adult or someone who is old and senile. No valid argument can be offered to prove the position that an innocent person may be killed. The fact that somebody is killed by painless means does not alter the basic injustice of his being forcibly deprived of the basic right to life. Whether a baby or an innocent old man is killed, and whether brutally or painlessly, it does not alter the injustice of violating their basic right to life.

**Voluntary Positive Euthanasia**   means that a patient procures for himself a painless death either without the cooperation of others or with the help of a physician or some other person. Death is not forced upon the patient but rather sought by him. In essence, this type of euthanasia is suicide or cooperation with others in committing suicide. It is a special case of suicide, however, because it is committed only to end unbearable pain or a "useless" life. This type of suicide was defended by certain philosophers in ancient times and was also practiced by certain nations. Jewish and Christian tradition, on the other hand, has always been against any form of suicide. Nevertheless, there have been a number of writers and philosophers in the Christian era who have defended man's freedom to commit suicide, for example, David Hume in his *Essay on Suicide.*

In the United States and other countries various pro-euthanasia groups campaign for the legalization of voluntary active euthanasia under certain restricted conditions. In America, for example, several state legislatures have discussed euthanasia bills but so far no voluntary positive euthanasia bill has been passed. Many nations, however, consider an incurably ill patient's request for euthanasia as a mitigating factor in a murder trial of those who comply with such a request. In Uruguay and Peru, the person who commits a homicide out of compassion and responding to the repeated request of an incurably ill patient is exempt from penalty.

In the United States, the law forbids any person to help an incurably ill patient commit suicide. Any accomplice in such a suicide is charged with manslaughter. However, if he is found guilty, he usually receives a light sentence. An example is the case of Robert C. Waters, who gave in to his gravely ill wife's pleas and helped her commit suicide. He put his wife in the family car in their garage, kissed her goodbye, turned on the ignition key and let her die of carbon monoxide poisoning. He pleaded *nolo contendere* to manslaughter charges and was sentenced to 30 months of probation and a fine of $3,750. In some cases the jury finds the defendant not guilty on the ground of temporary insanity.

The following arguments are usually proposed in favor of voluntary positive euthanasia.

1.   The life of a person who is suffering from terminal illness has become useless to his family, to society and to himself. A healthy person may not commit suicide because he has many duties he is morally obliged to fulfill toward his family, society and his own development. A person

suffering from a terminal illness, however, does not have any more duties to fulfill because he is simply incapable of doing anything for himself or others.

2.   Faced with the conflict of two evils, one has to choose the lesser evil. The prolongation of useless suffering, however, is a greater evil than procuring immediate death, a death which would come anyhow within a short time.

3.   It is inhuman and unreasonable to keep a terminally ill patient alive when he does not want to live any longer and an injection could painlessly end his misery.

4.   A person not believing in God can reasonably conclude that man is the master of his own life. Consequently, he may freely decide to terminate his own life either alone or with the help of others when he does not have any more duties to fulfill with regard to his family and society.

5.   Man's freedom to act should not be restricted unless there are convincing arguments that his freedom to act comes into conflict with the rights of others. No such conflict can be shown, however, in the case of a terminally ill person. Consequently, such a man has the right to die as he chooses.

6.   Voluntary positive euthanasia is an act of kindness toward one's family and society because the terminally ill person chooses not to burden them with his prolonged illness, expenses and all the work of caring for a gravely ill patient. It is better to free scarce medical and financial resources to be employed in curing those who can lead a useful life.

7.   Believers hold that God gave us our life. But it does not follow from this that we may not interfere in our lives, because God made us stewards of our lives. It is reasonable to assume, then, that God does not want us to suffer unnecessarily when we can easily terminate our misery.

What counter-arguments are we proposing? Western tradition and theistic philosophy have been against the direct killing of oneself either alone or with the help of others. The main argument for this position is that God has direct dominion over human life. We are managers of our own lives but we do not own them; consequently, we may not destroy them. Just as we cannot decide the beginning of our own life, we may not determine its end either. Although this argument is valid on the basis of theistic philosophy, it will not convince everybody, possibly not even the believer. Can any other reason be adduced?

When we speak of voluntary euthanasia, it is assumed that the patient freely asks for death. To avoid any misunderstanding or deception, the patient's request should be done in writing and signed in the presence of witnesses. Is a patient weakened by a terminal illness really in a position to evaluate his own situation and make a request with a clear mind? How can the witnesses testify that he made the request for his own death with sane and sound mind? Then there is the problem of freedom in making the decision. Can pressures be eliminated? The possibility of abuse is not imaginary but very real, given the conflicting financial and other interests of the patient's family and of society.

In addition, the exact time for the lethal injection must be determined. This looks very much like execution. Most countries did away with the death penalty because it is an inhuman form of punishment. It is cruel to tell a person the exact time of his death. Are we now willing to reintroduce execution by injection on a mass scale? Granted there is a difference between the execution of a criminal and the killing of a patient, but the gruesome dehumanizing circumstances of the execution and of the killing are the same.

Further, who will administer the lethal injection? Will physicians accept the role of dispensing death instead of healing? The person who injects the lethal substance need not be a physician for the simple procedure can be easily learned by others. Will there be a new profession whose task it is to deliver death, just as there are professional executioners who are paid for their "service"?

Someone might object that this description of euthanasia is exaggerated or even sarcastic. I don't think so. The concrete performance of euthanasia must not be overlooked. Taking all the circumstances into account, voluntary positive euthanasia is dehumanizing, it is not "dying with dignity." The possibility of abuses connected with the legalization of euthanasia might increase old people's fear that a serious illness is an occasion for the family or authorities to dispatch them from this world. It is much more in conformity with human dignity to let nature take its course and to accept death when it comes through factors which are not in the power of man to control.

Does it follow from the previous reasoning that everything possible must be done to prolong the life of a terminally ill patient? Are we allowed to omit or refuse useless treatment that does not cure a disease but only prolongs dying? The opponents of any form of euthanasia argue that we have the duty to keep terminally ill patients alive as long as modern medicine can because, from the moral point of view, omitting treatment is equivalent to killing a person. The generally accepted meaning of passive or negative euthanasia is the omission of a treatment. It means letting a person die of an incurable disease. It is the disease that terminates the patient's life and not a positive human intervention.

Passive euthanasia can be voluntary or involuntary. Voluntary passive euthanasia is simply the refusal of treatment. The right of a competent patient to refuse treatment is generally recognized in the Western legal tradition. It is another question whether it is morally justifiable. We have a moral duty to take care of our health in order to be able to fulfill the obligations our state of life imposes upon us. Consequently, it would be wrong to refuse treatment that can restore our health. It would not be wrong, however, to refuse treatment that is useless, that cannot cure a terminal illness and only prolongs the dying process.

Is there a natural right to die when our time comes? Rights are derived from natural needs and duties. People having a natural need for food, clothing and shelter are obliged to provide these necessities for themselves in cooperation with others. They have a moral claim, that is a natural right, to the means by which they can procure them. It follows from this that nobody is allowed to prevent them from pursuing this goal. Is death a duty? Can a right to die be derived from that duty? In a certain way, death is a part of human existence, as are the natural processes of birth, growth and mental development. These processes are imposed upon us by our nature; consequently, we have the right not to be prevented from fulfilling these natural duties. We do not like to speak about the obligation to die. Nevertheless, it is a necessity of human existence. Consequently, we have the right not to be subjected to futile therapies which try to forestall death when it is inevitably coming as a result of natural causes. In other words, man has a right to accept death peacefully when the time for dying arrives.

One of the practical difficulties of exercising the right to die is the fact that many patients are brought to a hospital in a critical condition that prevents them from revealing their will not to be placed on life supporting machines which can prolong the dying process for a long time. The *living will* is intended to remedy this situation. The essence of the various forms of a living will is the request of a person directed to all who care for him to let him die and not be kept alive by artificial means when there is no reasonable expectation of recovery. The living will is signed in the presence of witnesses and copies of it are given to the intestate's family, physician, lawyer, clergyman and others who might get involved with the medical facility caring for him in a critical illness.

California and seven other states have passed *"natural death"* legislation, assuring the right to die of terminally ill patients under carefully circumscribed legal conditions. Twenty-five more states are considering such legislation. The proposed aim of these laws is the defense of the patients' right to die. Do they achieve this goal? It seems that in practice exactly the opposite is happening. The patient's right is restricted by the requirement to write a living will, which has to be renewed from time to time according to various stipulations (in California, for example, every five years) to remain valid. How many people will take the trouble to write and renew a living will to protect the natural right they already have without any legislation? In California, more than 100,000 right-to-die forms were distributed in 1978. But according to a California Medical

Association report, they are not being used frequently. In late 1977, a sampling of 111 doctors who ordered a total of more than 11,000 copies, revealed that the right-to-die forms had been used only in 67 cases. Any critically ill patient brought to a hospital without a legally executed living will runs the risk of being subjected to useless treatment prolonging his dying. The attending physicians, being concerned about malpractice suits, will be reluctant not to start or to stop useless treatment in the absence of a legal document protecting them. The main concern of any natural death legislation should be to assure, in a practical way, the natural right of any person not to be subjected to useless treatment. The state does not grant this right to us. Rather, it is called upon to protect it, for we have it by our very nature.

Is it moral to let an incompetent terminally ill patient die by not starting or by stopping useless treatment? If a terminally ill and mentally competent patient may refuse useless therapy, the guardians of a mentally incompetent patient should have the same right. In the case of children, the right of parents to refuse useless treatment is recognized in medical practice. There have been a number of cases, however, where the hospital refused to accept the parents' decision and went to court to have treatment authorized. The case of Karen Ann Quinlan attracted international attention. Miss Quinlan, 21, collapsed and went into a coma on April 15, 1975. She did not recover consciousness and was being kept alive by a respirator and intravenous feeding for several months. Since there was no hope for her recovery, her parents asked the hospital to take her off the respirator. When the request was refused by her doctors, the parents went to court and asked the judge to be permitted to turn off the life sustaining machine. New Jersey Superior Court Judge, Robert Muir, Jr., on November 10, 1975, rejected the petition of Karen's father. The case was appealed to the New Jersey Supreme Court, which on April 1, 1976, ruled unanimously that the respirator could be removed. Karen was taken off the respirator but continued to breathe on her own without coming out of the coma. At the time of this writing, she is still in a comatose state in a New Jersey nursing home and is being kept alive only by intravenous feeding.

There are two questions with respect to involuntary negative euthanasia. 1. Is it morally right in the case of a terminally ill, mentally incompetent patient not to start useless treatment or to stop such therapy by turning off the machine or "pulling the plug" as it is popularly called? 2. Who is entitled to make such a decision?

1.  It follows from our previous discussion that it is morally right to allow every such patient to die. It is contrary to rational human nature to apply useless means. In an address to a group of anesthesiologists on

November 24, 1957, Pope Pius XII emphasized man's right to die in dignity. He used the [two] customary terms, ordinary and extraordinary means, and said rightly that there is no obligation to use extraordinary means to preserve life.

2.   Who is entitled to decide to let terminally ill patients die without prolonging the dying process? According to the order of nature, such a right belongs to those who have the duty to care for the person. These are the immediate family, parents, spouses, children, close relatives. This right does not belong to public authorities, for citizens are not the wards of the state. According to the principle of subsidiarity, public authorities have such a duty and right only when there are no competent family members or relatives to exercise this right.

The rights of parents to withhold treatment in the case of minors is generally recognized in America. There does not seem to be a clear policy, however, concerning mentally incompetent adults. The Massachusetts Supreme Court, in its ruling on November 28, 1977, referring to the case of Joseph Saikewicz, stated that the probate court has this authority. Such a decree, if it were recognized nationwide, would deprive families and those directly caring for the patient, of their natural right to make this decision. The court would arrogate the right it does not have, and in addition, it would be incapable of exercising it. There are so many such cases every day that the courts would become hopelessly cluttered. In the meantime all dying patients would be subjected to the torture of being placed on life sustaining machines. In order to avoid such an impossible situation, carefully drafted "Natural Death" legislation should clearly protect the natural right of the family and of all those who are directly involved in care of the dying.

The controversy over euthanasia is about the moral difference between *action and omission,* commission and omission. According to sound ethical principles, we are never allowed to perform an act that directly violates the right of others, but we are not always obliged to perform an act that would save others from injury. Not every omission is excusable, of course. The policeman omitting to patrol a street, bears responsibility, to a certain degree, for a burglary he could have prevented. An ordinary citizen, however, is not obliged to get up at night to patrol the streets. If we are dutybound to perform an act we have omitted, the results may be imputed to us. As we have seen, there are good reasons to hold that we are not obliged to apply useless therapy. The omission of such a therapy, then, is at least morally indifferent. In active euthanasia, or mercy killing, it is the lethal injection or some other means that directly kills the patient. In passive euthanasia, on the other hand, it is the disease, that is, a natural cause, that terminates the life of the patient. The omission of therapy is not direct killing.

Some physicians do not have any particular difficulty about not starting a useless therapy, but they are reluctant to stop it once it has been started. However, it is not turning off the respirator that kills the patient but the disease. Pulling the plug is not equivalent to giving a lethal injection.

Patients cannot make a well-informed decision about whether or not to refuse treatment unless doctors *tell them the truth about their illness.* It is an unpleasant task to tell a patient that his illness is terminal. One can understand why many doctors and nurses shirk this duty. They may inform the patient's family and then both the family and the doctors begin to play a game with the patient, concealing the truth and offering false hope. Is it morally obligatory to tell patients the truth or may the truth be concealed? According to solid ethical principles, everybody has a right to the truth unless he has forfeited his right to it or indicates that he does not want to hear the truth, does not want to be informed. A patient may indicate in some way that he does not want to hear the truth about his illness. In this case, the doctor has no moral obligation to inform him. Otherwise he owes the truth to his patient. The Patient's Bill of Rights, approved by the American Hospital Association's House of Delegates on February 6, 1973, affirms that "The patient has the right to obtain from his physician complete information concerning his diagnosis, treatment, and prognosis in terms the patient can be reasonably expected to understand. When it is not medically advisable to give such information to the patient, the information should be made available to an appropriate person in his behalf. He has the right to know by name the physician responsible for coordinating his care." It seems to me that the physician should not easily assume that truthful information would be harmful to his patient. Non-communication could be actually more harmful than the truth.

According to recent reports, there has been a major change in the attitude of doctors with respect to informing their patients of their illness. A questionnaire was submitted to doctors in 1961 to indicate their preference for telling their patients or keeping secret from them the fact that they had cancer. Ninety percent of the responding physicians expressed a preference for not telling their patients that they had cancer. In 1977, a similar questionnaire was submitted by the University of Rochester Medical Center. Ninety-seven percent of the doctors who responded expressed a preference for truthfully informing their patients of a cancer diagnosis. According to various surveys, the overwhelming majority of patients want to be informed about the nature of their illness, even if it is terminal.

We owe it to our fellow human beings to be truthful with them all the time, but especially when they are approaching the end of their earthly pilgrimage. We ourselves don't want less than compassionate sincerity in the last moments of our lives.

# The Right to Die

Bernard Bard and Joseph Fletcher

## A FATHER SPEAKS

My son, Philip, was born at 11:20 A.M. on December 2, 1962, at Booth Memorial Hospital, Flushing, New York. The pediatrician, Dr. F., a youngish man given to bow ties, met me in the corridor of the maternity floor. It was a boy, five pounds, thirteen ounces, he said, but added: "I'm not totally satisfied."

The vital organs were functioning normally, said the doctor, but there was something about the facial features, the extra-wide bridge between the eyes, the poor muscle tone, the weakness of the stomach muscles when the infant cried that showed abnormality.

"This is something we'll have to watch carefully, to see how the baby develops in the next twenty-four hours, or three to four days," said Dr. F. "But for the moment, the outlook is for an individual without a long life-span and not great mental development in the years ahead. Please call me by tomorrow."

My wife was still under anesthesia. I went out to buy flowers, and was in her room when she awakened. "How is the baby?" were her first words. I said he was fine. She smiled and went back to sleep.

I visited the nursery that afternoon and again that night. My baby was in a warmer. The nurse on duty assured me it was not an incubator, just a temperature-control device. I had been worried because Philip was premature, born four weeks ahead of schedule. But the nurse told me his weight was good. He looked beautiful. His face seemed round and healthy-looking. I detected none of the unusual facial configurations Dr. F. had mentioned. I began to grope for reassurance. I stopped another nurse to ask how my son appeared to her. "Fine," she said. "Don't let the warmer worry you."

At three the next day, I sat in Dr. F.'s office, on a residential side street a mile from the hospital. He closed the door, and began, quietly, to recite some of his observations. The ears were set back too far on the head. The

Copyright © 1968 by Bernard Bard and The Atlantic Monthly Company, Boston, Mass. Reprinted by permission of the authors and publisher. From *Atlantic Monthly*, April, 1968. Bernard Bard is a veteran reporter for the *New York Post,* currently on general assignments.

hands and feet were stubbier than normal. There was an in-turning of the final joint of the pinky fingers. There was a fold over each eyelid. There was a scruff of fat at the back of the neck. The hands and feet flexed back too far under pressure, but did not reflex. "The child is almost double-jointed." And the tongue was too large for the mouth.

The features and symptoms suggested hypertelorism, a word I immediately recognized as associated with mental retardation. The word for the infant's overall appearance and condition, said Dr. F., was mongolism. "All signs point to it." But still Dr. F. did not want to make his diagnosis final. He assured me tests could be taken, hip X-rays and chromosome counts. And he could consult with the chief of pediatrics at the hospital. "How sure are you?" I asked. "Is there perhaps a fifty-fifty chance you are wrong?"

No, said Dr. F., the odds were more likely ninety to ten that he was right. Few such children, he continued, live beyond the teens. Those that do survive into adulthood are incapable of reproduction. The outlook for "normal" mental development was about nil, he said, and only fifty-fifty that the child would be able to care for his own bodily functions, and not much more.

"Parents make either one of two decisions," said Dr. F. "Either they take the child home, and give him as much care as possible. Or, where there is another child at home, as in your case, the decision is sometimes made to institutionalize the mongolian child. Some parents take the child home for several months, or years, and then place it in a nursing home or training school."

That night I met Dr. L., the chief pediatrician at Booth. He emerged from the nursery, where he had just concluded his examination, and was still wearing his surgical mask and gown. "Wait till I shed this," he said. "I'll meet you in the father's waiting room."

There was no doubt at all about the diagnosis, said Dr. L. No tests were necessary. All the classic symptoms were present. The child, he said, would be vulnerable to heart trouble "of a severe sort," perhaps at age one or two. He would be peculiarly susceptible to digestive ailments and respiratory troubles. Life would, according to medical experience, be short. Mental development would be arrested at the age level of two or three.

Dr. L. said many parents institutionalize mongolian children, "particularly when there is another child at home, a normal child." But he declined firmly to offer any advice.

Two days after Philip was born, I gave Peggy the entire story. Until then she had only known there were symptoms that troubled the doctors. She tried to nurse, but the baby was too weak. Dr. F. ordered Philip be given a bottle in the nursery. I told my wife that I felt it best to have the baby cared for away from home, that this was a decision the doctors had not attempted to influence in any way, but one in which they concurred as the best. Dr. F. said, "He will grow up among children like himself, not aware that he is different."

In point of fact, the physicians I consulted said it was better to experience heartache now than to know a cumulative, greater anguish later on. To take the child home, one doctor said, would trap the family in "an irreversible situation." Peggy agreed, and said weakly: "Take me home."

Through friends, I learned in the next few days of a private sanitarium in Westchester County, said to be rated one of the best in the state. I called and found my son could be accepted immediately. The institution, I was told, was run "as a hobby" by a pediatrician with a flourishing practice with normal children.

He was a specialist in mentally retarded children. The price, to families receiving welfare assistance, was $160 a month. I was one of these. My income, in the middle range, had forced me to apply to the Nassau County Department of Public Welfare for aid in meeting the costs of institutional care.

Now, among close friends, I began to tell our story. I learned that there are such tragedies in many families. The sister of a neighbor, I learned, cares at home for a mongolian boy of fifteen. He is virtually helpless, still wears diapers. The mother has suffered three miscarriages because of the strain of lifting him.

A friend from my high school days told me of a cousin with mongolism, a woman of thirty-eight with the mind of a four-year-old. "I see her once in a while at a family social function," he said. "It's impossible to exchange more than a few words with her. Her mother's greatest fear is that she will be left alone, with no one to look after her, after the mother dies." The parents, I was told, were determined to have no more children for fear mongolism might strike again.

Another friend told of another mongolian child being raised at home. The mother has said openly: "I want to outlive him by just one day, so that I can know a single day of freedom." The child is in his teens. He often wanders away and gets lost in the neighborhood. The police bring him home.

On the weekend following Philip's birth, I visited the sanitarium which had been recommended to me. It was a large old mansion, constructed of brown and buff-colored stones. The premises looked solid, formidable, and cold; the design was turn-of-the-century; there was a small sign over the front entrance. The neighborhood was neat and partly residential.

Mrs. C., the chief nurse, gave me the admissions forms. I paused, conscious of her watchful eyes, as I answered each question—father's name, mother's name, age of infant, weight, and so on. My feelings of guilt were overpowering. I felt I was abandoning my child. My mind returned to the hospital nursery. The other infants now there would come into homes made ready to receive them. My child was forsaken.

"Would you like to look around?" asked Mrs. C. We went first to a room containing the newborn. Nine infants were in cribs, some asleep. Most were awake. There was no whimper, no cry. The babies were almost motionless. They lay as if in a trance. Their faces showed no expressions. Most showed the telltale facial characteristics of mongolism—eyes widely spaced, slight deformities of the ears, round, fat cheeks.

We passed down a corridor. Mrs. C. told me to wait while she closed a door. "The children in there have oversized heads," she said. "It might disturb you. We keep them together." On we went, into other rooms containing other children—mongoloids, brain-damaged; some were blind in addition to being mentally retarded. Some of the children seemed too large to be languishing helplessly in a crib; others seemed pitifully small.

In one room was a girl of four, wearing a red playsuit. She lay on her back in the crib, staring blankly into space or at the ceiling. She was the age of my older son, Stephen, but half his size. "Mongolian," said Mrs. C. She affectionately tickled the child's stomach to bring on a playful mood. But there was no response, no laughter, no smile. The face was void. For my child, I told myself, there would be a crib here. It was a thought beyond total understanding or complete acceptance.

In her office, Mrs. C. listened as I told her of my feelings. It was not for this, I said, that we wanted another baby. We would consider ourselves blessed, I went on, if there had been a miscarriage or a blue baby rather than this. Mrs. C. understood. I asked her how mongoloid children fared. While they live, she said, "they haven't a care in the world—it's the parents who suffer." Heart failure kills many the first year, she said, but with new drugs more and more survive that period. If they do, she said, some mongoloid children live for years.

On the trip home, I prayed for my child's death, cursing and damning myself as I did.

I went back to see Dr. F., our pediatrician, who was pleased with the sanitarium and the speed with which arrangements were completed. I raised with him the question of euthanasia in those instances where neurological damage is so severe that no matter how long a child may live, he will be little more than a body—unable to care for the most elemental needs, totally dependent on others for survival.

There was no shock on his face. Mongolism, said Dr. F., was incurable and the cause, usually, of gross retardation. If euthanasia were legal and professionally ethical, he said he would be more inclined to perform it on my child than on children afflicted with other diseases that were on the threshold of new discoveries. But for mongolism, he said, there was no cure and none on the horizon. Research was concentrating, he said, on birth defects so as to eliminate the prenatal causes of mongolism.

While medicine could not take Philip's life, said Dr. F., nothing would be done to prolong it. No operations would be performed; no miracle drugs would be administered. "Medical emergencies will be met, such as sudden bleeding or choking," said Dr. F., "and the child will be kept warm, fed, and sheltered. Nothing more."

I returned to the sanitarium in a day or two to meet Dr. K., the director. His offices were separated from the institution he ran by a narrow drive-way. On one side of the driveway was the sanitarium, with its population of retarded children. On the other was a pediatrician's office, with baby carriages parked at the door. Cutouts of clowns and Humpty-Dumpties adorned the bright yellow walls of Dr. K.'s waiting room. There was laughter, and an occasional shriek, and mothers chased after children intent on mild havoc. At a small table, a group of children read aloud from a picture book.

Dr. K. is a man in his fifties. He has been a specialist in mental retarda-tion among children for thirty years. He has examined every mongoloid child in Westchester County, it is said, either to confirm the diagnosis of other physicians or to contradict them. He spoke of mongolism in scientific terms, the papers he had written on it, the statistics compiled. Nothing, he said, had been discovered concerning precisely what goes wrong dur-ing pregnancy to cause the condition, marked by the presence of 47 chromosomes, one more than the normal human complement of 46. The research, he said, was attempting to find what body processes within the mother produce the extra chromosome.

I told Dr. K. that I wanted nothing done to extend my son's hold on life artificially. He assured me he understood. The sanitarium, he said, con-tains no oxygen. The children are given no inoculations against childhood diseases, unless parents insist. "There are churches on all sides of me," he said. "Every one of these ministers agrees with me that it would not be moral, or serving God's will, to prolong these lives."

At the suggestion of an official in the welfare department, a social case-worker took Philip to the sanitarium next day. I had brought her diapers, nightgowns, blankets, bunting, and bottles for his formula. A few hours after Philip's arrival, Dr. K. called to tell me he had died. "Heart failure and jaundice," he said. "Consider it a blessing." And I remembered what he had told me at our first meeting: "Some parents regularly visit their children here. They waste their lives trying to expunge a feeling of guilt that should not be there, instead of devoting themselves to their normal children. It is for them that they must and should live."

I did not know my son. I do not know his thousands of brothers and sisters, of whom it has been written, "Oh, what a mortal pity he was ever born," and I do not know the parents of these children. I do not speak for them, just for myself and perhaps for Philip. I believe that it is time for a sane and civilized and humane approach to euthanasia.

I do not know how it should be practiced, or what committee should have a voice in the decisions, or what pill or injection might best be employed. I do know that there are thousands of children on this earth who should never have been born. Their lives are a blank. They do not play; they do not read; they do not grow; they do not live or love. Their life is without meaning to themselves, and an agony to their families.

Why?

Bernard Bard

## A THEOLOGIAN COMMENTS

Bernard Bard is a loving man. He is not a vitalist—which is the label philosophers attach to those who make an idol of life. To them life is the highest good, regardless of the situation. But he loves people too much to absolutize mere biological process. He cares too much for human happiness and peace and kindness and loving concern to subordinate every other consideration to merely keeping breathing a sadly non- or un- or subhuman creature.

I agree with Mr. Bard that we ought to be able to do something about such tragedies, something that he calls "a sane and civilized and humane approach to euthanasia." There is no good reason why he and Mrs. Bard and Stephen and a host of friends and medical and paramedical helpers should quit in dumb resignation to that mysterious, disastrous forty-seventh chromosome.

Out of respect for the Mongols, by the way, and to keep the peace with my own son, who is a specialist historian of Central Asia, I prefer to speak of this pathology as an embryonic anomaly or, specifically, Down's syndrome.

Dr. F. has to act within the law, at least as far as policy goes. Nobody knows for sure what doctors do in practice, sometimes. For example, to stop the pain of terminal patients they sometimes give them rapidly increased doses of morphine in order to reach the fatal, toxic level. And at the other end of the life spiral, at delivery, they often refrain from respirating "monsters." But our statute and common law—that is, our official morality—is thoroughly idolatrous and vitalistic. It prohibits our ever ending a life directly, except when necessary in defense of one's own life.

In short, the official morality and conventional wisdom are not only vitalistic and idolatrous; they are selfishly so. "All life is sacred, and my life most of all."

It is the sacrosanct notion of life which is challenged by Bernard Bard. He is saying that we are not helpless and hopeless in the face of adversity and suffering. He rejects fatalism. Fatalism attributes cosmic evil (evil not due to human cause or choice) to God, perhaps, or nature, or chance, or to some weird combination of all three, and then it decides that we ought not to do anything about it even if and when we could!

Look carefully at what Dr. K. told him. The "sanitarium" where Philip was taken immediately from the hospital only cares for a Down's case physically, and only in a minimum way at that. They keep no oxygen, give no inoculations against disease. Nothing is done to keep death away. On the contrary, it is welcomed as a friend. Kant once said that if we will the end we will the means, and morally surely he was right. The official morality in this matter is plainly of the primitive taboo order. "Life is untouchable; don't dare the lightning of the gods." This is not rational or responsible.

This policy we can call *indirect* euthanasia, achieved by deliberately omitting to do what is possible to preserve life, thus bringing death about left-handedly. It is really dys-thanasia, not euthanasia; a bad death, ugly and prolonged, rather than a good death, merciful and quick. One morality lets death drag out, willy-nilly, the other shortens it by a morally authentic decision.

Dr. F.'s professed policy, in which death is desired but not devised, is public simply because it has general acceptance. To give him the credit due, Dr. F. did say to Mr. Bard that if euthanasia were legal, he would be inclined to end the lives of grossly retarded infants like Philip. But behind the reigning official morality lurks a religious or taboo morality. In formal teaching Roman Catholics, Protestants, and Jews, at least as far as their moral theologians and ethicists can speak for them, are agreed that we are not obliged in conscience to preserve a life, just so long as we don't do anything directly to end it. Pope Pius XII, in saying so in 1957, added that we may never choose to let sufferers "go" except when extraordinary means would be required to keep them alive. Doctors and moralists, however, cannot agree about what is extraordinary, and even if they could, it would become ordinary very quickly because of the rapid advances of medical care.

Whether at the start of life, as with fetal and neonatal defects, or later on; in terminal and senile illnesses, the moral problem is essentially the same; if we can justify wanting death to come, is it ethical to sit by waiting fatalistically for whatever blind, brute nature happens to "do" about it?

There are some who object that "the end does not justify the means." This is an old bromide, and basically quite an irrational one. Nothing at all can justify what we do, or make good sense of it, except the goal or purpose which gives an act its character as a "means," or to put it differently, makes it meaningful. Otherwise any act would be random, pointless, non-sense.

The only serious ethical question about means and ends is, "Is the flame worth the candle?" Is the cost of the necessary means proportionate to the value of the end sought? Is the payoff worth the input? This is a decision which depends on the facts in each situation; there are no general formulas, no absolute or universal requirements and prohibitions. In dealing with Down's cases, it is obvious that the end everybody wants is death. What is at issue is the means. Shall it be indirect, by omission, as in the official policy, just letting it all hang on chance? Or shall it be direct, by commission, resulting from responsible choice?

What Mr. Bard is pleading for, on behalf of millions of blameless and miserable people, is *direct* euthanasia. I almost said "honest" or "straightforward" euthanasia. Bard's belief is that it is dishonest or phony to will the end but not the means. I agree with him. Absolute taboos, with their underlying mystique about life, make a farce of human freedom.

All such taboos cut the ground from under morality because nothing we do lies in the moral order if it is not humanly chosen. The atom bomb dropped on Hiroshima in 1945 (tragic and debatable as it was) was morally significant, but the Krakatoa volcanic earthquake off Sumatra in 1883 wasn't. If Philip's life, such as it was, had been brought mercifully to a close, that would have had ethical value; but with its sudden end by "heart failure and jaundice," neither his life nor his death had any moral meaning whatsoever.

Pause for a moment to consider preventive abortion, of the kind that so many women underwent during the thalidomide snafu a few years ago. There is no reason in the world (other than the vitalist mystique in its extreme form) why a pregnancy should not be stopped at once if there is a solid ground to believe or even to fear that it will result in a mentally or physically deformed child.

This is, in a manner of speaking, fetal euthanasia. Mrs. Finkbine was on a morally sound course when she went to Sweden for an abortion after an Arizona court found that our American laws are too vitalistic to allow her to make a morally responsible decision.

Now, then, if through ignorance or neglect or sheer chance (like the forty-seventh chromosome) the damage has not been ended prenatally, why should it not be ended neonatally? To have given birth innocently to a Down's case, when we would not have done so if we had known the truth, does not of itself justify our extending the tragedy. By stubbornly persisting we only compound the evil; we make ourselves "accessories" after the fact of a monstrous accident. We cannot be blamed for what we did not know, but we can be blamed when we do know.

The only difference between the fetus and the infant is that the infant breathes with its lungs. Does this make any significant difference morally or from the point of view of values? Surely not. Life and human *being* is a process, not an event; a continuum, not an episode. It is purely superstitious to assert that life "occurs" at fertilization or nidation or embryonic formation or fetal animation (movement) or birth or at school or voting age.

To be a human is to be self-aware, consciously related to others, capable of rationality in a measure at least sufficient to support some initiative. When these things are absent, or cannot ever come to be, there is neither a potential nor an actual person. To be a person is a lot more than just to be alive—as any student of the human struggle for maturity and well-being knows perfectly well. The fact that a biological organism functions biologically does not mean that it is a human being. There *is* a difference between a man and a brute. Even if it is a difference only of degree, it is still a difference.

There are many variants or variables situationally, of course. What has been said here is directed only against absolute prohibitions of euthanasia, maintained legalistically and regardless of relative circumstances. On the other hand, however, there is no logic in slipping into the opposite error and absurdity—insisting that euthanasia is always the right thing to do in all cases of retardation! This would simply be a reverse legalism. There is, on the contrary, a strong case to be made for the medical distinction between idiots, cretins, and morons.

The Kennedy Foundation will no doubt help us eventually to correct the condition of some retardates. Whether we ought to do so or not should depend on each particular situation. Neonatal intensive-care units in maternity hospitals are having increasing success in overcoming hypoxia (lack of oxygen), hypoglycemia (lack of sugar), bilirubin (a blood chemical causing jaundice and anemia), and infections of the central nervous system. But the core of the moral problem is still the freedom of people to choose, to be responsible, in every situation.

How strange and contradictory it is that people should deliberately assume the responsibility to *initiate* a life, and to control its creation contraceptively, but still fail or refuse to *terminate* it, no matter what the actual situation is. Some vitalists, the archaically intransigent ones, flatly refuse to terminate reproductive failures either before or after birth, and in a way perhaps this kind of whole-hog opposition makes more sense than a willingness to do it before respiration (abortion) but not afterward (euthanasia). The archaists at least have consistent and radical fatalism.

People in the Bards' situation have no reason to feel guilty about putting a Down's syndrome baby away, whether it's "put away" in the sense of hidden in a sanitarium or in a more responsible lethal sense. It is sad, yes. Dreadful. But it carries no guilt. True guilt arises only from an offense against a person, and a Down's is not a person. There is no cause for remorse, even though, certainly, there is for regret. Guilt over a decision to end an idiocy would be a false guilt, and probably unconsciously a form of psychic masochism.

There is far more reason for real guilt in keeping alive a Down's or other kind of idiot, out of a false idea of obligation or duty, while at the same time feeling no obligation at all to save that money and emotion for a living, learning child. The learning child might be a retarded one with a viable potential, or just an orphan in need of adoption.

To "feel" obligation to prolong "life" in the Down's case while failing utterly to see or accept any responsibility in the promising child's case is moral confusion worse confounded. From a human or moral point of view it is irresponsible.

Theologically oriented people often get the idea that life is God's alone, to deal with as He wills or pleases. (They stick to this idea even if they practice birth control! The really *consistent* vitalists are across the board opposed equally to contraception, abortion, sterilization, euthanasia—that is, to any form of human initiative and responsibility whatsoever.) One moralist has said that euthanasia is a "destruction of the temple of God and a violation of the property rights of Jesus Christ." But this divine-monopoly theory logically militates against medicine itself, which is trying to lengthen life and defend it from "nature's" threats.

The belief that God is at work directly or indirectly in all natural phenomena is a form of animism or simple pantheism. If we took it really seriously, all science, including medicine, would die away because we would be afraid to "dissect God" or tamper with His activity. Such beliefs are a hopelessly primitive kind of God-thought and God-talk, but they hang on long after theologians generally have bid them good-bye.

The notion that life is sacrosanct is actually a Hindu idea, although Hindus practice things like suttee. It is not Christian or biblical. If it were, all heroism and martyrdom would be wrong to say nothing of carnivorous diet, capital punishment, and warfare. The sanctity (what makes it precious) is not in life itself, intrinsically; it is only extrinsic and *bonum per accidens, ex casu*—according to the situation. Compared to some things, the taking of life is a small evil, and compared to some things, the loss of life is a small evil. Death is not always an enemy; it can sometimes be a friend and servant.

Life is sometimes good, and death is sometimes good. Life is no more a good in itself than any other value is. It is good, when and if it is good, because of circumstances, because of the context. When it is not good, it deserves neither protection nor preservation. Our present laws about "elective death" are not civilized. It is high time we had some constructive guidance, perhaps from a model code committee of the American Law Institute. Let the law favor living, not mere life.

**Joseph Fletcher**

# SUGGESTIONS FOR FURTHER READING FOR PART SIX

## Chapter 13: The Future of Humanity

Beauchamp, Tom L. and James F. Childress. *Principles of Biomedical Ethics.* New York: Oxford U. Press, 1979.

Callahan, Daniel. *The Tyranny of Survival: On a Science of Technological Limits.* New York: Crowell-Collier and Macmillan, 1973.

Fletcher, Joseph. *Humanhood: Essays in Biomedical Ethics.* Buffalo, N.Y.: Prometheus, 1979.

Hamilton, Michael, ed. *The New Genetics and the Future of Man.* Grand Rapids, Mich.: Eerdmans, 1972.

McCormick, Richard A., S.J. *How Brave a New World: Dilemmas in Bioethics.* Garden City, N.Y.: Doubleday, 1981.

Ramsey, Paul. *Fabricated Man.* New Haven, Conn.: Yale University Press, 1970.

Reiser, Stanley Joel, Arthur J. Dyck, and William J. Curran, eds. *Ethics in Medicine: Historical Perspectives and Contemporary Concerns.* Cambridge, Mass.: M.I.T. Press, 1977.

Shannon, Thomas A., and James J. DiGiacomo. *An Introduction to Bioethics.* New York: Paulist Press, 1979.

Varga, Andrew C. *The Main Issues in Bioethics.* New York: Paulist Press, 1980.

Watson, James D., and John Tooze. *The DNA Story: A Documentary History of Gene Cloning.* San Francisco: Freeman, 1981.

## Chapter 14: Abortion

Gardner, Robert F. R. *Abortion: The Personal Dilemma.* Grand Rapids, Mich.: Eerdmans, 1973.

Noonan, John T. *The Morality of Abortion: Legal and Historical Perspectives.* Cambridge, Mass.: Harvard University Press, 1970.

—.*A Private Choice: Abortion in America in the Seventies.* New York: Free Press, 1979.

Patterson, Janet, and R. C. Patterson, Jr. *Abortion: The Trojan Horse.* Camden, N.J.: Nelson, 1974.

Perkins, Robert L., ed. *Abortion: Pro and Con.* Cambridge, Mass.: Schenkman, 1974.

Potts, Malcolm, Peter Diggary, and John Peel. *Abortion.* Cambridge: Cambridge University Press, 1977.

## Chapter 15: Euthanasia: Elective Death

Downing, A. B., ed. *Euthanasia and the Right to Death.* New York: Humanities Press, 1970.

Grisez, Germain, and Joseph M. Boyle, Jr. *Life and Death with Liberty and Justice.* Notre Dame, Ind.: U. of Notre Dame Press, 1979.

Kohl, Marvin. *Beneficent Euthanasia.* Buffalo, N.Y.: Prometheus, 1975.

Maguire, Daniel C. *Death by Choice.* Garden City, N.Y.: Doubleday, 1974.

Mannes, Marya. *Last Rights.* New York: Morrow, 1974.

Steinfels, Peter, and Robert M. Veatch. *Death Inside Out.* New York: Harper & Row, 1975.

Vaux, Kenneth. *Will to Live/Will to Die: Ethics and the Search for a Good Death.* Minneapolis: Augsburg Publishing House, 1978.

Wilson, Jerry B. *Death by Decision.* Philadelphia: Westminster Press, 1975.